BRAZIL:
BOOM, BUST,
and the **ROAD** to
RECOVERY

EDITORS
Antonio Spilimbergo and Krishna Srinivasan

I N T E R N A T I O N A L   M O N E T A R Y   F U N D

Cataloging-in-Publication Data
IMF Library

Names: Spilimbergo, Antonio. | Srinivasan, Krishna. | International
Monetary Fund.
Title: Brazil: boom, bust, and the road to recovery / editors: Antonio
Spilimbergo and Krishna Srinivasan.
Description: [Washington, DC] : International Monetary Fund, 2018. |
Includes bibliographical references.
Identifiers: ISBN 978-1-48433-974-9 (paper)
Subjects: LCSH: Brazil—Economic conditions. | Economic development—
Brazil. | Fiscal policy—Brazil.
Classification: LCC HC187.B73 2018

Please send orders to:
International Monetary Fund, Publication Services
P.O. Box 92780, Washington, DC 20090, U.S.A.
Tel.: (202) 623-7430   Fax: (202) 623-7201
E-mail: publications@imf.org
Internet: www.elibrary.imf.org
www.imfbookstore.org

Contents

PART IV. STRENGTHENING THE FISCAL FRAMEWORK

PART V. CHALLENGES TO THE MONETARY AND FINANCIAL FRAMEWORK

PART VI. FIGHTING CORRUPTION

Acknowledgments

This book has been a collective endeavor involving both IMF staff and senior policymakers, as well as leading academics and others from Brazil. We would like to thank the contributing authors for their close collaboration and enthusiasm to work on topics chosen in the book. The research presented in this book has been drawn from work done by IMF staff in the context of the annual Article IV policy consultations with the Brazilian authorities and other stakeholders, and has benefited from comments and feedback provided by several individuals at the IMF and elsewhere, including Alejandro Werner, director, Western Hemisphere Department, and Alfredo Cuevas, assistant director, European Department. Valentina Flamini, senior economist, and Nina Biljanovska, economist—both of the Western Hemisphere Department—provided valuable assistance in finalizing various chapters.

Linda Kean and Linda Long of the IMF's Communications Department efficiently managed all aspects related to the production of the book, and we are grateful for their excellent work. Excellent research assistance provided by Henrique Barbosa and Genevieve Lindow, and administrative assistance by Cristina Barbosa, is gratefully acknowledged.

Antonio Spilimbergo and Krishna Srinivasan
Editors

Foreword

From World War II until the 1980s and again for much of the 1990s, Brazil was a fast-growing emerging economy, with growth averaging about 8 percent a year. The recession of 1981, with the onset of the Latin American debt crisis, was an adverse turning point, with Brazil experiencing a contraction in activity for the first time in three decades. It also marked a structural downshift in growth, which has averaged just over 2.6 percent per year since then. Brazil has seen falling productivity, with only short-lived upturns in growth and the economy reverting to a slower long-term trend.

Brazil's lackluster growth performance, however, masks important improvements in the quality of institutions and macroeconomic frameworks in the 1990s, beginning with the *Plano Real* in 1994, the floating of the *real*, the adoption of inflation targeting, and the passing of the Fiscal Responsibility Law by Congress. These reforms contributed to greater stability and significant social progress in the 2000s. The global financial crisis produced another change in fortunes for Brazil, as both unfavorable external conditions and domestic policy shortcomings morphed into a deep and prolonged recession. Brazil now faces a moment of opportunity, with the economy emerging gradually from the recession, albeit with significant domestic and external downside risks.

Brazil can turn the corner by pursuing much-needed reforms to place the economy on a stronger footing. But this will require strong political leadership, a sustained commitment by policymakers to make the right, albeit difficult choices, and partnership among all stakeholders, many of whom are fatigued by reform and have experienced falling living standards. In this regard, this book is timely and important in many respects. It provides rich analysis by assessing Brazil's economic performance over the past several years from a variety of angles, with a view to understanding the factors that have shackled growth and social progress, and examining policies that have worked well and those that have not. The book draws upon and synthesizes extensive work done at the IMF and in Brazil by leading policymakers, academics, and think tanks, and serves as a fresh platform to deepen our close engagement and policy dialogue with policymakers, academics, and civil society.

I hope the book will spark interest and healthy debate on the economic challenges facing Brazil, and help guide policy choices to place the country on the path to greater prosperity and social progress.

David Lipton
First Deputy Managing Director
International Monetary Fund

PART I

OVERVIEW

CHAPTER 1

Overview: Brazil's Road to Recovery

ANTONIO SPILIMBERGO AND KRISHNA SRINIVASAN

The recession of 1981 was a watershed moment in Brazilian economic history. After several decades of impressive growth, averaging about 8 percent a year from the 1950s through the 1970s, Brazil experienced a contraction in activity for the first time. Against the backdrop of a collapse in the terms of trade, rising debt, and soaring inflation, many saw a recession coming. But few could fathom this would mark a structural shift in growth prospects, because until then Brazil had not experienced a significant downturn, let alone prolonged periods of economic distress, and its growth performance ranked among the best in Latin America. Economic success in the period leading up to the recession had, however, masked serious microeconomic distortions and macroeconomic imbalances in the economy, and it was clear that a turn of events was on the anvil—it was a question of when, and not whether! In any event, the recession was a harbinger of difficult times ahead, and Brazil's economic performance since then has been rather uninspiring.

Following the turbulent 1980s, marked by political upheavals, economic volatility, hyperinflation, debt defaults, and large social inequities, the launch of the *Plano Real* in 1994, a set of measures to stabilize the economy, was a turning point in policymaking in Brazil. It was extremely successful in taming hyperinflation. But economic volatility endured, led by twin external and fiscal deficits, and called for further economic reforms. In response, the *real* was allowed to float, Brazil moved to adopt inflation targeting, and soon thereafter the Congress approved the Fiscal Responsibility Law. The policy tripod—floating *real*, inflation targeting, and fiscal responsibility—formed the basis for improved economic performance in the following years. It took several years of distress—marked by economic and political volatility and growth slumping to 2.5 percent a year on average over the 1980s—before Brazil took important steps to address the large macroeconomic imbalances and microeconomic distortions plaguing the economy. But reforms beginning with the *Plano Real* were unprecedented and pathbreaking, lending support to the notion that "no crisis should go to waste."

The early 2000s was a period marked initially by political uncertainty, but subsequently by the triumph of reason over fear and largely unexpected economic success, anchored by an upturn in the commodity cycle and prudent

Figure 1.1. Real GDP Growth
(Percent; 10-year average)

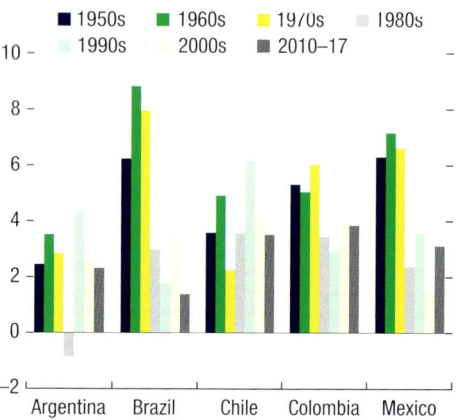

Sources: Global Finance Database (GFD); IMF, World Economic Outlook (April 2018) database; and IMF staff calculations.
Note: For Argentina, Brazil, Colombia, and Mexico, data prior to 1963 are from GFD. For Chile, data prior to 1961 are from GFD. All other years are from WEO.

policymaking. Brazil was one of the best-performing emerging market economies in the early 2000s. But economic success was short-lived—with the global financial crisis leading to a change in fortunes, because of both unfavorable external conditions and serious policy mistakes—and eventually morphed into a deep and historic recession.

In sum, over the past 40 years or so since the recession of 1981, Brazil's economic performance has been mediocre, marked by more downs than ups, with annual GDP growth averaging 2.6 percent. This translates to per capita GDP growth of 0.9 percent a year on average, which compares very poorly with 3 percent for other emerging market and developing economies and 1.7 percent for developed economies. Any significant upturn in growth has been short-lived, with the economy reverting quickly to the underwhelming long-term trend. Hence, the prospects of converging toward the income levels of advanced economies, which looked promising in the late 1970s, now appear to be a goal too far. But evidence from the past suggests hope that Brazil can turn the corner by focusing on much-needed macroeconomic and structural reforms to place the economy on a stronger footing. But this will require strong leadership and unwavering resolve, anchored by a sense of responsibility and partnership among all stakeholders.

The analysis in this book examines Brazil's economic performance over the past several years, with a view to assessing factors that have shackled growth and

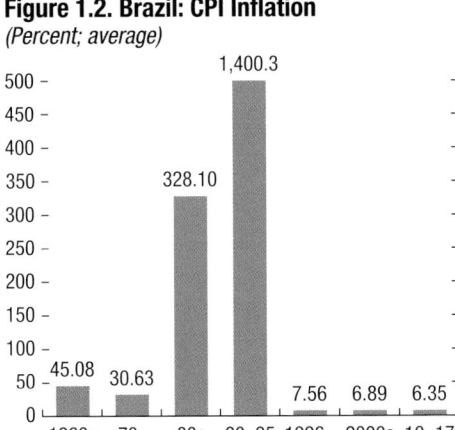

Figure 1.2. Brazil: CPI Inflation
(Percent; average)

Sources: IMF, World Economic Outlook (April 2018)
database; and IMF staff calculations.
Note: Data for the 1960s are from 1964–69. CPI =
consumer price index.

social progress and identifying macroeconomic policy and structural reform priorities that could help secure strong, balanced, and durable growth.

PRODUCTIVITY AND GROWTH

Putting things in context, *Alfredo Cuevas, Antonio Spilimbergo, Krishna Srinivasan,* and *Alejandro Werner* elaborate, in Chapter 2, on reforms in Brazil's policymaking and institutional framework since the 1990s. They argue that poor growth in recent years reflects backpedaling on some of these reforms, owing largely to the role of an activist state and its distrust of markets; riskier macroeconomic policy choices; and, most importantly, structural factors, including, but not limited to, fiscal malaise and the closed nature of the Brazilian economy. The authors go on to argue that long-term prospects for Brazil hinge on how the country addresses macroeconomic imbalances—notably the unsustainable fiscal position, through a focus on certain Brazil-specific characteristics of public spending and the earmarking of revenues. Tackling structural impediments to boosting productivity, which has been on a trend decline, and growth is essential. The authors stress that reforms aimed at opening up the economy, closing infrastructure gaps, improving the efficiency of credit allocation, and improving the functioning of the state hold the key to improving the economy's productive potential.

Characterizing Brazil's growth experience over the past four decades as a series of short boom-and-bust cycles, *Armando Castelar Pinheiro* and *Paulo de Carvalho Lins* argue, in Chapter 3, that it would take the country more than 100 years to double its per capita income, based on the growth it has registered since the 1981

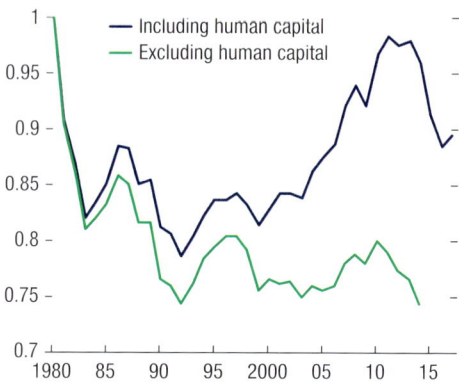

Figure 1.3. Total Factor Productivity
(1980 = 1)

Sources: IMF staff calculations using *World Economic Outlook* and Penn World Tables data.

recession. Growing even at this historic pace would be hard, they argue, given demographic changes, unless there is a huge boost to productivity, which in their view has plummeted since 1980. Noting that low productivity plagues all sectors of the Brazilian economy, the authors call for reforms aimed at reviving the manufacturing sector, notably through competitive pressure to push corporations to invest more in research and development and integrate into global supply chains. To this end, they identify six policy priorities, including significant fiscal changes (that is, consolidation) that can pave the way for a policy mix that reduces the high cost of capital borne by Brazilian firms; sweeping tax reforms to reduce the cost of doing business; reducing infrastructure gaps and improving the business environment; privatization of state-owned enterprises; greater integration of Brazil into the world economy; and reducing the role of the state, which in their view has promoted inefficient and zombie firms.

Similar to *Pinheiro* and *Lins*, *João Manoel Pinho De Mello, Isabela Duarte, and Mark Dutz* analyze, in Chapter 4, Brazil's productivity performance, in aggregate and across sectors, and conclude that in both absolute and relative terms productivity growth over the past several decades has been uninspiring. And low productivity, they argue, is pervasive across all sectors of the economy and cannot be attributed to misallocation of factors between sectors. Brazil's challenge is to forge a business environment that stimulates businesses across all sectors of its economy to change and improve *how* they produce and not *what* they produce. They argue that as entrepreneurs are encouraged to allocate their talent toward productive activities—investing in technology and frontier innovation rather than in rent-seeking activities—the reward will be sustainable growth with more and better jobs for all. To this end, they call for improving

Brazil's business environment so that there are no impediments to starting a business, the tax system is simple and transparent, the judicial system upholds contracts, credit is readily available, and producers can benefit from greater trade integration.

Clearly structural reforms are the key to boosting productivity, which has been on a trend decline, and improving Brazil's long-term growth prospects. But successful reform requires clear policy priorities, because of both capacity constraints and since such reforms can be extremely challenging and require political capital, which is always in limited supply. *Nina Biljanovska* and *Damiano Sandri* examine, in Chapter 5, Brazil's reform priorities in two steps. They first analyze the impact of various reforms—notably pertaining to the banking sector, labor markets, the legal system, product markets, and trade openness—on productivity, and then use survey data to assess the degree of public support for each of the reforms. They conclude that banking sector reforms, aimed at limiting state intervention in credit markets, would generate the largest productivity gains and have the highest level of public support. They extend the analysis to argue that banking sector reforms would be relatively easy to legislate and could generate significant fiscal savings. Beyond the banking sector, reforms of the legal system, aimed at strengthening legal protection for individuals and property rights, would also mean large productivity gains and find favor with the citizenry.

With trade flows averaging a woeful 25 percent of GDP, Brazil is one of the world's least-open economies. In addition to high average tariff rates, the use of nontariff barriers—including antidumping duties and local content production requirements—is rampant. Despite significant trade reforms in the 1990s, import duties, notably on manufactured goods, remain high and compare unfavorably with other emerging market economies. This has, among other things, resulted in very low participation in global value chains, denying Brazil the benefits of booming global trade over the past several years. Drawing on evidence of the benefits of trade liberalization, *Marcello de Moura Estevão Filho* and *Fernando Coppe Alcaraz* call, in Chapter 6, for Brazil to open up its economy. Unilaterally reducing import tariffs should come first, including on basic production inputs, as well as on information technology and capital goods. Elimination of local content rules the pursuit of deeper trade agreements with more and larger trade partners must follow.

Trade liberalization will, all else equal, boost Brazil's productive potential and growth prospects, but it will likely affect labor markets, employment, and wages. Using a computable general equilibrium model with labor frictions and heterogeneity in productivity, *Carlos Góes, Alexandre Messa, Carlos Pio, Eduardo Leoni*, and *Luis Gustavo Montes* examine, in Chapter 7, the effects of trade liberalization on regional labor markets. They conclude that labor markets in regions that now enjoy higher trade protection are more likely to suffer from trade liberalization. Given the limited mobility of labor in Brazil's domestic market, they argue that trade liberalization must be accompanied by active labor market policies and a

Figure 1.4. Trade Openness, 2017
(Percent of GDP)

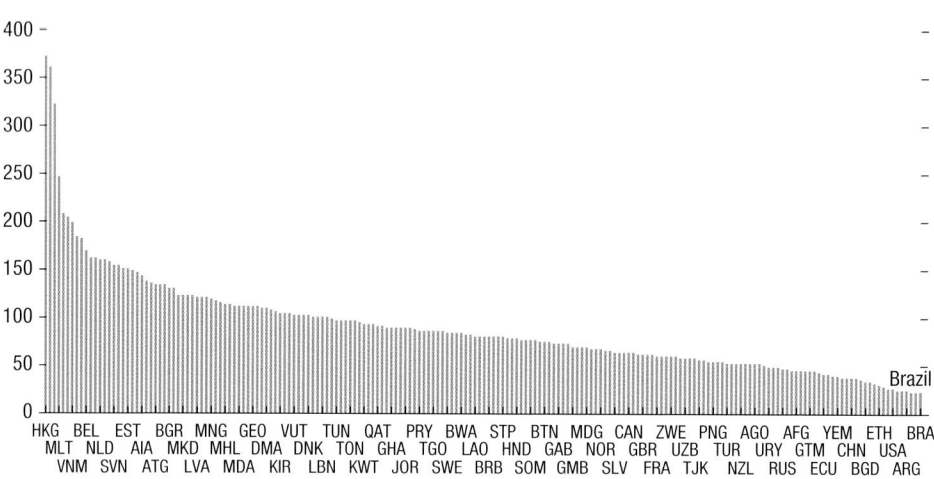

Sources: IMF, World Economic Outlook (April 2018) database; and IMF staff calculations.
Note: Trade openness is the sum of exports and imports of goods and services. Data labels use International Organization for Standardization (ISO) country codes.

skills enhancement program, so that would workers hurt by trade can acquire new skills for sectors and industries that benefit from the economy's opening.

SOCIAL PROGRESS

Historically, Brazil has been marked by more inequality than most countries in the world. Despite the economic boom in the decades preceding the 1981 recession, dismal growth since then led to a worsening of poverty and inequality in Brazil. Indeed, at the turn of the century, close to 40 percent of the population lived below the poverty line. Since then, however, Brazil has made tremendous progress in reducing poverty and inequality. The poverty rate fell by more than half, to below 20 percent by 2014, and income inequality—as measured by the Gini coefficient—dropped from 0.60 to 0.52 in the context of the recent commodity boom. This reflects concerted policy efforts and social programs, such as Bolsa Familia, that have boosted labor income growth, enhanced higher schooling levels, and increased labor formalization.

Izabela Karpowicz and *Carlos Góes* examine, in Chapter 8, trends in inequality in Brazil since the early 2000s. Using a new methodology that allows for adjustment of incomes of households according to price-level differences across states, they argue that the decline in overall inequality in Brazil was led by a decrease in both intra- and interstate inequality, albeit for different reasons. They conclude that the decline in inequality within individual states has been

Figure 1.5. Progress with Reducing Inequality in Brazil
(Gini units)

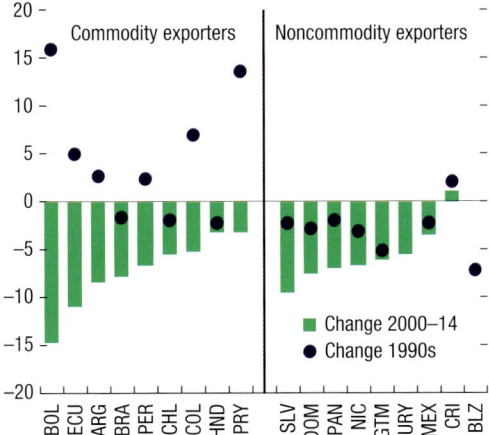

Sources: Inter-American Development Bank, SIMS database; World Bank, World Development Indicators database; and IMF staff calculations.
Note: Colombia uses 2003 and Brazil uses 2001 values for 2000 given data availability. Data labels use International Organization for Standardization (ISO) country codes.

driven, among other things, by strong growth of the poor household incomes and convergence of household incomes in the middle of the distribution. The decline in inequality between states has been led by stronger overall income growth in poorer states.

In Chapter 9, *Ravi Balakrishnan, Frederik Toscani,* **and** *Mauricio Vargas* put inequality and poverty developments in Brazil into a regional perspective. They argue that even though Latin America as a whole made significant progress in the 2000s in reducing poverty and inequality, improvement has been particularly pronounced in commodity-exporting countries. They argue that the commodity price boom led to lower labor income inequality, owing to a decline in the skill premium and the expansion of services and lower-skill jobs. Combined with social transfers, these factors yielded lower overall inequality and poverty. Against this backdrop, they argue, absent policy measures and with lower future commodity prices and limited fiscal space in countries in Latin America, including Brazil, are at significant risk of a slower decline in poverty and inequality. To preserve or improve social progress they call for maintaining the quality of social spending by increasing revenues and reprioritizing other spending, boosting the flexibility of labor markets and deploying policies aimed at retooling workers, and improving education outcomes.

Figure 1.6. Commodity Terms of Trade and Poverty

Average Commodity Terms of Trade Growth and Change in Poverty Headcount Ratio
(During boom period 2000–14)

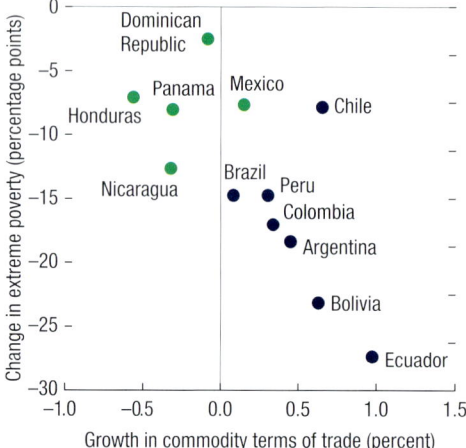

Sources: Inter-American Development Bank, SIMS database; and IMF staff calculations.
Note: Green dots correspond to CAPDR and Mexico, and dark blue dots to South America. CAPDR comprises Central America, Panama, and the Dominican Republic. Chile uses 2013 values for 2014 poverty headcount ratio due to data availability.

RESTORING FISCAL DISCIPLINE

It is clear that improving Brazil's short- and long-term prospects depends critically on curing the fiscal malaise and restoring debt sustainability, notably by addressing structural fiscal idiosyncrasies and modernizing and improving fiscal institutions. *Paulo Medas* argues, in Chapter 10, that Brazil's fiscal framework is very complex. Budgetary rigidity, as a result of many competing constitutional and legal mandates and rules, and a highly constrained budgetary process, because of excessive revenue earmarking and mandatory spending limit the fiscal policy's ability to adjust to shocks or changes in priorities and promotes procyclicality and a deficit bias. Medas calls for a revamp of the institutional framework to limit the deficit bias, improve spending efficiency, and increase accountability. He underscores the need for a medium-term expenditure framework based on a deep transformation of the annual budget process, including a substantial reduction in rigidity, modernizing the public financial management framework, and designing new fiscal rules anchored by a debt target.

Beyond the immediate future, when Brazil's precarious fiscal scenario weighs on the road to recovery and growth, fiscal pressure from population aging

Figure 1.7. Brazil: Expenditure on Pensions
(2014 or latest available estimate)

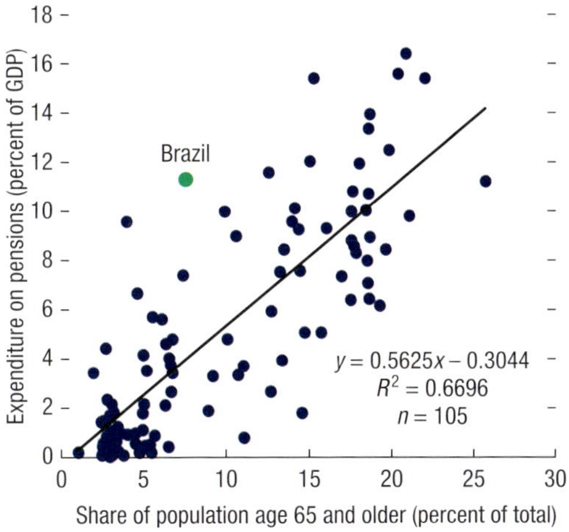

Expenditure on pensions (percent of GDP)

Brazil

$y = 0.5625x - 0.3044$
$R^2 = 0.6696$
$n = 105$

Share of population age 65 and older (percent of total)

Sources: World Bank, World Development Indicators; and IMF staff estimates based on a sample of 184 countries.

presents an enormous challenge. *Alfredo Cuevas, Izabela Karpowicz, Carlos Mulas-Granados, Mauricio Soto, Marina Mendes Tavares,* and *Vivian Malta* argue, in Chapter 11, that unlike in other countries, where demographic disequilibrium points to difficult times ahead, the Brazilian pension system is already showing large cash deficits owing to structurally high, and growing, spending. This problem has been exacerbated by lower contributions as a result of the recent recession. More important, they note that public age-related spending (on retirement and other pensions) is projected to be fiscally unsustainable within the next decade. Given the situation, they elaborate several options to address the problem. They argue that a combination of reforms, including a higher retirement age, changing the benefits indexation formula, and removing existing payroll tax exemptions has the potential to contain future deficits and maintain the integrity of the system. They advocate beginning reforms without delay, because the recurrent pension deficits will put growing pressure on the public finances as a whole, and the necessary reforms will only become more difficult the longer the system continues to operate according to its current rules.

The fiscal situation in Brazil appears even more daunting when one examines the balance sheet of subnationals. *Guillerme Merces, Fabian Bornhorst,* and *Nayara Freire* examine, in Chapter 12, the impact of the recession on the public finances of Brazilian states and review recent modifications to the subnational fiscal framework. They argue that a history of subnational bailouts by the federal government since the 1980s has shaped today's intergovernmental relations and the fiscal responsibility legislation. They note that only a few, albeit important, states face high debt, but point out that the recession uncovered structural fiscal problems similar across all states, centered around high and rigid personnel and social security expenditures. Arguing that the fiscal recovery regime is a vehicle to overcome liquidity problems, they emphasize that implementation of structural reforms at the state level must advance with greater urgency to secure the sustainability of subnational fiscal accounts.

Brazil's public-sector wage bill is high and, after social secutity, is the biggest item in the budget. *Izabela Karpowicz* and *Mauricio Soto* in Chapter 13 consider various aspects of the wage bill, comparing it with the private sector and wage bill in other countries. Lowering the wage bill is necessary to comply with the federal government expenditure ceiling, stimulate administrative efficiency, and bring more equity into the system. A reform should include subnational governments where most of the public employment is concentrated and where the wage bill has grown more pronouncedly in recent years. Because Brazil's wage bill grows inertially due to automatic progression rules, to contain its growth it is necessary to cut salaries in real terms and shrink employment through attrition. In the medium term, a review of the compensation structure should simplify the numerous wage grids, merge allowances into the base wage, and align public sector compensation to private wages in low-skilled professions.

IMPROVING THE MONETARY AND FINANCIAL FRAMEWORK

Following the global financial crisis, emerging markets have experienced a sizable decline in their neutral real interest rates, reflecting both a decline in the rates of interest and output growth in advanced economies and improved domestic fundamentals. Brazil is not different from others in this regard, but the country still features one of the highest real interest rates among peers. *Roberto Perrelli* and *Shaun K. Roache* examine this topic, in Chapter 14, and conclude that domestic factors, including inflation gaps, financial deepening, public debt, and sovereign risk account for high neutral rates in Brazil and for the bulk of the changes in the rate since the inception of the inflation target regime.

The conventional view among economists is that higher interest rates reduce inflation. However, the prolonged period of low inflation and low interest rates in advanced economies following the global financial crisis appears to be inconsistent with this view. This has sparked a debate in Brazil on whether lower interest rates increase inflation (the conventional view) or lead to lower inflation (the so-called Neo-Fisherian view). *Troy Matheson* examines this issue and finds strong evidence, in Chapter 15, in favor of the conventional view of monetary policy transmission in Brazil. He argues that while lower inflation and lower nominal interest rates can be achieved over the long term by targeting a lower level of inflation, this is likely to come at the cost of lower output (and employment) in the short term—a cost that can be mitigated by enhancing monetary policy transparency and credibility. He concludes that monetary policy transmission could be made more efficient by reducing distortions and improving the allocation of resources in the financial sector.

Frequent macroeconomic instability in Brazil has prevented the development of free market finance beyond short-term finance. Historically such situations motivate policymakers to use state intervention in the provision of longer-term finance. State-directed credit makes up half of total credit and amounts to about a quarter of GDP, and such finance largely benefits older, lower-risk, and larger firms, often with the intent of promoting national champions. *Steen Byskov* argues, in Chapter 16, that credit market interventions in Brazil have not delivered the economic benefits they were designed for and have led to high fiscal costs, with subsidies, explicit and implicit, embedded in directed credit peaking at 2.1 percent of GDP in 2015. Such lending, generally provided at regulated interest rates, has, he argues, impeded monetary transmission and led to greater volatility in free market interest rates. He calls for reducing subsidies, as in the recent *Taxa de Longo Prazo* (TLP) reform, both to lower fiscal costs and improve monetary transmission, but also to reduce the resistance to reforming the provision of such credit away from powerful vested interests that receive directed credit.

Following several years of inflation expectations exceeding the midpoint of the central bank's target, and amid a rapid disinflationary process that began in late 2016, inflation forecasts in Brazil are now broadly aligned with the central bank's target. These subdued inflation dynamics are the reflection of a large output gap; hence they are cyclical in nature. Against this background, ensuring that inflation expectations remain well anchored is a policy priority. *Yan Carrière-Swallow* and *Juan Yépez* in Chapter 17 argue that strengthening the Central Bank of Brazil's (CBB) transparency framework and communication strategies—that is, how openly and how well the central bank communicates in guiding markets—could make monetary policy decisions more predictable and keep medium-term inflation expectations firmly anchored. The CBB should continue with its recent practice of providing clear public guidance about the conditional future direction of monetary policy and the balance of risks to inflation reaching the target within the policy horizon.

FIGHTING CORRUPTION AND IMPROVING GOVERNANCE

Corruption has long been recognized as a key problem also for macroeconomic performance in many countries. Corruption and weak governance have been a problem for Brazil. This section looks at three different aspects of the issue. First, how does Brazil compare with other countries in the region? Second, what has Brazil done to improve the institutional framework? Third, is the experience of Brazil unique and what can we learn from other countries experiencing a wave of corruption scandals, such as Italy?

In general, countries in Latin America compare unfavorably with advanced economies regarding perceptions of corruption. However, there is significant variation within the region. Unfortunately, Brazil fares worse than expected, especially given its level of development. In Chapter 18, *Carlos Goncalves* and *Krishna Srinivasan* examine the effect of corruption on economic performance. They find that improvements in perceptions of corruption could boost a country's GDP per capita anywhere from 12 percent to 35 percent, depending on the assumptions. Getting rid of corruption requires an institutional big push, one that revamps the de facto law enforcement capabilities, under strong political leadership and with the support of society, including free and active media.

Brazil has already started the fight against corruption and to improve governance. *Richard Berkhout*, in Chapter 19, discusses the progress in the 20 years since Brazil first joined international efforts against money laundering, terrorism financing, and corruption, and points out that some of the current successes against money laundering and corruption are the result of legal progress several years ago. Yet challenges remain, and further progress is critical. This chapter examines Brazil's progress against money laundering and related corruption, as well as the main risks and mitigation measures, and presents recommendations for further improvement.

What does the future have in store? Brazil has experienced an unprecedented wave of scandals and investigations, which uncovered a network of corruption at the highest level. This wave of scandals has not only economic implications but also deep social and political implications. Is the experience of Brazil unique? And what are the lessons for the future? To answer these questions, *Cristina Pinotti*, in Chapter 20, and *Alessandro Merli*, in Chapter 21, compare the *Lava Jato* experience in Brazil with *Mani Pulite* in Italy. These two scandals have many similarities because both involve an entire political class and had deep and economic implications. For instance, the entire party system, which had dominated Italy for almost 50 years, disappeared in a couple of years. But also, worrisomely, Italy's relative decline accelerated in those years. It is too early to say what the long-term consequences will be for Brazil but, given the important tasks ahead, it is important for Brazil to emerge with a strong political system that can carry on the reforms discussed in this book.

CHAPTER 2

An Eventful Two Decades of Reforms, Economic Boom, and a Historic Crisis

ALFREDO CUEVAS, ANTONIO SPILIMBERGO, KRISHNA SRINIVASAN, AND ALEJANDRO WERNER

INTRODUCTION

After ending hyperinflation in the early 1990s, Brazil embarked on a remarkable economic journey at the beginning of this century. The first part of this chapter reviews this journey, which began with Brazil testing new macroeconomic policy institutions in an environment marked by fear and uncertainty as the first national elections of the new century brought to power a new set of leaders. But Brazil overcame this period of market uncertainty and intense fear, and transitioned to a period of rapid and unexpected economic success, facilitated by a favorable external environment. This was, however, followed by a historic economic collapse, triggered by the global financial crisis, leading eventually to a tentative emergence from the abyss. A truly remarkable journey, with many sharp ups and downs, and all in a matter of less than two decades.

The chapter then elaborates on the underlying forces that drove the Brazilian economy during this journey, leading up to the recent crisis. Policy mistakes were an important part of the process, including the continuation of countercyclical policies, introduced to deal with the effects of the global financial crisis, beyond the point where they were helpful. But fundamental structural weaknesses have also played a role—in fact, an increasingly important one, as the fall in demand during the recession exacerbated their effects.

A durable exit from the crisis will thus require addressing longstanding weaknesses in the public finances, notably those related to the social security system, and in the determinants of productivity and investment, which are key for economic growth. The chapter finally elaborates on possible options to address these weaknesses, concluding that while the economy is now on a gradual mend, it will require strong leadership and unwavering resolve, anchored by a sense of responsibility and partnership among all stakeholders, to place it on a path of strong, sustainable, and inclusive growth.

HISTORIC REFORMS, EXTERNAL TAILWINDS, AND GLARING CONTRADICTIONS

The Closing Years of the Last Century

Brazil's macroeconomic policy framework and institutions evolved significantly toward the end of the 20th century. A key component was the launching of *Plano Real,* spearheaded by Fernando Henrique Cardoso, who was first Minister of Finance and subsequently became President. *Plano Real*—which involved the introduction of a new currency (the real) as part of a comprehensive stabilization program—ended hyperinflation in the mid-1990s. Subsequently in 1999, under considerable pressure from capital flight, Brazil moved to an inflation-targeting framework anchored by a flexible exchange rate regime. Soon thereafter in 2000, the Congress approved the Fiscal Responsibility Law. These three elements— inflation-targeting, flexible exchange rate, and fiscal responsibility—known as the macroeconomic policy tripod, came at the end of previous steps to modernize macroeconomic policy institutions, and would form the basis for improved economic performance in subsequent years.[1] At the same time, efforts at beefing up financial regulation in line with international standards helped improve the resilience of the financial system. In addition, the government also sold (or reduced its stake in) companies such as Telebras and Vale, and privatized several government-owned national and subnational banks. It, however, retained control of some of the large corporations in Brazil, notably Petrobras and Eletrobras, while accepting private minority shareholders in a bid to modernize their governance. The government also retained ownership of Banco do Brasil and the Caixa Economica, two of the largest deposit-taking institutions in Brazil, and the national development bank, BNDES—the Brazilian Development Bank, which it used actively to pursue its development goals.

In sum, against the backdrop of the turbulent 1980s, Brazil embarked on serious reforms in the 1990s, beginning with the *Plano Real*, aimed at liberalizing the economy by addressing large macroeconomic imbalances and structural distortions in the system, but the state remained an important player and a significant participant in the production of goods and services in key sectors of the economy.

The Lula Presidency

After three failed attempts, the Workers' Party candidate, Ignacio Lula da Silva (Lula), won Brazil's presidency in 2002. The prospects of a win by Lula in the 2002 elections had caused significant turbulence and panic in markets in the closing months of the electoral campaign. The Brazilian currency depreciated sharply, requiring the central bank to hike interest rates and intervene heavily in the foreign exchange market. The yield on sovereign bonds skyrocketed as

---

[1]See da Nobrega (2016) and Loyola (2016).

Figure 2.1. Brazil: Daily Asset Prices, 2002–04

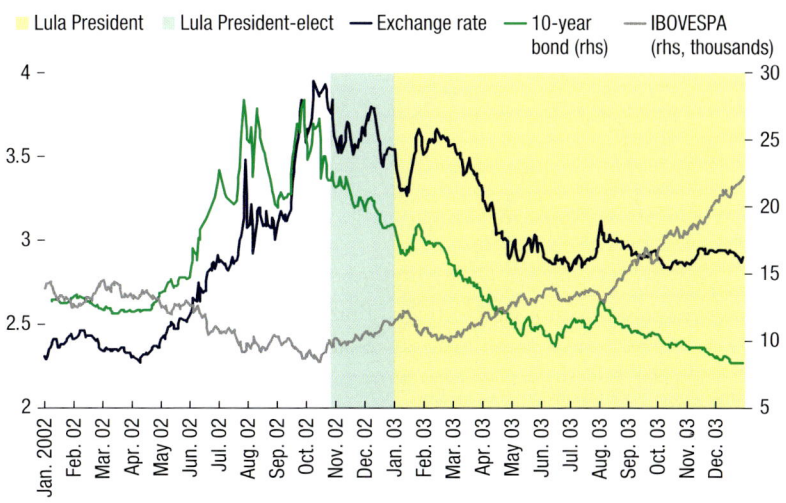

Source: Bloomberg Finance LP.
Note: IBOVESPA = Bovespa Index; rhs = right-hand scale.

investors fled Brazil in fear that a government formed by the Workers' Party would make a strong departure from the macroeconomic policies of the previous eight years (Figure 2.1).

But markets were pleasantly surprised, as President Lula's government pursued successfully prudent macroeconomic and progressive social policies. It made a point of overperforming on the targets included in the IMF-supported economic program negotiated in the closing year of the previous administration, notably pertaining to the primary fiscal balance. The successful implementation of the IMF-supported program was reflected in Brazil's improved access to market financing, which, in turn, helped it repay early, in December 2005, the loans from the IMF.

Strong fiscal performance, with primary surpluses exceeding 3 percent of GDP every year from 2003 to 2008, led to a decline of public debt from 74 to 62 percent of GDP (Figure 2.2). Recognizing the strong fiscal effort, international credit rating agencies gave an "investment grade" to Brazilian sovereign bonds in 2008. In a similar vein, the fiscal record gradually enabled the government to issue bonds in local currency with increasingly long maturities, improving the resilience of the public finances, even as large capital inflows allowed the country to strengthen its international reserves position.

Real GDP growth exceeded 4 percent a year during 2003–08, reflecting, in part, stronger average investment growth than in the previous decade. In addition to fiscal discipline, a favorable external environment helped Brazil strengthen investment and external balances. Brazil benefitted from improved

Figure 2.2. Brazil: Primary Balance and Gross Debt
(Percent of GDP)

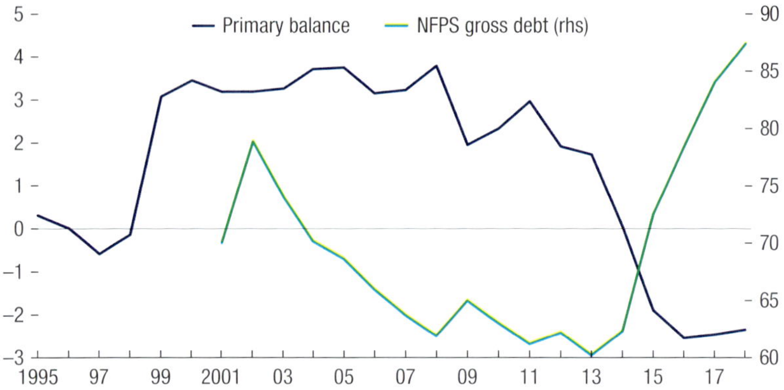

Sources: Country authorities' data; and IMF staff estimates.
Note: NFPS = nonfinancial public sector; rhs = right-hand scale.

terms of trade and registered small current account surpluses during 2003–07. Against this background, the discovery of large reserves of oil bore the promise of turning Brazil into a large producer and even an exporter of oil, and contributed to the rising enthusiasm about the economy's longer-term prospects. At the same time, however, the risks to governance posed by the rapid growth of the oil industry would eventually prove larger than anyone could anticipate at the time.

Going beyond anchoring macroeconomic stability, the government launched important social assistance programs, of which the most well-known initiative was the *Bolsa Familia* conditional-grant scheme. Bolsa Familia remains to date an efficient program, delivering significant "bang" at a modest fiscal cost. A key attribute underpinning the program's success is the focus on children and their mothers, leveraging well-targeted cash stipends to boost both school attendance and the use of public health services. Moreover, real wages also increased considerably from 2002 through 2009 owing, in large part, to the increase in minimum wages. Because of the social programs and other factors, income inequality, measured by the Gini coefficient, fell from 59 to 54 percent during the Lula administration.

The Global Financial Crisis

Although a relatively closed economy, Brazil was not spared by the global recession that followed the global financial crisis. Real GDP growth turned negative in 2009, hurt by falling exports and an abrupt deceleration in credit growth. Like other countries around the world, the government responded with countercyclical policies. It pursued orthodox fiscal stimulus, reflected in a decline of the primary balance by two percentage points of GDP, as well as "quasi-fiscal" expansion in the form of an increase in the lending operations of the public banks ("policy lending"). Notably, BNDES received significant funding from the National Treasury in the form of government bonds, which it sold in the open market to obtain resources for its own lending operations (carried out mostly at the Taxa de Juros de Longo Prazo or TJLP, a below-market rate set quarterly by the government). Owing to these actions, and to the rebound in the terms of trade, the economy responded energetically in 2010, with real GDP growth exceeding 7 percent.

The exit from recession seems to have been a moment of change in the orientation of economic policies in Brazil. The immediate success in reviving the economy strengthened the government's self-confidence as a manager of the economy, notably at a moment when the global financial crisis was viewed by many as proof that market economies could not be trusted to regulate themselves and that stability and development required strong state leadership.

Many of the changes in economic policy in Brazil that began during Lula's second term, in large part as a response to the recession, would become permanent under President Rousseff, who succeeded Lula in January 2011. The expansion in the activity of public banks continued, and the injection of funds to BNDES would go on for several years, reaching a cumulative amount of nearly 9 percent of GDP by 2014. Although the initial wave of policy lending did have a positive impact on activity, the multiplier effects of policy lending declined over time as conditions improved in global and domestic financial markets.[2]

This approach to government-led development came to be popularly known as the *new matrix of economic policies.* While maintaining formal allegiance to the tripod, the new matrix was characterized by a larger presence of the state in the economy, a distrust of markets, and riskier macroeconomic policy choices. State intervention increased in the electricity sector, for example, because of which lower tariffs for end users were imposed in a context of high generation costs, leading producers and distributors to increase their borrowing—debt financing—in the expectation of future compensation from the state. Similarly, the expansion of lending by public banks would boost investment and growth, while interest rates were kept low even as inflation remained stuck near the upper limit of the target band and despite an ongoing credit-fueled consumption boom, in the expectation that low rates would push the economy into a superior equilibrium characterized by fast growth and low inflation.[3]

Petrobras, the state-owned oil company, offers a useful prism to view the detrimental impact of some of the new policies. The company pursued ambitious expansion plans, as it was viewed as a lever for the development of the domestic industrial sector, even though the strategy was highly cost ineffective. This is best

---

[2]The evidence suggests that the expansion of lending by public banks became progressively less important for economic activity (IMF 2016a). In fact, BNDES loans were in large part directed to large companies with access to market financing. There were extreme cases in which BNDES loans did not fund capital expenditure in Brazil as much as they did purchases of foreign assets or government securities.

[3]See Almeida (2013).

exemplified by the contracting of local shipyards to build deep-sea platforms despite their high production costs and long delivery delays. Meanwhile, despite high world oil prices that made expansion so attractive, Petrobras was losing money in its downstream activities, as it had to sell fuels (some of which were imported) domestically at below-market prices. In addition, as police investigations would later reveal, Petrobras was routinely overpaying its contractors and suppliers, who acted in collusion with strategically placed Petrobras executives in a corrupt scheme that also involved notable figures in the political system as well as political parties, according to federal prosecutors.[4] As a result, owing to an ambitious growth strategy financed by massive borrowing, and burdened with secondary objectives, mismanagement, and corruption, Petrobras became the most leveraged oil major in the world by 2014.

The deterioration of macroeconomic policy management, including the inconsistency of policies, had a deleterious effect on credibility. When the central bank tightened monetary policy in 2013, it found itself working against the continuing expansion of lending by public banks. In the case of fiscal policy, the primary surplus declined continuously until it vanished by 2014. Nevertheless, the desire to continue showing healthy primary fiscal balances even as the government pursued an accommodative stance led to the use of practices that masked the underlying state of public finances. This included the frequent recourse to tax amnesties, the anticipation of dividends from state-owned enterprises to boost revenues temporarily, and the exclusion of some expenditures from the computation of the fiscal balances subject to annual limits or "targets" established by Congress in line with the dictates of the Fiscal Responsibility Law—which thus lost much of its relevance and credibility as an anchor of the government's fiscal stance.[5] Some of these practices, however, went beyond "window dressing," and amounted to what the National Accounting Tribunal in 2015 considered to be de facto lending to the government by the state-owned banks, which is forbidden by the Fiscal Responsibility Law.

Opaque practices were also being followed in some states, which adopted ad hoc accounting conventions to facilitate the observance of the limits prescribed in the Fiscal Responsibility Law, notably on the states' wage bill as a share of their revenues.[6] Resorting to these practices was spurred by the continuous deterioration in the finances of several states, especially arising from the increasing cost of

---

[4]The illicit practices uncovered by the justice system were part of these Brazilian contractors' operating procedures in their dealings outside Brazil as well, in many cases with officials at the highest level in foreign governments.

[5]See Mendes (2014) and Almeida (2013).

[6]For example, in the state of Rio de Janeiro the wage bill (which includes the benefits paid to retired former civil servants) was reported until 2015 net of oil royalties earmarked for the financing of pensions. When oil prices collapsed, the accounts showed steep increases in expenditure. See FIRJAN System (2017).

Figure 2.3. Brazil: Real GDP per Capita Growth, 1902–2017
(Yearly percentage change)

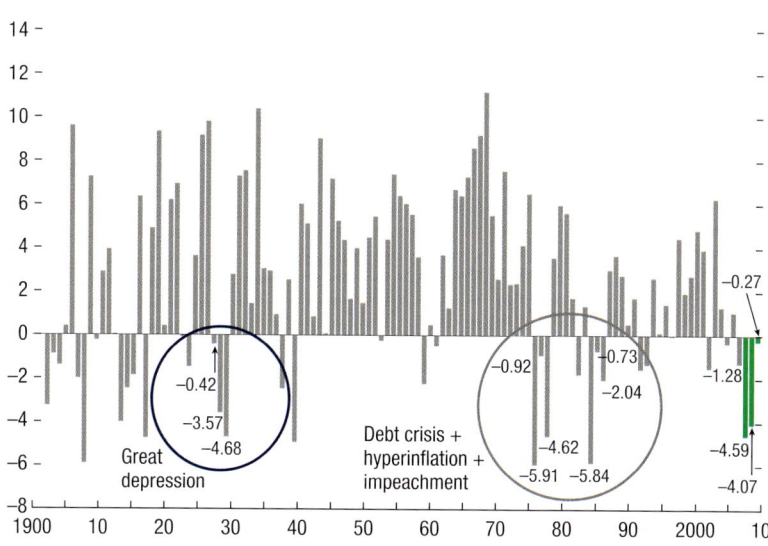

Source: Authors' calculations based on data from Haddad (1975) and IBGE (2007).

retirement benefits for former state government employees. Such deterioration would accelerate with the recession.

BRAZIL'S WORST RECESSION IN MEMORY

The recession that began in late 2014 in Brazil deepened to historic proportions, before bottoming out in early 2017 (Figure 2.3). The recession was the result of an interplay of external and domestic, economic and political, structural and conjunctural factors, and cut across many sectors of the economy. It must be stressed, however, that the recession did not morph into a balance of payments or a financial crisis. The soundness of the banks and the strong external reserves of the country undoubtedly helped keep the recession, which had a major fiscal aspect, from reaching into those other dimensions.

The recession's key driver was a sharp contraction in investment, arising in large part from a (perceived) deterioration in the country's medium-term prospects (Figure 2.4). This can, in turn, be attributed to a combination of the adverse business environment owing to interventionist government policies, declining policy credibility, heightened political and policy uncertainty, and the end of the commodity super-cycle, which had been greatly beneficial for Brazil. The last factor is more important than one might imagine at first blush. For sure, Brazil is a large and diversified economy, but in the years preceding the recession, Petrobras alone was making capital expenditures in the order of 2 percent of GDP per year. The

Figure 2.4. Brazil: Decomposition of Gross Fixed Capital Formation Growth
(Quarter-over-quarter growth, deviations from average, accumulated since 2014:Q1)

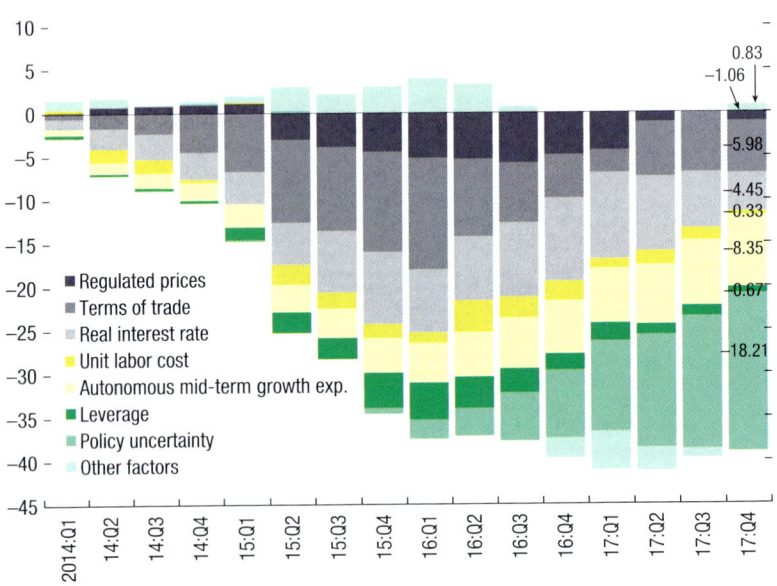

Source: IMF (2016) updated to the fourth quarter of 2017.

collapse of international oil prices in 2014, even more than the corruption scandal, would force a drastic cutback in Petrobras' expansion program.

The deepening economic malaise was compounded by a political crisis. The Petrobras corruption scandal dried up financing for tainted construction companies and fostered a climate of uncertainty. Moreover, policy uncertainty also increased with the surprising change of policy direction foreshadowed immediately after the October 2014 election. President Rousseff was reelected on a platform of continuity with the policies of her first term. However, soon after winning in the second-round vote in October 2014, her government acknowledged that various aspects of the economy required correction, but this admittance did not resonate with her base.

The appointment of a new Finance Minister was viewed by markets as a sign of willingness to correct course, garnering the government some support among investors. However, policy uncertainty remained high, as the cabinet was divided on economic policy issues, undermining policy coherence. For example, while it was pushing for cuts in discretionary spending, the government renewed for another four years the indexation formula for the minimum wage, which would raise mandatory expenditures. Moreover, different branches of government could not agree on a policy direction, and sometimes adopted unexpected and inconsistent positions. For instance, "fiscally conservative" legislators in Congress repealed the *fator previdenciario*, a provision that encouraged delayed retirement and had been introduced when these legislators' parties had been in power to help contain social security deficits. This forced Rousseff to employ offsetting consolidating measures, further distancing her from her political base.

A further driver of the recession was the procyclical nature of some otherwise necessary consolidation policies. The monetary policy tightening cycle, well justified by the behavior of inflation expectations, would take the policy interest rate (Sistema Especial de Liquidação e Custodia, or SELIC) from 11 percent in the summer of 2014 to 14.25 percent by July 2015.[7] On the fiscal policy side, for example, besides discretionary spending cuts, the government increased fuel excises—just as Petrobras was increasing its ex-refinery domestic fuel prices towards import parity. The government also announced that it would not compensate electricity distributors for the losses incurred in past years. This would lead to a very large increase in electricity tariffs, averaging some 57 percent in the first quarter of 2015.[8]

These much-needed measures affected demand but did not restore policy credibility, because of the continuing policy uncertainty generated by intra-cabinet and executive-legislature conflicts, nor did they provide confidence of an improvement in economic prospects over the medium-term. Investment continued to decline, dragging activity down. The weakening weighed, in turn, on tax revenues, exacerbating concerns over the fiscal accounts. These concerns deepened with the relaxation of the fiscal targets mid-year, and subsequently, in August, with a draft 2016 budget targeting a primary fiscal deficit. In the absence of a well-articulated fiscal strategy, the repeated modifications of the fiscal targets dashed expectations of a quick turnaround. Rating agencies and markets reacted negatively, downgrading the sovereign debt to "junk" status in late 2015 and pushing up the sovereign borrowing costs and the value of the dollar in local currency. Indeed, the Brazilian currency touched its trough of nearly R4.3 per US dollar in September, reflecting a worsening of the debt dynamics and concerns of fiscal dominance (Figure 2.5).

The policy response was to tighten interest rates further (although the policy rate never quite matched the rise in yields in bond markets), extend foreign exchange (FX) intervention (the notional stock of FX swaps would eventually rise to US$110 billion), and further squeeze discretionary spending while trying to resurrect the financial transactions tax. But soon it became clear that cutting discretionary spending would be insufficient to restore fiscal viability, and equally clear that the Congress was unwilling to approve new taxes. By May 2016, a new Finance Minister was in office who underscored the need for comprehensive social security reform to control the trajectory of mandatory government spending.

---

[7]SELIC is the Brazilian Central Bank's system for performing open market operations in execution of monetary policy.

[8]Policy lending was discontinued as well, after one last transfer to BNDES in December 2014, although it is unclear whether this decision had much additional impact in an environment of falling demand for credit.

Figure 2.5. Brazil: Exchange and Policy Rates

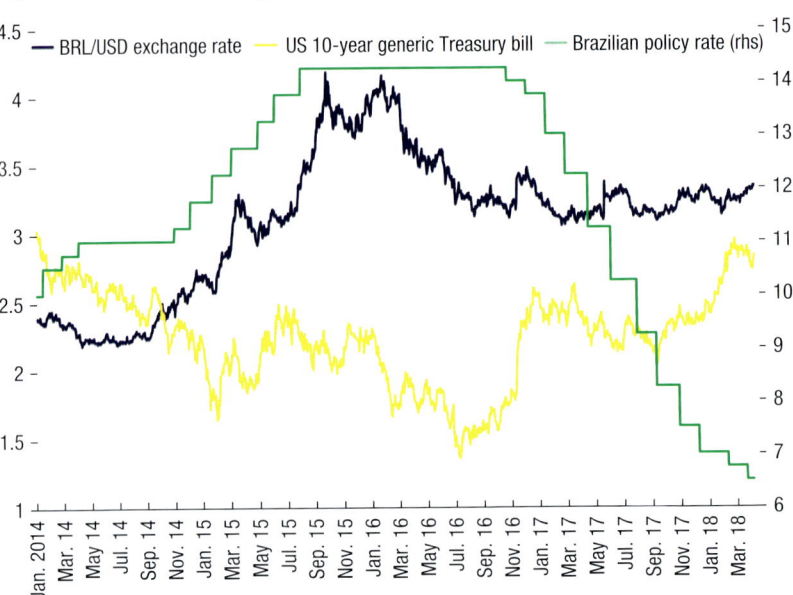

Source: Bloomberg Finance LP.
Note: rhs = right-hand scale.

But by then it was too late for the government to chart the course of events, as political capital was exhausted owing to a deepening of the ongoing recession (real GDP fell by 3.5 percent in 2015, and a further severe contraction was forecast for 2016) and a widening corruption scandal originating in the schemes to defraud Petrobras and other schemes, which by now had engulfed a large number of company executives and politicians at the highest levels. Against this background, the Lower House opened impeachment proceedings against President Rousseff, throwing the country even deeper into political uncertainty. In May 2016, the Lower House suspended President Rousseff and Vice-President Temer became acting President.

The new government announced a strategy to address the underlying fiscal crisis and the recession. The government's plan aimed to shore up policy credibility by initiating a constitutional amendment mandating expenditure rationalization over the medium term through the imposition of a cap on noninterest federal spending (excluding mandatory transfers to subnational governments and other items). The cap, indexed to consumer price index (CPI) inflation, was designed to be effective beginning in 2017 (though not immediately binding) and to be in place in its initial form for nine years, following which the President could initiate legislation to change the cap's indexation mechanism. The amendment was expected, in turn, to confront Congress with the need to introduce

Figure 2.6. Financial Conditions Index

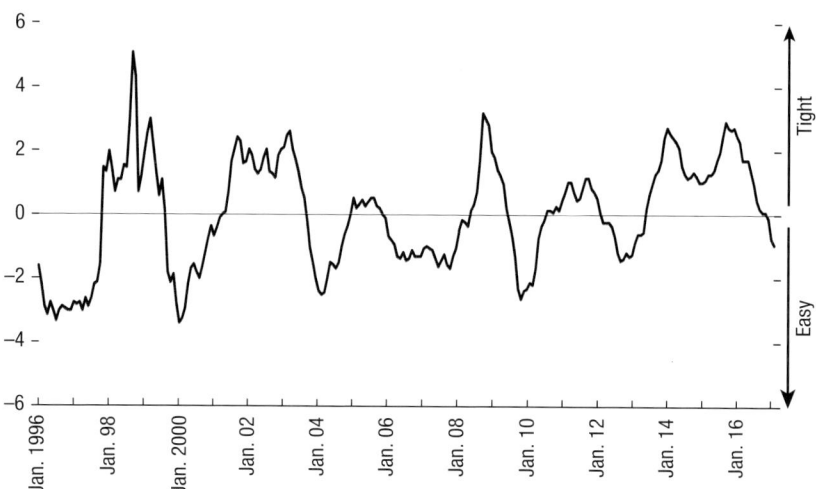

Source: IMF staff estimates.

reforms, notably of social security (pension), to contain the automatic growth in spending over the medium term. This road map somewhat eased market concerns regarding the path of fiscal policy and public debt over the medium term, thereby allowing to set the initial level of the cap at a level that would provide some space to relax fiscal consolidation in the very near term.

The initial phases of the strategy worked well, allowing market conditions to ease (Figure 2.6). The constitutional amendment introducing the expenditure cap was passed in December 2016, and subsequently an ambitious and well-designed pension reform featuring the introduction of a minimum retirement age was submitted to Congress. In early 2017, the government turned to the political task of securing the votes to pass social security reform, trading off some weakening of the original reform for the promise of broad support in Congress.

The process was interrupted by the release in May 2017 of tapes of a conversation between President Temer and a businessman enmeshed in a new and large corruption scandal. This episode dramatically altered the political situation in Brazil, with survival becoming the priority for the government. The President survived a series of legal and judicial challenges. But pension reform never made it to the floor of Congress, and no other initiatives to control mandatory spending materialized.

The evolution of government expenditure is now subject to two conflicting principles: a constitutional norm that limits the growth of nominal noninterest federal spending to the rate of inflation and other constitutional norms (and legislation) which, coupled with forces such as population aging, are working to drive up nominal expenditure at a rate faster than the growth of nominal GDP. This conflict remains to be resolved.

THE DEEPER ROOTS OF BRAZIL'S ECONOMIC CHALLENGES

Fiscal Malaise

The fiscal crisis in Brazil has been long in the making.[10] Two sets of factors dominate in this regard: underlying fundamental forces driving expenditures up and challenging revenues to play catch up, and a budgetary process that, despite all the institutional advances culminating in the Fiscal Responsibility Law, remains highly distorted because of political fragmentation.

Starting with the budget process, a fundamental factor is the high degree of fragmentation of political representation.[11] No less than 27 political parties are represented in the Federal Congress. In the presence of such fragmentation, the approval of any legislation requires the formation of large coalitions, which are cemented, in the best of cases, by decisions over the allocation of public spending. For years, Congress has habitually revised upwards revenue forecasts made by the government so that it can allocate the additional "revenue" to various spending projects. The executive would then endeavor to under-execute some of the spending added by the Congress to the annual federal budget employing the so called *contingenciamentos*. In time, Congress would come to approve tighter rules for these contingenciamentos. The 2016 constitutional amendment aimed to overhaul this process by imposing a hard budget constraint in the form of the expenditure cap. Despite all these measures, Brazil remains one of the countries with the highest public expenditure as a share of GDP among the countries in the region (Figure 2.7).

One effect of this type of process has been the proliferation of revenue earmarking in Brazil, as each interest and cause aims to secure a permanent revenue source, which makes the budget highly rigid. Widespread earmarking implies that even when the economy is doing well, the positive impact on fiscal outcomes is muted by the need to increase certain categories of spending in line with the buoyant revenues. The constitutional amendment that introduced the expenditure cap also simplified some of the main earmarking schemes, but retained the obligation to allocate at least a given real (CPI-indexed) amount to health and education.

A key underlying driver of spending in Brazil is the social security system. Despite still having a relatively young population, Brazil's spending on social security is on par with countries that are more advanced in their demographic transition. The reason is a combination of schemes with generally easy qualification rules, including low effective retirement ages, relatively high replacement rates, and generous formulas for updating benefits, which go beyond cost-of-living adjustment. Two examples:

- In the general pension scheme for private sector workers, the payment to existing beneficiaries grows at nearly the same rate as total contribution

---

[10]An essential reading on the long-term drivers of fiscal pressure in Brazil is Almeida, Lisboa, and Pessoa (2015).

[11]For a discussion in an international comparative context see IMF (2016).

Figure 2.7. LA6: Government Expenditures

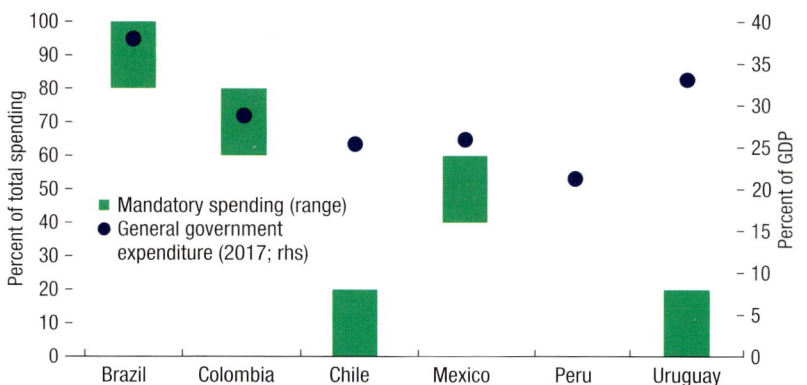

Source: Celasus, Oya, and others (2015).
Note: Shadowed areas are ranges. LA6 = Brazil, Colombia, Chile, Mexico, Peru, Uruguay; rhs = right-hand scale.

revenue, leaving insufficient contribution revenue growth to pay for the increase in the number of beneficiaries, which takes place at a rate of 3.5 percent a year.[12]

- Teachers tend to retire not long past age 50, often with a pension equal or close to their full salary, which increases every year at the same rate as the salaries of active teachers. The aging of the body of state civil servants is a main factor contributing to the deterioration of state government finances. In some states, such as Rio Grande do Sul, the annual cost of pension benefit payments already exceeds the cost of the salaries paid to active civil servants.

And with the population aging, all pension systems will come under increasing financial stress over time: precisely the reason why reform is so important to ensure the long-term viability of the social security system.

At times, a positive environment allowed revenue to grow as a ratio to GDP, offsetting the growth in the spending ratio (itself contained during those positive times). But every so often, new taxes had to be legislated to help revenue keep up with spending—and failing that, debt had to be issued. Revenue ratios should improve from their recent lows as the economy emerges from the recession; but nothing suggests, let alone guarantees, that revenue can permanently keep up with expenditure without new tax increases (Figure 2.8). However, as illustrated by the failure to enact anew the financial transactions tax in 2015–16, Brazil is finding it increasingly difficult to address its expenditure problem with new sources of revenue. Thus, social security reform and other forms of expenditure rationalization are needed to bring the deficit and debt trajectories under control and to meet the new constitutional limits on federal noninterest spending in an orderly way. Increasing efficiency in spending will moreover be

---

[12]See Cuevas and Karpowicz (2016) and their contribution in this book.

Figure 2.8. Brazil: General Government Expenditure and Revenue, 1996–2017
(Percent of GDP)

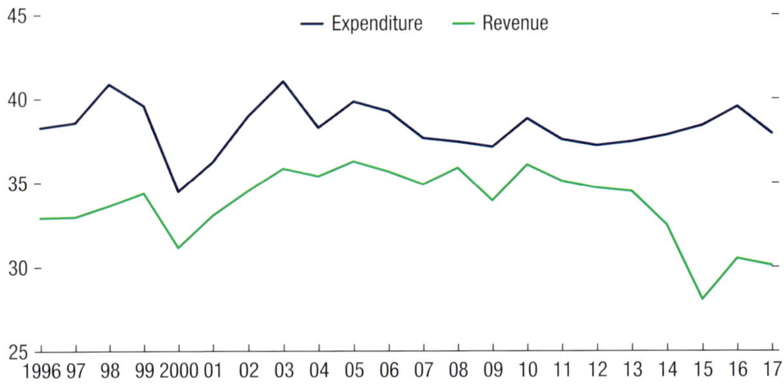

Sources: Country authorities' data; and IMF staff estimates.

necessary to ensure that the government continues to operate effectively under tighter budget limits.

Finally, the fiscal system remains very inefficient. Not only is the tax burden high, it is highly distortionary, owing to legacy factors and the compulsions of a fragmented political system. In a similar vein, tax expenditures are also high and highly distortionary. And last, but not least, the tax code is so complicated that its interpretation is very contentious, giving rise to several appeals, which in the context of an inefficient and slow judiciary system, increases the real burden for the taxpayers. The silver lining is the broad consensus across most stakeholders on the urgent need and scope to rethink the architecture of the tax system.

Productivity and Growth—Stuck in Low Gear

Over the last 40 years, the Brazilian economy has grown on average by 2.7 percent per year (Figure 2.9). This is remarkable for two reasons. First, growth has been mean reverting, whereby, notwithstanding any shock to the economy, growth has always gone back to the disappointing long-term trend. Second, growth has been driven solely by population growth and capital accumulation, even as productivity growth has essentially remained constant. The picture is grimmer once the contribution of human capital is taken out, with labor productivity averaging less than 1 percent per year over the last 10 years, significantly below levels in other upper-middle income countries. In essence, weak productivity is undoing the positive effect of the massive investment in human capital, which has, in turn, contributed to undermining the economy's competitiveness. This underscores the need for reforms aimed at alleviating the structural impediments to growth.

Although a range of factors have contributed to weak productivity and growth, this chapter focuses on four of them, which seriously shackle Brazil's productive

Figure 2.9. Productivity and Real GDP

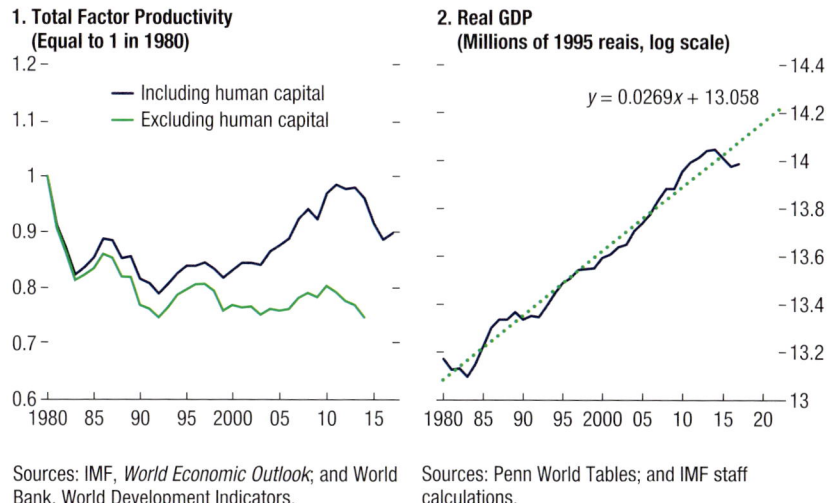

1. Total Factor Productivity
(Equal to 1 in 1980)

— Including human capital
— Excluding human capital

2. Real GDP
(Millions of 1995 reais, log scale)

$y = 0.0269x + 13.058$

Sources: IMF, *World Economic Outlook*; and World Bank, World Development Indicators.

Sources: Penn World Tables; and IMF staff calculations.

potential. These include the relatively closed nature of the economy, poor infrastructure, inefficient allocation of credit, and an inefficient state.

Trade woes. Brazil remains a relatively closed economy, with limited integration into global value chains, and structural trade indicators compare poorly with peers and other G20 countries (Figure 2.10). Brazil's goods trade—at about 25 percent of GDP in 2017—is about half the size of that in China, India, Peru, Russia, and about a third of the size of trade in Chile and Mexico, while the volume of trade in goods and services relative to GDP is among the lowest in the Brazil, Chile, Colombia, Mexico, and Peru (the "LA5") and BRICs—Brazil, Russia, India, and China. Low trade integration can be explained, in part, by Brazil's relatively restrictive system of trade taxes. Good imports face a weighted average applied most favored nation (MFN) tariff of about 10 percent, the highest among LA5 and peers in BRICS, even as they are subject to a complex system of internal taxes. And Brazil's network of preferential trade agreements covers a relatively small share of world trade compared to its peers.

Despite its traditionally closed economy, Brazil made important strides between 1988 and 1994 in opening its economy, notably by drastically reducing tariff and nontariff barriers. But such reforms were short lived, and growing current account deficits following the 1990s trade liberalization led to a distinct reversal in the path toward a more open and market-based economy. Indeed, beginning in the early-2000s, Brazil introduced several nontariff barriers, began taxing numerous imports, and introduced measures to protect the domestic industry. As a sign of continuing protectionism, nontariff barriers, especially anti-dumping measures, increased considerably following the global financial crisis. Inward-looking policies, notably tariffs on capital goods have impeded

Figure 2.10. Selected Trade Policy Indicators
(0 = least open country in G20; 1 = most open country in G20)

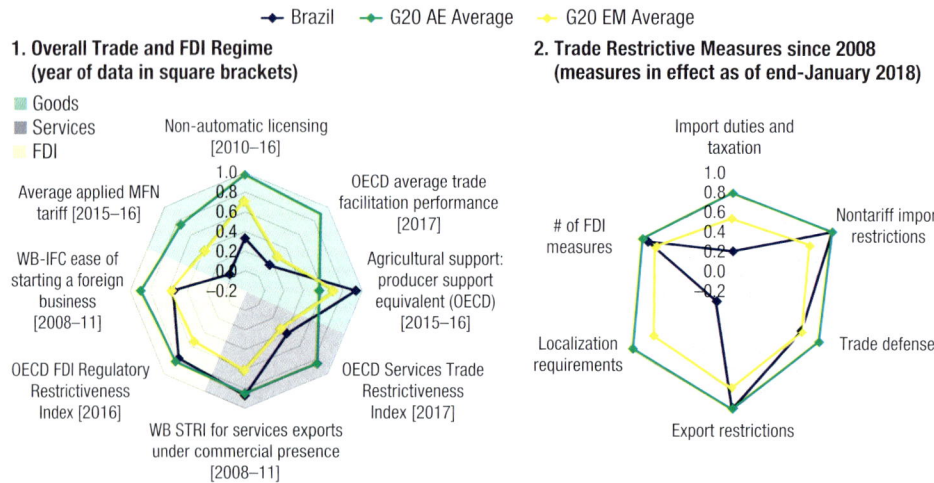

Sources: Tariff data are from the World Trade Organization (WTO), World Tariff Profiles; the import licensing measure is based on UNCTAD TRAINS and COMTRADE data; the average trade facilitation performance, agricultural support measure, Services Trade Restrictiveness Index (STRI), and FDI Restrictiveness Index are from the OECD; WB STRI is from the World Bank; the post-global financial crisis indicators are from Global Trade Alert.
Note: The indicators reflect no judgment as to WTO compliance of underlying measures, nor whether certain measures (such as trade defense) are an appropriate response to the actions of other countries. The "ease of starting a business" indicator is based on perceptions as part of an established IFC survey process. AE = advanced economy; EM = emerging market economy; FDI = foreign direct investment; G20 = Group of Twenty; IFC = International Finance Corporation; MFN = most favored nation; OECD = Organisation for Economic Co-operation and Development.
[1] Import (export) coverage ratio, except for the case of FDI (number of measures).

domestic investment and productivity, even as ill-conceived industrial policies have lowered the overall competitiveness of the Brazilian economy.

Poor infrastructure. Brazil's limited trade integration both within Latin America and with rest of the world can be explained, at least in part, by poor infrastructure, which has also been a drag on domestic investment. The gap in Brazil's infrastructure is large when compared to other emerging economies, its trade competitors, and relative to the country's level of development. On an overall score for infrastructure quality, Brazil ranked 120 out of 144 countries surveyed by the World Economic Forum in 2014, with particularly poor results for roads and air transport quality, while in other areas it ranked in the bottom third of countries surveyed. Most strikingly, the quality of infrastructure in Brazil compares very poorly with most of its major export competitors—this is particularly true for all areas of transport infrastructure—roads, ports, railroads, and air transport (Figure 2.11). Even in areas where it has invested more recently, such as electricity and telecommunication, outcomes have fallen short of expectations. For instance, according to the 2017 World Bank Enterprise Survey, nearly 50 percent of firms in Brazil indicated that electricity was a major constraint to

Figure 2.11. LAC6 and Trade Competitors: Quality of Infrastructure, 2007–18
(Index, 7 = best)

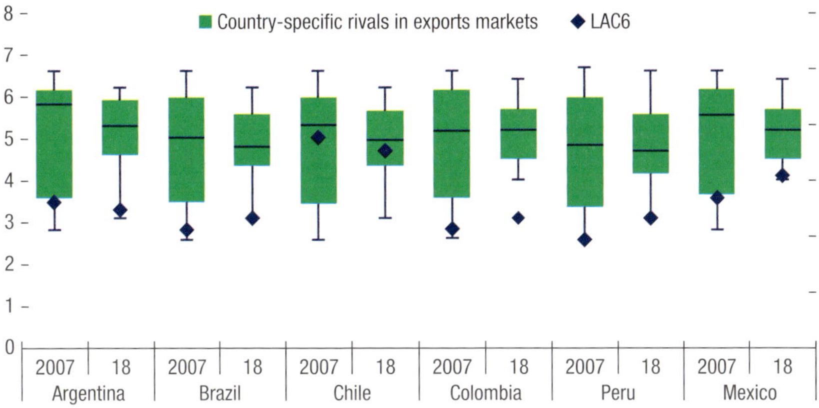

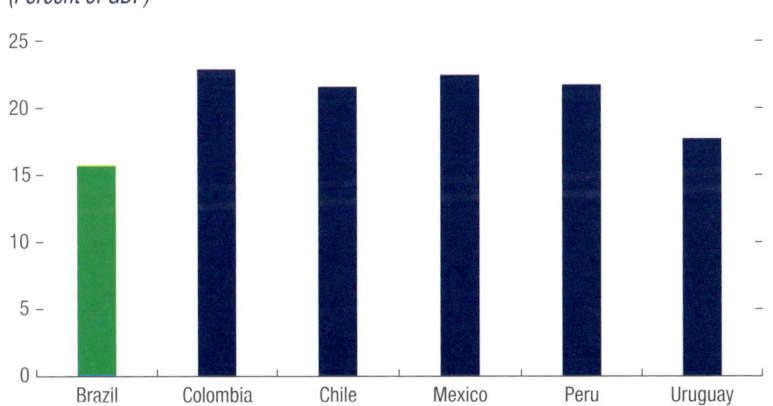

Source: Cerra and others (2016), with updated data.
Note: LA6 = Argentina, Brazil, Chile, Colombia, Mexico, Peru.

activity, compared to 38 percent in rest of Latin America. Quantitative indicators of infrastructure paint a similarly grim picture—for instance, in a country which relies a lot on road transportation for moving goods within and across borders, less than 15 percent of Brazil's roads are paved, which leads to congestion and high costs, significantly undermining competitiveness and growth (Figure 2.12).

Impaired credit and capital markets. Brazil's infrastructure gap is attributed, in large part, to prolonged period of underinvestment relative to other countries. Indeed, infrastructure investment in Brazil has declined from an average of 5.2

Figure 2.12. Gross Fixed Capital Formation, Current Prices
(Percent of GDP)

Source: World Economic Outlook database.

percent of GDP in the early 1980s to an average of 2¼ percent of GDP over the last two decades, and compares unfavorably with other major emerging economies—the decline is explained, in part, by a sharp decline in public infrastructure investment, reflecting limited fiscal space given growing budgetary rigidities and mandatory current spending. The slack was, however, not offset by a pickup in private investment, which has remained lackluster, owing, in part, to underdeveloped capital markets—market capitalization in Brazil still lags other major emerging markets. The private sector has therefore had to rely on bank financing. In recent years, about half of the available credit has been subsidized, with state banks playing a key role, even as interest margins remained very high. Because of this inefficient financial intermediation, investment, and savings in Brazil remain low, with investment, at 15.7 percent of GDP in 2017, being particularly low compared to other emerging markets and reflected in the poor state of infrastructure (Figure 2.12).

An inefficient state. Inefficiency is evident in the tax system, regulation, labor markets, and credit and commercial policies. The federal tax system in Brazil remains inefficient in many aspects—indirect federal taxes (PIS/COFINS—Program of Social Integration/Contribution for the Financing of Social Security) are exceedingly complex, and contribute to unduly large compliance costs, creating opportunity for corruption. According to the World Bank's *Doing Business Indicators,* the cost of paying taxes in Brazil is higher than the average in Latin America and has been increasing over the last several years. Similarly, regulations governing the establishment of a business are more onerous in Brazil compared to other Latin American countries; trading across borders is particularly difficult, in terms of both time and cost, with Brazil ranking 149 in the world; state efficiency, including corruption and quality of bureaucracy, is very low in Brazil, given its level of income; and local content requirements are also distortionary and contribute to the low productivity growth. Finally, public wages in Brazil have a relatively high premium when compared with wages in the private sector. In addition to the large fiscal cost, this has underpinned significant distortion in the labor markets.

THE LONG ROAD TO STRONG AND DURABLE GROWTH

Brazil is slowly emerging from a long and deep recession, but the road ahead to secure strong, durable and inclusive growth is likely to be long and, possibly, tortuous. It will test the verve, resolve, and commitment of the leadership and will require sacrifice and burden sharing by all stakeholders, including the citizenry. In addition to macroeconomic stability, underpinned by an appropriate policy framework, securing the growth objectives will require ambitious structural reforms.

The Near-Term Policy Mix

The policy mix going forward should be geared towards sustaining the nascent recovery, safeguarding against potential risks, and putting the economy back on a sure footing. Over the near to medium-term, a continued focus on fiscal

Figure 2.13. Qualitative Indicators

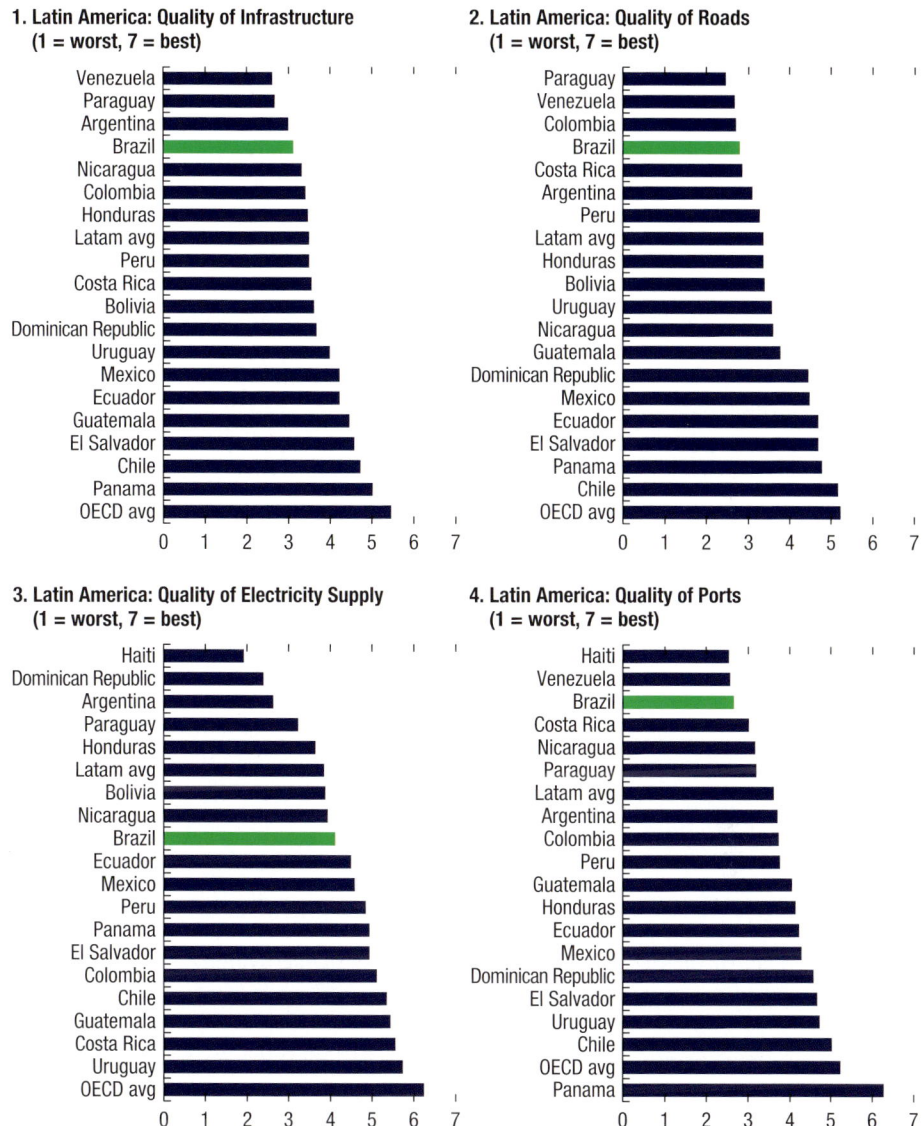

1. Latin America: Quality of Infrastructure
(1 = worst, 7 = best)

2. Latin America: Quality of Roads
(1 = worst, 7 = best)

3. Latin America: Quality of Electricity Supply
(1 = worst, 7 = best)

4. Latin America: Quality of Ports
(1 = worst, 7 = best)

Source: World Economic Forum.
Note: Latam = Latin America; OECD = Organisation for Economic Co-operation and Development.

consolidation will remain crucial for underpinning macroeconomic stability and restoring market confidence in policymaking in Brazil. More on the fiscal below. Monetary policy should remain data dependent, focusing on the evolution of inflation and expectations, market signals, external conditions, and the progress with fiscal consolidation. The flexible exchange rate regime is an important cornerstone of the policy framework, and monetary policy should respond to exchange rate fluctuations only to offset possible second-round effects on inflation, while intervention in the foreign exchange market should be limited to episodes of excessive market volatility.

Improving the central bank's credibility. In the context of falling inflation, the merits of lowering the inflation target for 2019 are being debated in Brazil. While such a move would clearly bring the inflation target closer in line with targets adopted by other inflation-targeting centrals banks across both advanced and emerging market economies, and possibly improve credibility, policymakers should internalize fully the reduction in the space for monetary easing that such an action would entail. On balance, given the current state of the economy and the need for fiscal prudence for the foreseeable future, there is little merit in lowering the inflation target at this juncture.

Improving the inflation targeting framework in Brazil. Reforms to this end could include improving transparency, notably the specification of a well-defined medium-term inflation target, and strengthening the central bank's independence. These policy actions would go a long way in enabling the public understand and anticipate better central bank decisions, help align their medium-term inflation expectations with the central bank's objective, and thus strengthen the effects of monetary policy changes. Moreover, the key to implementing a sustained counter-cyclical monetary policy response, even when supply shocks lead to a rise in inflation above the target, is a sound communication strategy. In this regard, the central bank could improve efforts to provide clear public guidance about the conditional future direction of monetary policy and the balance of risks to inflation reaching the target within the central bank's policy horizon. Explicitly providing guidance on policy "bias" in the run-up to monetary policy decisions, including the publication and discussion of fully endogenous inflation and policy rate projections, could help improve the transmission of policy rates to long-term inflation compensation measures.

A Strategy for Medium-Term Fiscal Consolidation

A key pillar of the policy framework for restoring market confidence in Brazil's ability to secure the growth objectives centers around measures that would help restore fiscal and debt sustainability.

Capping expenditures. As noted previously, in December 2016, Brazil legislated a ceiling on federal noninterest spending, whereby such spending is indexed to the rate of consumer price inflation in the previous year, with the reform including provisions that would trigger a series of corrective measures in case the rule is breached.[13] With this constitutional limit, noninterest expenditure as a

---

[13]The rule will be in effect for 20 years, with an opportunity to modify the ceiling's indexation mechanism after the first 9 years. A few items are excluded from the ceiling, most notably transfers to subnational entities arising from the revenue-sharing system. At the same time, the approval of Congress in 2016 of a legal instrument releasing the earmarking on 30 percent of federal taxes through 2023, should help in meeting the spending ceiling.

share of GDP should decline over the medium term, assuming nominal GDP growth exceeds consumer price inflation. The expenditure cap is a welcome measure, as it lays the basis for gradually exiting a period marked by primary fiscal deficits and very large increases in public debt. This said, it is important that the implementation of the expenditure cap does not lead to creative accounting practices, including the shifting of spending off-budget. This, in turn, begs the question whether the expenditure cap is credible without complementary reforms.

An ambitious social security reform is an imperative. It is needed to ensure the viability of both the expenditure cap and, more importantly, the social security system. Since spending on social security accounts for more than 40 percent of federal government spending, it would be extremely difficult for the government to adhere to the legislated ceiling on expenditures without an ambitious reform of social security. At the same time, a reform of social security is also crucial because of the system's large and rising cash and actuarial imbalances arising from increasing dependency and replacement ratios. The key elements of such reforms should include a higher mandatory retirement age—albeit with some transition rules—and an effective reduction in replacement ratios. In addition, efforts should be made to unify the rules governing the public and private pension systems, since such a move would reduce inequalities arising from the relatively large benefits granted by some of the schemes for government employees, who already command a premium on their salaries.

A road map for medium-term consolidation aimed at restoring sustainability. Notwithstanding the large and rising public debt, fiscal consolidation efforts have been timid and back-loaded. Indeed, under current plans and policies, primary balances will improve only gradually and the public debt-to-GDP ratio would begin to decline several years from now, posing significant risks, especially if the economic environment turns less favorable. There is also a risk of "adjustment fatigue" arising from the incessant talk about adjustment, without any significant progress. This calls for transparency, aimed at laying out clearly and explaining to all stakeholders the need for fiscal adjustment and the potential risks if such adjustment is not pursued, accompanied by a rolling medium-term fiscal framework that clarifies and updates the goals for debt stabilization.

Elements of the medium-term fiscal framework. A medium-term budget framework would bolster policy credibility through the identification of expenditure policies that could be rolled out over time to keep the budget consistent with the expenditure ceiling. In this context, it is important to recognize that social security reform, while essential, will not be enough to meet the expenditure ceiling over the next several years, since its benefits will materialize over a longer horizon. Hence, additional measures are needed. These could include reducing rigidities in expenditures, including those mandated by legislation, and ending the earmarking of revenues to facilitate greater flexibility in the allocation of budgetary resources; revisions to the minimum wage indexation formula, since this is a key driver of social security and other benefit spending; and linking closely wage increases of civil servants to productivity and streamlining their allowances. Moreover, some of these measures, including pension reform, wage restraint, and greater transparency, could be usefully transported to the level of sub-nationals, notably the states and municipalities, many of whose finances are in dire straits. Finally, the credibility of the fiscal framework could be bolstered by further empowering the Independent Fiscal Institution, which was established in 2016 and is attached to the Senate, with a view to improving fiscal forecasts and strengthening the budget process.

Structural Reforms

Structural reforms targeted at opening the economy, improving the efficiency of capital markets, reducing the costs of doing business, and fostering investment are essential to raise the economy's productive capacity and potential growth over the medium-term. While reforms are needed on many fronts, some of them are more critical than others.

Opening the economy. Reducing tariffs, especially on capital goods, eliminating nontariff barriers to trade, including frequent resort to anti-dumping, and eliminating local content requirements would enhance efficiency and boost potential growth. Likewise, pursuing free-trade negotiations, notably outside Mercosur, would help increase competition and foster productivity gains. To avoid the mistakes of the past and ensure that future governments do not retreat from commitments to open the economy, the opening should be enshrined in multilateral treaties. In this context, the prospect of Organisation for Economic Co-operation and Development (OECD) accession can foster trade integration and avoid further backpaddling on structural reforms.

Simplifying the tax system. To boost domestic investment and promote greater trade integration, both within the region and with rest of the world, greater efforts are needed to simplify the federal tax system, especially concerning the distortionary indirect taxes. This should include a simplification of the State Tax on the Circulation of Goods and Services and the PIS/COFINS, which has a complex base, and continuing to work on harmonizing federal and state tax regimes, with a view to reducing taxpayer compliance costs and improving resource allocation and productivity.

Improving credit efficiency. An efficient allocation of capital should play a key role both on the supply side (by increasing efficiency) and, at the same time, on the demand side (by decreasing the cost of capital and increasing investment). The efficiency of capital markets has been undermined by macroeconomic instability, the intrusive role of the state, and regulatory uncertainty. Some progress has been made recently, notably with the reform of the TJLP by linking it to government bond rates, which augurs well for rethinking and reducing durably the role of the state in the allocation of credit. But much more needs to be done, including by reestablishing macroeconomic stability. The financial system has proven resilient to severe macroeconomic shocks, but interest rates for the non-earmarked credit are still too high and an impediment to investment and growth. Various measures could help reducing the interest margins, including simplifying reserve requirements, promoting credit bureaus, establishing a centralized market for receivables, and improving further the bankruptcy frame-work (recovery rates are still below 16 percent of the value). Some of these measures could be implemented by the Central Bank of Brazil, while others require an improvement of the legal system.

Improving infrastructure. From a medium-term perspective, making gains in spatial and social integration by expanding the transport network and improving access to basic infrastructure services in an equitable way remains paramount for development. Given the fiscal constraints, Brazil will have to "do more with less" by leveraging private finance, optimizing costs and eliminating inefficiencies in service provision. While reform needs are numerous, the focus should be on scal-ing up efforts to boost private sector participation in investment financing, improving investment returns, and increasing efficiency. Projects with private participation should also have transparent accounting practices that recognize contingent liabilities that could impact the public finances. In this context, the infrastructure concessions program is critical and ongoing efforts to make the program more attractive to investors while maintaining high standards of gover-nance and program design should continue.

Labor reforms. Ongoing reforms to increase labor market flexibility and reduce excess litigation in labor courts should continue. The flexibility should help reduce labor market informality among the poor, but the potential impact on formal labor market duality remains unclear. Other reforms, notably pertain-ing to labor protection regulations, should be considered alongside policies to support the unemployed.

Tackling corruption. Brazil should continue pursue reforms to further strengthen the governance and anti-corruption framework. The fight against corruption is ongoing, driven by some strong and independent law enforcement and judicial authorities. Changing societal norms that enable and promote cor-ruption requires continuing and intensifying current efforts for years to come. Authorities should continue to empower strong and independent law enforce-ment and judicial authorities that can investigate and prosecute corruption cases at all levels of society. At the same time, to reduce corruption risks in the long term, repression alone will be insufficient to support lasting changes, and other reforms will be necessary. A lesson learned from earlier corruption drives is that authorities must continue to improve the effectiveness of the criminal justice system, and implement preventive actions to reduce money laundering and cor-ruption risks in the longer term.

CONCLUSIONS

Following a remarkable journey starting from the beginning of this century, Brazil finds itself in a difficult situation, marked by a modest and tentative eco-nomic recovery in the context of deep political uncertainty. Transitioning from here to a path of strong and durable growth will require addressing deep-seated economic problems, notably an unsustainable fiscal position, and serious struc-tural impediments, including the economy being relatively closed to trade, inefficiencies in the functioning of the state and in credit intermediation, large infrastructure gaps, and weak governance. Addressing these challenges is not easy and will require strong leadership and unwavering resolve, anchored by a sense of responsibility and partnership among all stakeholders.

REFERENCES

Almeida, Mansueto. 2013. "About Tax Tricks and Creative Accounting." Blog of Mansueto Almeida, January 8.

———. 2015. "The Frst Year of the New Economic Matrix—2012." Blog of Mansueto Almeida.

———, Marcos Lisboa, and Samuel Pessoa. 2015. "The Inevitable Adjustment or the Country That Got Old Before It Developed." Blog of Mansueto Almeida, July 1.

Brazilian Institute of Geography and Statistics. (IBGE). 2007. *System of National Accounts: Reference 2000*. Rio de Janeiro.

———. 2012. *Demographic Census 2010. General Characteristics of the Population, Religion and People with Disabilities*. Rio de Janeiro.

Celasus, Oya, and others. "Fiscal Policy in Latin America: Lessons and Legacies of the Global Financial Crisis." Staff Discussion Note, International Monetary Fund, Washington, DC.

Cerra, Valerie, Alfredo Cuevas, Carlos Góes, Izabela Karpowicz, Troy Matheson, Issouf Samake, and Svetlana Vtyurina. 2017. "Highways to Heaven: Infrastructure Determinants and Trends in Latin America and the Caribbean." *Journal of Infrastructure, Policy and Development* (1): 2 168–89

Crivelli, Ernesto, Sanjeev Gupta, Carlos, Mulas-Granados, and Carolina Correa-Caro. 2017. "Fragmented Politics and Public Debt." In *Fiscal Politics*, edited by Vitor Gaspar, Sanjeev Gupta, and Carlos Mulas-Granados. Washington, DC: International Monetary Fund.

Cuevas, Alfredo, and Izabela Karpowicz. 2016. "The Urgent Case for Pension Reform in Brazil," IMF Diálogo a fondo blog, December 1.

da Nobrega, Mailson. 2016. "'Construction and Dismantling of Fiscal Institutions." In *Public Finances: From Creative Accounting to the Rescue of Credibility*, edited by Felipe Salto and Mansueto Almeida. Rio de Janeiro: Editora Record.

FIRJAN System. 2017. "Economic Conjuncture: The Fiscal Situation of The Brazilian States." FIRJAN System blog, April.

Haddad, Claudio Luiz da Silva. 1975. "Real Product Growth in Brazil, 1900–1947" *Brazilian Journal of Economics* (29).

International Monetary Fund (IMF). 2016. "Brazil Selected Issues." Country Report 16/349, Washington, DC.

———. 2016a. Country Report 16/348, Washington, DC.

———. 2016b. 2016 Article IV—Press Release; Staff Report; and Statement by the Executive Director Country Report 16/348, Washington, DC.

Loyola, Gustavo. 2016. "The Relations between Fiscal Policy and Monetary Policy in Brazil." In *Public Finances: From Creative Accounting to the Rescue of Credibility*, edited by Felipe Salto and Mansueto Almeida. Rio de Janeiro: Editora Record.

Mendes, Marcos. 2014. "What is 'Creative Accounting?'" Brasil Economia Governo, Braudel Institute, São Paulo.

PART II

Growth

CHAPTER 3

Current Constraints on Growth

ARMANDO CASTELAR PINHEIRO AND PAULO DE CARVALHO LINS

After ranking among the world's top-performing economies for most of the 20th century, in the early 1980s Brazil entered a long cycle of low and volatile growth that shows no sign of ending. This dramatic slowdown reflects a large drop in labor productivity growth, a symptom of the inability of the Brazilian economy to move a large enough number of workers to higher-productivity jobs, despite their increasing levels of schooling. This chapter discusses three possible explanations for this poor performance: the failure to complete market-oriented reforms, the adoption of industrial policies focused on protecting inefficient incumbents, and the expansion of policies aimed at favoring small, unproductive firms. The chapter concludes by highlighting six policy focus areas for bringing back sustained growth.

INTRODUCTION

In 1981 Brazil fell into a recession. Despite clear signs that the country's economic fundamentals had significantly deteriorated, as evidenced by a rising foreign debt and soaring inflation, few believed the crisis would be long-lasting. Skepticism was warranted: Brazil's GDP had not contracted in nearly 40 years, and, throughout the 20th century, only as a consequence of major international catastrophes, such as the two World Wars and the Great Depression.

But the good times never did return. Since 1980, brief moments signaled that the good times might be back, but they soon gave way to another crisis. These short boom-and-bust cycles have so fascinated analysts that the dismal performance of the Brazilian economy over this period as a whole has gone nearly unnoticed. Between 1980 and 2017 Brazil grew strikingly little—the country's per capita income rose by just 0.7 percent per year, on average, compared with 1.7 percent in developed countries and 3.0 percent in emerging market and developing economies over the same period. At this rate, it will take Brazil 100 years to double its per capita income.

Following nearly three years of deep recession, Brazil is once again experiencing a moment of hope for a lasting rebound. But what can be done to ensure the country does not once again plunge into a crisis? What can be done to sustain durable and strong growth?

This chapter endeavors to answer these questions, arguing that, while is no silver bullet, a broad set of issues must be addressed. The next section covers Brazil's long-term economic performance and is followed by a discussion of the failed policies of the period after 1980. The final section summarizes the main arguments and suggests six areas that should be the focus of growth-oriented policies.

STYLIZED FACTS REGARDING ECONOMIC PERFORMANCE

Between 1900 and 1980, Brazil's was one of the world's fastest-growing economies, with GDP expanding by about 5.5 percent per year. Between 1951 and 1980, GDP expanded by an average 7.4 percent per year, more than in most other countries in the world and considerably ahead of the rest of Latin America, trailing only Japan and the Republic of Korea. Since 1981, however, Brazil's economic performance has been mediocre at best (Table 3.1). The drastic growth slowdown that marked the period 1981–93 and the modest growth during 1994–2017 were not unique to Brazil, but in both periods the country performed more poorly than the rest of the world and as badly as the rest of Latin America. Particularly noteworthy is that Brazil's economy has systematically underperformed countries such as Chile and Colombia.[1]

These facts suggest that the post-1980 economic slowdown has deep structural roots that may be predominantly homegrown. That is, most regions in the world grew more slowly post-1980 than before, particularly in the 1980s, but the slowdown was much more pronounced in Brazil than most everywhere else. To better understand the cause of this dramatic deterioration in economic performance, consider these four stylized facts (Table 3.2):[2]

- Demographic growth stayed below that of employment throughout the post-1981 period. Only in 1964–80 was the difference between these two growth rates larger than after 1980. This means that the decline in per capita income growth did not result from an unfavorable demographic change, but rather almost exclusively from slower labor productivity gains.

- Human capital per worker increased more significantly in 1981–2017 than in previous periods.

- Investment as a share of GDP was generally lower after 1980 than in previous periods, causing capital per worker to expand much more slowly.

---

[1]The Mexican economy, however, has historically followed a path similar to that of Brazil.

[2]Economic growth was decomposed using the Cobb-Douglas production function $Y = A K^{\alpha} H^{\gamma} L^{1-\alpha-\gamma}$, the inputs of which are labor (L), physical capital (K), and human capital (H), where $\alpha = 0.3$ and $\gamma = 0.5$ (Mankiw, Romer, and Weil 1992; Pinheiro and others 2005). Dividing both sides of the equation by L, taking the logarithm and the derivative over time, yields the following breakdown:

$$\Delta \frac{Y}{L} = \Delta TFP + \alpha \Delta \frac{K}{L} + \gamma \Delta \frac{H}{L}, \text{ where } \frac{d}{dt} log(A) = \Delta TFP.$$

Table 3.1. Comparison of GDP Growth from 1930 to 2000

(Percent)

Country	1931–50[1]	1951–80	1981–93	1994–2017[2]
Brazil	4.6	6.8	2.1	2.4
Argentina	2.9	3.4	1.7	2.2
Mexico	4.1	6.4	1.7	2.5
Chile	2.7	3.4	4.0	4.2
Colombia	3.9	5.2	3.7	3.3
Rep. of Korea	0.6	7.5	9.6	4.4
Japan	1.6	7.9	3.9	1.0
United States	3.2	3.6	3.1	2.4
Latin America & Caribbean	3.6	5.2	2.1	2.7
World	1.8	4.5	3.2	3.8

Sources: Pinheiro and others (2005); and authors' calculations using IMF data.
[1]1930–50 for Latin America and World.
[2]2016 and 2017 values reflect IMF estimates.

- Total factor productivity growth in the post-1980 period was far lower than in all previous periods.[3]

One way to explain these numbers is that, from 1980 onward, Brazil no longer managed to move workers to higher-productivity jobs. Before the 1980s, the country had succeeded in shifting workers across sectors or reallocating them to more productive jobs within sectors. But the country lost its ability to do so; workers who joined the labor force after 1980, although better-schooled than the workers they were replacing, were mostly absorbed by low-productivity sectors, especially traditional services, which saw the greatest increase in number of jobs during this period. Pecora and Menezes-Filho (2014) show that, between 2002 and 2009, skilled workers were in excess supply, so the wage difference between skilled and unskilled workers decreased (see also Menezes-Filho, Fernandes, and

Table 3.2. GDP, Capital, Labor Force, and Human Capital Growth

(Percent, annual average)

	1931–50	1951–63	1964–80	1981–93	1994–2017
GDP	5.14	6.88	7.79	2.10	2.36
GDP per Capita	3.19	3.83	5.19	0.33	1.07
Population	1.95	3.05	2.60	1.78	1.29
Employment	1.84	2.81	3.25	2.17	1.61
GDP/Worker	3.30	4.07	4.54	−0.07	0.75
Contribution to GDP/Worker Variation (percentage points)					
Physical Capital/ Worker	1.04	1.76	1.71	0.13	0.23
Human Capital/ Worker	0.19	0.24	0.08	0.92	0.80
Total Factor Productivity	2.07	2.08	2.75	−1.11	−0.28

Sources: Pinheiro and others (2005); and Lee and Lee (2016).

---

[3]The stagnation of labor productivity (and of total factor productivity) has been reviewed by many Brazilian scholars and is the primary focus of numerous studies. For further reading, see Bonelli, Veloso, and Pinheiro (2017) and the World Bank (2018a).

Picchetti 2006 and Barbosa Filho and Pessôa 2008). Ottoni (2017) presents similar results and shows that workers went to sectors in which their higher schooling was basically lost.[4]

The next three sections analyze three policies that explain why Brazil failed so badly at creating enough higher-productivity jobs: incomplete market reforms, industry policies that protected entrenched companies, and the expansion of policies that favored both formal and informal small companies with low levels of productivity.

INCOMPLETE MARKET REFORMS

Through most of the period of rapid growth, Brazil relied on an import-substitution development model. Although initially pursued without much policy coordination, import-substitution industrialization became the explicit mainstay of economic policy in the 1950s. Trade policy was designed to favor Brazilian industry by, among other things, manipulating the exchange rate, barring certain imports, and subsidizing exports (Pinheiro 2016).[5] The government also relied on state-owned enterprises (SOEs) and public banks, which often supplied industry with low-cost inputs and credit at subsidized rates.

With such widespread incentives, Brazil underwent a rapid structural transformation, reallocating low-productivity agricultural laborers to other, higher-productivity jobs, generally in industry and services. More than 40 percent of the decline in the productivity gap between Brazil and the United States between 1950 and 1980 can be accounted for by this massive structural transformation (Ferreira and Fonseca 2015).

But the economy began to lose steam once the country's sectoral structure approached that of more advanced economies. By then, the perverse incentives embedded in import-substitution policies had begun to hamper growth, and the government turned to propping up growth with public and private debt and tax subsidies. A faltering economy coupled with a rising foreign debt, the second oil crisis, high US interest rates, and foreign investors' growing aversion to Brazilian assets culminated in the 1981–83 crisis.

The economic downturn was then attributed to two interconnected problems. One problem was a lack of control over key macroeconomic variables—as reflected in extremely high inflation and recurrent foreign debt crises, in particular—that paralyzed investment and harmed economic efficiency. Brazil has not entirely overcome these issues to this day, although the Real Plan and the

---

[4]Some argue that increased schooling was concomitant with a decrease in average educational quality such that the true increase in human capital was less than the numbers suggest. The World Bank (2018b) supports this analysis and concludes that Brazilian schools do not teach skills that allow students to be competitive and productive workers.

[5]In practice, the combination of import tariffs and export subsidies on manufactured products, together with an overvalued exchange rate, generated a kind of double exchange system that taxed commodity exporters and favored industry.

fiscal reforms of the late 1990s went a long way to ensure macroeconomic stability. The other problem was the lack of public funds to sustain policies that relied heavily on government subsidies. This limited the government's ability to extend subsidized loans and have SOEs invest significantly in areas like infrastructure.

In the 1990s the government enacted several reforms aimed at reducing its influence in microeconomic decisions. It suspended some export-subsidy programs, removed most nontariff barriers on imports, reduced import tariffs, privatized some SOEs, and deregulated various markets. The idea was to give the private sector a greater role in making investment and resource allocation decisions. However, that policy shift was more the result of lack of alternatives than a wholehearted conversion to a market-friendly development strategy, and this weak commitment was reflected in the depth, breadth, and stability of reforms. As a result, the impact of the reforms of the 1990s was positive but modest.

Thus, despite all the reforms, the government continued to intervene heavily in the economy. Public banks still hold great sway, with Banco do Brasil, Brazilian Development Bank (the BNDES), Caixa, Banco da Amazônia, and Banco do Nordeste do Brasil accounting for 42 percent of total assets, 35 percent of equity, and 49 percent of loan portfolios of Brazilian banks in 2017. And the government owns shares in several private companies through the BNDES and SOE pension funds, both of which are controlled by the federal government (Lazzarini 2011).

Furthermore, the government continued to subscribe to the idea of protecting entrenched companies against competition from domestic, international, and new businesses, which weakened not only natural market selection but also incentives to innovate and seek efficiency gains. Examples of this protection include the loans extended by the BNDES. Bonomo, Brito, and Martins (2015) show that the largest, oldest, and most conservative companies were the primary beneficiaries of BNDES lending. The authors find that these companies have the lowest financial cost compared with nonrecipients, but the effects of these loans on investment are statistically insignificant. Lazzarini and others (2015) also find that companies that had received BNDES loans experienced a decline in their cost of capital, but that this had no effect on investment. In other words, by directing loan subsidies almost entirely to conservative, well-established companies that already had access to the credit market, the BNDES created a barrier to entry and was complicit in the private sector not expanding its investments.

In addition to the incompleteness of structural reforms, the unbalanced nature of macroeconomic policy also contributed to Brazil's inability to sustain economic growth. Specifically, the massive increase in public sector spending, which was driven by higher expenditures on social transfers and services—social security, education, health, basic income, and so on—and by the subsidies extended to businesses, began in the mid-1980s and continued unabated in the following decades. The government's fiscal expansionism forced the central bank to keep monetary policy in contractionary mode, especially once inflation was brought under control in 1994. The results were high cost of capital, currency appreciation, and a severe foreign-debt crisis in the late 1990s. Following that period, the government began to fund its escalating public spending by raising taxes—considerably increasing the complexity and instability of the tax structure—and limiting public investment, which also weakened capital accumulation and the pursuit of efficiency gains.

THE RETURN OF PRO-MANUFACTURING POLICIES

The modest impact of the market reforms of the 1990s encouraged some politicians and economists to more loudly defend a return to policies aimed at increasing the manufacturing share of GDP. Their primary arguments in support of a larger manufacturing sector included the following:

- Factory workers are more productive than workers in the agriculture and services sectors. Thus, when more people are employed in manufacturing, productivity levels should be higher.

- Manufacturing posts a higher rate of productivity growth, so the greater the share of this sector in GDP, the faster the gains in productivity.

- Manufacturing attracts higher levels of research and development, generating spillovers that benefit other sectors through the spread of ideas and the availability of more technologically advanced capital goods.

- Commodity exports are more volatile than those of manufactured goods; therefore, the more manufactured goods a country sells, the less volatile its balance of trade and exchange rate. Macroeconomic stability fosters a higher rate of investment as a share of GDP.

The ensuing policy prescriptions were then put into practice during the da Silva and Rousseff administrations.[6] The primary instruments of industrial policy in that period included the following (ABDI 2014):

- Higher import tariffs on selected products

- Multiple tax exemptions, including lower taxes on capital goods and construction materials, as well as cuts in social security taxes levied on most manufacturing industries (Werneck 2013)

- Local content requirements in the oil and gas sector, both for Petrobras procurement processes and for drilling operations, as well as preferences for domestic manufactured goods in government procurement contracts (in

---

[6]In 2004 President Lula da Silva launched the Industrial, Technological and Foreign Trade Policy Program (PITCE), designed to encourage innovation, increase efficiency, and expand exports of manufactured goods. In 2008, the PITCE was replaced by the Manufacturing Development Policy Program, which was also designed to encourage innovation, competition, entrepreneurship, and exports. During 2011–12 manufacturing policy was revamped under the Brasil Maior Plan, which sought to increase the technological content and exports of manufactured goods. Among its many goals, the Brasil Maior Plan endeavored to raise private investment in science and technology from 0.55 percent to 0.90 percent of GDP and to increase manufacturing as a share of GDP by 1.2 percentage points.

several cases, the government agreed to purchase domestic manufactured goods that cost as much as 25 percent more than identical foreign-made products)

- Massive subsidized credit channeled primarily through the BNDES, including some lines of credit that operated at negative real interest rates (from 2004 to 2015, BNDES disbursements averaged 3 percent of GDP)

Overall, these policies had only a negligible effect on productivity. Indeed, manufacturing has not shown itself to be the propeller of productivity growth that these policies presumed: manufacturing productivity has been steadily decreasing for years, on average by 1.5 percent annually between 1997 and 2015 (Bonelli and Pinheiro 2016). Furthermore, the available empirical evidence does not support the premise that a higher share of manufacturing in GDP would significantly improve average labor productivity. And, one way or another, those policies failed to meet their primary goal of putting the brakes on Brazil's deindustrialization. Two problems in particular seem to have undermined their efficacy.

First, the policies sought to protect entrenched companies from domestic and international competition. Thus, when the government, under da Silva and Rousseff, raised import barriers, it focused its efforts not on nascent industries but on industries in which Brazil had little, or a decreasing, competitive edge. In 2012 the goods that benefited from import tariffs greater than 25 percent were concentrated in the textile, clothing, footwear, automobile, truck, and toy industries (Baumann and Kume 2013). Similarly, the BNDES policy of "national champions" relied on credit subsidies that supported the merger of competitors instead of supporting new entrants, for instance. Therefore, in large part, the government's industrial policy sought not to increase productivity but to keep noncompetitive companies afloat.

Second, the policies pursued in that period produced harmful side effects for the manufacturing sector. Examples abound. Incentives were funded by expansionist fiscal policies, which led to an increase in the unit cost of labor. The growing fiscal deficit and the rapid rise in public debt forced the central bank to keep interest rates high, which caused the exchange rate to appreciate and unfairly harmed those companies that did not have access to subsidized loans. Furthermore, by limiting competition, the government discouraged companies from investing in research and development (Pinheiro 2016). The final outcome was more economic uncertainty and less investment.

Another consequence of the industrial policies pursued by the da Silva and Rousseff administrations was that they discouraged greater integration of Brazilian manufacturing into global value chains. Their local content requirement policies demanded that manufacturers operated vertically integrated with local suppliers, which is inconsistent with integration into global value chains. Indeed, an explicit objective of industrial policy during that period was to deepen the compactness of supply chains, fostering the use of domestically produced intermediate goods. The result, as Rios and Tavares (2013) observe, was that these policies led Brazilian manufacturers to operate under a standard of vertical integration typical of the mid-20th century.[7]

Finally, the tax benefits extended to Brazilian companies also made it difficult for new competitors to enter the market, because the benefits created a comparative advantage for entrenched companies already profiting from assistance. And these benefits amounted to no small sum. According to the World Bank (2018a), in 2016 the federal government spent nearly 4.5 percent of GDP on a combination of tax exemptions, subsidized loans, and transfers to specific industries and companies. These assistance policies had minimal to no effect on productivity (IDB 2017; World Bank 2018a). The IDB (2017) study is perhaps the most comprehensive attempt to measure the effects of Brazil's manufacturing incentive program.[8] The companies that received support boasted survival rates higher than those of the average Brazilian company, but practically none of the programs managed to increase company productivity.

PROTECTING SMALL, INEFFICIENT COMPANIES

The growth slowdown can also be explained by endogenous factors: the country's inability to create high-productivity jobs meant that many workers could only find work at small, often informal, companies. In turn, these companies wielded outsized political influence, which led to initiatives ranging from tolerating informal employment and regulatory arrangements to granting a variety of benefits to small businesses, many with low levels of productivity, owing to the lack of scale, capital, technology, and good management.

Thus, another explanation for Brazil's low productivity is the atypically high percentage of small, unproductive companies. These companies continue to operate for much longer than the international average, proof that the Brazilian economy's natural selection process is flawed, because otherwise less productive companies would be weeded out, clearing a path for more productive companies to enter and thrive.

At least three explanations are behind the high number of small, unproductive companies in Brazil. The first is the excessive informality, which enables companies that do not pay taxes or comply with various laws to compete in a market with more productive companies that do honor their legal obligations. Ulyssea (2014) finds that 44.5 percent of informal establishments are unproductive and survive only by avoiding taxes and skirting the law. He also finds that another

---

[7]See Ferraz, Gutierre, and Cabral (2015) for more evidence of the excessive vertical integration of Brazilian industry and the negative consequences thereof on integration into global value chains.

[8]For this study, the authors reviewed data from 34 programs endorsed by nine Brazilian institutions and combined the findings with data from another four government institutions. They reviewed an 11-year period, from 2002 to 2012. Unfortunately, because of the complexity of institutional arrangements for Brazilian manufacturing incentives and the difficulty of correctly identifying causality, the authors were forced to limit their analysis to companies that benefited from just one of the six programs selected.

38.7 percent of those firms are productive enough to survive in the formal sector but prefer to remain informal so they can increase profits. This illustrates the fact that informality also hinders productivity growth by limiting scale, as informal business prefer to stay small to avoid calling the authorities' attention.

The second reason for the existence of so many small, unproductive companies is the legal advantages enjoyed by micro and small businesses. Various tax laws in Brazil, such as the Simples and Supersimples tax regimes, benefit those companies. Barbosa Filho and Corrêa (2017) find evidence that these benefits keep companies with low levels of productivity in business. Moreover, these policies discourage the growth of efficiently run micro and small businesses, because growth would force them to operate under more hostile tax and regulatory regimes.

Barbosa Filho and Corrêa (2017) find that this pattern of many low-productivity firms coexisting with large, more productive companies also exists at the sector level, particularly in the commerce, hotel, restaurant, and other services industries. They note that low average productivity in these sectors is explained by the high percentage of low-productivity companies. And it is these traditional services industries that have seen the greatest increase in worker schooling (Ottoni 2017); that is, most young workers, who are better educated than their parents, are absorbed by businesses with low levels of productivity, which may explain the minimal effect of increased schooling on worker productivity.

The many barriers to closing inefficient companies, starting with an ineffective bankruptcy law, likely compound the problem. Brazil's expensive and slow bankruptcy process discourages the closing of businesses with low levels of productivity, which continue to compete for market share and inputs that could otherwise be used to help more productive businesses to grow. In 2005 Brazil restructured the bankruptcy law, leading to an increase in companies' total long-term debt and a reduction in their cost of debt, with an increase in private lending to companies as a percentage of GDP (Araujo, Ferreira, and Funchal 2012). The law also changed how businesses behave. Ponticelli and Alencar (2016) find that, following the new bankruptcy law, cities with less burdened courts saw a greater increase in loans to the manufacturing sector, business investments, and production.[9] Nevertheless, the current view is that the new law leaves much to be desired, and many of the old problems remain.

Both Ulyssea (2014) and Meghir, Narita, and Robin (2015) find that intensifying the inspections of informal businesses increases overall economic efficiency. Ulyssea (2014) finds that reducing the costs of entering the formal sector is not as effective in reducing informality, even though doing so leads to substantial gains in well-being and increases GDP and wages. And Meghir, Narita, and Robin (2015) show that stepping up inspection increases wages, overall production, and well-being, and does not raise unemployment. These positive effects of expanding inspections of informal businesses can be explained by the fact that, once unproductive businesses are taken out of the market, workers are better

---

[9]In other words, those capable to better apply the law and more swiftly try bankruptcy cases.

allocated to more productive jobs and the formal market benefits from increased competition.

These findings show that it makes sense to decrease the amount of money spent on subsidies intended to formalize companies and to invest in inspections and in penalizing those companies that remain informal. Brazil spends tens of billions of reais on policies that formalize businesses and workers under the Simples and MEI (Microempreendedor Individual) tax regimes. These policies do facilitate the crossover to formality, but it is scale, capital, technology, and management that truly make businesses productive. Companies that embrace these elements are almost always formal entities, but their formality is a consequence and not a cause. It is not the assignment of a company tax number or the issuance of a social security card that will cause business and labor productivity in Brazil to increase.

WHAT CAN BE DONE TO BRING ABOUT CHANGE

As discussed earlier, low Brazilian growth stems from the difficulty to allocate workers to more productive jobs, which results in low investment in physical capital and a drop in total factor productivity. The previous section posited that this scenario is the result of misguided economic policies pursued since 1980, the more damaging of which is, perhaps, the government's ongoing intervention in the economy, playing a major role in corporate decision making and in determining which sectors receive more investment.

These policies have failed to increase productivity and have brought about the negative consequences of drastically increasing public spending, reducing competition, complicating and raising taxes, shrinking government investment, and sustaining a restrictive monetary policy, thereby increasing companies' cost of capital. In turn, limited competition has enabled inefficient companies, both large and small, to survive. As it stands, Brazil has an atypically high share of inefficient companies, a result of tolerance for informality and of well-intended but, in practice, ineffective policies meant to increase productivity.

Considering this diagnosis, what can be done to ensure the country does not once more plunge into crisis?

Brazil must pursue six concurrent policies. First, the government must undertake significant fiscal reforms so that it can pursue a more balanced macroeconomic policy that reduces the high cost of capital borne by Brazilian companies.

Second, Brazil must institute sweeping tax reforms that eliminate the perverse incentives inherent in the current tax structure. This overhaul includes replacing the various taxes currently in place with a single value-added tax on all products in all sectors, with a single tax rate (see Appy 2017). The administrative cost of meeting tax obligations must also be reduced, and frequent changes to tax laws must cease. Ideally, the government must also reduce the tax burden by reining in public spending, which is feasible if the government respects the spending limit enshrined in the Constitutional Amendment 95, preferably for the 20 years foreseen in this legislation.

Third, other business regulations must improve, specifically regarding legal risk, covering laws and other legislation that need to be better drafted, more stable, and more uniformly interpreted across courts and over time. For infrastructure, in which at least twice as much investment is needed and where efficiency must improve considerably, the problem of legal risk is critical; unless this concern is addressed, it is unlikely that private firms will invest in the sector, notwithstanding the attractive expected rates of return the sector offers.

Fourth, Brazil must embark on a long and broad process of privatization, which entails not only selling SOEs but also divesting the myriad shares held by government banks and SOE pension funds. Furthermore, government banks and development agencies must concentrate their loans and subsidies on socially attractive projects, using more and better evaluations. The new legislation that requires the BNDES to pay market interest rates when borrowing from the Treasury is a first step in the right direction, for this will demand that credit subsidies be included in the government budget and approved by Congress. But further changes are needed. BNDES, for example, could act more like a bank, gathering and processing information and monitoring clients, and less like a clearinghouse for subsidies mandated by the Treasury, a practice that should be restricted.

Fifth, Brazil must better integrate its economy into the world economy. Economic integration will facilitate access to less expensive, more modern capital goods and inputs and will increase effective and potential competition. Better integration and more competition are also essential for the services sector, particularly for financial, insurance, engineering, and similar services. A reduction in average Brazilian tariffs and fewer restrictions on international trade will increase not only imports but also exports and the country's overall economic efficiency (SEAE 2018).

Sixth, Brazil must increase competition to properly allow for the natural selection of more efficient businesses. Competitive pressure will also encourage companies to innovate in technology and management, so that they remain healthily in the market. Striving toward more competition implies abolishing policies that protect entrenched companies, inspecting and correctly penalizing companies that do not follow the rules, and suspending policies that disproportionly benefit small businesses, especially where taxes are concerned.

These reforms must be pursued concurrently; most notably, if competition is increased without creating conditions to increase investments, workers will be pushed out of companies forced to be more competitive and into informal activities or less-competitive sectors, since workers will not remain idle. The magic formula, therefore, consists of simultaneously establishing conditions for those companies with the technology, capital, good management, and scale to grow or enter the market, while putting pressure on those businesses that do not bear these characteristics and show no sign of pursuing them, so that they shut their doors for good. This is exactly what occurred between 2003 and 2009, when

Brazil posted its most recent increase in productivity: 87 percent of the increase came from the transfer of workers from informal to formal businesses in the same sector.

If these six changes are implemented concurrently, Brazil's economy will once again create jobs in which workers can be more productive. But if they are not, it will be difficult to maintain a high and stable rate of growth, and Brazil will run the risk of yet another painful cycle of boom and subsequent bust.

REFERENCES

Appy, Bernard. 2017. "Taxation and Productivity in Brazil." In *Anatomy of Productivity in Brazil*, edited by Regis Bonelli, Fernando Veloso, and Armando C. Pinheiro. Rio de Janeiro: Elsevier, 323–60.

Araujo, Aloisio P., Rafael Ferreira, and Bruno Funcha. 2012. The Brazilian Bankruptcy Law Experience. *Journal of Corporate Finance* 18 (4): 994–1004.

Barbosa Filho, Fernando Holanda, and Paulo Correa. 2017. "Distribution of Labor Productivity among Firms and Aggregate Labor Productivity in Brazil." In *Anatomy of Productivity in Brazil*, edited by Regis Bonelli, Fernando Veloso, and Armando C. Pinheiro. Rio de Janeiro: Elsevier, 109–42.

Barbosa Filho, Fernando Holanda, and Samuel Pessôa. 2008. "Returns on Education in Brazil." *Research and Economic Planning* 38 (1).

Barbosa Filho, Fernando Holanda, and Fernando A Veloso. 2016. "Stylized Facts of Labor Informality in Brazil." In *Causes and Consequences of Informality in Brazil*, vol. 1, edited by Fernando de Holanda Barbosa Filho, Gabriel Ulyssea, and Fernando Veloso. Rio de Janeiro: Elsevier, 3–34.

Baumann, Renato, and Honorio Kume. 2013. "New Patterns of Trade and Tariff Policy in Brazil." In *The Future of Industry in Brazil,* edited by Edmar Bacha and Monica de Bolle. Rio de Janeiro: Editora Civilização Brasileira.

Bonelli, Regis, and Armando C. Pinheiro. 2016. "Industry Boom and Decline in Brazil." In *The Brazilian Crisis of Growth*, edited by Regis Bonelli and Fernando Veloso. Rio de Janeiro: Elsevier.

Bonelli, Regis, Fernando Veloso, and Armando C. Pinheiro, eds. 2017. *Anatomy of Productivity in Brazil*. Rio de Janeiro: Elsevier.

Bonomo, Marco, Ricardo D. Brito, and Bruno Martins. 2015. "The After Crisis Government-Driven Credit Expansion In Brazil: A Firm Level Analysis." *Journal of International Money and Finance* 55: 111–34.

Brazilian Industrial Development Agency (ABDI). 2014. "Plano Brasil Maior: Monitoring Report on Systemic Measures." Brasilia.

Ferraz, Lucas, Leopoldo Gutierre, and Rodolfo Cabral. 2015. "Brazilian Industry in the Age of Value Chains." In *Industry and Productive Development in Brazil*, edited by N. Barbosa, N. Marconi, M. C. Pinheiro, and L. Carvalho. Rio de Janeiro: Elsevier.

Ferreira, Pedro Cavalcanti, and Leonardo Fonseca. 2015. "Structural Transformation and Productivity in Latin America." *BE Journal of Macroeconomics* 15 (2): 603–30.

Inter-American Development Bank (IDB). 2017. "Evaluation of Business Support Programs in Brazil." Washington, DC.

Lazzarini, Sérgio G. 2011. *Capitalism of Ties: Brazil's Owners and Their Connections*. Rio de Janeiro: Elsevier.

Lazzarini, Sergio G., Aldo Musacchio, Rodrigo Bandeira-de-Mello, and Rosilene Marcon. 2015. "What Do State-Owned Development Banks Do? Evidence from BNDES, 2002–09." *World Development* 66: 237–53.

Lee, Jong-Wha, and Hanol Lee. 2016. "Human Capital in the Long Run." *Journal of Development Economics* 122: 147–69.

Mankiw, N. Gregory, David Romer, and David N. Weil. 1992. "A Contribution to the Empirics of Economic Growth." *Quarterly Journal of Economics* 107 (2): 407–37.

Meghir, Costas, Renata Narita, and Jean-Marc Robin. 2015. "Wages and Informality in Developing Countries." *American Economic Review* 105 (4): 1509–46.

Menezes-Filho, Aquino Naercio, Reynaldo Fernandes, and Paulo Picchetti. 2006. "Rising Human Capital but Constant Inequality: The Education Composition Effect in Brazil." *Brazilian Economic Review* 60 (4): 407–24.

Ottoni, Bruno. "Education, Sectors of Activity and Productivity." In *Anatomy of Productivity in Brazil*, edited by Regis Bonelli, Fernando Veloso, and Armando C. Pinheiro. Rio de Janeiro: Elsevier.

Pecora, Alexandre Reggi, and Naercio Menezes-Filho. 2014. "The Role of Supply and Demand for Qualification in the Evolution of the Wage Differential by Educational Level in Brazil." *Economic Studies (São Paulo)* 44 (2): 205–40.

Pinheiro, Armando C. 2016. Brazil's Deindustrialization. Unpublished.

———, Indermit S. Gill, Luís Servén, and Mark Thomas. 2005. "Brazilian Economic Growth, 1900–2000: Lessons and Implications." In *Sources of Growth in Latin America: What Is Missing?* edited by Eduardo Fernández-Arias, Rodolfo Manuelli, and Juan S. Blyde. Washington, DC: Inter-American Development Bank.

Ponticelli, Jacopo, and Leonardo S. Alencar. 2016. "Court Enforcement, Bank Loans, and Firm Investment: Evidence from a Bankruptcy Reform in Brazil." *Quarterly Journal of Economics* 131 (3): 1365–413.

Rios, Sandra, and Jose Tavares. 2013. "Industrial Performance and Comparative Advantages." In *The Future of Industry in Brazil*, edited by Edmar Bacha and Monica de Bolle. Rio de Janeiro: Editora Civilização Brasileira.

Special Secretariat for Strategic Affairs (SEAE). 2018. "Trade Opening for Economic Development." Report Number 3, Brasilia.

Ulyssea, Gabriel. 2018. "Firms, Informality and Development: Theory and Evidence from Brazil." *American Economic Review* 108 (8): 2015–47.

Werneck, Rogerio. 2013. "Openness, Competitiveness and Tax Relief." In *The Future of Industry in Brazil*, edited by Edmar Bacha and Monica de Bolle. Rio de Janeiro: Editora Civilização Brasileira.

World Bank. 2018a. "Employment and Growth: The Productivity Agenda." Washington, DC.

———. 2018b. "Skills and Jobs: An Agenda for Youth." Washington, DC.

CHAPTER 4

Brazil's Productivity Challenge: Structural Change versus Economy-Wide Innovation-Based Improvements

João M. P. De Mello, Isabela Duarte, and Mark Dutz

Brazil's productivity growth over the past several decades has been uninspiring. Low productivity is pervasive across all sectors of the economy and cannot be attributed to misallocation of factors between sectors. Brazil's challenge is to forge a business environment that stimulates businesses across all sectors of its economy to improve how they produce, not what they produce. To this end, impediments to starting a business should be reduced, the tax system should be made simple and transparent, the judicial system should uphold contracts, credit should be readily available at competitive prices to creditworthy firms, and trade integration should be promoted.

INTRODUCTION

The goal of this chapter is to analyze determinants of Brazil's productivity performance. It starts by exploring aggregate data, including an aggregate measure of productivity computed at the country level. The sluggishness of Brazil's productive performance over the past few decades is confirmed. The weakness of Brazil's relative productivity growth is shown in comparison with the growth of developed economies and, more generally, in most international comparisons.

Sector-level productivity and the employment share of each sector in the economy are decomposed. This decomposition identifies the sources of low productivity. In particular, it addresses the following question: are all industries and sectors economy-wide unproductive largely because of insufficient innovation or upgrading of capabilities by most firms, or is the country allocating labor to more unproductive industries and sectors and therefore should focus on promoting a few specific industries and sectors? To achieve this goal, two simulation exercises are performed based on the work of Veloso and others (2017). In the first exercise, sector-level employment is changed, keeping sector-level productivity constant, to understand the effects on aggregate productivity of reallocating production factors to more productive sectors. In the second exercise, sector-level productivity is changed but sector shares in the economy are kept constant, to understand the effects on aggregate productivity of innovation-driven increases in productivity economy-wide across all sectors, without reallocating production factors between them. The results indicate that aggregate productivity in Brazil is disappointing because of low productivity across all sectors, and not because production factors are misallocated across sectors. Based on the conclusions reached from these exercises, general recommendations for Brazil's way forward are presented. The empirical result of low productivity across sectors in Brazil holds several policy implications. The discussion focuses on three of them: access to credit, trade openness, and market competition.

In summary, Brazil's productivity problem is not what its firms produce but how they produce it. Brazil's challenge is to create a business environment that stimulates enterprises across all industries and sectors of its economy to innovate and improve the way in which they produce—by adopting existing better technologies that are new to the firm and generating new frontier technologies, and then by using these technologies to produce better products at lower cost. As entrepreneurs across the economy face incentives to allocate their talent toward productive activities, investing in technology adoption and frontier innovations rather than investing in rent-seeking activities, Brazil's reward will be sustainable growth with more and better jobs for all.

BRAZIL'S PRODUCTIVITY IMPERATIVE: AGGREGATE EVIDENCE

Analyzing aggregate economic growth jointly with the factors that determine it over time is useful to understand Brazil's poor growth performance. Figure 4.1 presents GDP growth between 1960 and 2014. It decomposes Brazil's economic performance since 1960 into the three factors that determine production growth: labor, capital, and productivity (as measured by total factor productivity). Brazil experienced robust production growth only from 1960 until the end of the 1970s (Figure 4.1). From 1980 onward, Brazil has alternated between periods of production growth and periods of stagnation or even recession.

Between 1960 and 2014, Brazil relied mostly on the expansion of labor and capital as sources of growth (Figure 4.1). Throughout this period, Brazil experienced the initial and middle stages of its demographic transition. Its population increased from 71 million to 190 million between 1960 and 2010.[1] The percentage of potential workers participating in the workforce also increased considerably, especially in the past two decades. The labor force participation rate increased from 53.2 percent in 1960 to 66.5 percent in 2014.[2] The expansion of investment in human capital was also a major attribute of the period. The literacy

---

[1]Brazilian Institute of Geography and Statistics—Instituto Brasileiro de Geografia e Estatística (IBGE).

[2]International Labour Organization.

Figure 4.1. Brazil's Economic Performance (1960–2014)
(Percent)

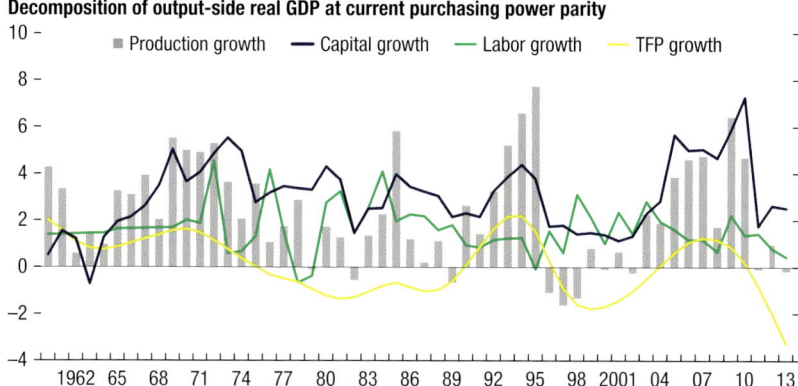

Decomposition of output-side real GDP at current purchasing power parity

■ Production growth   — Capital growth   — Labor growth   — TFP growth

Source: Fernández-Arias (2017).
Note: TFP = total factor productivity.

rate in the country increased from 74.5 percent in 1980 to 91.7 percent in 2014.[3] Human capital investment accelerated beginning in 2000. Educational attainment data for Brazil reveal that average years of total schooling increased from 3.9 in 1985 to 7.9 in 2010.[4] Investment in physical capital played a prominent role in the period. Between 1970 and 2016, gross fixed capital formation amounted to 20 percent of Brazil's GDP, on average.[5] Nevertheless, investment in Brazil has historically relied heavily on public rather than private funds. Numerous public policies were implemented with the intention of boosting public investment in physical capital. In the past decades, the federal government has put in place several ambitious multiyear investment plans led by public outlays.[6] As a result, the share of gross capital formation by the private sector in Brazil dropped from about 90 percent in the beginning of the 1980s to roughly 80 percent in 2011.[7] In addition to investing directly, the public sector has influenced private

---

[3]United Nations Educational, Scientific, and Cultural Organization (UNESCO) Institute for Statistics. The adult literacy rate is the percentage of people aged 15 and older who can both read and write with understanding a short, simple statement about their everyday life.

[4]Barro-Lee Educational Attainment Data.

[5]World Bank national accounts data and OECD National Accounts data files.

[6]Some examples are the Programa de Ação Econômica (PAEG), from 1964 to 1967; the two Planos Nacionais de Desenvolvimento (PND I, from 1972 through 1974, and the PND II, from 1974 through 1979); and the more recent Planos de Aceleração do Crescimento (PACs), in the years 2000 and early 2010. See Lara Resende (2014), Carneiro (2014) for PAEG and the PNDs. For the more recent period, see Dutz (2018).

[7]World Bank national accounts data and OECD National Accounts data files.

investment through several interventionist mechanisms involving public expenditures, such as direct subsidies, tax exemptions, and subsidized credit.

Productivity growth contributed to production growth in Brazil only for brief periods. The general trend, since the 1980s, is that even periods of economic prosperity were marked by poor productivity growth. The evolution of productivity in Brazil can be tracked by comparing it with productivity at the frontier (that is, productivity in the United States). Data from the Conference Board Total Economy Database can be used to analyze the evolution of Brazil's productivity levels—measured as labor productivity—as a proportion of productivity in the United States over time. To attain a sustainable economic development and be included in the group of higher-income countries, Brazil would need to either accumulate massive amounts of capital and labor or converge in productivity to the level observed at the frontier (or both). The available data reveal that from 1960 until the end of the 1970s, Brazil's productivity did converge to the frontier. The ratio between Brazil's productivity and productivity at the frontier reached 40 percent in 1980. From 1980 onward, convergence stalled and productivity declined relative to the frontier. In 2017 Brazil's productivity level was 25 percent of the level observed at the frontier.

Brazil's productivity growth is also disappointing compared with other developing economies. Figure 4.2 shows the evolution of the ratio between productivity in a group of developing economies—measured as output per employed person in 2016 US dollars—and productivity in the United States. In 1980 the productivity level in Brazil was behind only the levels in Chile and Mexico. Between 1980 and 2016, Brazil's productivity distanced itself from the frontier. As a result, by 2016 only China and India lagged behind Brazil. Despite still being farther from the frontier than Brazil, India's and China's performances are both impressive because between 1980 and 2014 their productivity levels more than doubled.

During the past few decades, Brazil has relied mostly on the accumulation of labor and capital as inputs for its economic development, which did compensate for its lagging productivity. Looking forward, this might no longer be achievable. Brazil can no longer rely on substantial expansions of its labor force because it is about to reach the final stages of its demographic transition. In contrast, significant physical capital growth could still occur in Brazil. The country is faced with crumbling infrastructure and its investment rates lag behind some of its peers'.[8] Nevertheless, unlike in the past, Brazil cannot rely on public funds. Brazil has recently reached a level of public sector indebtedness unsustainable for a

---

[8]According to World Bank data, gross fixed capital formation amounted, on average, to 20 percent of Brazil's GDP between 1970 and 2016. This is roughly the same average observed across Latin America. Nevertheless, categorizing countries according to income level reveals that Brazil's performance is unsatisfactory. Between 1970 and 2016 the average ratio between gross fixed capital formation and GDP was 23 percent for high-income countries, 22 percent for lower-middle-income countries, 26 percent for middle-income countries, and 27 percent for upper-middle-income countries.

Figure 4.2. Labor Productivity—Output per Employed Person
(2016 US dollars; as percentage of US productivity)

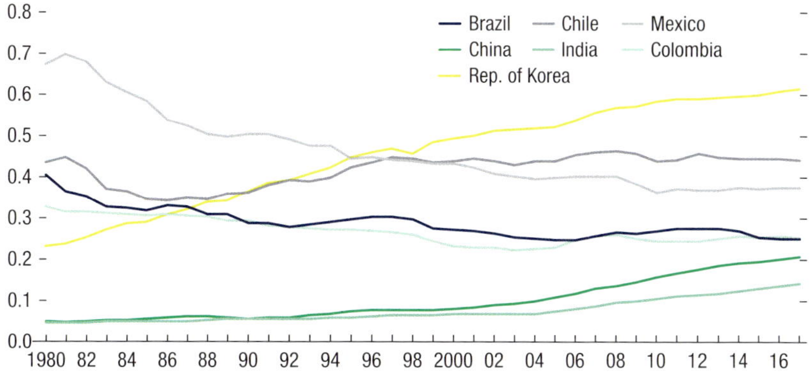

Source: Conference Board, Total Economy Database.

middle-income country.[9] Fiscal space for government-induced capital spending is severely limited, and any future development strategies for the country must be designed with consideration for the urgent need to reduce government spending. Brazil can no longer rely solely on factor accumulation for economic growth. If Brazil is to initiate a process of sustainable economic development and converge to the income level of developed economies, it must face its productivity challenge.

Brazilian policymakers should promote a policy and institutional framework that stimulates productivity. The potential rewards for such a strategy are promising. Figure 4.3 illustrates a series of simulations based on a simple growth accounting framework. If Brazil's total factor productivity growth remains negligible, the investment rate remains at the recent low level of 17 percent of GDP, and the growth of the labor force is set at 1 percent per year, with improvements in the quality of human capital also kept at 1 percent per year (roughly the level of each of these factors, on average, over the past decade), the resulting potential growth rate is 1.8 percent per year. Considering that labor force growth is projected to decline to zero by 2035 and to –0.7 percent by 2050, potential growth falls to 1.2 percent and 0.7 percent, respectively. Assuming an increase in the investment rate to 21.5 percent of GDP—the level observed in the 1970s—potential growth would increase to 2.5 percent over the coming decade but would fall below 1 percent in the long term because of diminishing returns to capital. Alternatively, boosting total factor productivity growth to 2.5 percent per year—a rate achieved in Brazil in the 1960s and 1970s—would raise Brazil's growth potential permanently to 4.4 percent even without an increase in investment. Of

---

[9]According to data from the IMF, Brazil's general government gross debt reached 72 percent of GDP in 2015. Indebtedness is greater in Brazil than in Chile (17.3 percent), China (41.1 percent), Colombia (50.6 percent), Mexico (52.9 percent), and India (69.6 percent).

Figure 4.3. Brazil: Real GDP Growth Rate Potential
(Percent)

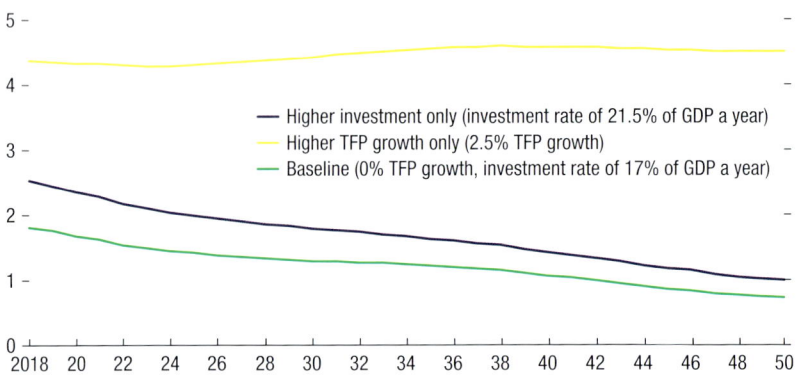

Source: Dutz (2018).
Note: Figure shows increase in growth of potential GDP from increases in investment and TFP.
Simulations use the Public Capital Extension of the Long-Term Growth Model (LTGM-PC) calibrated
to Brazil, assuming 1 percent human capital growth.
TFP = total factor productivity.

course, the gains to Brazil's potential growth would be even higher if national savings and investment rates could be raised alongside productivity growth.[10] Adequate promotion of a policy and institutional framework that could enable faster productivity growth depends on a proper understanding of the underlying microeconomic reasons for Brazil's poor performance.

MICROFOUNDATIONS OF AGGREGATE PRODUCTIVITY

This section decomposes aggregate productivity into its microeconomic foundations and shows that productivity at the country level is a result of the interaction of firms across sectors.

Productivity for the entire economy can be measured as the sum of the productivity of each sector weighted by sectoral employment shares (Timmer and Szirmai 2000). Specifically, consider an economy with $j = 1, 2, \ldots, J$ sectors. Each sector produces output Y_j and employs L_j workers. Aggregate output (Y_a) is the sum of output produced by each sector ($Y_a = \sum_{j=1}^{J} Y_j$). Likewise, the total number of workers (L_a) is the sum of workers employed by each sector ($L_a = \sum_{j=1}^{J} L_j$). Let P_a represent aggregate productivity, measured as labor productivity.

---

[10]The framework underlying these projections is based on a simple Cobb-Douglas production function calibrated to Brazil's recent historical averages, with a labor share in output of 0.56 and a capital-to-output ratio of 3.5. See the introductory chapter in Dutz (2018). Data are taken from the Penn World Tables and the IMF Fiscal Affairs Department database.

Aggregate productivity is the ratio of aggregate output to the country's workforce. Aggregate productivity can be decomposed in the following manner:

$$P_a = \frac{Y_a}{L_a} = \sum_{j=1}^{J} \frac{Y_j}{L_j} \times \frac{L_j}{L_a}.$$

Aggregate productivity is determined by the relationship between sectoral productivity (Y_j/L_j) and sectoral employment shares (L_j/L_a).

In a similar way, the productivity of each sector can be decomposed into firm-level productivity. Thus, one way to understand the determinants of sectoral and aggregate productivity is to investigate what determines productivity at the firm level.

Syverson (2011) surveys the literature on the determinants of productivity at the firm level, focusing on the reasons why firms differ so much in their ability to combine inputs into output. The available evidence reveals that many factors influence the productivity of a given firm. These factors can be divided into internal and external factors. Internal factors are those within the firm's scope of influence, while external factors are those outside this scope.

Internal factors include managerial talent, information technology, research and development, product innovation, the firm's decision-making structure, and the quality of inputs. A labor force with more education, training, experience, or tenure tends to be more efficient. Likewise, the production process is generally determined by how much technological progress is embodied in the capital. It is reasonable to assume that these internal factors are distributed unevenly across sectors. Some sectors attract more talented managers or invest more in research and development than others, for example. Hence, internal factors determine not only differences in productivity between firms but also between sectors, given their heterogeneous exposure to each factor.

External factors include productivity spillovers, market competition, regulation, and flexibility of input markets. External factors not only are relevant in determining firm-level productivity but also influence the allocation of production factors between firms. External factors determine whether more efficient firms will perform better and have a higher survival rate than less productive firms. They also influence the process through which more efficient entrants replace existing businesses. This reallocation of production factors between firms is one of the most powerful engines of productivity growth. Take competition as an example. Greater competition can boost productivity through two main mechanisms. First, market shares move toward more productive firms. Second, competition induces firms to invest in costly actions that can have a positive impact on productivity. Likewise, flexible input markets increase productivity by helping firms adapt to innovation and by facilitating the process of transferring inputs from less efficient to more efficient firms. These external factors can have a role in determining differences in sectoral productivity only if they have a heterogeneous impact across sectors. More specifically, sectoral differences in productivity caused by external factors come from differences between sectors in competition, regulation, and input-market characteristics. External factors that are not sector specific tend to influence productivity levels across all sectors simultaneously.

Understanding how external factors determine productivity is of particular interest because these factors are often more closely related to government policy than are some internal factors. The next section shows how productivity at the sector level can be used to gain a better understanding of the reasons behind Brazil's low aggregate productivity levels. Based on the results of this exercise, the subsequent section discusses how external factors should be adjusted to promote more appropriate incentives.

A SECTORAL ANALYSIS OF BRAZIL'S PRODUCTIVITY

As mentioned, the traditional measures of productivity are an aggregation of productivity observed at the sector and firm levels. Internal and external factors determine how much is going to be produced with a given amount of inputs. The distribution of firms across sectors determines sectoral productivity. Aggregate productivity, in turn, is determined by sectoral productivity and by the share of workers allocated to each sector. Specifically, aggregate productivity is the average of productivity in each sector weighted by the share of workers employed by each sector.

The decomposition presented in the previous section indicates that the difference in productivity across countries can result from two separate mechanisms: (1) differences in productivity across sectors (which is also influenced by the level and distribution of productivity across firms within each sector, and which in turn is influenced by investments by firms in innovation, including the adoption and use of existing new-to-the-firm technologies), and (2) differences in the distribution of workers across sectors.

From the previous argument, two alternative explanations for Brazil's poor productivity performance can be proposed. In the first explanation, Brazil's weak productivity is the result of an inadequate distribution of workers across sectors. According to this explanation, the productivity of some sectors is satisfactory. Nevertheless, the productivity increase observed in these sectors is not reflected in aggregate measures of productivity because these sectors employ a small share of the factors of production. Thus, Brazil's productivity performance is poor because the share of workers allocated to inefficient sectors is too large.

In the second explanation, inefficiency in the production process is a common economy-wide feature of firms across sectors. According to this account, Brazil's weak productivity level and growth results from an inability to increase productivity across sectors. Firms within every sector are incapable of initiating a sustainable process of productivity growth driven by investments in innovation.

A different set of policy recommendations can be outlined for each of these alternative interpretations. The policies to promote productivity across sectors do not necessarily coincide with the policies to promote a more efficient distribution of the workforce. Determining which of the previous interpretations is more plausible is crucial to design and implement public policy. That is the intent of this section.

An analysis that closely resembles Veloso and others (2017) is undertaken to perform two counterfactual exercises for Brazil.[11] The first exercise maintains the actual productivity of each sector and simulates aggregate productivity if the distribution of workers across sectors in Brazil were the same as the distribution in other countries. The second exercise maintains the distribution of workers across sectors and simulates the aggregate productivity if each sector in Brazil reached the productivity level observed in other economies.

For both exercises, productivity and the share of workers employed in each sector are calculated using information from the Socio Economic Accounts (SEA) database. Specifically, average productivity and the share of employed workers are calculated for 56 sectors in a group of 43 countries for 2014. The sample is composed of high- and upper-middle-income countries, as well as some large emerging market economies (Table A1 in the Appendix contains the complete list of countries included in the data set). In the SEA database, productivity is measured as value added per person engaged, in local currency. To compare productivity measures across countries, purchasing power parity (PPP) data from the Penn World Table database are used. With this information in hand, implementing the two proposed exercises is straightforward.

Consider the classic division of the economy across three sectors: agriculture, manufacturing, and services. The international evidence suggests that firms in manufacturing are more productive than those in agriculture. The evolution of average productivity within the services sector is particularly interesting. Traditionally, the services sector has been considered a less dynamic sector. Yet technological breakthroughs in the information and communication industries have profoundly altered this view. As a result, breaking down the services sector into two subsectors—a modern, dynamic one and a traditional one—has become common practice. The following exercises ask what would be the average productivity if the Brazilian economy had the same sectoral composition as in other countries.

The first exercise intends to evaluate the extent to which Brazil's productivity would increase if its workforce were concentrated in the more dynamic sectors. Figure 4.4 summarizes the results. Vertical bars indicate the increase (or decrease) in Brazil's aggregate productivity if its workforce were distributed to reflect the workforce distribution observed in a given country. Figure 4.4 shows that structural changes can improve the productivity of the Brazilian economy. By

---

[11]Note that this a static exercise. The exercise considers only a counterfactual scenario for the productivity level. An example of a dynamic exercise is presented by Alam and others (2008) to evaluate the productivity growth of the economies of Eastern Europe and the former Soviet Union. The objective of Alam and others (2008) is to answer the following question: is overall productivity growth driven mainly by sectoral or by within-sector productivity gains? To answer this question, the study performs a shift-share analysis. The analysis decomposes economic growth into three parts: (1) a within effect that intends to evaluate the contribution of within-sector productivity growth over aggregate productivity, (2) a between effect that aims to represent the productivity gains resulting from a reallocation of employment from less productive to more productive sectors, and (3) a cross effect that measures the impact of reallocating workers into sectors with growing productivity.

Figure 4.4. Counterfactual 1—Productivity Growth
(Percent)

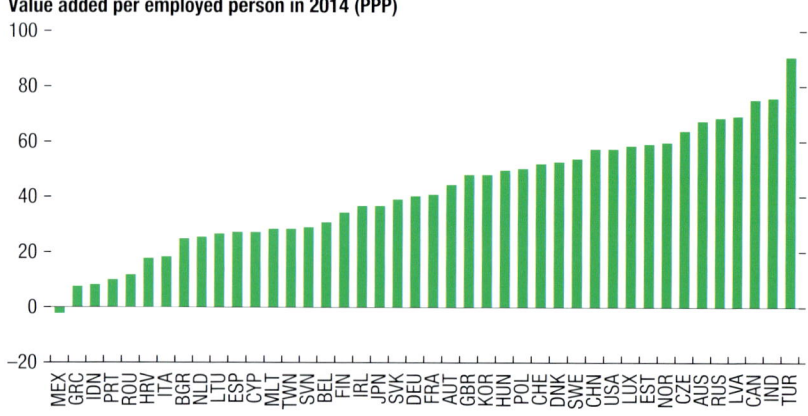

Source: World Input-Output Database Socio Economic Accounts.
Note: Counterfactual 1 maintains the actual productivity of each sector and simulates aggregate productivity if the distribution of workers across sectors in Brazil were the same as the distribution in other countries. Data labels in figure use International Organization for Standardization (ISO) country codes. PPP = purchasing power parity.

reproducing Korea's structure, a much-cited example in the Brazilian public debate on industrial policy, value added per worker would increase by almost 50 percent. If Brazil's workforce distribution were to replicate the average workforce distribution in the sample, productivity would increase by 41.6 percent, as shown in Table 4.1.

Table 4.1 also shows the impact of within-sector structural changes. Most of the gain in productivity from changing the allocation of labor among different subsectors comes from manufacturing, that is, from reallocating labor within manufacturing subsectors.[12]

The second exercise evaluates how average productivity would change if Brazil were to achieve the sectoral productivity observed in other economies. The aim is to investigate whether there is evidence that weak productivity is a widespread phenomenon across sectors. Figure 4.5 depicts the results of this exercise. Vertical bars indicate the extent to which aggregate productivity would increase (or decrease) in Brazil if the productivity of its workforce were the same as that of

---

[12]Following the taxonomy in Veloso and others (2017), traditional services are construction; administrative and support service activities; public administration and defense; education; human health and social work activities; activities of households as employers; arts, entertainment, and recreation; accommodation and food service activities; and wholesale and repair trade. Modern services are activities of extraterritorial organizations and bodies; professional, scientific, and technical activities; real estate activities; financial and insurance activities; information and communication; and transporting and storage. Table A2 in the Appendix defines all the subsectors included in the analysis.

Table 4.1. Counterfactual 1—Productivity Growth in 2014 (%)

Value added per employed person *(current purchasing power parity)*

Counterfactual Country	Total	Agriculture	Manufacturing	Traditional Services	Modern Services
Australia	67.38	−0.03	111.26	13.98	24.54
Austria	44.52	2.59	26.04	14.12	23.29
Belgium	30.60	−0.74	17.58	26.87	−19.41
Bulgaria	24.96	−1.36	32.23	20.66	12.29
Canada	74.71	5.54	95.60	16.71	41.40
People's Republic of China	57.25	3.14	82.81	10.58	117.92
Croatia	17.96	1.02	20.32	16.71	−20.28
Cyprus	27.26	0.22	9.31	9.62	2.47
Czech Republic	63.92	3.46	33.17	17.94	40.73
Denmark	52.77	2.43	27.54	16.96	37.27
Estonia	59.12	10.17	17.31	22.16	36.16
Finland	34.31	6.80	20.81	21.71	−1.88
France	40.96	−0.10	10.17	23.33	12.71
Germany	40.14	0.15	32.53	13.97	8.01
Greece	7.70	−0.51	26.18	15.02	−25.17
Hungary	49.64	0.43	22.57	27.08	30.05
India	75.45	3.02	3.71	10.72	255.07
Indonesia	8.49	6.60	38.50	8.66	41.97
Ireland	36.30	8.05	59.77	13.13	−7.08
Italy	18.25	0.33	5.09	2.61	−6.03
Japan	36.82	2.43	17.88	13.82	0.60
Republic of Korea	47.98	0.48	24.51	14.55	21.60
Latvia	69.21	8.33	30.14	13.55	60.76
Lithuania	26.49	2.32	1.16	16.98	10.94
Luxembourg	58.57	0.10	10.93	16.60	−0.56
Malta	28.26	6.78	1.80	18.75	−14.64
Mexico	−2.67	−0.95	20.32	6.81	−35.92
Netherlands	25.56	−1.83	7.09	17.00	−7.80
Norway	59.36	12.41	111.20	25.90	7.65
Poland	50.36	−0.98	65.67	24.05	14.31
Portugal	9.94	−0.43	−6.65	12.23	6.58
Romania	12.03	−1.80	49.58	18.92	−13.47
Russia	68.57	−2.67	107.79	16.71	122.32
Slovak Republic	39.06	11.26	24.63	20.82	2.91
Slovenia	28.60	0.71	38.74	16.33	−20.02
Spain	27.06	0.63	15.15	9.74	15.30
Sweden	53.51	13.97	31.71	19.60	27.16
Switzerland	51.63	−1.78	32.96	16.76	17.22
Taiwan Province of China	28.48	4.40	13.44	8.51	30.94
Turkey	90.07	−0.84	28.67	15.29	231.27
United Kingdom	47.97	0.20	23.26	11.59	20.19
United States	57.45	9.62	46.90	32.86	27.49
SEA Mean	41.57	2.70	33.08	16.43	26.88

Source: World Input-Output Database, Socio-Economic Accounts.

Figure 4.5. Counterfactual 2—Productivity Growth
(Percent)

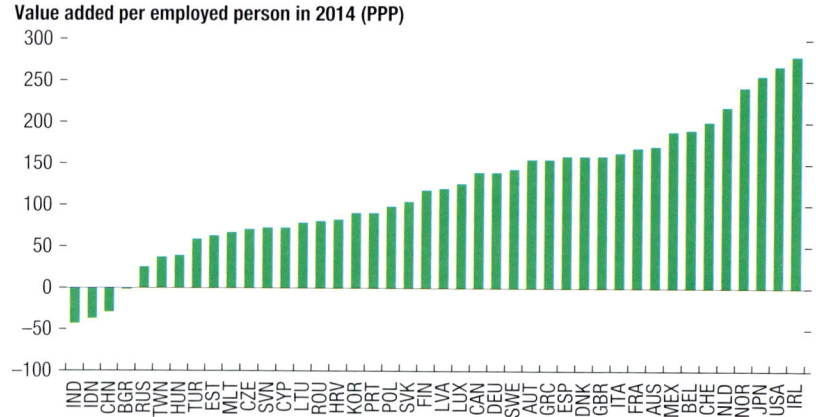

Value added per employed person in 2014 (PPP)

Source: World Input-Output Database Socio Economic Accounts.
Note: Counterfactual 2 maintains the distribution of workers across sectors and simulates the aggregate productivity if the productivity in each sector were the same as the productivity in other countries. Data labels in figure use International Organization for Standardization (ISO) country codes. PPP = purchasing power parity.

other countries in each sector, keeping the sectoral labor distribution constant. If the Brazilian worker were to be as productive as the Korean worker in each sector, the average value added per worker would increase by 90 percent. If the Brazilian workforce were to achieve the sample's average productivity, value added per person would increase by 117.7 percent, as shown in Table 4.2.

Table 4.2 also shows the impact of replicating the productivity of individual sectors in other countries. Most of the gain in productivity would come from agriculture, a somewhat surprising result because Brazilian agriculture is widely believed to be productive. However, all sectors, except for modern services, would have productivity gains of more than 100 percent.

In summary, simple counterfactual exercises show that Brazil's productivity would increase almost three times as much if Brazil were to reach the sectoral productivity observed in more productive countries than if it were to reproduce the sectoral labor distribution of more productive countries (almost 120 percent compared with a little more than 40 percent).

A comparison of the results obtained from these two exercises reveals that the second interpretation of Brazil's productivity challenge (i.e., that weak productivity is a widespread economy-wide issue across sectors and industries) seems more reasonable. To promote a process of significant and sustainable development, Brazil needs to address the pervasive inefficiency of its firms, including spurring more firm-level investments in innovation. As previously noted, this diagnosis leads to a specific set of policy recommendations, as addressed more closely in the next section.

Table 4.2. Counterfactual 2—Productivity Growth in 2014 (%)

Value added per person engaged *(current PPP)*

Counterfactual Country	Total	Agriculture	Manufacturing	Traditional Services	Modern Services
Australia	171.60	710.78	190.06	161.07	71.00
Austria	154.97	136.64	208.67	189.54	59.15
Belgium	191.08	376.20	207.80	203.63	122.81
Bulgaria	−1.59	−5.96	−0.91	2.49	−7.62
Canada	139.42	624.80	173.70	126.94	38.30
People's Republic of China	−29.55	−22.18	−9.66	−29.77	−47.70
Croatia	83.49	86.85	39.54	108.09	82.81
Cyprus	73.63	210.64	18.23	99.85	55.28
Czech Republic	71.15	294.71	60.26	87.20	13.99
Denmark	159.19	368.71	238.39	155.88	57.04
Estonia	62.15	295.72	54.16	74.92	5.69
Finland	118.66	144.55	136.26	149.25	51.71
France	170.07	401.57	188.11	189.99	80.65
Germany	140.21	249.60	174.63	151.27	73.17
Greece	155.04	81.19	78.46	103.18	314.30
Hungary	39.36	206.85	35.60	48.34	−2.54
India	−42.71	−62.89	−53.22	−19.45	−65.65
Indonesia	−37.63	−37.12	22.25	−50.79	−68.93
Ireland	278.81	213.30	368.36	285.22	204.31
Italy	163.27	354.27	155.12	167.97	127.29
Japan	255.62	92.53	179.72	465.73	28.53
Republic of Korea	89.68	155.27	184.22	83.09	6.32
Latvia	119.80	49.07	40.25	245.59	8.12
Lithuania	78.43	87.44	111.97	99.40	15.70
Luxembourg	125.08	105.10	91.97	196.98	46.79
Malta	67.51	273.94	18.64	106.36	11.18
Mexico	188.57	−10.45	76.53	341.67	86.83
Netherlands	219.01	595.88	329.58	182.54	109.55
Norway	241.18	397.17	306.38	238.04	160.79
Poland	97.95	49.92	76.34	167.67	18.39
Portugal	91.22	29.17	76.03	121.70	69.05
Romania	79.80	−3.53	75.26	76.74	104.01
Russia	25.84	−27.76	17.84	80.33	−40.98
Slovak Republic	104.87	788.69	93.53	82.67	20.72
Slovenia	73.30	25.06	74.75	109.92	24.82
Spain	158.94	382.31	199.27	161.31	78.86
Sweden	142.81	144.45	185.70	173.39	58.68
Switzerland	200.48	152.92	209.11	280.65	78.81
Taiwan Province of China	37.58	50.95	37.53	64.37	−6.04
Turkey	59.43	46.91	42.79	93.02	24.47
United Kingdom	160.36	251.38	210.88	193.08	49.67
United States	267.10	937.54	330.61	245.81	119.76
SAE Mean	117.74	219.10	125.11	143.21	53.31

Source: World Input-Output Database, Socio-Economic Accounts.

RECOMMENDATIONS FOR BRAZIL'S WAY FORWARD

The sectoral-level evidence shows that Brazil's aggregate productivity could increase greatly if the country were to reach the level of sectoral productivity observed in more developed economies. An increase of this magnitude could not be achieved if Brazil were only to reallocate its workforce toward more productive sectors. This result leads to the conclusion that inefficiency in the production process is a common economy-wide issue affecting the performance of firms across industries and sectors.

If inefficiency is common across industries and sectors, then it is probably the result of external factors that influence the behavior of all firms in all sectors. A business environment that provides the wrong incentives will harm the performance of most firms; consequently, it will have a negative influence on aggregate productivity. This thesis is borne out by the evidence: Brazil has performed poorly in evaluations of its business environment. In the 2018 edition of the *Doing Business* report—a World Bank study (World Bank 2018) that evaluates the processes of opening, operating, and closing a business across countries—Brazil ranked 125th out of 190 countries. To promote an adequate business environment, a country must provide a policy and institutional framework in which there are no unnecessary obstacles to starting a business; the tax system is simple and transparent, and paying taxes is straightforward; entrepreneurs are not excessively punished for business failures; the judicial system guarantees contracts and provides legal security for business transactions; credit is readily available; and producers can benefit from access to international trade. The *Doing Business* report shows that Brazil has a lot of room to improve in all these dimensions. The following discussion focuses on three main dimensions: access to credit, openness to trade, and market competition.

To democratize economic opportunities and promote entrepreneurship, a country's institutional framework must address the market failures that limit access to credit. In 2018 Brazil ranked 105th out of 190 countries on the "Getting Credit" indicator of the *Doing Business* report. Brazil's poor performance on the *Doing Business* evaluation indicates the need to promote creditors' rights and to implement policies that reduce information asymmetries. Promoting credit markets in Brazil also means implementing a rational strategy for earmarked credit. By the end of 2015, earmarked credit represented almost half of total credit in Brazil, a policy with high fiscal cost[13] and no clear evidence of positive impact (Pazarbasioglu and others 2017).

Brazil imposes a broader series of barriers to trade than comparator countries do. Moreover, tariff rates in the country exceed the average observed for countries with similar income levels.[14] Brazil is also one of the world leaders in antidumping

---

[13]According to Pazarbasioglu and others (2017), 1.5 percent of GDP for 2015.

[14]In 2012, according to data from the World Bank, the weighted average of applied tariffs was 7.8 percent in Brazil, 4.6 percent in upper-middle-income countries, 4.86 percent

measures.[15] As a result, international trade amounts to only a quarter of Brazil's GDP.[16] Brazil is significantly less integrated into international trade than other emerging economies of similar size.[17] An increase in Brazil's openness to trade could benefit the country in at least two ways. First, Brazilian firms could gain substantially from access to cheaper and better inputs from abroad. These inputs include adoption of existing new-to-the-firm technologies that could enhance the production process, promote specialization, and increase the probability that Brazilian firms integrate into and benefit from global value chains. Second, the availability of goods from abroad would pressure Brazilian firms to reduce costs, seek and use new technologies, and avoid waste. Competition from imported goods could promote the efficiency of Brazilian firms.

An institutional framework that fails to promote entrepreneurship and competition will increase the survival rate of inefficient firms and industries, preventing both innovation and the reallocation of production factors toward more efficient use. The environment for competition is influenced not only by trade openness but also by public policies that directly encourage competition. In the past decade, Brazil has implemented several policies to promote specific industries or sectors, the so-called national champions or *campeões nacionais*. These policies took the form of tax exemptions, tax credits, subsidized credit, or payment of direct subsidies (see Dutz 2018). As became clear over time based on careful data analysis, policies that promote specific industries or firms—unless designed to outweigh economic externalities—harm competition and innovation, stimulate inefficient allocation of resources in the economy, and promote rent seeking. As a result, these policies are also likely to negatively influence productivity.

The conclusion reached from this analysis is twofold. First, Brazil needs to promote a set of public policies to deal with the factors that impede firm-level and aggregate productivity growth. These policies should promote efficiency and include investments in innovation for firms in every sector and industry. Second, Brazil would benefit greatly from regulatory reforms that promote a pro-business institutional framework, open Brazil's economy to international trade, eliminate policies intended to promote specific sectors or industries, and improve the functioning of credit markets.

---

in middle-income countries, 1.66 percent in high-income countries, and 9.58 percent in low-income countries.

[15]According to the World Trade Organization, Brazil had 156 antidumping measures in force by the end of 2016, lagging behind the United States with 286 measures in force and India with 244 measures in force.

[16]World Bank national accounts data and OECD National Accounts data files.

[17]OECD Economic Surveys: Brazil, February 2018.

CONCLUSION

This chapter aims to answer the question: how can Brazil converge to the income level observed in more developed economies? The evidence suggests this convergence can be made possible only by a productivity-led process of income growth. This process presents some challenges.

In the past few decades, aggregate productivity performance in Brazil has been disappointing at best, but not because of inadequate allocation of production factors among sectors. This chapter's analysis shows that inefficiency in the production process is a common economy-wide feature of firms across industries and sectors. Accordingly, policies aimed at improving Brazil's productivity must target the business environment facing all firms, including incentivizing and supporting firm investments in innovation.

The analysis also reveals that there is much room for improvement. Brazil has a lot to gain from regulatory reforms that promote a more business-friendly environment that spurs innovation, including opening the country's economy to international trade, rationalizing past policies intended to promote specific sectors and industries, and improving the functioning of credit markets. The good news is that the issue of productivity growth has taken center stage in Brazil's policy debate in the past few years. As a result, in early 2018 Brazil's Ministry of Finance created a secretariat with the purpose of promoting productivity—the Secretariat for Productivity and Competition Advocacy.[18] Recognizing productivity as a pressing issue is the first step toward a more reasonable development strategy. The road ahead is full of challenges, but it is also full of opportunities.

REFERENCES

Alam, A., P. A. Casero, F. Khan, and C. Udomsaph. 2008. *Unleashing Prosperity: Productivity Growth in Eastern Europe and the Former Soviet Union.* Washington, DC: World Bank.

Banerjee, A. V., and A. F. Newman. 1993. "Occupational Choice and the Process of Development." *The Journal of Political Economy* 101(2): 274–98.

Carneiro, D. D. 2014. "Crisis and Hope 1974–1980." In *The Order of Progress: Two Centuries Economic Policy in Brazil.* Rio de Janeiro: Elsevier.

Dutz, M. 2018. *Employment and Growth: The Productivity Agenda.* Washington, DC: World Bank.

Fernández-Arias, E. 2017. *Productivity Database 2017.* Washington, DC: Inter-American Development Bank.

Galor, O., and J. Zeira. 1993. "Income Distribution and Macroeconomics." *The Review of Economic Studies* 60: 35–52.

Lara Resende, A. 2014. "Stabilization and Reform, 1964–1967." In *The Order of Progress: Two Centuries Economic Policy in Brazil.* Rio de Janeiro: Elsevier.

Organisation for Economic Co-operation and Development (OECD). 2015. *The Future of Productivity.* OECD Publishing, Paris.

---

[18]Presidential Decree Nº 9.266, January 15, 2018

————, and Inter-American Development Bank (IDB). 2016. "Boosting Productivity and Inclusive Growth in Latin America." OECD Latin America and Caribbean Regional Programme, OECD Publishing, Paris.

Pazarbasioglu, Ceyla, S. Byskov, M. Bonomo, I. Carneiro, B. Martins, and A. Perez. 2017. "Brazil—Financial Intermediation Costs and Credit Allocation." Discussion Paper for Workshop. World Bank, Washington, DC.

Syverson, C. 2011. "What Determines Productivity?" *Journal of Economic Literature* 49(2): 326–65.

Timmer, M. P., and A. Szirmai. 2000. "Productivity Growth in Asian Manufacturing: The Structural Bonus Hypothesis Examined." *Structural Change and Economic Dynamics* 11(4): 371–92.

Timmer, M. P., E. Dietzenbacher, B. Los, R. Stehrer, and G. J. de Vries. 2015. "An Illustrated User Guide to the World Input–Output Database: The Case of Global Automotive Production." *Review of International Economics* 23: 575–605.

Veloso, F., S. Matos, P. C. Ferreira, and B. Coelho. 2017. "Brazil in International Comparisons of Productivity: A Sectoral Analysis." In *Anatomy of Productivity in Brazil*. Rio de Janeiro: Elsevier and FGV/IBRE.

World Bank. 2018. *Doing Business*. Washington, DC.

ANNEX 4.1

Annex Table 4.1.1. Country Codes

Country	Code
Australia	AUS
Austria	AUT
Belgium	BEL
Brazil	BRA
Bulgaria	BGR
Canada	CAN
People's Republic of China	CHN
Croatia	HRV
Cyprus	CYP
Czech Republic	CZE
Denmark	DNK
Estonia	EST
Finland	FIN
France	FRA
Germany	DEU
Greece	GRC
Hungary	HUN
India	IND
Indonesia	IDN
Ireland	IRL
Italy	ITA
Japan	JPN
Republic of Korea	KOR
Latvia	LVA
Lithuania	LTU
Luxembourg	LUX
Malta	MLT
Mexico	MEX
Netherlands	NLD
Norway	NOR
Poland	POL
Portugal	PRT
Romania	ROU
Russia	RUS
Slovak Republic	SVK
Slovenia	SVN
Spain	ESP
Sweden	SWE
Switzerland	CHE
Taiwan Province of China	TWN
Turkey	TUR
United Kingdom	GBR
United States	USA

Annex Table 4.1.2. List of Sectors

Sector Code	Sector Description
A01	Crop and animal production, hunting and related service activities
A02	Forestry and logging
A03	Fishing and aquaculture
B	Mining and quarrying
C10-C12	Manufacture of food products, beverages, and tobacco products
C13-C15	Manufacture of textiles, wearing apparel, and leather products
C16	Manufacture of wood and of products of wood and cork, except furniture; manufacture of articles of straw and plaiting materials
C17	Manufacture of paper and paper products
C18	Printing and reproduction of recorded media
C19	Manufacture of coke and refined petroleum products
C20	Manufacture of chemicals and chemical products
C21	Manufacture of basic pharmaceutical products and pharmaceutical preparations
C22	Manufacture of rubber and plastic products
C23	Manufacture of other nonmetallic mineral products
C24	Manufacture of basic metals
C25	Manufacture of fabricated metal products, except machinery and equipment
C26	Manufacture of computer, electronic, and optical products
C27	Manufacture of electrical equipment
C28	Manufacture of machinery and equipment not elsewhere classified
C29	Manufacture of motor vehicles, trailers, and semitrailers
C30	Manufacture of other transport equipment
C31_C32	Manufacture of furniture; other manufacturing
C33	Repair and installation of machinery and equipment
D35	Electricity, gas, steam, and air-conditioning supply
E36	Water collection, treatment, and supply
E37-E39	Sewerage; waste collection, treatment, and disposal activities; materials recovery; remediation activities and other waste management services
F	Construction
G45	Wholesale and retail trade and repair of motor vehicles and motorcycles
G46	Wholesale trade, except of motor vehicles and motorcycles
G47	Retail trade, except of motor vehicles and motorcycles
H49	Land transport and transport via pipelines
H50	Water transport
H51	Air transport
H52	Warehousing and support activities for transportation
H53	Postal and courier activities
I	Accommodation and food service activities
J58	Publishing activities
J59_J60	Motion picture, video, and television program production; sound recording and music publishing activities; programming and broadcasting activities
J61	Telecommunications

(Continued)

Annex Table 4.1.2. *(continued)*

J62_J63	Computer programming, consultancy, and related activities; information service activities
K64	Financial service activities, except insurance and pension funding
K65	Insurance, reinsurance, and pension funding, except compulsory social security
K66	Activities auxiliary to financial services and insurance activities
L68	Real estate activities
M69_M70	Legal and accounting activities; activities of head offices; management consultancy activities
M71	Architectural and engineering activities; technical testing and analysis
M72	Scientific research and development
M73	Advertising and market research
M74_M75	Other professional, scientific, and technical activities; veterinary activities
N	Administrative and support service activities
O84	Public administration and defense; compulsory social security
P85	Education
Q	Human health and social work activities
R_S	Other service activities
T	Activities of households as employers; undifferentiated goods- and services-producing activities of households for own use
U	Activities of extraterritorial organizations and bodies

CHAPTER 5

Structural Reform Priorities for Brazil

Nina Biljanovska and Damiano Sandri

Over the past few decades, stagnant productivity has caused Brazil to experience relatively weak economic growth. To boost productivity, Brazil should embark on an ambitious structural reform process. In doing so, it is crucial that authorities select a few reform priorities, to avoid dispersing political capital over an overly broad reform agenda. This chapter identifies Brazil's reform priorities in two steps. First, it estimates the impact that different reforms would have on Brazil's productivity. Second, it analyzes survey data to assess the extent of public support for reforms. The results show that banking sector reforms would generate the largest productivity gains and have the highest level of public support. Moreover, these reforms would be relatively easy to legislate and would generate significant fiscal savings.

INTRODUCTION

Over the past few decades, Brazil has experienced relatively weak economic growth (Figure 5.1). Since 1980 real GDP has grown at only about 2.6 percent per year, well below the rates of other major emerging market economies. Brazil's weak growth performance is largely because of stagnant total factor productivity (TFP), which has been roughly constant for about 40 years. In fact, if human capital accumulation is excluded, using the estimates provided by the Penn World Tables up to 2014, TFP today is considerably lower than it was in the early 1980s.

To raise productivity and potential growth, Brazil should adopt ambitious structural reforms. A large and growing empirical literature finds that structural reforms have positive effects on GDP growth, especially by boosting productivity. Most of the literature has focused on advanced economies for which structural reform indicators are more broadly available (Bouis and Duval 2011; IMF 2016). However, recent papers have documented that structural reforms can also raise productivity in emerging markets and low-income countries (Ostry, Prati, and

Prepared by Nina Biljanovska and Damiano Sandri (both staff in the IMF Western Hemisphere Department). The authors thank Chris Papageorgiou and Minsuk Kim for sharing the data used in IMF (2015) and John Bluedorn and Romain Duval for helpful comments. Henrique Barbosa provided excellent research assistance.

Figure 5.1. Brazil GDP and Productivity Growth

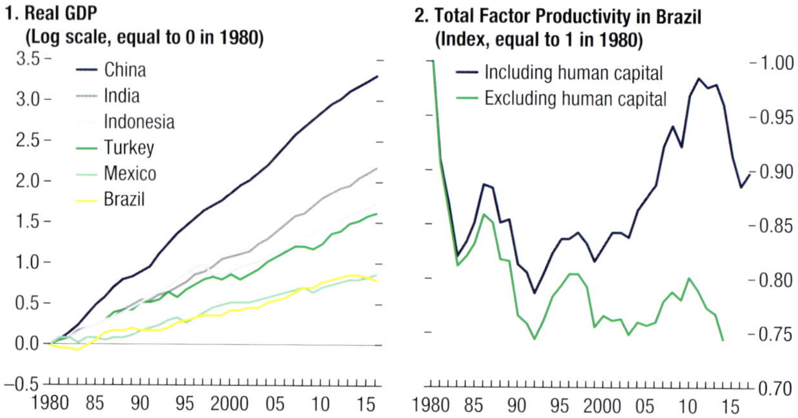
1. Real GDP
(Log scale, equal to 0 in 1980)
China
India
Indonesia
Turkey
Mexico
Brazil
3.5
3.0
2.5
2.0
1.5
1.0
0.5
0.0
–0.5
1980 85 90 95 2000 05 10 15
2. Total Factor Productivity in Brazil
(Index, equal to 1 in 1980)
Including human capital
Excluding human capital
1.00
0.95
0.90
0.85
0.80
0.75
0.70
1980 85 90 95 2000 05 10 15

Sources: World Bank, World Development Indicators; IMF, *World Economic Outlook;* Penn World Tables; and IMF staff calculations.

Spilimbergo 2009; Prati, Onorato, and Papageorgiou 2013). These papers have focused on the *economic* aspects of reforms, neglecting the *political economy* of consensus. This chapter fills that gap.

A successful reform process requires that clear policy priorities be set. Undertaking structural reforms is often an arduous political task. Despite generating benefits for society at large, reforms raise fierce opposition from those individuals that gain from existing market distortions and barriers to competition. Rather than dispersing political capital across an overly broad reform agenda, concentrating the reform efforts in a few critical areas would be a preferable path.

This chapter provides guidance on how to identify the main structural reform priorities for Brazil. It does so in two steps. First, the impact that several different structural reforms are likely to have on Brazil's productivity is estimated. Second, survey data are used to assess the extent of public support for specific reforms. By drawing on the insights from these two steps, those reforms that are likely to have the *highest growth payout* at the *lowest political cost* are identified. Reforms are also differentiated depending on their legislative requirements and fiscal impacts. Additional considerations that can influence the choice of reform priorities are presented, and the conclusion summarizes the key insights of the analysis.

PRODUCTIVITY GAINS FROM STRUCTURAL REFORMS

This section identifies the structural reforms in Brazil that are most likely to boost productivity. First, the impact that several different structural reforms have on productivity is estimated based on a sample of both advanced and emerging market economies. Second, these estimates are used to assess the impact on Brazil's productivity if it undertakes reforms that bring its structural indicators up to the average levels in advanced economies.

A broad range of structural reform indicators are considered. Measuring the degree of structural reforms is notoriously difficult. In most instances, structural reforms are associated with policy measures that support free market outcomes, for example, by removing barriers to entry and reducing state intervention. However, structural reforms can also include measures to address market failures, for example, by improving banking regulation and supervision. This paper considers several indices of structural reforms taken from Prati, Onorato, and Papageorgiou (2013) and IMF (2015):

- **Banking sector:** This index is based on the methodology in Abiad and Mody (2005) and Abiad, Detragiache, and Tressel (2010), which captures the presence of interest rate controls, directed credit, public banks, restrictions to bank competition, and the quality of banking supervision and regulation.

- **Labor market:** Labor reforms are measured as the average of two indices from the Global Competitiveness Report compiled by the World Economic Forum, capturing the ease with which employers can hire and fire workers and the extent to which wages can be freely determined at the firm level rather than being set through collective bargaining.

- **Legal system:** This index, assembled by the Fraser Institute, gauges the legal protections afforded to persons and their property, considering the rule of law, property rights, the independence of the judiciary, and the impartial and effective enforcement of the law.

- **Product market:** This index, constructed by the Economist Intelligent Unit, measures the extent to which government policies curb monopoly power and promote competition.

- **Trade openness:** Rather than measuring trade openness using tariffs that in previous studies have been found to be unrelated to productivity, this analysis uses an index introduced by Quinn (1997) that captures restrictions to payments associated with the international trade of goods and services.

All indices are normalized between zero and one, with higher values corresponding to higher levels of structural reforms. Some of these indices, especially those for the labor market and the legal system, are constructed using surveys of public perceptions and should thus be interpreted with caution.

A notable shortcoming of the analysis is the absence of established structural indicators for fiscal reforms. To make up for this, IMF (2015) presents several case studies that demonstrate the importance of structural fiscal reforms for macroeconomic performance. In Brazil, reforms to simplify the federal tax system, harmonize federal and state tax regimes, and remove distortionary tax exemptions can play an important role in raising productivity.

Figure 5.2. Brazil's Structural Reform Gaps
(Index between 1 and 0)

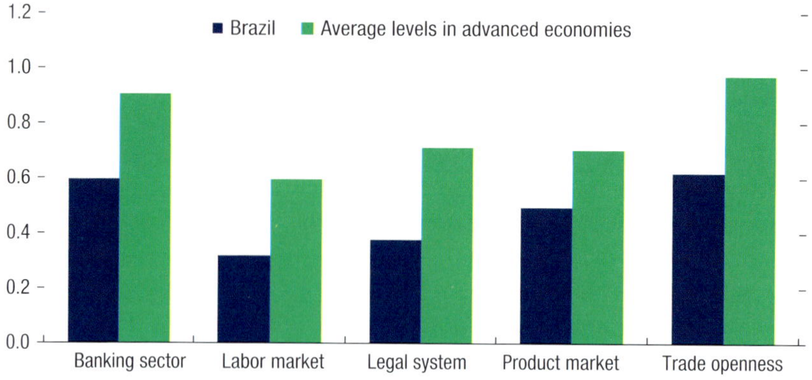

Source: IMF staff calculations.
Note: Higher values correspond to higher structural reforms.

To estimate the impact of structural reforms on productivity, the econometric approach in IMF (2015) is followed. The growth rate of TFP, $gTFP_{i,t}$, is regressed over the one-year lagged values of the structural reform indices, according to the following equation:

$$gTFP_{i,t} = \alpha + \beta \cdot \ln TPF_{i,t-1} + \gamma \cdot SR_{i,t-1} + \mu_t + \nu_i + \varepsilon_{i,t}.$$

The regression controls for the level of TFP and includes time and country fixed effects denoted by μ_t and ν_i, respectively. The estimation is performed on a sample of 86 advanced and emerging market economies with data between 1970 and 2011 based on the data set used in IMF (2015).

The regression results show that structural reforms have positive effects on productivity growth. Columns (1)–(5) in Table 5.1 report the estimates of the regression coefficients γ, which capture the impact of a given structural reform indicator on the one-year-ahead growth rate of TFP. In line with the literature, the coefficients are positive and statistically significant. Columns (6)–(7) show that reforms to the banking sector and legal system also have a positive impact on real investment growth. Therefore, in addition to raising productivity, they also stimulate capital accumulation.

To assess the impact of structural reforms on Brazil's productivity, the regression coefficients are interacted with Brazil's structural gaps. Brazil's structural gaps are measured relative to the average levels prevailing in advanced economies.[1] Figure 5.2 shows that Brazil lags significantly behind advanced economies across all structural reform indicators. Multiplying Brazil's structural gaps by the

---

[1]To calculate structural gaps, the structural reform indicators for Brazil are updated to the most recent available year.

Table 5.1. Impact of Structural Reforms on TFP and Investment Growth

	(1)	(2)	(3)	(4)	(5)	(6)	(7)
	TFP					Investment	
Banking Sector	3.68***					6.72***	
	(0.71)					(2.52)	
Labor Market		3.48***					
		(0.88)					
Legal System			2.33***				7.83***
			(0.77)				(2.92)
Product Market				2.64**			
				(1.11)			
Trade Openness					1.24*		
					(0.73)		
Observations	1,840	1,283	2,349	848	2,389	1,695	2,200
R^2		0.12	0.31	0.19	0.28	0.10	0.08	0.12
Number of Countries	62	83	71	53	77	60	70

Source: Authors' calculations.
Note: TFP = total factor productivity. Standard errors are in parentheses.
***$p < 0.01$; **$p < 0.05$; *$p < 0.1$.

regression coefficients in Table 5.1 yields an estimate of the extent to which TFP growth would increase if Brazil were to undertake reforms that raise its structural indicators to the average levels in advanced economies.

The results show that banking sector reforms are likely to have the strongest impact on productivity. Figure 5.3 illustrates the impact on productivity growth from undertaking structural reforms that would bring Brazil up to the average level in advanced economies. Structural reforms to the banking sector are predicted to have the largest effects on productivity, raising one-year-ahead TFP growth by almost 1.2 percent.

Figure 5.3. Impact of Structural Reforms on Brazil's Productivity
(Percent)

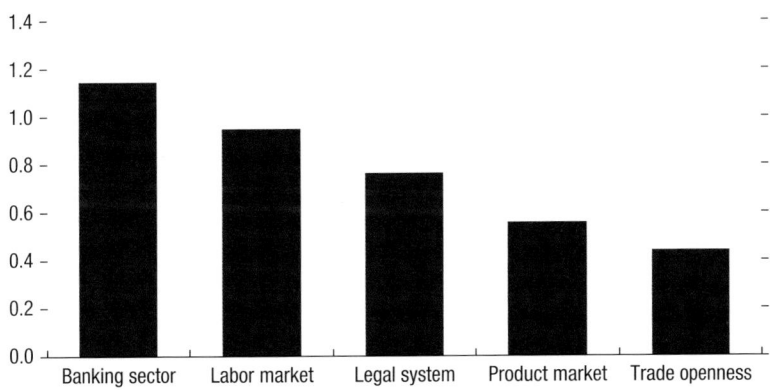

Source: IMF staff calculations.
Note: Figure shows impact on one-year-ahead total factor productivity growth.

Bank reforms should aim to reduce state intervention in credit markets and promote privatization. The structural reform indicator for the banking sector is an average of several subcomponents, following the methodology presented in Abiad and Mody (2005) and Abiad, Detragiache, and Tressel (2010). By examining the subcomponents, specific areas for which structural reforms are needed the most can be identified. Brazil fares relatively well in the areas of bank supervision, low levels of entry barriers, and free setting of interest rates by private banks. However, Brazil scores poorly because of pervasive state intervention in credit allocation and the presence of large public banks.

Labor market reforms also have a significant impact on productivity, but the analysis may overestimate the scope for further reforms. The structural indicators for the labor market are based on employers' perceptions, surveyed before September 2017, about rigidities in hiring and firing and wage setting. Therefore, they do not yet reflect the improvements associated with the labor reform that came into effect in November 2017. The scope for further labor reforms might thus be more limited than suggested by the analysis.

In addition to banking reforms, Brazil would benefit greatly from measures to improve the legal system. Figure 5.3 shows that legal reforms would boost productivity significantly. For example, authorities should consider measures to increase the efficiency of the court system, such as preventing the abuse of appeals provisions and statutes of limitations in legal proceedings. These reforms would also assist in reducing corruption, which also is likely to raise productivity. The structural indicator for legal reforms used in the analysis is indeed strongly correlated with corruption indices provided by the World Governance Indicators and the International Crisis Risk Guide, suggesting that the productivity gains associated with improvements in the legal system are likely to also capture the benefits from curbing corruption.

The effects of product market and trade reforms appear more limited, but still sizable. Measures to enhance competition and further open the economy to international markets would have a positive impact on productivity in Brazil. Nonetheless, the effects are more limited, equal to about half the gains that can be seized with banking sector reforms. Trade and product market reforms fare relatively better when considering the impact on long-term GDP growth, as documented in OECD (2018).

PUBLIC SUPPORT FOR STRUCTURAL REFORMS

This section uses survey data to identify which structural reforms have the highest support among the public in Brazil. Data are drawn from the Latin Barometer Survey and the Pew Global Attitudes and Trends Survey, both of which collect information over time and across countries on people's views about various economic, political, and social issues. This analysis focuses on questions that address economic issues, from which public attitudes toward specific structural reforms can be inferred.

Figure 5.4. Public Support for Market Economy

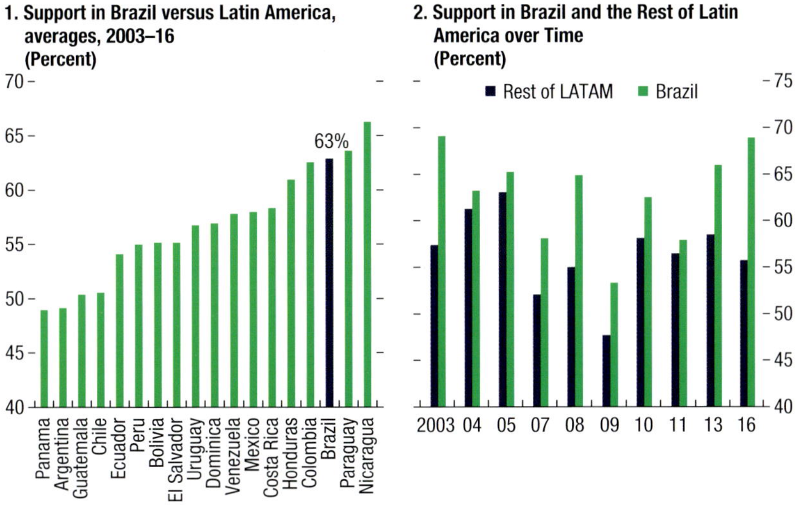

1. Support in Brazil versus Latin America, averages, 2003–16 (Percent)

2. Support in Brazil and the Rest of Latin America over Time (Percent)

Source: Latin Barometer.
Note: LATAM = Latin America.

The analysis begins by considering the extent of public support for a free market economy. Public opinion over time and across 18 Latin American countries is assessed by looking at the following Latin Barometer question: *Q: The market economy is the only system with which the country can become developed.*[2] Over the period 2003–16,[3] 63 percent of the Brazilian public, on average, agreed or strongly agreed with the statement, suggesting that the majority believe that a free market system is essential for development. When compared with the rest of Latin America, support for free markets in Brazil is among the highest in the region (Figure 5.4, panel 1).[4]

Public support for a market-based system has been high in Brazil over time and is consistently above the Latin American average (Figure 5.4, panel 2). Nonetheless, public support for free markets dropped sharply in 2009, from 65 percent to 53 percent. This decline likely reflected concerns with the financial deregulation process in advanced economies that led to the global financial crisis. In contrast, support for free markets reached its highest level in 2016, at almost

---

[2]The respondents can choose from five possible answers: (1) strongly agree, (2) agree, (3) disagree, (4) strongly disagree, and (5) don't know. Support for the market economy variable is constructed by adding the share of people who "strongly agree" and "agree" with the statement.

[3]Participants were asked this question in every survey during the period 2003–16.

[4]Rest of Latin American countries: Argentina, Bolivia, Chile, Colombia, Costa Rica, Dominican Republic, Ecuador, El Salvador, Guatemala, Honduras, Mexico, Nicaragua, Panama, Paraguay, Peru, Uruguay, Venezuela.

70 percent, in conjunction with Brazil's recent recession. Given that Brazil's 2015–16 recession was highly idiosyncratic, the higher support for free markets could be explained by the desire to correct the structural imbalances present in the domestic economy.

Growth increases support for free markets. The comovement between public support for free markets and real output growth is now examined more systematically, controlling for other macro variables. The following regression equation is estimated for a panel of 18 Latin American countries over the period 2003–16:[5]

$$Mrkt_{i,t} = \alpha + \beta \cdot gdp_{i,t} + \gamma \cdot X_{i,t} + +\varepsilon_{i,t}.$$

The variable $Mrkt_{i,t}$ denotes the percentage of people in country i and year t who agree or strongly agree with the statement that the market economy is the only system with which the country could become developed; $gdp_{i,t}$ denotes the real growth rate of GDP; $X_{i,t}$ is a vector of macroeconomic variables, including the fiscal impulse, inflation, and the unemployment rate. The regression results are shown in Table 5.2. Across all specifications, real GDP growth is positively associated with higher public support for free market reforms. Accommodative fiscal policy may be marginally promoting support, whereas inflation and unemployment do not play an important role.

The positive effect of growth on free market support is robust to using instrumental variables. One concern that arises with the baseline specification is the risk of omitted variable bias. Other factors that are not being controlled for may indeed be driving both growth and support for free markets, resulting in biased estimates. To address this problem, an instrumental variables regression is estimated using real global growth as an instrument for real domestic growth. The coefficient on real domestic growth remains highly statistically significant and becomes somewhat larger. The results are also robust to estimating the baseline

Table 5.2. Support for a Market Economy and Macroeconomic Variables

	(1) OLS	(2) OLS	(3) OLS	(4) OLS	(5) IV
GDP Growth	0.64***	0.83***	0.89***	0.89***	1.74***
	(0.19)	(0.25)	(0.26)	(0.26)	(0.42)
Fiscal Impulse		0.76*	0.70	0.69	0.54
		(0.42)	(0.42)	(0.43)	(0.46)
Inflation			0.18	0.18	0.22
			(0.15)	(0.15)	(0.16)
Unemployment				0.01	0.12
				(0.39)	(0.41)
Observations	178	105	104	104	104
R^2	0.07	0.14	0.16	0.16	
Number of Countries	18	11	11	11	11

Source: Authors' calculations.
Note: IV = instrumental variables; OLS = ordinary least squares. Standard errors are in parentheses.
***$p < 0.01$; **$p < 0.05$; *$p < 0.1$.

---

[5]See footnote 4 for the list of countries included in the regression analysis in addition to Brazil.

Figure 5.5. Brazil: What Is Most Important for the Development of Brazil?

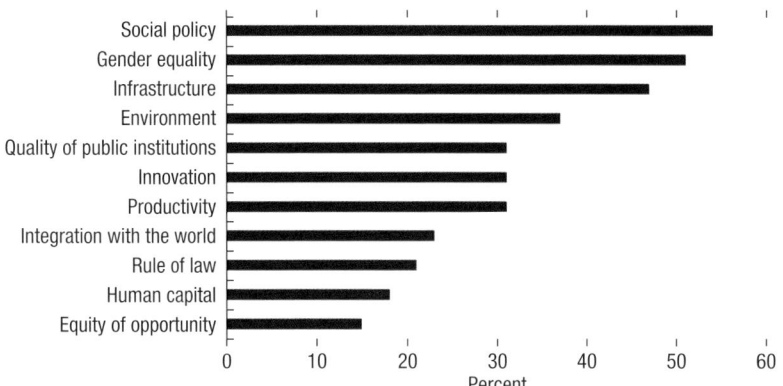

Source: 2016 Latin Barometer.

regression equation with the dependent variable specified in first differences rather than levels.

Which structural reforms does the public most support? To identify the specific structural reforms supported by the public, the following question from the Latin Barometer Survey is analyzed:[6]

Q: What is most important for the development of Brazil?

The range of choices includes (1) social policy, (2) gender equality, (3) infrastructure, (4) environment, (5) innovation, (6) productivity, (7) quality of public institutions, (8) integration with the world, (9) rule of law, (10) equity of opportunity, and (11) human capital.[7] Although this question does not ask respondents directly about structural reforms, it communicates views on what aspects of the economy need to be strengthened for the country's development. Based on respondents' answers (Figure 5.5), the measure of public support for structural reforms is built.

As illustrated in Table 5.3, matching survey responses to structural reforms involves some judgment. Matching certain reforms with survey responses is straightforward. For example, "integration with the world" can be interpreted as indicative of the public's support for free trade reforms. Similarly, respondents' choices of "rule of law" and "quality of public institutions" can be interpreted as signaling public support for legal system reforms. The procedure is more challanging when matching product market and banking sector and labor market

---

[6]Ideally, a survey data set would be used that asks participants questions about their views on specific structural reforms (for example, Baker 2000). However, these types of questions are generally not covered by population-representative surveys such as the Latin Barometer, Pew Global Attitudes Project, Latin American Public Opinion Project, and Datafolha (Brazil).

[7]Respondents can select multiple responses.

Table 5.3. Matching Survey Responses to Structural Reforms

Survey Response(s)	Structural Reform
Integration with the World	Trade openness
Rule of Law	
Quality of Public Institutions	Legal system
Productivity	
Innovation	Banking and product markets
Equity of Opportunity	Labor market

reforms. Under the assumption that product market and banking reforms can bolster productivity and innovation, these two reforms are tied to support for "innovation" and "productivity." Finally, people's demand for "equity of opportunity" is interpreted as a measure of public support for a more equitable and meritocratic labor market.[8] To validate this matching procedure for banking sector, product market, and labor market reforms, the next paragraph considers their correlation with structural reform indicators.

Measures of public support for specific reforms are correlated with structural reform indicators, supporting the matching procedure. Figure 5.6 shows the relationship between people's support for "innovation" and "productivity" and the level of product market and banking sector reforms measured using the indices described previously. In countries where product market and banking reforms are weak, respondents consider "innovation" and "productivity" to be more beneficial for development. Similarly, respondents report "equity of opportunity" to be an

Figure 5.6. Structural Reform Indices versus Public Support for Reforms

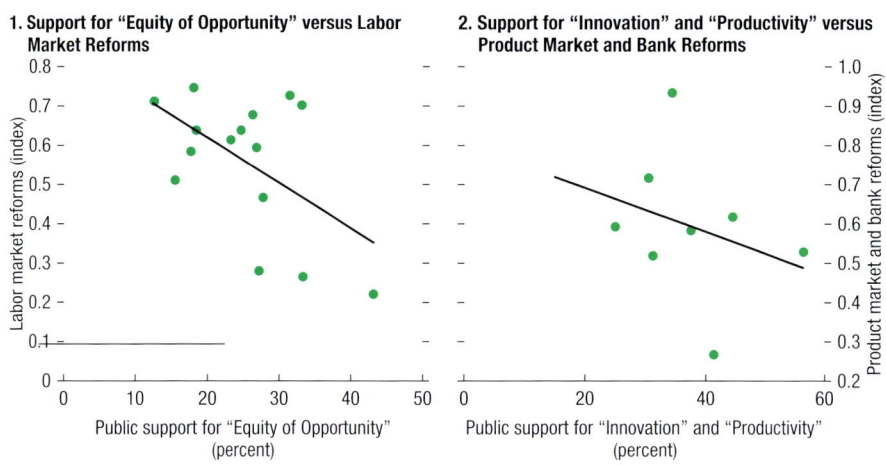

Source: IMF staff calculations.
Note: Structural reform indices vary between 0 and 1, with higher values corresponding to higher structural reforms.

[8]The rest of the answers from the question do not correspond to structural reforms and were therefore omitted.

Figure 5.7. Brazil: Public Support for Structural Reforms
(Percent)

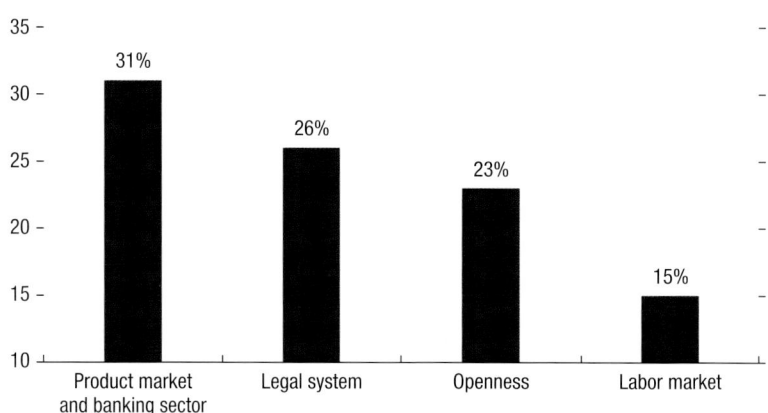

Source: IMF staff calculations.

important factor for development, especially in countries with rigid labor markets. These results provide some support to the matching algorithm that uses "innovation," "productivity," and "equity of opportunity" as proxies for public support for product market, banking sector, and labor market reforms, respectively.

Product market, banking sector, and legal system reforms receive the highest level of public support in Brazil (Figure 5.7). Based on the analysis, about 30 percent of the sample surveyed in Brazil supports product market and banking sector reforms. Similarly, about a quarter of the respondents believe that legal system reforms are important for development. Trade reforms are supported by 23 percent of respondents. Only 15 percent believe that improving labor laws could contribute to development.

Discontent with the banking sector and legal system is also evident in the Pew Global Attitudes Survey. To corroborate the findings and ensure they are not specific to the Latin Barometer, the following two questions from the Pew Global Attitudes Survey are examined:

Is the influence of banks and other financial institutions good?

Is the influence of the Court System good?

More than half of the respondents in the sample consider the influence of financial institutions to be "somewhat bad" or "very bad." In addition, more than 70 percent of respondents consider the court system to have a poor influence, suggesting that there is scope for improvement through structural reforms (Figure 5.8).

Micro-level data from the Latin Barometer are used to identify the segments of society more likely to support reforms. The priority list of reforms may vary across different groups because the costs and benefits associated with reforms may

Figure 5.8. Brazil: Public View of Financial and Legal Institutions

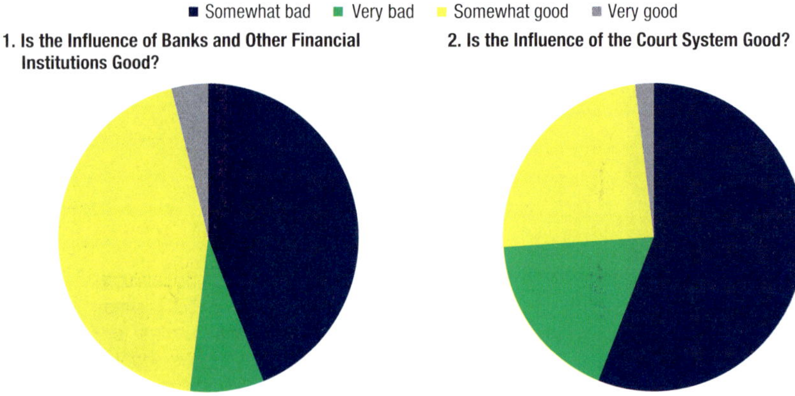

■ Somewhat bad ■ Very bad ■ Somewhat good ■ Very good

1. Is the Influence of Banks and Other Financial Institutions Good?

2. Is the Influence of the Court System Good?

Source: Pew Global Attitudes & Trends Survey.

differ by demographic and socioeconomic characteristics. To account for this possibility, the following regression equation is estimated based on 2016 Latin Barometer Survey data for Brazil:

$$Support\_Reform_i^s = \alpha + \beta \cdot EDU_i + \gamma_1 \cdot AGE_i + \gamma_2 \cdot AGE_i^2 + \delta \cdot EMPL_i + \varphi \cdot GENDER_i + \varepsilon_i.$$

$Support\_Reform_i^s$ is a dummy variable that denotes individual i's support for reform s, where s stands for product market and banking sector, legal system, labor market, or trade reforms; the explanatory variables include the individual's years of education, age, age squared (to account for nonlinearities), employment status, and gender.

Level of education is a strong predictor of support for reforms. The regression coefficients associated with years of education are positive and statistically significant across all reform categories in Table 5.4. Little variation is detected across other demographic and socioeconomic characteristics, suggesting that support for reforms is homogeneous across the population. Employment status matters only for labor market reforms, with the unemployed or self-employed being more supportive of labor reforms. Age appears to affect people's views about trade, with older people being less supportive of reforms.

The survey regressions further corroborate the procedure for assessing public support for labor market reforms. Given that unemployed and self-employed individuals are, on average, more supportive of labor market reforms than the rest of the population—this suggests that the survey answer "equity of opportunity" is a good proxy for public support for labor market reforms. Hence, the approach is also validated by micro-level data.

Despite broad public support, the reform agenda may be undermined by special interests. One caveat to the analysis is that public support does not necessarily translate into political action because special interest groups can have a powerful

Table 5.4. Brazil: Support for Reforms by Population Groups

	Product Market and Banking	Legal System	Labor	Trade
Years of Education	1.46***	0.56**	1.01***	1.16***
	(0.39)	(0.28)	(0.32)	(0.35)
Age	(0.24)	(0.51)	(0.24)	−1.03**
	(0.47)	(0.34)	(0.37)	(0.42)
Age Squared	0.00	0.00	0.00	0.01**
	(0.01)	(0.00)	(0.00)	(0.00)
Self-Employed	1.68	1.99	6.40*	(0.85)
	(4.75)	(3.23)	(3.84)	(4.06)
Salaried in Public Sector	1.93	7.17	4.99	4.43
	(6.98)	(5.15)	(5.50)	(6.43)
Salaried in Private Sector	5.61	2.45	2.06	3.82
	(5.83)	(4.00)	(4.46)	(5.09)
Unemployed	7.90	6.83	11.47**	5.69
	(6.73)	(4.92)	(5.50)	(5.93)
Outside of Workforce	0.18	(2.52)	(1.16)	(5.74)
	(5.69)	(3.63)	(4.24)	(4.64)
Student	(3.62)	7.41	2.08	(10.19)
	(9.43)	(7.90)	(7.31)	(8.38)
Male	4.06	(1.09)	3.65	3.83
	(2.82)	(2.05)	(2.24)	(2.59)
Observations	1,148	1,148	1,148	1,148
R^2	0.03	0.03	0.02	0.04

Source: Authors' calculations.
Note: Standard errors are in parentheses.
***$p < 0.01$; **$p < 0.05$; *$p < 0.1$.

impact on the legislative process. The political science literature has not yet taken a definite stand on the extent to which public opinion influences policymakers' decisions.[9] Studies suggest that the balance of power between public support and special interest groups depends on the prominence of the subject, the degree of agreement among the public, the intensity with which opinions are held, and the extent of organized support for and against the opposition. Nonetheless, even though public opinion may not be the only driver for political action, it certainly plays a significant role.

BRAZIL'S REFORM PRIORITIES

This section combines the findings about the effects on TFP and the extent of public support to identify Brazil's structural reform priorities. Figure 5.9 presents a scatterplot of the structural reforms considered in the analysis, showing the estimated effects on TFP growth on the horizontal axis and the degree of public

---

[9]On the one hand, Monroe (1998), Page and Shapiro (1992), and Stimson, Mackuen, and Erikson (1995) argue that policymakers follow public support; on the other, Zaller (1992) and Kingdon (2003) find that policy elites sway public opinion toward their viewpoint.

Figure 5.9. Economic Impact and Public Support for Reforms

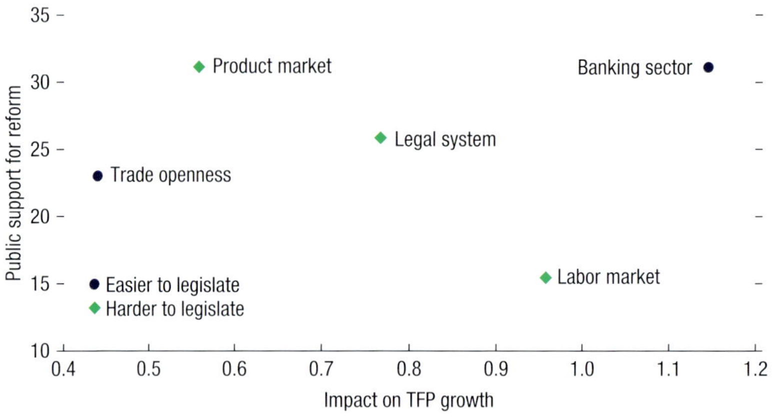

Source: IMF staff calculations.
Note: TFP = total factor productivity.

support on the vertical axis. Thus, those structural reforms closer to the top-right corner are the ones likely to boost productivity the most while gathering the largest support among Brazil's population.

Banking sector reforms have both the strongest impact on TFP and the highest level of public support. Therefore, they should be placed at the top of the structural reform agenda for Brazil. As previously discussed, the structural indicator for the banking sector suggests that policy efforts should focus on improving credit allocation by limiting state intervention. Legal reforms should also be given high priority, especially if they contribute to reducing corruption. They are supported by a large proportion of the population and have strong positive effects on productivity.

In addition to the effects on TFP and the extent of public support, legislative considerations can also influence the choice of reforms. Table 5.5 lists several structural reforms that have recently been adopted or are under consideration in Brazil, together with their legislative requirements. Some policy measures can be adopted relatively easily by the government without requiring approval from Congress. These include recent initiatives to reform the Brazilian Development Bank and Federal Savings Bank—Caixa Econômica Federal and measures to foster trade integration. At the opposite end of the spectrum, some measures require congressional approval through ordinary law—for example, labor reforms. Finally, in some cases, the government can adopt measures on a temporary basis through provisional laws that later need to be confirmed by Congress.

An additional factor in favor of banking sector reforms is that they are relatively simple to legislate. Table 5.5 shows that important banking reforms can be enacted by the government alone because they do not require congressional approval. This is also the case for several trade reforms. In contrast, labor market,

Table 5.5. Legislative Requirements for Structural Reforms

Structural Reform Category	Measures	Legislative Requirements
Banking Sector	TLP reform to reduce subsidies on long-term rates (law 13483)	Provisional law
	Reform of BNDES's business model	Congressional approval not required
	Reform of CAIXA's governance and business model	Congressional approval not required
Labor Market	Labor reform (law 13467)	Ordinary law
	Outsourcing of core business activities (law 13429)	Ordinary law
	Migration reform (law 13455)	Ordinary law
Legal System and Corruption	Ten measures against corruption (PLC 27/2017)	Ordinary law
	Bankruptcy law	Ordinary law
	Limits on cancellation of greenfield contracts (PLS 774)	Ordinary law
Product Market	Privatization and PPP reforms (PL 9463)	Ordinary law
	Bolstering of regulatory agencies (PL 6621)	Ordinary law
	SOE governance reforms (PL 9215, PLS 555)	Ordinary law
Trade Openness	OECD accession	Congressional approval not required
	Bilateral agreement between MERCOSUR and European Union	Congressional approval not required

Source: Authors' calculations.
Note: BNDES = Brazilian Development Bank; MERCOSUR = Southern Cone Common Market (Argentina, Brazil, Paraguay, Uruguay, Venezuela); OECD = Organisation for Economic Co-operation and Development; PPP = public-private partnership; SOE = state-owned enterprise; TLP = Taxa de Longo Prazo ("long-term rate").

legal system, and product market reforms are more cumbersome from a legislative standpoint because they need to be passed with ordinary laws.

The structural reform agenda can also be influenced by fiscal space considerations. By boosting productivity and raising economic growth, structural reforms tend to have positive effects on the sustainability of fiscal accounts over the long term. However, some reforms may involve significant short-term fiscal costs, as discussed in IMF (2017). For example, labor market reforms may require higher spending on unemployment benefits or active labor market policies as workers are gradually reallocated into more productive employment opportunities. Fiscal considerations are particularly important at the current juncture in Brazil given the high and rising level of public debt.

Banking sector reforms can yield significant fiscal gains. As discussed, Brazil scores poorly in the banking sector structural reform index because of pervasive state intervention. About half of total credit to households and nonfinancial firms is provided by public banks through earmarked programs, often at subsidized rates. According to authorities' estimates, the fiscal costs from subsidized lending amounted to 2.1 percent of GDP in 2015. Reducing public intervention in credit markets can thus result in considerable fiscal savings.

ADDITIONAL CONSIDERATIONS FOR IDENTIFYING REFORM PRIORITIES

Does sequencing matter? This chapter identifies the key reform priorities for Brazil by examining the impact on productivity and the extent of public support. However, reform choices can be shaped by several additional factors, which are briefly discussed in this section. A first issue concerns the optimal sequencing of reforms—some reforms should be undertaken first because they can boost public support for or strengthen the economic benefits of subsequent reforms.

For example, it is generally argued that trade liberation and domestic financial reforms should precede capital account liberalization. This consideration dates to the work of McKinnon (1973), who argues that allowing for free capital flows before trade liberalization would likely exacerbate the allocative distortions owing to trade barriers. Similarly, free capital flows could lead to overborrowing, possibly in foreign currency, if the financial sector is not properly supervised and free of distortions. Ostry, Prati, and Spilimbergo (2009) find empirical evidence that shows a stronger positive impact on growth if trade reforms precede capital account liberalization.

Evidence also indicates that trade liberalization can increase support for domestic financial reforms. Rajan and Zingales (2003) argue that competition associated with international trade weakens domestic monopolists, thus reducing their political influence against domestic financial liberalization. Hauner, Prati, and Bircan (2013) present empirical evidence in line with this hypothesis. Trade liberalization is found to be a leading indicator of domestic financial liberalization across a broad sample of both high- and low-income countries.

Furthermore, product market reforms can facilitate labor market reforms. Blanchard and Giavazzi (2003) developed a model to provide an understanding of the interactions between product and labor market liberalization. By fostering competition and lowering prices, product market reforms increase real wages. This outcome facilitates labor market liberalization, which tends instead to reduce wages (while increasing employment). Furthermore, product market reforms reduce the size of rents seized by incumbent firms, which weakens workers' incentives to unionize and oppose labor reforms to appropriate part of the rents.

In addition to considerations about optimal sequencing, reform priorities can also be affected by the state of the economic cycle. Recent model-based and empirical studies find that the impact of reforms can vary significantly depending on macroeconomic conditions. More specifically, some structural reforms tend to be more beneficial when they are implemented under strong economic conditions. This is especially the case for labor market reforms, which can even become

Figure 5.10. Virtuous Circle between Growth, Public Support, and Reforms

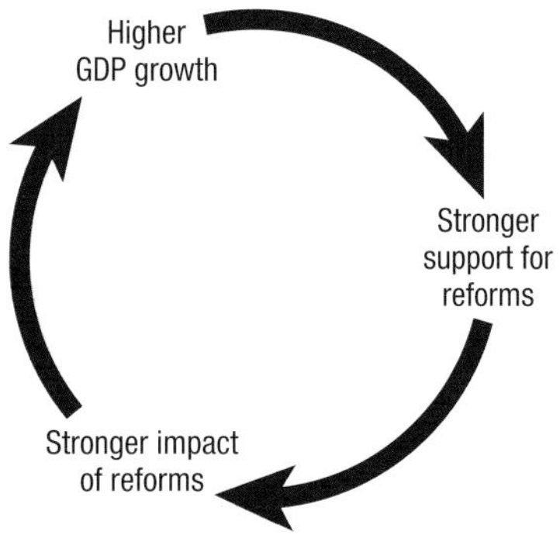

Source: Authors' graphic.

contractionary in periods of economic downturns, as is documented in IMF (2016), for example. In this regard, the ongoing economic recovery in Brazil provides a crucial window of opportunity for enacting structural reforms.

The academic literature has also proposed that reform priorities be selected based on the most binding constraint for economic growth. Hausmann, Rodrik, and Velasco (2008) argue that policymakers should first identify the most important impediment to economic development and then prioritize structural reforms to address the source of the problem. For example, they argue that Brazil's economic growth is constrained primarily by limited credit supply, which hinders private investment. To increase private financing, they call for fiscal consolidation to reduce crowding-out effects. They also attribute credit constraints to high intermediation margins in the financial sector. Their focus on boosting credit supply is consistent with the call in this chapter for banking sector reforms that are expected to ultimately raise private investment by improving credit allocation and reducing intermediation margins.

CONCLUSIONS

The analysis suggests that banking sector reforms should be given priority. In Brazil, banking reforms to limit state intervention in credit markets would have the highest impact on productivity and enjoy broad public support. Furthermore, they are relatively easy to legislate and can generate significant fiscal savings. Labor market reforms can also create large productivity gains, but the full impact of the 2017 labor reform should be assessed before further measures are contemplated. In addition to reforming the banking sector, authorities should focus on reforms to the legal system that can also generate large productivity gains while gathering broad public support. Reforms should strengthen the legal protection provided to individuals and their property and include measures to curb corruption.

The ongoing economic recovery in Brazil offers a crucial opportunity to enact reforms. This chapter uses survey data primarily to identify which structural reforms should be given priority. However, survey data also provide important information about when to enact reforms. In this regard, the analysis finds that public support for structural reforms tends to increase with the pace of economic growth. The level of support for reforms in Brazil, already high relative to other Latin American countries, is thus expected to rise further as the economic recovery strengthens. Because structural reforms tend to have more beneficial effects when the economic cycle is strong (IMF 2016), the virtuous circle illustrated in Figure 5.10 may arise. Therefore, periods of sustained economic growth provide a crucial opportunity to adopt structural reforms by exploiting stronger public support and maximizing the economic impact.

REFERENCES

Abiad, Abdul, Enrica Detragiache, and Thierry Tressel. 2010. "A New Database of Financial Reforms." *IMF Staff Papers* 57 (February): 281–302.

Abiad, Abdul, and Ashoka Mody. 2005. "Financial Reform: What Shakes It? What Shapes It?" *American Economic Review* 95 (January): 66–88.

Baker, Andy. 2000. "Economic Policy Debates and Voter Choice in Brazil: Issues and Economy in the 1998 Presidential Elections." Paper presented at the 2000 meeting of the Latin American Studies Association, Miami, March 16–18.

Blanchard, Olivier, and Francesco Giavazzi. 2003. "Macroeconomic Effects of Regulation and Deregulation in Goods and Labor Markets." *Quarterly Journal of Economics* 118 (March): 879–907.

Bouis, Romain, and Romain Duval. 2011, "Raising Potential Growth after the Crisis: A Quantitative Assessment of the Potential Gains from Various Structural Reforms in the OECD Area and Beyond." *OECD Working Paper* No. 835, Organisation for Economic Co-operation and Development, Paris.

Hauner, David, Alessandro Prati, and Cagatay Bircan. 2013. "The Interest Group Theory of Financial Development: Evidence from Regulation." *Journal of Banking and Finance* 37 (March): 895–906.

Hausmann, Ricardo, Dani Rodrik, and Andres Velasco. 2008. "Growth Diagnostics." In *The Washington Consensus Reconsidered: Towards a New Global Governance*, edited by J. Stiglitz and N. Serra. New York: Oxford University Press.

International Monetary Fund (IMF). 2015. "Structural Reforms and Macroeconomic Performance: Initial Considerations for the Fund—Staff Report." IMF Policy Paper, Washington, DC.

———. 2016. "Time for a Supply-Side Boost? Macroeconomic Effects of Labor and Product Market Reforms in Advanced Economies." *World Economic Outlook*, Chapter 3, Washington, DC.

———. 2017. "Labor and Product Market Reforms in Advanced Economies: Fiscal Costs, Gains and Support." Staff Discussion Note No. 17/03, Washington, DC.

Kingdon, John W. 2003. *Agendas, Alternatives, and Public Policies.* New York: Longman.

McKinnon, Ronald I. 1973. *Money and Capital in Economic Development.* Washington, DC: Brookings Institution.

Monroe, Alan D. 1998. "Public Opinion and Public Policy, 1980–1993." *The Public Opinion Quarterly* 62 (January): 6–28.

Organisation for Economic Co-operation and Development (OECD). 2018. *OECD Economic Surveys: Brazil*. Paris.

Ostry, Jonathan D., Alessandro Prati, and Antonio Spilimbergo. 2009. "Structural Reforms and Economic Performance in Advanced and Developing Countries." IMF Occasional Paper No. 268, International Monetary Fund, Washington, DC.

Page, Benjamin I., and Robert Y. Shapiro. 1992. *The Rational Public: Fifty Years of Trends in Americans' Policy Preferences*. Chicago: University of Chicago Press.

Prati, Alessandro, Massimiliano Gaetano Onorato, and Chris Papageorgiou. 2013. "Which Reforms Work and under What Institutional Environment? Evidence from a New Data Set on Structural Reforms." *Review of Economics and Statistics* 95 (March): 946–68.

Quinn, Dennis. 1997. "The Correlated of Change in International Financial Integration." *The American Political Science Review* 91 (March): 531–51.

Rajan, Raghuram, and Luigi Zingales. 2003. "The Great Reversals: The Politics of Financial Development in the Twentieth Century." *Journal of Financial Economics* 69 (1): 5–50.

Stimson, James A., Michael B. Mackuen, and Robert S. Erikson. 1995. "Dynamic Representation." *The American Political Science Review* 89 (March): 543–65.

Zaller, John. 1992. *The Nature and Origins of Mass Opinion*. New York: Cambridge University Press.

CHAPTER 6

Brazil in the New World Economic Order

MARCELLO ESTEVÃO AND FERNANDO COPPE ALCARAZ

Brazil is one of the most closed economies in the world; it has comparatively high import tariffs, numerous local-content programs, and few and shallow trade agreements. However, the country's trade and international economic policies have undergone important changes since mid-2016, indicating an attempt to become more integrated into international trade flows. These changes include a request for accession to the Organisation for Economic Co-operation and Development, the acceptance of the country as an observer to the World Trade Organization's Government Procurement Agreement, and a more pragmatic attitude toward trade agreements. But there is still room for improvement. Economic theory and the empirical literature show that trade openness leads to higher levels of productivity and welfare gains. This chapter therefore argues that Brazil should be more open to international trade, starting by reducing import tariffs for basic production inputs and for information technology and capital goods, by eliminating its local-content rules, and by pursuing deeper trade agreements with more and larger trade partners.

INTRODUCTION

Despite being one of the largest countries in the world in territory, population, and GDP, Brazil has traditionally been a relatively closed economy, with comparatively high tariffs and few trade agreements. Indeed, with one of the lowest trade-to-GDP ratios in the world (even though this figure is 50 percent higher now than the average of the last four decades of the 20th century), Brazil has taken little advantage of the well-known growth benefits from international trade and greater insertion into global value chains.

Moreover, from 2003 to 2015, the Brazilian government emphasized diplomatic and economic relationships with the developing world, in part guided by the ideology of the political party in power. That strategy has sometimes

The views expressed in this article are the authors' own and do not reflect the views of, and should not be attributed to, the Brazilian government or any of its ministries, bodies, or institutions. The authors would like to thank José Henrique Martins, Rafael Quirino, Emerson Gazzoli, and Vivian Macedo for their suggestions and contributions.

constrained Brazil's positions in key multilateral institutions and bilateral relationships with other key trading partners. The mix of a protectionist culture, a foreign economic policy often at odds with the true interests of the country, and state dirigisme has stifled economic growth and helped create the conditions for the deep economic crisis seen in 2015–16.

Since the crisis, changes in domestic policies and in the international arena have contributed to some correction in the country's relationships with the rest of the world. Brazil's foreign economic policy has turned to a more pragmatic approach by getting closer to Organisation for Economic Co-operation and Development (OECD) partners—a source of wealth and good governance—especially after sending a request for accession to the institution in 2017, and to the other BRICS countries (Russia, India, China, South Africa)[1]—a source of growth—through new agreements and increased activity by the New Development Bank. Policymakers have continued their historically strong advocacy of key national and emerging market interests in Bretton Woods institutions as well as active participation at regional development banks, and at the World Trade Organization (WTO), although with a more balanced and productive attitude. As part of Mercosur,[2] the country is aiming to conclude an ambitious trade agreement with the European Union, one of its main trading partners.[3] That bodes well for the future, especially if the agreement is a harbinger of a movement toward more trade agreements coupled with lower tariffs and rationalized nontariff protections.

This chapter discusses how Brazil's insertion into the world economy has evolved, with a focus on trade policies and trade flows. The next section shows how Brazil compares with other countries in integration into international trade flows. The chapter then briefly examines the factors that seem to explain this low level of trade integration, followed by an exploration of some of the possible consequences of Brazil's low levels of international trade. Some important changes in Brazil's trade policy stance since mid-2016 are then explored. The last two sections suggest an agenda for the future and conclude the chapter.

BRAZIL'S INTEGRATION INTO INTERNATIONAL TRADE FLOWS

Brazil is still one of the most closed economies in the world (Table 6.1), despite some increase in trade as a share of GDP in the past 20 years (Figure 6.1).

On the export side, this very low level of trade integration may be surprising if only commodity export data are reviewed. Brazil is, after all, among the world's

---

[1]Brazil is the "B" in BRICS.

[2]Mercosur, officially Southern Common Market is a South American trade bloc; full members are Argentina, Brazil, Paraguay, and Uruguay. Venezuela is a full member but has been suspended since December 1, 2016.

[3]Originally written in April 2018.

Table 6.1. International Trade as a Share of GDP

(2016, in percent)[1]

Highest Proportions (trade/GDP)		Lowest Proportions (trade/GDP)	
1. Luxembourg	407.4	1. Sudan	22.4
2. Hong Kong SAR	372.6	2. Brazil	24.6
3. Singapore	318.4	3. Pakistan	25.1
4. Malta	268.2	4. Argentina	26.3
5. Ireland	221.2	5. United States	26.6
6. United Arab Emirates	205.3	6. Yemen	28.4

Source: World Bank, World Development Indicators.[2] Elaboration by authors.

[1]As additional benchmarks, the trade-to-GDP figures are 77.7 percent in the Republic of Korea, 56.1 percent in Chile, 46.3 percent in Russia, 39.8 percent in India, and 37.1 percent in China.

[2]Series description: "The sum of exports and imports of goods and services measured as a share of gross domestic product."

top exporters for its three most exported products: soybeans (second in the world, behind only the United States), iron ore (second only to Australia) and sugar (first in the world).[4] However, Brazil is not a particularly successful exporter of other goods and is only the 27th largest exporter of goods in the world. On the import side, the picture looks even bleaker, with Brazil reaching only 30th position among the world's top goods importers.

Figure 6.1. Brazil: Ratio of Trade to GDP

(Percent)

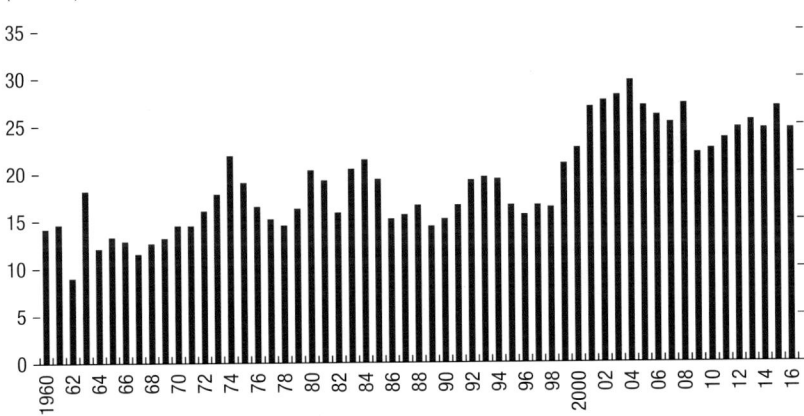

Source: World Bank, World Development Indicators (November 2017).

---

[4]These were the three top products in Brazil's exports in 2016 (in that order) according to the WTO Trade Profiles. The source for the data on the largest commodity exporters in the world is the Trade Map database provided by the International Trade Center. For simplicity, 2016 four-digit Harmonized System data were used for the three products.

Table 6.2. Largest Countries by Total GDP and Their Rank as Traders in Goods and Services

Country	GDP (190 countries)	Exports of goods and services (BoP, current US$, 156 countries)	Imports of goods and services (current US$, 171 countries)
United States	1	1	1
China	2	2	2
Japan	3	4	6
Germany	4	3	3
France	5	5	5
United Kingdom	6	6	4
India	7	14	12
Brazil	8	24	24
Italy	9	10	11
Canada	10	12	9

Source: World Bank, World Development Indicators (2016 data).
Note: BoP = balance of payments.

These indicators compare unfavorably to the country's position among the world's 10 largest economies (Table 6.2), revealing that Brazil has been following a distinct path on international trade when compared with other major world economies.

WHY IS BRAZIL SO CLOSED TO TRADE?

As economic theory and numerous empirical studies show, many factors can explain a country's degree of trade openness. Among these factors are size, distance to trading partners, and trade policy variables. All else equal, the larger the country and the farther it is from its actual or potential trading partners, the less it will trade as a proportion of its domestic production.

Regarding trade policy, the lower the tariffs on and nontariff barriers to imports and exports, the lower the cost to trade and the more the country will trade. This is true both for barriers that apply to all import origins, the so called most-favored-nation tariffs, and nontariff barriers, as well as for the usually lower barriers that apply to bilateral trade flows under preferential trade agreements.

Brazil is a large country—the fifth largest in the world in both territory and population. It is also among the 10 largest economies in the world in GDP. These factors, however, cannot in isolation explain why Brazil is so closed to trade. For instance, trying to explain Brazil's trade-to-GDP ratio by taking only population into account would lead to a trade-to-GDP ratio of 48.6 percent, a figure well above the actual ratio (Figure 6.2).

The explanation for Brazil's lack of openness to trade, therefore, should lie mostly in its own trade policy and institutions.

Figure 6.2. Ratio of Trade to GDP (percent) and Population (2012–16)

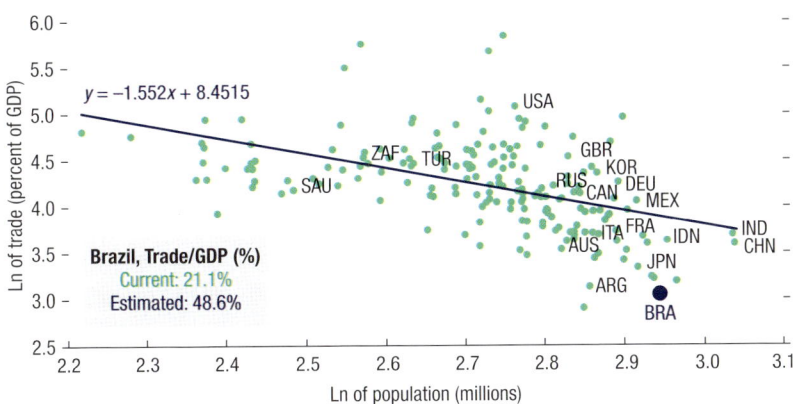

Source: World Bank data.
Note: Data labels in figure use International Organization for Standardization (ISO) country codes. Ln = natural logarithm. Ln = natural logarithm.

Policy Variables

Brazil's trade policy consists mainly of comparatively high tariffs, numerous antidumping duties and local-content programs, and relatively shallow trade agreements that do not cover most of the country's foreign trade.

Exploring the underlying reasons for Brazil's comparatively protectionist trade policy is outside the scope of this paper. However, empirical work by Baumann and Messa (2017) suggests that firms' lobbying has influenced Brazil's trade policies more than other countries', notably in the period between 2005 and 2013. The authors assert the following:

> The Brazilian government, between 2005 and 2010, gave a heavy weight (25%) to the corporate lobby in its decisions on trade policy; this same weight, between 2011 and 2013, had a growth level of little more than 35%. For comparison, Goldberg and Maggi (1999) found, for the United States, in 1983, a weight of 2% for lobbying pressures. In turn, Gawande, Krishna and Olarreaga (2009) estimated, for the Brazilian economy in 1998, a weight for the lobby of 3.8%.[5]

The subsections that follow describe Brazil's policies on tariffs, local-content rules (LCRs), antidumping duties, and trade agreements.

Brazil's Tariffs

Brazil's average applied tariff is among the highest in the world (Table 6.3).

In addition, Brazil's trade-weighted average tariff is twice as high as Colombia's and more than eight times higher than Chile's or Mexico's. Brazil also has the

---

[5]Baumann and Messa (2017).

Table 6.3. WTO Members with Highest and Lowest Effective Applied Tariffs

(Percent)

Highest Tariffs		Lowest Tariffs	
1. Gabon	18.89	1. Norway	0.75
2. Central African Republic	18.34	2. Iceland	0.76
3. Chad	18.16	3. Georgia	1.20
4. Brazil	**13.56**	4. Brunei Durassalam	1.21
5. Senegal	13.09	5. Albania	1.44
6. Côte d'Ivoire	13.09	6. Mauritius	1.45

Source: World Integrated Trade Solution (UNCTAD Trade Analysis Information System). 2016 data retrieved in January 2018.

highest number of tariff lines above 10 percent (OECD 2018, 49). These comparatively high tariffs apply not only on average but specifically on imported goods that are deemed essential for firms' competitiveness and for the country's productivity, such as capital goods (Table 6.4).

Brazil's Local-Content Rules

On top of its high tariffs, Brazil's highly protectionist trade policy also includes numerous LCRs. Stone, Messent, and Flaig (2015) show that the country is the third most active user of local-content policies in the world after Indonesia and the United States.

LCRs tend to be particularly pernicious because of their lower level of transparency in comparison with more typical trade policy tools, such as tariffs and trade remedies. This is usually the case because, while tariffs and trade remedies are allowed under WTO rules,[6] typical LCRs violate the WTO Agreements,[7] so governments tend to disguise LCRs' discriminatory aspects. One example is Brazil's former Inovar-Auto Program, which included numerous automotive-sector LCRs wrapped up in a program that proclaimed only to promote innovation and safety standards and to reduce pollution.

Brazil's local-content policies exist in different forms and cover different sectors and regions. Some examples of LCRs that either are still in force or were recently terminated include the following:

- Inovar-Auto, in the automotive sector (in force between 2012 and 2016)
- Informatics Law, for information technology (IT) goods
- Manaus Free Trade Zone, a special tax regime for the Manaus region in the Amazon
- Government procurement rules that grant preferences for domestic goods, services, and providers

---

[6]Provided the relevant upper limits (for example, the bound tariff for each tariff line and the margin of dumping for every antidumping duty) and procedural rules are respected.

[7]Depending on their characteristics, LCRs may violate General Agreement on Tariffs and Trade Articles III.2, III.4, and III.5, as well Article 3.1(b) of the Agreement on Subsidies and Countervailing Measures.

Table 6.4. G20 Members: Tariffs Applied to Capital Goods (2015[1])

(In descending order by group of countries)

G20: Developing Economies		G20: Developed/High-Income Countries	
Brazil	**13.1**	South Korea	5.89
China	9.10	Australia	2.59
India	7.80	European Union	2.01
Indonesia	5.44	United States	1.61
Saudi Arabia	4.15	Canada	0.90
Russia	4.00	World Average	**5.87**
Mexico	2.91		
Turkey	2.11		
South Africa	1.99		

Source: World Bank.

[1]Except for the European Union (2014), Saudi Arabia (2014), and India (2013). Retrieved from the World Bank website (World Integrated Trade Solution) on February 9, 2017.

- Several programs that cover information and communication technology, including PADIS, which covers semiconductors, displays, and inputs used in the production of these goods; PADTV, which covers inputs and equipment for digital television transmission (expired in January 2017); and the Digital Inclusion Program, which covers several digital consumer goods

The automotive sector deserves special attention. Brazilians pay a 35 percent tariff to import a car, the highest tariff applied by the country to any industrial product. On top of this high tariff, the Inovar-Auto program granted domestic producers better internal taxation treatment in the form of lower domestic taxes than the ones that applied to imported cars and car parts, hindering the beneficial effects that foreign competition would bring to productivity growth in the industry and lower prices for consumers. The tax rate differential could reach up to 30 percentage points. To benefit from this preferential treatment, producers had to comply with minimum performance requirements and LCRs. LCRs compounded the relative protection of domestic sectors—at the input as well as the output level—and raised the costs of producing and buying cars in Brazil.[8]

Because the program discriminated against imported cars and car parts, a WTO panel found that Inovar-Auto was inconsistent with Brazil's WTO obligations under Article III[9] of the General Agreement on Tariffs and Trade, which mandates national treatment for foreign goods, and under Article 3.1(b) of the WTO Agreement on Subsidies and Countervailing Measures, which prohibits "subsidies contingent . . . upon the use of domestic over imported goods."[10]

---

[8]This is a very short description of a very complex program. For more information, see Alcaraz (2016, 22–29).

[9]More specifically, Articles III.2, which deals with international taxation, and III.4, which deals with "all laws, regulations and requirements affecting . . . internal sale, offering for sale, purchase, transportation, distribution or use."

[10]For these specific findings of the panel, see WTO (2017).

Table 6.5. Brazil's Trade Agreements with Its Main Trading Partners (2017)

Country	Part. in Brazil's Exports (%)	Part. in Brazil's Imports (%)	Part. in Brazil's Trade Flows (%)	FTA with Brazil
China	21.8%	18.1%	20.3%	No
European Union	16.0%	21.3%	18.2%	No
United States	12.3%	16.5%	14.0%	No
MERCOSUR	10.4%	7.9%	9.4%	Yes
Japan	2.4%	2.5%	2.4%	No

Source: Brazil's Ministry of Foreign Trade, Industry and Services. Elaboration by authors.
Note: FTA = free trade agreement; MERCOSUR = Southern Cone Common Market (Argentina, Brazil, Paraguay, Uruguay, Venezuela).

Antidumping Duties

From 2013 to 2016, Brazil was the world leader in imposing antidumping duties, a "tariff-like" nontariff measure.[11] Although the imposition of new measures has declined significantly since then, Brazil remains a relatively more important antidumping user than importer among the largest economies in the world. As Alcaraz and others (2018) show, Brazil accounts for 9.7 percent of the world's total antidumping measures but only 0.9 percent of the world's total imports, which indicates the national authorities' above-average tendency to resort to antidumping measures.

Brazil's antidumping duties also exhibit a feature particularly detrimental to firms that operate in the country: about 80 percent of the measures currently in force[12] are imposed on imports of inputs, contributing to higher production costs in the country, thus hurting the competitiveness of Brazilian goods and services.

Trade Agreements

In addition to the significant trade barriers described above, Brazil, individually or as a member of Mercosur, has focused its actions on trade agreements with developing countries, especially in Latin America. As a result, Brazil has a reasonable network of free trade agreements (FTAs) in South America,[13] but it has no FTAs with any of its large trading partners in the North. For instance, Brazil has no FTAs with its three main trading partners—China, the European Union (EU), and the United States (Table 6.5).

---

[11]The expression "tariff-like" is used because antidumping duties are applied in a manner that closely resembles ad valorem or specific tariffs, although they are applicable only to the specific origins against which dumping, injury, and causal link were found. The nonuniversal (most favored nation), temporary, and conditional nature of antidumping duties, as well as the procedural requirements necessary for their application, make them a nontariff measure (NTM; Chapter D in UNCTAD's classification of NTMs, page 3, UNCTAD [2013]).

[12]Alcaraz and others (2018). Data available as of February 12, 2018. For the data set, see Ministry of Industry, Foreign Trade and Services (2018).

[13]A complete list of Brazil's trade agreements can be found at Organization of American States.

Brazil's lack of FTAs contrasts with the experience of other important emerging economies in Latin America. Chile, for instance, has a wide network of FTAs, covering, among others, the Mercosur countries, Australia, Canada, the EU, the European Free Trade Association (EFTA), Japan, Korea, China, and the United States. Similarly, Mexico has FTAs with, among others, the EU, EFTA, Israel, Japan, the United States, and Canada (through the North America Free Trade Agreement). Except for the Mercosur customs union and Israel, Brazil (individually or through Mercosur) has not signed FTAs with any of the aforementioned countries or trade blocs.

Moreover, Brazil's trade agreements are relatively shallow. With a few exceptions,[14] the country's trade agreements cover only trade in goods and do not include rules or market access commitments in important areas, such as trade in services and investment.

Even in goods trading, some agreements are more diplomatic formalities than relevant tools for international trade. One example is the trade agreement between Mercosur and India, which covers only 450 to 452 tariff items (out of more than 10,000) and in most cases grants only a 10 percent or 20 percent reduction of the tariff that would normally be paid.[15]

POSSIBLE CONSEQUENCES

Gains from Trade: A Brief Theoretical Description

Economists are in consensus that, under most circumstances, trade openness leads to welfare gains for consumers through lower prices and access to more and better varieties of goods and services.

On the producers' side, trade openness leads to higher levels of productivity through a variety of channels, including (1) a competitive push that leads to reallocation effects, with resources shifting from less productive to more productive firms and sectors; (2) a competitive push that produces intrafirm effects, in which exposure to foreign competition creates incentives for existing domestic firms to invest in better processes and products; and (3) access to higher technology embodied in imported inputs (high-tech inputs become less costly after trade liberalization).

Numerous studies have shown how these productivity-enhancing effects operated in different countries and situations so that trade openness led to higher levels of productivity, which, in turn, are essential for long-term economic growth. The following discussion describes a few examples that cover different regions of the world. For the trade liberalization observed in Brazil in the late 1980s and in the 1990s, Lisboa, Menezes Filho, and Schor (2010) show that the main productivity gain came from reducing input tariffs, allowing domestic firms

---

[14]Such as Mercosur and the agreements with Peru, Colombia, and Chile.

[15]Ongoing negotiations aim to strengthen and deepen the agreement. Source: Ministry of Industry, Foreign Trade and Services.

Table 6.6. World Economic Forum's Global Competitiveness Index's Pillars of Competitiveness

1) Institutions	7) Labor market efficiency
2) Infrastructure	8) Financial market development
3) Macroeconomic environment	9) Technological readiness
4) Health and primary education	10) Market size
5) Higher education and training	11) Business sophistication
6) Goods market efficiency	12) Innovation

Source: World Economic Forum 2017.

to use more efficient inputs and raise their markups. Similarly, in a study covering Indonesia, Amiti and Konings show that a reduction of both input and output tariffs increases productivity, although the effect from reducing input tariffs was found to be higher: "a 10 percentage point fall in input tariffs leads to a productivity gain of 11 percent for importing firms" (2005, 18) and of 3 percent for firms as a whole. In a paper using panel data across 12 European countries covering the period 1996–2007, Bloom, Draca, and van Reenen (2016) show that "Chinese import competition increase[ed] innovation within surviving firms, [. . . and led them to] create more patents, raise their IT intensity, and increase their overall level of productivity."

Productivity and Competitiveness in Brazil: A Link to Trade?

The next paragraphs explore the links between Brazil's trade policy options and its levels of productivity and competitiveness.

Brazil's position in the World Economic Forum's Global Competitiveness Index provides a good indicator of how poorly Brazil's trade policy performs in comparison with both other countries and other public policies in Brazil. The underlying idea of this index is that competitiveness is defined as "the set of institutions, policies, and factors that determine the level of productivity of a country. The level of productivity, in turn, sets the level of prosperity that can be reached by an economy" (Alcaraz 2016, 99).

To measure competitiveness, the Global Competitiveness Index considers the 12 pillars set out in Table 6.6.

Brazil ranks as the 80th most competitive country in the 2017–18 edition of the index (out of 137 countries). The pillar most directly affected by the country's low openness to trade is "goods market efficiency," for which Brazil ranks as the 122nd most competitive economy, its second-worst position among the 12 pillars.

In the indicators that lead to the overall result for goods market efficiency, the negative impact of Brazil's lack of openness to trade is even clearer. In the subpillar "foreign competition," Brazil ranks 132nd out of 137 countries, ahead of only Venezuela (137th), the Islamic Republic of Iran, Ecuador, Yemen, and Chad (133rd; Table 6.7).

Because the Global Competitiveness Index claims to analyze the factors that determine a country's level of productivity and has indicated how poor Brazil's

Table 6.7. Brazil's Performance on the Global Competitiveness Index

Pillar/Indicator	Rank (out of 137)
Global Competitiveness Index	80
Basic requirements	104
Institutions	109
Infrastructure	73
Macroeconomic environment	124
Health and primary education	96
Efficiency enhancers	60
Higher education and training	79
Goods market efficiency	122
Prevalence of nontariff barriers	130
Trade tariffs	121
Imports/GDP	126
Labor market efficiency	114
Financial market development	92
Technological readiness	55
Market size	10
Innovation and sophistication factors	65
Business sophistication	56
Innovation	85

Source: World Economic Forum 2017.

trade policy performance is, it is worth examining the way in which the country's productivity has evolved recently (see Figure 6.3).

Brazil's Participation in Global Value Chains

Brazil's high tariffs on inputs and capital goods make them more expensive. As a result, Brazilian firms add fewer imported inputs into their products, which, in

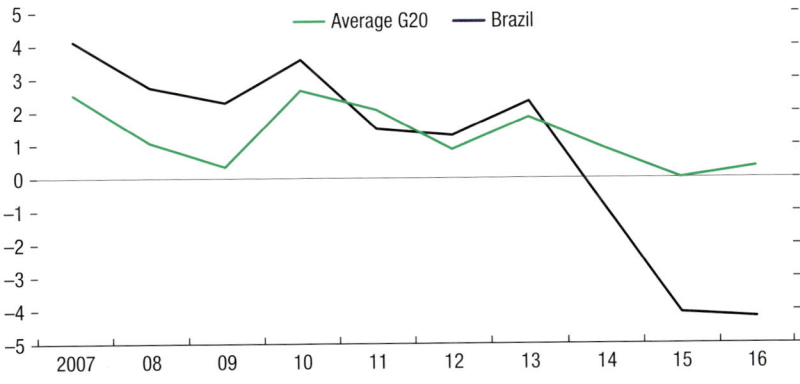

Figure 6.3. Labor Productivity Change, Brazil versus G20 Average
(Percent, output per hours worked)

Source: Conference Board Total Economy Database (adjusted version), November 2016.
Note: G20 = Group of Twenty.

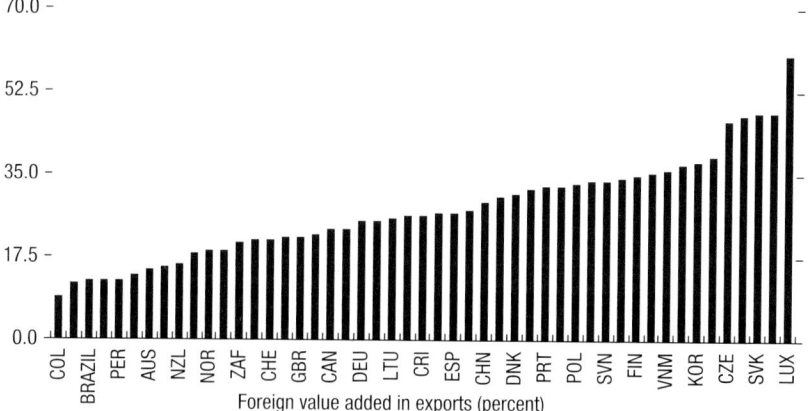

Figure 6.4. Backward Participation in Global Value Chains[2]
(Percent)

Source: Organisation for Economic Co-operation and Development (2018).
Note: Data labels in figure use International Organization for Standardization (ISO) country codes.

turn, makes the goods costlier and the firms less competitive internationally.[16] This plays a relevant part in Brazil's very low participation in global value chains.

The high cost of importing inputs leads to low participation in global value chains through two mechanisms. First, the direct and first-order effect of the high cost of importing inputs is to reduce backward participation in global value chains (Figure 6.4). Second, by making Brazilian exports more expensive and, therefore, less competitive internationally, the high cost of imports in Brazil also ends up contributing to a less significant presence of Brazilian exports in other countries' exports (Figure 6.5).

RECENT CHANGES

Since mid-2016, numerous actions have indicated that policymakers have been altering the relationship between the Brazilian economy and the rest of the world. For example,

- Brazil requested to become an OECD member in May 2017. Acceding to the OECD will lead to higher exposure to best international practices and may lead to better public policies for Brazil in numerous areas because OECD members' policies are constantly submitted to rigorous and sophisticated—although not legally binding—peer-review discussions.

- Brazil's request to accede, as an observer, to the WTO's Government Procurement Agreement was accepted by the WTO's relevant committee in

[16]Brambilla, Chauvin, and Porto (2017) show that Brazilian companies add the fewest imported inputs to their products among all Latin American and emerging market economies, which has contributed to low productivity at the firm level.

Figure 6.5. Forward Participation in Global Value Chains[1]
(Percent)

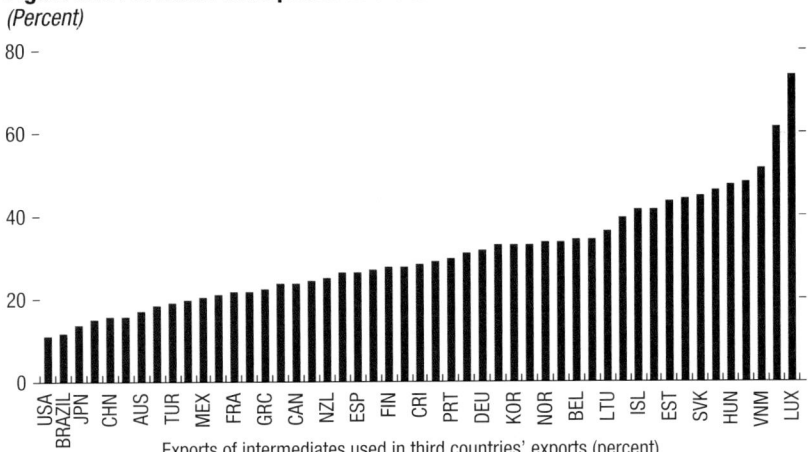

Exports of intermediates used in third countries' exports (percent)

Source: Organisation for Economic Co-operation and Development (2018).
Note: Data labels in figure use International Organization for Standardization (ISO) country codes.

October 2017. This clearly indicates the country's willingness to be exposed to best practices in the area. If, in the future, Brazil takes a step further by requesting and becoming a party to the agreement, then further gains in transparency and efficiency may be made by preventing future discriminatory policies against imported products and foreign service providers, given that such policies are, in general, prohibited under Article IV of the agreement.

• Brazil has shifted the focus of its trade negotiations, including a renewed effort to conclude a deal with the European Union, its main trading partner, and the beginning of negotiations with Canada and Korea, breaking with the previous administration's focus on developing and Latin American countries.

• Brazil has increased its integration with the Pacific Alliance, a group that is more open to international trade, including by having significantly lower tariffs and more ambitious trade agreements than Mercosur.

• The imposition of new antidumping duties has declined and there has been an increased use of the public interest test to avoid the imposition of measures in cases where a measure's negative impact over the economy as a whole is larger than the private benefits for the domestic industry requesting imposition of the duties.[17]

---

[17]An example is the decision in January 2018 by the Foreign Trade Board/Chamber (Câmara de Comércio Exterior—CAMEX) to not charge an antidumping duty on imports of one specific type of steel based on a proposal presented by the Ministry of Finance. The ministry's studies showed that, if the duty had been imposed and charged, the negative impacts on inflation and total GDP would surpass the private benefits that would accrue to steel producers.

- The BRICS movement has deepened, with speedier setup of the New Development Bank's operations and increased trade, investment, and diplomatic ties among its members.

AN AGENDA FOR THE FUTURE

Notwithstanding the important recent changes highlighted in the previous section, there is still room for additional improvement in the medium term.

Reducing tariffs is perhaps the most obvious first move. In a country so closed to trade as Brazil and where empirical work has shown that firms' lobbying is relevant in trade policymaking (Baumann and Messa 2017), the best way to proceed would be to gradually reduce tariffs on capital goods and IT goods and inputs.[18]

Such a first step in a tariff reform would be easier to implement for several reasons. From a political economy perspective, most producers would gain from a reduction in their costs. From a regulatory point of view, because of a Mercosur waiver valid until 2021, Brazil has the flexibility to change its national tariffs on capital and IT goods without obtaining authorization from the trade bloc. Moreover, the productivity-enhancing and investment-boosting effects of starting with a tariff reduction on machinery and inputs would probably serve as a stimulus to further liberalization. Computable general equilibrium model simulations show that the positive impact on the economy as a whole far exceeds the limited negative impact on IT and capital goods producers (Ferraz, Ornelas, and Pessoa 2018), many of whom would become more productive in the new lower-tariff environment.

Regarding LCRs, Brazil should start to remove the import-discrimination component present in some of its programs. Inovar-Auto, for instance, would not have been such an inefficient program[19] if it had only reasonably stimulated investments in research and development, safety, and efficiency instead of leading to higher indirect taxes on imported cars and car parts. Empirical studies indicate the results for the economy would have been positive. In a computable general equilibrium simulation, Araújo and Flaig (2016) show that reducing import tariffs on intermediate goods to the minimum OECD rates and ending LCR programs could lead to, among other results, increases in production (0.62 percent), investment (0.59 percent), labor demand (0.61 percent), and exports (7.69 percent).

Regarding antidumping duties, more active and more frequent use of the public interest test by the Foreign Trade Chamber (CAMEX), leading to the nonapplication or suspension of duties in cases in which these measures would

---

[18]Ideally, the gradual tariff reduction on IT goods should lead, at the end of the process, to a zero tariff being applied to imports of these goods and to Brazil's adherence to the WTO Information Technology Agreement (ITA), which would lock this tariff level and prevent further changes. Such a permanent change would probably require a Mercosur decision, either to adhere to the ITA as a bloc or to allow individual members to do so separately.

[19]See Sturgeon, Chagas, and Barnes (2017).

have relevant negative impacts over the economy as a whole, would be fundamental. As in any aspect of policymaking, broad public interest should come ahead of the interests of particular groups.

Continuing to pursue trade agreements with countries and blocs that exhibit high levels of productivity and of participation in the world economy, as well as trying to expand the coverage of old FTAs, would be an important complement to horizontal measures to liberalize trade. A focus on agreements with these types of countries would also alleviate some of the trade-diversion effects that usually result from trade agreements.

As trade liberalization advances, the country should review and, when necessary, make specific adjustments to its labor policies and regulations, including its active labor market policies, to facilitate and speed up adjustment.[20] Brazil's reform of its Labor Law, approved in 2017, brought more flexibility to its labor markets and was a good first step.

CONCLUSIONS

This chapter shows that Brazil is still one the economies most closed to trade in the world, seemingly because of the protectionist trade policies the country adopted in several areas until mid-2016.

However, some positive signs indicate that this trade policy stance has been changing. Nevertheless, better policies could still be adopted that could lead to a more productive economy in which firms and citizens could enjoy better access to a wider variety of goods and inputs.

As a first step, Brazil could reduce its tariffs on capital and IT goods, as well as on some selected inputs. New trade agreements should be negotiated with more relevant trading partners, and the coverage of old agreements should be expanded. For nontariff barriers, eliminating LCRs and reducing the imposition of anti-dumping duties on inputs would complement the trade-liberalizing agenda needed to improve Brazil's overall levels of productivity and competitiveness.

A more ambitious trade liberalization agenda should, of course, be accompanied by adjustments to Brazil's active and passive labor market policies aimed at facilitating and speeding up the reallocation of labor between firms and sectors necessary to fully reap the benefits of trade openness.

REFERENCES

Alcalá, Francisco, and Antonio Ciccone. 2004. "Trade and Productivity." *The Quarterly Journal of Economics* 119(2): 613–46.

Alcaraz, Fernando Coppe. 2016. "Trade Policy in Brazil: Main Characteristics, Political Economy Determinants and Some Legal and Economic Consequences." Master's thesis. World Trade Institute of the University of Bern.

---

[20]For an analysis and suggestions of transition policies, see Brasil Presidency of the Republic (2018, 29–38).

Alcaraz, Fernando C., J. H. Martins, F. S. Nicoli, and D. M. Marques. 2018. "Dumping and Predatory Pricing: Conceptual Differences and the Case of Brazil." *Brazilian Journal of Foreign Trade*.

Amiti, Mary, and Jozef Konings. 2005. "Trade Liberalization, Intermediate Inputs and Productivity: Evidence from Indonesia." IMF Working Paper No. 05/146, International Monetary Fund, Washington, DC.

Araújo, S., and D. Flaig. 2016. "Quantifying the Effects of Trade Liberalisation in Brazil: A Computable General Equilibrium Model (CGE) Simulation." OECD Economics Department Working Paper No. 1295, OECD Publishing, Paris.

Baldwin, Richard. *Multilateralising 21st Century Regionalism*. Paris: OECD Publishing.

Baumann, R., and A. Messa. 2017. "The Political Economy of Commercial Policy in Brazil." In *The Brazilian Commercial Policy in Analysis*. Brasília: Alexandre de Gusmão Foundation.

Bloom, Nicholas, Mirko Draca, and John van Reenen. 2016. "Trade Induced Technical Change? The Impact of Chinese Imports on Innovation, IT and Productivity." *The Review of Economic Studies* 83(1): 87–117.

Brambilla, I., N. Depetris Chauvin, and G. Porto. 2017. "Examining the Export Wage Premium in Developing Countries." *Review of International Economics* 25(3): 447–75.

Brasil Presidency of the Republic—Secretariat for Strategic Affairs. 2018. Trade Openness for Development. Brasília.

Canuto, Otaviano, Cornelius Fleischhaker, and Philip Schellekens. "Why Is Brazil's Economy Closed to Trade?" Regional Agenda, World Economic Forum, Cologny, Switzerland.

European Commission. 2018. EU-Mercosur Association Agreement. Brussels.

Ferraz, L.P.C., E. Ornelas, and J. P. Pessoa. 2018. "Economic Consequences of Brazil's Reducing Import Tariffs on Capital Goods." FGV-SP, Unpublished.

International Trade Centre (ITC). Trade Map. Geneva.

Lisboa, Marcos B., Naercio A. Menezes Filho, and Adriana Schor. 2010. "The Effects of Trade Liberalization on Productivity Growth in Brazil: Competition or Technology?" *Brazilian Journal of Economics* 64(3): 277–89.

Messa, Alexandre, and Oliveira, Ivan (eds.). 2017. The Brazilian Commercial Policy in Analysis. Brasilia: Institute of Applied Economic Research.

Ministry of Industry, Foreign Trade and Services. 2018. Antidumping Measures in Force. Brasilia.

Narlikar, Amrita. 2010. "New Powers in the Club: The Challenges of Global Trade Governance." *International Affairs* 86(3): 717–28.

Organisation for Economic Co-operation and Development (OECD). 2018. OECD Economic Surveys: Brazil. Paris: OECD Publishing.

Stone, S., J. Messent, and D. Flaig. 2015. "Emerging Policy Issues: Localisation Barriers to Trade." OECD Trade Policy Papers, No. 180, OECD Publishing, Paris.

Sturgeon, T., L. L. Chagas, and J. Barnes. 2017. "Inovar Auto: Evaluating Brazil's Automotive Industrial Policy to Meet the Challenges of Global Value Chains." Background paper, World Bank Group, Washington, DC.

United Nations Conference on Trade and Development (UNCTAD). 2013. *Non-tariff Measures to Trade: Economic and Policy Issues for Developing Countries*. Geneva: United Nations.

Villela, André. 2015. "Ever Wary of Liberalism: Brazilian Foreign Trade Policy from Bretton Woods to the G-20." In *Brazil on the Global Stage: Power, Ideas, and the Liberal International Order*, edited by Oliver Stuenkel and Matthew M. Taylor. New York and London: Palgrave Macmillan.

World Economic Forum (WEF). 2017. *The Global Competitiveness Report 2017–2018*. Cologny, Switzerland.

World Trade Organization (WTO). 2017. Brazil–Certain Measures Concerning Taxation and Charges. WTO Disputes. Panel Reports. Geneva.

———. Trade Profiles: Brazil. Geneva.

CHAPTER 7

Trade Liberalization and Active Labor Market Policies

CARLOS GÓES, ALEXANDRE MESSA, CARLOS PIO, EDUARDO LEONI, AND LUIS GUSTAVO MONTES

Trade liberalization will boost Brazil's productive potential and growth prospects, but it will also affect labor markets, including employment and wages. Using a computable general equilibrium model with labor frictions and heterogeneity in productivity, this chapter examines the effects of trade liberalization on regional labor markets. Labor markets in regions that now enjoy higher trade protection are more likely to suffer from trade liberalization. Given the limited mobility of labor in Brazil's domestic market, trade liberalization must be accompanied by active labor market policies and a skills enhancement program, so that workers hurt by trade can acquire new skills for sectors and industries that benefit from the economy's opening.

INTRODUCTION

The trade liberalization that took place in Brazil in the 1990s increased aggregate productivity in manufacturing both directly, through the pressure of foreign competition that materialized with the greater availability of imported goods, and indirectly, through the lower cost of machinery, equipment, and inputs for Brazilian firms (Rossi and Ferreira 1999; Lisboa, Menezes-Filho, and Schor 2002).

Trade liberalization affected the regions within Brazil differently. This regional disparity occurred because sectors are geographically concentrated, so the scale of a relative price shock varied from one region to another, and the adjustments in the labor market occurred much more slowly than the accepted consensus on the effect of trade shocks.

This chapter investigates the extent of the relative price shocks across regions and the labor market adjustment, using estimates of heterogeneous regional effects of liberalization on the labor market, and analyzes the implications of that heterogeneity for policymaking for the labor market.

This chapter summarizes the results presented in SAE (2018) and Góes, Messa, and Leoni (forthcoming).

Figure 7.1. Brazil: Relationship between Total Trade and Structural Variables

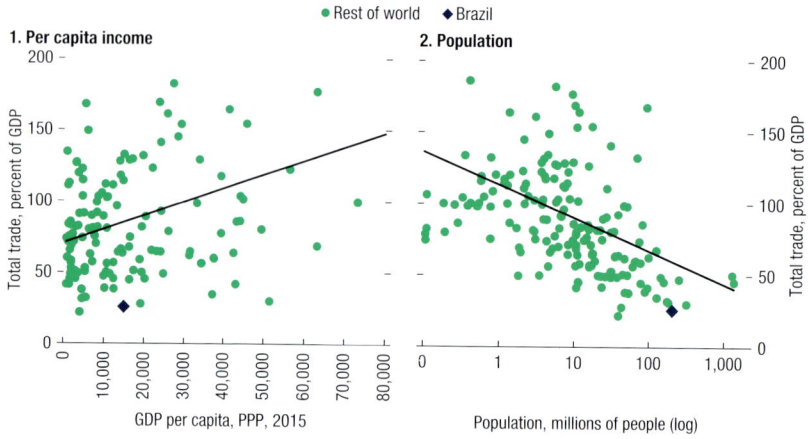

Source: World Bank, World Development Indicators.
Note: PPP = purchasing power parity.

Consistent with conclusions by Dix-Carneiro and Kovak (2017), this chapter finds that regions facing greater price shocks because of trade liberalization would suffer relatively greater impacts on their labor markets. So, despite low levels of permanent variation in employment, the outcomes indicate regional differences in the effect of trade on the labor market.

Public policies can ease the inclusion into the labor market of workers exposed to transitional negative impacts of the trade shock, offsetting the limited mobility of labor in Brazil's domestic market. These policies would maximize the gains from trade while avoiding disproportionate losses concentrated in a minority of workers.

Active labor policies can build on the current programs. An efficient active labor market policy must incorporate information on three essential issues: (1) which regions are most likely to be affected by the trade shock, (2) which productive sectors are likely to experience growth (or decline) in employment after the trade opening, and (3) which skills are in demand, and their dynamic evolution, in each region. This chapter gives a first contribution to answer these questions.

CONTEXT: TRADE PROTECTION IN BRAZIL

Brazil's international trade flows amount to about 25 percent of its GDP, making it one of the world's most closed countries. In terms of trade, Brazil was the second most closed country in the world from 2012 to 2015, surpassed only by Sudan. In terms of income and population brackets, Brazil is also closed to international trade compared with countries with similar features (Figure 7.1).

Figure 7.2. Brazil: Nominal and Effective Protection, by Sector, 2014
(Percent)

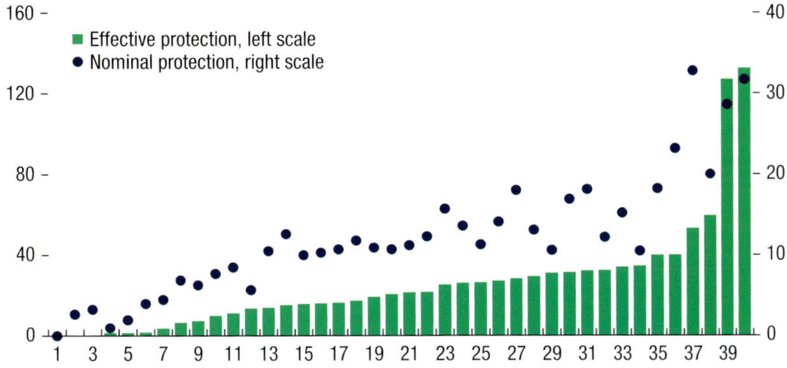

Source: Castilho and others (2014).
Note: 1 Oil and natural gas; 2 Livestock and fisheries; 3 Other in the extractive industry; 4 Oil refining and coke; 5 Iron ore; 6 Cement; 7 Agriculture, forestry, logging; 8 Newspapers, magazines, records; 9 Pharmaceutical products; 10 Non-ferrous metal metallurgy; 11 Wood products, excluding furniture; 12 Chemical products; 13 Electricity and gas, water, sewage and urban cleaning; 14 Medical and hospital devices and instruments, measuring and optical; 15 Alcohol; 16 Office machines and computer equipment; 17 Other transport equipment; 18 Machinery and equipment, including maintenance and repairs; 19 Other non-metallic mineral products; 20 Miscellaneous chemical products; 21 Manufacture of steel and its byproducts; 22 Cellulose and paper production; 23 Metal products, excluding machinery and equipment; 24 Rubber and plastic products; 25 Pesticides; 26 Electrical machinery, apparatus and material; 27 Furniture and products of miscellaneous industries; 28 Paints, varnishes, enamels and lacquers; 29 Food and beverages; 30 Parts and accessories for motor vehicles; 31 Leather and footwear; 32 Electronic material and communications equipment; 33 Perfumery, hygiene and cleaning; 34 Manufacture of resins and elastomers; 35 Appliances; 36 Textiles; 37 Clothing articles and accessories; 38 Tobacco products; 39 Cars, vans and utility vehicles; 40 Trucks and buses.

On average, Brazil has higher import tariffs for manufactured goods than for raw materials. That average, however, hides a broad range of sectoral variations. Some sectors, especially intermediate goods such as petrochemicals, cement, and metallurgy, are subject to low levels of protection. Other final goods, such as automobiles, trucks, textiles, and garments, are subject to high levels of protection. This variation holds both for nominal protection (that is, import duties levied on that sector) and for the effective level of protection (that is, considering the sector's input structure and the degree of protection on the value added by that sector to the final product).

The dispersion of Brazil's tariff structure is just as important as the average levels of nominal protection. Whenever nominal tariffs on intermediate goods are reduced but the high nominal tariffs on final goods remain unchanged, the effective level of protection on final goods is higher. This dispersion in nominal tariffs explains why effective protection in specific sectors, particularly the automobile industry, is significantly higher than the Brazilian average (Figure 7.2).

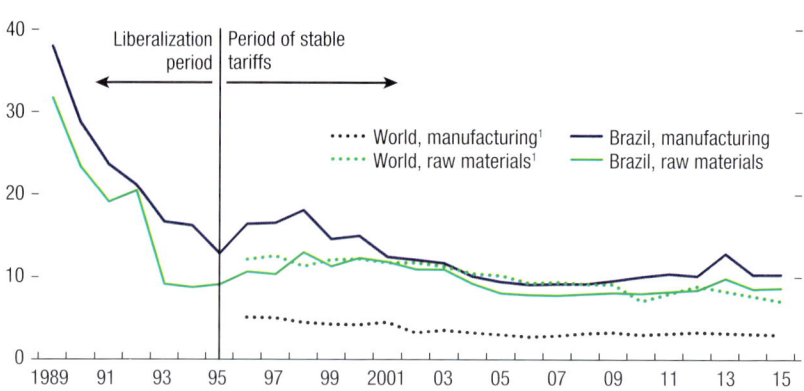

Figure 7.3. Brazil and the World: Applied Tariffs in Major Sectors
(Percent)

Source: Authors' calculations using World Bank data.
[1]Global average weighted by trade flows.

HETEROGENEOUS EFFECTS OF TRADE LIBERALIZATION ON REGIONAL LABOR MARKETS: PAST EVIDENCE

The tariff structure in Brazil can be divided into two periods over the past 30 years. From 1990 to 1995, Brazil's import duties fell significantly, both for manufactured goods (from 37 percent to 12 percent) and for raw materials (from 31 percent to 9 percent). Since 1995, Brazil's import duties have been relatively stable (Figure 7.3).

Even so, the tariff structures for manufactured goods and raw materials are different. While Brazil's average tariffs for raw materials converged to a rate near the world average (about 8 percent in 2015), Brazil's manufacturing sector is still much more protected than those of the rest of the world. In 2015, average duties effectively levied on imported manufactured goods in Brazil were about 10 percent, compared with the global average of 3 percent.

The decline in tariffs improved efficiency. Labor productivity in industry, which had fallen in the late 1980s, grew strongly after trade liberalization (Rossi and Ferreira 1999). Productivity gains in industry were achieved both directly, from the pressure of foreign competition through more imports, and indirectly, from the lower cost of machinery, equipment, and inputs for Brazilian firms (Lisboa, Menezes-Filho, and Schor 2002).

Despite the sectoral effects of liberalization in the 1990s, long-term nationwide aggregate effects on the labor market were minor. However, Kovak (2013) and Dix-Carneiro and Kovak (2017) find that the country's regions that previously specialized in the industries most affected by trade liberalization experienced a greater reduction in formal sector employment than did other regions in the country. Those studies estimate that the impact on formal employment continued for more than 20 years after the trade liberalization process began, and they conclude the following:

- The level of trade protection differs across regions and depends on the geographic concentration of each industry; therefore, the post-liberalization trade shock is also heterogeneous.

- Although the aggregate impact on formal employment and income is minor, regional impacts are significant.

- Costs are concentrated because of the low degree of integration of labor markets and, possibly, the rigidity of labor laws, inducing workers to shift from the formal to the informal sector in regions more affected by liberalization.

These outcomes are consistent with other analyses that find a low degree of integration in Brazil's domestic labor market (Góes and Matheson 2017). Those conclusions indicate that estimates of the regional effects on the labor market of future trade liberalizations can be helpful in designing public policies that favor adjustments in the labor market, facilitating the migration of affected workers from one sector to another.

HETEROGENEOUS EFFECTS OF TRADE LIBERALIZATION ON REGIONAL LABOR MARKETS: FORWARD-LOOKING ESTIMATES

The estimates presented here were derived using a general equilibrium model that aggregated information on production, employment, wages, prices, imports, and exports in 57 economic sectors in Brazil and other countries. The complete methodology, including the estimated equations and statistical appendices, are available in Góes, Messa, and Leoni (forthcoming).

The analysis employs a computable general equilibrium model using input-output matrices for 57 economic sectors in Brazil and another 25 countries, the European Union, and an aggregate for the rest of the world. As seen in Caliendo, Dvorkin, and Parro (2015), the exercise extends the study done by Eaton and Kortum (2002) to multiple sectors, modeling the interaction between them using input-output matrices from each country covered by the analysis. Trade between countries arises from differences in productivity, making the sensitivity of trade flows to variations in tariff rates dependent on the degree of dispersion of that productivity.

The model includes some 2.5 million equations that describe interactions between firms and workers, who maximize their utility and change sectors based on a cost-benefit analysis. The model also estimates the probability that workers in a given sector will move to another in the following period. The model is assumed to be in equilibrium in the initial period. Following a shock introduced exogenously, which represents a change in Brazil's tariff structure, the changes in

Figure 7.4. Brazil: Net Expected Variation in Employment, per Sector, 20 Years after a Trade Liberalization
(Percent)

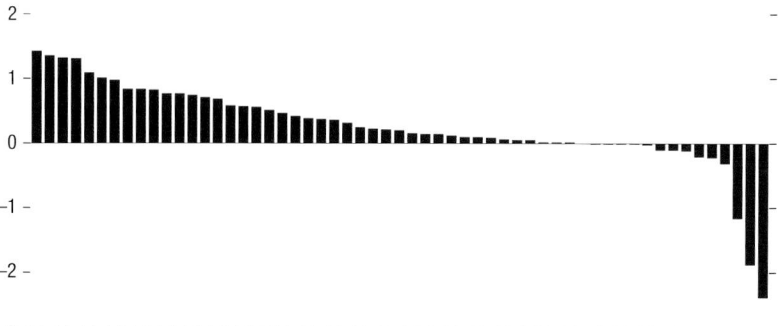

Source: Authors' calculations based on the computable general equilibrium model described in Góes, Messa, and Leoni (forthcoming).
Note: 1 Gas; 2 Oil; 3 Coal; 4 Other ores; 5 Petroleum products; 6 Oilseeds; 7 Wheat; 8 Other grains; 9 Other crops; 10 Non-ferrous metals; 11 Meat *in natura*; 12 Other meat; 13 Sugar; 14 Livestock; 15 Paper; 16 Fruits and vegetables; 17 Sugar cane; 18 Other animal products; 19 Plant fibers; 20 Vegetable oils; 21 Gas distribution; 22 Rice *in natura*; 23 Fish; 24 Forest products; 25 Other transportation equipment; 26 Iron and steel; 27 Electricity; 28 Chemicals; 29 Other food products; 30 Other transport; 31 Wood; 32 Water transport; 33 Processed rice; 34 Non-metallic minerals; 35 Air transport; 36 Business services; 37 Communications; 38 Water; 39 Financial intermediation; 40 Trade; 41 Milk; 42 Insurance; 43 Dairy products; 44 Construction; 45 Wool; 46 Recreation; 47 Government; 48 Residences; 49 Electronic equipment; 50 Cars and car parts; 51 Beverages and tobacco; 52 Other machinery; 53 Other manufactures; 54 Metal products; 55 Leather; 56 Textiles; 57 Clothing.

prices, production, imports, exports, wages, and jobs in the different sectors of the economy evolve dynamically. After a given period, the economy reaches a new, stationary equilibrium and the long-term effect for the aggregate economy and for each of the 57 sectors covered by the model can be observed.

The results from the estimation suggest that, following trade liberalization, workers tend to move out of sectors that had been more protected—and less competitive—into more competitive sectors. The total level of employment remains substantially unchanged because the main effect is intersectoral migration.[1] During the entire period that followed the trade liberalization, 75 percent of the sectors of Brazil's economy expanded their employment and, 20 years later, only three sectors of Brazil's economy are expected to experience more than a 0.5 percent reduction in employment (Figure 7.4).

Nationwide outcomes were used as sectoral shocks that, combined with the geographic distribution of the sectors and the heterogeneous regional elasticities, caused a net effect on employment in each sector of the economy in each of Brazil's 558 microregions. The weighted sum of the sectoral effects in each region

---

[1]More precisely, a 0.015 percent reduction in unemployment is expected.

Figure 7.5. Brazil: Net Expected Variation in Employment, 20 Years after a Trade Liberalization by Microregion
(Percent)

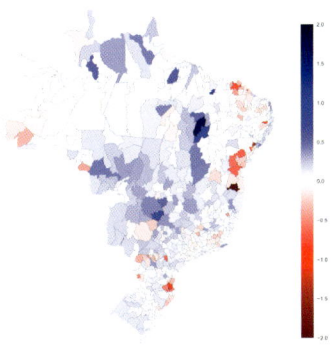

Source: Authors' calculations based on the computable general equilibrium model described in Góes, Messa, and Leoni (forthcoming).

led to the net regional effect, aggregating all sectors of the economy for each microregion (see Annex 7.1 for details). In about two-thirds of Brazil's 558 microregions, the long-term effect of liberalization on formal employment is positive. In 85 percent of the microregions, the effect on formal employment varies from –0.25 percent to +0.25 percent. Even the most extreme cases are within the range of –2 percent to +2 percent of the workforce.

This exercise identifies which regions are far from the average. The Center-West is slightly above the national average, as are southern Piauí and Maranhão, and some microregions in Pará, Amazonas, Roraima, and Amapá, with gains in formal employment of up to 2 percent. In other regions, the expected effect is basically zero, except for the Itajaí Valley in Santa Catarina, southern Bahia, and a cluster of microregions in northwestern Ceará where a reduction in formal employment may occur in sectors now active (Figure 7.5).

These variations are largely explained by the regional concentration of Brazil's different economic sectors, along with their different tariff levels. Microregions have varying levels of trade protection because their labor forces and regional production sectors can be concentrated in sectors with higher degrees of protection. These microregions are the ones that will tend to be more affected by trade liberalization (Figure 7.6).

The level of tariff protection can be computed for each microregion by weighting the duties levied nationally on imports of diverse goods and services by the sectoral makeup of the region's labor force (see Annex 7.2 for details). This calculation reveals the disparate geographic distribution of tariff protection in Brazil. Although 80 percent of the country's microregions have tariff protection of less

Figure 7.6. Brazil: Regional Tariffs by Microregion
(Effective average tariff, ad valorem percent; average weighted by the sectoral distribution of the labor force)

Source: Authors' calculations.

than 12 percent, a few specific microregions have much higher levels of protection, greater than an ad valorem tariff of 20 percent.

Because regions currently have different levels of trade protection, trade liberalization takes place to different degrees in each of them. As expected, the microregions with higher tariff protection today tend to have more negative long-term outcomes regarding permanent reductions of formal employment (Figure 7.7).

Another factor that influences the expected outcome of a trade shock on the labor market is the size of the microregions. Those more concentrated on the positive and negative extremes of expected variations in employment tend to have smaller populations. Larger cities tend to present variations close to zero. This outcome is intuitive because the economic structure of larger cities is more diversified. Therefore, in response to price shocks imposed by a trade opening, workers in those cities simply migrate to other sectors in the same microregion, with a net variation of zero.

ACTIVE LABOR MARKET POLICIES TO CATALYZE ADJUSTMENT TO TRADE LIBERALIZATION

In the context of labor market impacts during Brazil's trade liberalization, active labor market policies are preferable for two main reasons:[2]

---

[2]Public policies for the labor market can be divided into passive and active policies. Passive policies provide complementary income for individuals during periods of unemployment (such as unemployment insurance). Active labor market policies, in contrast, seek to reduce unemployment by improving workers' skills (through retraining programs), to reduce asymmetries in market

Figure 7.7. Brazil: Net Expected Variation in Employment and Regional Tariffs by Microregion
(Bubbles are proportional to the microregion's workforce.)

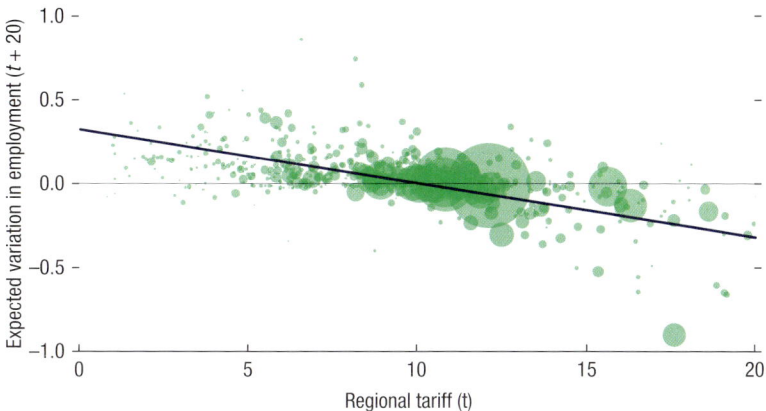

Source: Authors' calculations based on the computable general equilibrium model described in Góes, Messa, and Leoni (forthcoming).

- Evidence suggests that, because of the limited integration and flexibility of the Brazilian labor market, passive policies may not be sufficient to minimize the regional effects of liberalization.
- The regions and sectors that will be most affected both positively and negatively during the transition period can be identified in advance, and resources can be focused more efficiently, thus facilitating the transition of workers from declining to expanding sectors.

Brazil's most significant recent active labor market policy is the National Program for Access to Technical Education and Employment (Pronatec). Despite significant progress, Pronatec has not achieved its main objective, which is to ensure significantly more employment and income for its graduates. The main reason for this shortfall lies in the mismatch between the supply of courses and the demand for training in the market. While the market was signaling greater demand for workers with STEM (science, technology, engineering, and mathematics) skills, the bulk of the program's courses were for administrative assistants and computer operators.

In addition to Pronatec, different federal agencies began to launch slightly different programs to achieve the same goal of retraining Brazilian professionals,

---

information (the distance between job seekers and job providers), or to give companies incentives to hire workers in specific categories (such as special regimes for apprentices and youth). These policies are aimed at keeping individuals active in the labor market and facilitating their reintegration into the labor force by fighting market imperfections.

Figure 7.8. Brazil: Pillars of an Active Labor Market Policy, Adapted to the Context of Trade Liberalization

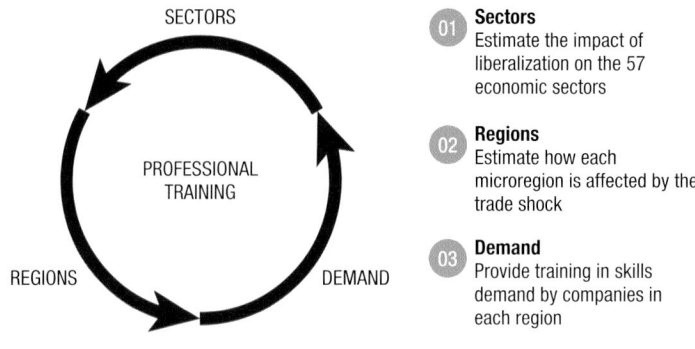

01 **Sectors**
Estimate the impact of liberalization on the 57 economic sectors

02 **Regions**
Estimate how each microregion is affected by the trade shock

03 **Demand**
Provide training in skills demand by companies in each region

Source: SAE (2018).

thus creating a veritable public policy laboratory for comparing various alternatives. One variation of Pronatec, implemented by the Ministry of Industry, Foreign Trade and Services, included a mechanism for identifying regional demand for skills in cities and regions, using an official database from companies surveyed about their real need for skilled workers. O'Connell and others (2017) found that graduates of this program had a significantly higher (approximately 8 percent) probability of being employed, especially in sectors reliant on STEM skills, some of whom displayed marginal employability gains higher than 10 percent. The rest of Pronatec not run by the Ministry of Industry, Foreign Trade and Services—which did not use local information on demand for skills—showed no statistically significant postcourse gains in employability or income (Barbosa Filho, Porto, and Delfino 2015).

By introducing changes in its existing programs, Pronatec can be reformed to help the labor market better adjust to the new reality of an open economy. To make such an active labor market policy efficient and suitable for accommodating the trade shock, three kinds of information must be combined:

- What regions will be most affected by the trade shock?
- In which sectors will employment expand (or contract) after trade opening?
- What skills are in demand, and how will that demand evolve, in each geographical area?

Designing an active labor market policy to be applied alongside a trade liberalization process would help maximize welfare and mitigate transitional costs likely to be borne by specific regions and groups of workers (Figure 7.8). In addition, because a trade opening tends to shift investment and production from less-productive and profitable sectors into more efficient sectors, a policy to facilitate individuals' access to new skills would be essential for workers to shift from negatively affected sectors into those favored by the new context.

CONCLUSIONS

Using a computable general equilibrium model with labor frictions and heterogeneity in productivity, this chapter estimates the heterogeneous regional effects of trade liberalization on labor markets in a forward-looking analysis. It uses two different lines of research: the inclusion of frictions and heterogeneity into forward-looking analytical models and the regionally heterogeneous labor effects of trade shocks in backward-looking empirical models.

The main results show a heterogeneous effect of trade on regional labor markets. In about two-thirds of Brazil's 558 microregions, trade liberalization is estimated to have positive, but small, long-term effects on formal employment.

The heterogeneity of estimated regional effects, explained largely by the spatial concentration of various sectors of Brazil's economy, coincides with the conclusions of Dix-Carneiro and Kovak (2017): regions that now enjoy higher regional trade protection are likely to experience relatively greater impact on their labor markets.

The methodology developed in this study has major implications for public policy. Using this methodology, policymakers can anticipate uneven effects and design active labor market policies to mitigate the impact of trade liberalization on the most affected regions and facilitate the intersectoral and interregional migration of workers. Doing so would allow aggregate gains from trade to be achieved without penalizing disproportionately specific workers for the costs of a transition toward a more open economy.

REFERENCES

Artuç, Erhan, Shubham Chaudhuri, and John McLaren. 2010. "Trade Shocks and Labor Adjustment: A Structural Empirical Approach." *American Economic Review* 1003: 1008–45.

Autor, David H., David Dorn, and Gordon H. Hanson. 2016. "The China Shock: Learning from Labor-Market Adjustment to Large Changes in Trade." *Review of Economics* 8(1): 205–40.

Barbosa Filho, F., R. Porto, and D. Delfino. 2015. *Pronatec Bolsa-Formação: Uma Avaliação Inicial Sobre Reinserção no Mercado de Trabalho Formal.* Brasília: Ministério da Fazenda/SPE.

Caliendo, Lorenzo, Maximiliano Dvorkin, and Fernando Parro. 2015. "The Impact of Trade on Labor Market Dynamics." NBER Working Paper 21149. National Bureau of Economic Research, Cambridge, MA.

Caliendo, Lorenzo, and Fernando Parro. 2015. "Estimates of the Trade and Welfare Effects of NAFTA." *The Review of Economic Studies* 82(1): 1–44.

Dix-Carneiro, Rafael. 2014. "Trade Liberalization and Labor Market Dynamics." *Econometrica* 82(3): 825–85.

Dix-Carneiro, Rafael, and Brian K. Kovak. 2017. "Trade Liberalization and Regional Dynamics." *American Economic Review* 107(10): 2908–46.

Eaton, Jonathan, and Samuel Kortum. 2002. "Technology, Geography, and Trade." *Econometrica* 70(5).

Edwards, Sebastian. 1993. "Openness, Trade Liberalization, and Growth in Developing Countries." *Journal of Economic Literature* 31(3): 1358–93.

Federative Republic of Brazil, Special Secretariat for Strategic Affairs (SAE). 2018. "Trade Opening for Economic Development." Report of Conjuntura no. 3. Brasília: National Press.

Frankel, Jeffrey A., and David Romer. 1999. "Does Trade Cause Growth?" *The American Economic Review* 89(3): 379–99.

Góes, Carlos, and Izabela Karpowicz. 2017. "Inequality in Brazil: A Regional Perspective." IMF Working Paper 17/225, International Monetary Fund, Washington, DC.

Góes, Carlos, and Troy Matheson. 2017. "Domestic Market Integration and the Law of One Price in Brazil." *Applied Economics Letters* 24(5): 284–88.

Góes, Carlos, Alexandre Messa, and Eduardo Leoni. Forthcoming. "Anticipating the Heterogeneous Effects of Trade Shocks on Regional Labor Markets." IPEA Discussion Paper. Institute of Applied Economic Research, Brasília.

Kovak, Brian K. 2013. "Regional Effects of Trade Reform: What Is the Correct Measure of Liberalization?" *American Economic Review* 103(5): 1960–76.

Lisboa, Marcos B., Naércio Menezes-Filho, and Adriana Schor. 2002. "The Effects of Trade Liberalization on Productivity: Competition or Technology." Technical report from the proceedings of the Meeting of the Brazilian Society of Econometrics.

O'Connell, Stephen D., Lucas Ferreira Mation, João Teixeira Bastos Bevilaqua, and Mark Dutz. 2017. "Can Business Input Improve the Effectiveness of Worker Training? Evidence from Brazil's Pronatec-MDIC." Policy Research Working Paper No. WPS 8155, World Bank, Washington, DC.

Pesaran, M. Hashem, and Ron Smith. 1995. "Estimating Long-Run Relationships from Dynamic Heterogeneous Panels." *Journal of Econometrics* 68(1): 79–113.

Rossi Jr., J. L., and P.C. Ferreira. 1999. "Evolution of Brazilian Industrial Productivity and Trade Liberalization." *Research and Economic Planning* 29(1): 1–34.

Wacziarg, Romain. 2008. "Trade Liberalization and Growth: New Evidence." *World Bank Economic Review* 22(2): 187–231.

ANNEX 7.1 DATA USED TO ESTIMATE REGIONAL EFFECTS

The production and trade data used in this analysis come from the Global Trade Analysis Project (GTAP), version 9, base year 2011. Each simulation involved 27 economic regions: Argentina, Bolivia, Brazil, Canada, Chile, China, Colombia, Egypt, India, Indonesia, Japan, Korea, Malaysia, Mexico, Nigeria, Paraguay, Peru, Russia, Saudi Arabia, South Africa, Switzerland, Turkey, the United States, Uruguay, Vietnam, the European Union, and the rest of the world grouped as a single region. From those 27 economic regions, each was broken down into 57 sectors using the maximum disaggregation of the GTAP Sectoral Classification, Revision 2, data for domestic production, input-output matrices, and bilateral trade flows, and bilateral tariffs were extracted.

The labor market data come from the Annual Social Information Report (RAIS), published by the Ministry of Labor. Each year since 1976, the RAIS has organized individualized information about workers employed in the formal Brazilian labor market.

The labor census uses forms completed and filed by employers, with individualized data on each formal labor relationship in their companies. Because employers can be fined for not filing the forms on time or for providing false information, they have strong incentives to answer the census correctly. Data from the RAIS are therefore considered to be of high quality.

The public version of the RAIS data provides, among other products, anonymized data on each worker that cover the economic sector of the employer company, wages, age of the worker, and so on. This analysis used only the number of employees in the employer's economic sector, including only active labor contracts.

To allow RAIS data to fit into the GTAP sectors, a transition matrix was built that matches the codes in Brazil's National Economic Activities Register, used for the RAIS, with those sectors. Based on the local and national aggregations produced by that matrix, the computable general equilibrium model and local elasticity estimates were calibrated.

To obtain local elasticities and calibrate the computable general equilibrium model, time series were constructed with RAIS data from 2002 to 2016, for each sector–microregion dyad. National and state aggregates were then created, with the sum of the sectoral workforce in each of the states calculated as follows:

$$e_{g,t} = \sum_{s=1}^{27} e_{s,g,t} = \sum_{s=1}^{27} \sum_{m=1}^{M_s} e_{m,s,g,t}$$

in which $e_{m,s,g,t}$ is employment in microregion $m = [1, \ldots, M_s]'$ of state $s = [1, \ldots, 27]'$ in sector $g = [1, \ldots, 57]'$ and in year $t = [2002, \ldots, 2016]'$.

The elasticities were combined with the results of the computable general equilibrium model—that is, national variations in employment, for each sector, after a specific tariff shock, for a specific horizon. Assuming elasticities to be homogeneous in each state-sector, the exercise arrived at the employment variations expected for each sector in each microregion following liberalization:

$$\Delta e^*_{m,s,g,t+k} = \phi_{m,s,g} \Delta e^*_{g,t+k}, \phi_{m,s,g} = \phi_{s,g} \forall m$$

in which the asterisks denote simulated values; t denotes the year of liberalization, k represents the simulated future horizon, $\phi_{m,s,g}$ represents the specific elasticity for each microregion and sector, and $\Delta e^*_{g,t+k}$ represents the cumulative variation in employment simulated for each sector g between liberalization year t and the simulation horizon k.

Finally, the expected net effect on employment was calculated for each microregion by computing a weighted average that incorporates the weight of each sector g for each microregion $\lambda_{m,s,g}$:

$$\Delta e^*_{m,s,t+k} = \sum_{g=1}^{57} \lambda_{m,s,g} \phi_{m,s,g} \Delta e^*_{g,t+k}.$$

ANNEX 7.2 METHODOLOGY FOR CALCULATING REGIONAL TARIFFS

Using the methodology described in Dix-Carneiro and Kovak (2017) and Kovak (2013), the level of tariff protection for each microregion can be calculated by weighting national duties levied on various imported goods and services with the sectoral composition of the regional labor force, as follows:

$$\tau_{m,s,g} = \sum_{m,s}^{M,S} \beta_{m,s,g} \tau_g$$

$$\beta_{m,s,g} = \frac{\lambda_{m,s,g} \frac{1}{\chi_{m,s,g}}}{\sum_{m,s}^{M,S} \lambda_{m,s,g} \frac{1}{\chi_{m,s,g}}}$$

in which, for each sector g in each microregion of different states r,g, $\lambda_{m,s,g}$ is the initial share of labor allocated to sector g in microregion m,s, which is heterogeneous between microregions; $\chi_{m,s,g}$ is the share of remuneration of factors except for labor in sector g, which is heterogeneous between different sectors; and τ_g is the nationwide tariff levied on sector g caused by the change in tariffs.

A heterogeneous regional tariff that is eliminated during trade liberalization can therefore be calculated using the expected tariff variation for different sectors of the national economy:

$$\Delta\tau_{m,s,g} = \sum_{m,s}^{M,S} \beta_{m,s,g} \Delta\ln\left(1 + \tau_{m,s,g}\right)$$

$$\Delta\tau_{m,s,g} = \sum_{m,s}^{M,S} \beta_{m,s,g}\left[\ln\left(1 + \tau_{m,s,g}^{t+k}\right) - \ln\left(1 + \tau_{m,s,g}^{t}\right)\right]$$

$$\tau_{m,s,g}^{t+k} \equiv \tau_g^{t+k} \forall m, s, t.$$

PART III

Social Progress

CHAPTER 8

Inequality in Brazil: A Closer Look at the Evolution in States

CARLOS GÓES AND IZABELA KARPOWICZ

Using a novel methodology that allows households' incomes to be adjusted for price-level differences across states, this chapter analyzes the evolution of income inequality in Brazil during the period 2004–14. Inequality declined both within and between states. The decline was sharper in more unequal states. The decline in within-state inequality was driven by, among other factors, strong growth of incomes of poor households, while between-state inequality declined because overall income growth was stronger in poorer states.

INTRODUCTION

During the period 2004 to 2014, income inequality declined sharply in Brazil. The Gini coefficient for household per capita income fell from 0.54 in 2004 to 0.49 in 2014.[1] The key drivers of this decline in inequality included sustained economic growth, which boosted incomes of the poor, and deliberate income and social inclusion policies, such as increases in the minimum wage and targeted social programs. Particularly noteworthy is the Bolsa Família program, which has played a significant role in reducing income inequality since 1995.[2] In addition, progressive taxation, as well as schooling, demographic changes, and labor market segmentation, contributed to reducing inequality (Lustig, Pessino, and Scott 2014; Menezes-Filho and de Oliveira 2014; Paes de Barros and others 2010). The overall country-level decline in inequality and the focus on national policies, however, mask regional disparities in income inequality (Figure 8.1). This is not a trivial issue, especially because Brazil is a very large country and the

---

[1]Brazilian Institute of Statistics, IBGE.

[2]See Neri (2010), Neri and Ferreira de Souza (2013), Azzoni and Silveira-Neto (2012), Soares and others (2006), and Mauricio (2014). Using the Rental Price Index (RPI) adjustments, Góes and Karpowicz (2017) show that, although most of the change in Gini can be explained by income growth, higher schooling levels, labor formalization, and the targeted social program Bolsa Família also contributed to income convergence. Civil servants' wage growth has, in contrast, slowed gains in equality.

heterogeneity in the distribution of income across states is often pronounced. This is the primary focus of this chapter.

The main challenge in studying income inequality within large countries is that price levels differ across states and regions. This variation causes a systematic bias because poorer areas have lower price levels, and the differences in the level of *real* incomes could be smaller than what a comparison of *nominal* incomes would suggest. For these reasons, in both advanced and emerging market economies researchers have resorted to constructing deflators specific to the region, state, or metropolitan area, often based on information contained in consumer price indices.[3]

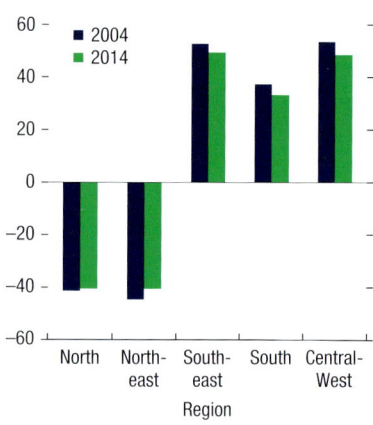

Figure 8.1. Real GDP per Capita
(Percent distance from the national mean)

Source: IBGE.

This chapter constructs a novel rental spatial price deflator, RPI, using the rental prices declared by households in the annual Pesquisa National de Amostra de Domicílios (PNAD). The RPI is used to adjust households' incomes that are aggregated from individual and household survey data, which allows comparison of nominal incomes across states with unequal living standards. The techniques developed by Milanović and his co-authors, and recently updated in Lakner and Milanović (2015), who study global income inequality, are then used to gain insights into both within- and between-state inequality in Brazil.

The chapter shows the following:

- The decline in overall inequality in Brazil was led by a decrease in both intrastate and interstate inequality.

- The decline in inequality was more significant in states with higher initial inequality.

- Most of the convergence in incomes over time occurred at about the middle of income distributions in states.

The chapter is organized as follows. First, the evolution of inequality in Brazil during 2004–14, a period preceding the historic decline in economic activity in Brazil and for which consistent data are available, is described. Second, cost-of-living adjustments are presented. Third, regional inequality trends are examined. Last, the chapter concludes.

---

[3]The US Bureau of Economic Analysis recently released regional price parities for the 325 Standard Metropolitan Statistical Areas and the 50 state nonmetropolitan areas in the United States.

Figure 8.2. Gini Coefficients

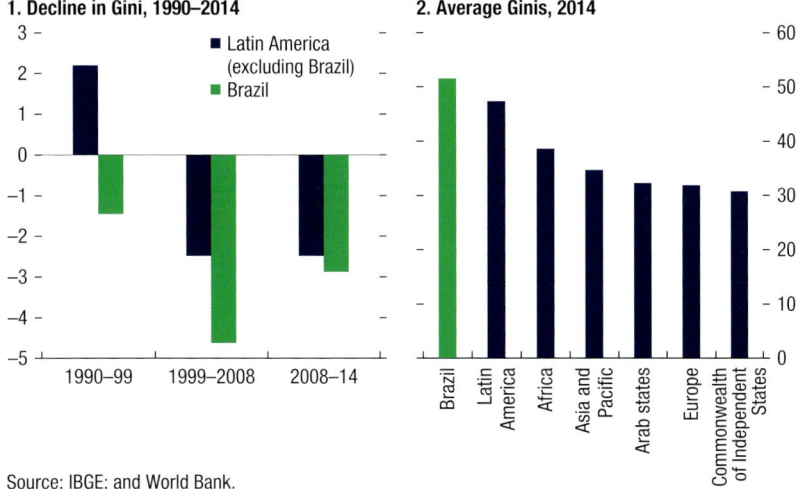

Source: IBGE; and World Bank.

OVERALL INEQUALITY TRENDS IN BRAZIL

Although many other countries in Latin America have witnessed a decline in inequality, Brazil's record is remarkable. Yet inequality remains high: the share of labor income of the top decile of the income distribution is 40 percent of the labor income of all Brazilians, and that of the top 1 percent is 12 percent.[4] Indeed, Brazil's income distribution still is one of the most unequal in Latin America and in the world (Figure 8.2).

Changes in household consumption patterns also reflect the decline in inequality. Income growth over the past decade has allowed the poorer segments of the population to increase their consumption of durable goods. With access to electricity being nearly universal across all income levels in 2004, access to durable goods, such as refrigerators, color TVs, washing machines, personal computers, and mobile phones, increased substantially for all households in the subsequent 10 years, with poorer households benefiting relatively more. Figure 8.3 shows the percentage of households with access to selected durable goods by decile in 2004 and 2014.

But how have incomes changed at the regional level, and how do intrastate and interstate income inequality today compare with those in the previous decade?

---

[4]Data from the 2014 PNAD.

Figure 8.3. Brazil: Convergence in Goods Consumption by Household, 2004–14
(Percent of total households in that quantile of the distribution)

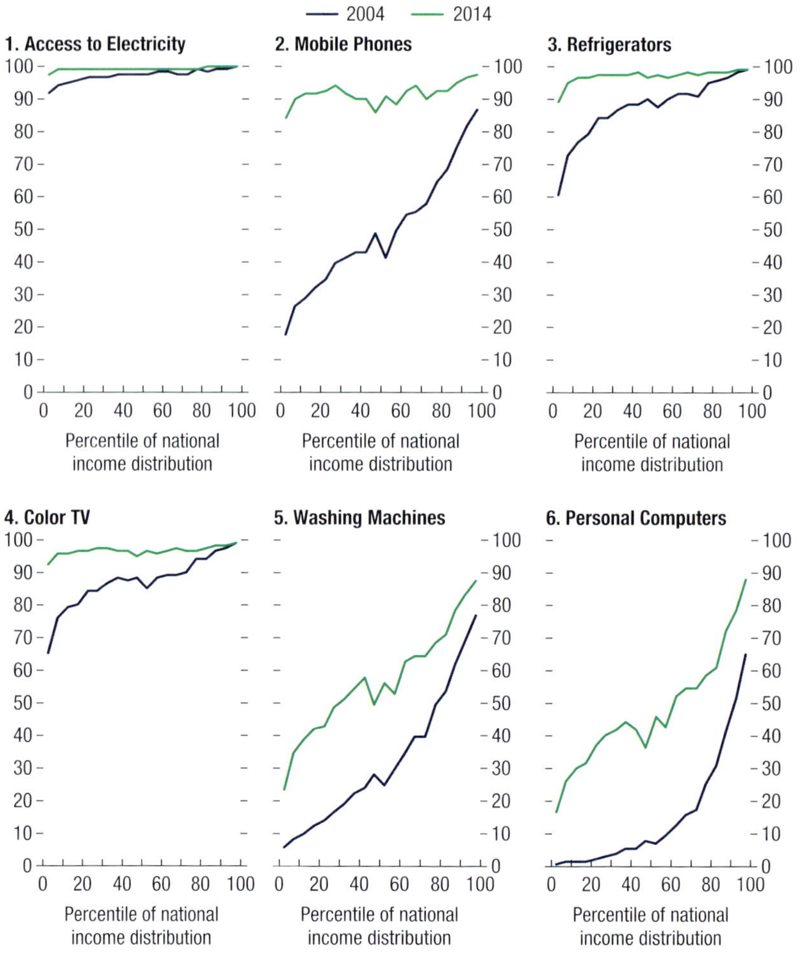

Sources: PNAD (Pesquisa Nacional por Amostra de Domicilios, National Household Sample Survey); and IMF staff calculations.

THE COST OF LIVING ADJUSTMENT

Inequality measures must consider differences in the cost of living across countries to distinguish between nominal and real differences in incomes. Cross-country inequality studies, such as Lakner and Milanović (2015) or Dollar, Kleinberg, and Kraay (2013), for instance, typically correct between-country income statistics using purchasing-power-parity conversions, often based on national price indices. Adjusting for living standards is also important when studying inequality within large countries because the Balassa-Samuelson effect may cause richer regions to show permanently higher price levels (see Deaton and Dupriez 2011). Indeed, price levels are not homogeneous across Brazilian states. Góes and Matheson (2017) document large divergences of product-specific price dynamics, particularly for nontradables, across different metropolitan areas. Almeida and Azzoni (2016) show that overall price levels can deviate from the national average in Brazil's metro areas between –19 percent and +14 percent.

However, microdata for consumer price–level differences are not available in Brazil. Moreover, consumer price indices are available for only 12 metropolitan areas, which is insufficient for capturing the potentially significant differences in living cost dynamics across Brazilian states. To overcome this obstacle, Deaton and Dupriez (2011), for instance, construct indices for India and Brazil based on food prices. Proxies based on traded goods prices are, however, flawed because they ignore the fact that spatial price dispersion is more pronounced for nontraded goods prices, especially housing, including in Brazil. Li and Gibson (2014), for example, use data on dwelling sales in urban China to develop spatially disaggregated indices of house prices, which they use as spatial deflators for both provinces and core urban districts.

This chapter uses information on rental prices as a proxy for the cost of living. The RPI is constructed using data on declared household rent prices from the PNAD and other characteristics of the dwelling (such as the number of rooms or area in square meters), and household incomes are adjusted for spatial price differences. A potential drawback of using the RPI is that it does not consider differences in price levels of goods that represent a significant share of the consumption basket (notably primary goods that are typically consumed in greater shares by poor households), although the RPI is a superior measure compared with a deflator that uses only information from traded-goods prices.

First, for each subregion $k = [1,2, \ldots ,7]'$ of each state $s = [1,2, \ldots ,27]'$ and each year $t = [2004, \ldots ,2015]'$, an *RPI* is constructed that measures the percentage deviation of the per room average rental price from the national average:

$$r_{s,k,t} = \frac{m_{s,k,t}/n_{s,k,t}}{m_t^*/n_t^*} - 1.$$

The term m is the average monthly rent price for the cluster s,k; n is the average number of rooms per household for the cluster; and the asterisks denote national averages.

The distribution of spatial price differences across the 189 clusters for which indices were created shows substantial variability of rent price levels in Brazil (Figure 8.4).

Using data on price-level differences in 12 metro areas estimated by Almeida and Azzoni (2016) from the households budget survey (Pesquisa de Orçamento Familial), overall spatial price differences can be expressed as a linear function of housing spatial price differences (Figure 8.5). The regression coefficient ϕ, assumed to be homogenous across regions, and the heterogeneous RPI can be used to fit an overall spatial price difference index $\hat{p}_{s,k,t} = \phi r_{s,k,t}$. Finally, $\hat{p}_{s,k,t}$ is used to obtain adjusted household incomes, which are then used in the analysis

Figure 8.4. Distribution of Spatial Difference in Rent Prices
(Deviations from national average)

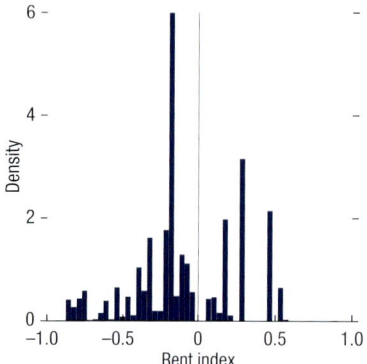

Source: Authors' calculations based on PNAD.

Figure 8.5. Brazilian Metro Areas: Correlation between Overall and Housing Spatial Price Differences
(Deviations from national averages)

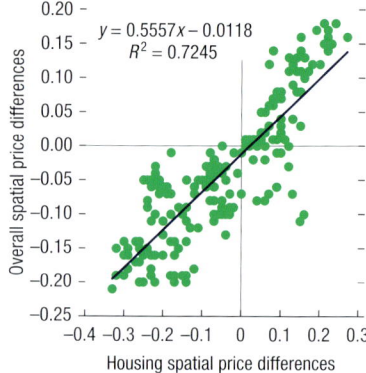

Sources: Almeida and Azzoni 2016; PNAD microdata; and IMF staff calculations.

of income distributions and their trends (Figure 8.6).

Richer regions have higher price levels; conversely, poorer regions have lower price levels. Thus, adjusting for spatial price differences compresses nominal differences in incomes and decreases the overall inequality indicator. On average, for the period 2004–14, correcting for spatial price differences reduces the Gini by 4 percent. The "RPI-adjusted" Gini index shows a decline in inequality at the country level from 0.55 to 0.50 over 2004–14, which is broadly the same reduction implied by the unadjusted Gini. Therefore, the inequality measure displays a level effect while maintaining the same trend.

Figure 8.6. Brazil: National Gini Coefficient (2004–14)
(Index, 0 = absolute equality)

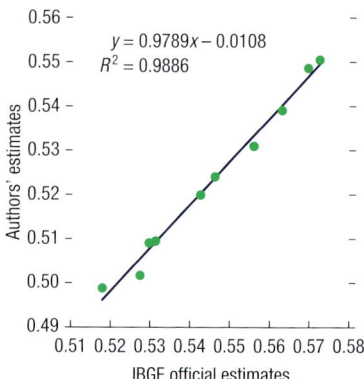

Source: IBGE; and authors' calculations based on PNAD.
Note: IBGE = Brazilian Institute of Geography and Statistics.

TRENDS IN INEQUALITY IN STATES (2004–14)

This section analyzes the historical trends in regional income inequality in Brazil based on PNAD data adjusted for spatial price differences. Because data on household incomes are being used, the analysis focuses on inequality of outcomes; inequality of opportunities, such as access to health-care, clean water and

Figure 8.7. Brazil: Income Inequality in Brazilian States: A Dynamic Decade
(Average real income growth per year; average across states per quantile; adjusted for spatial-price differences)

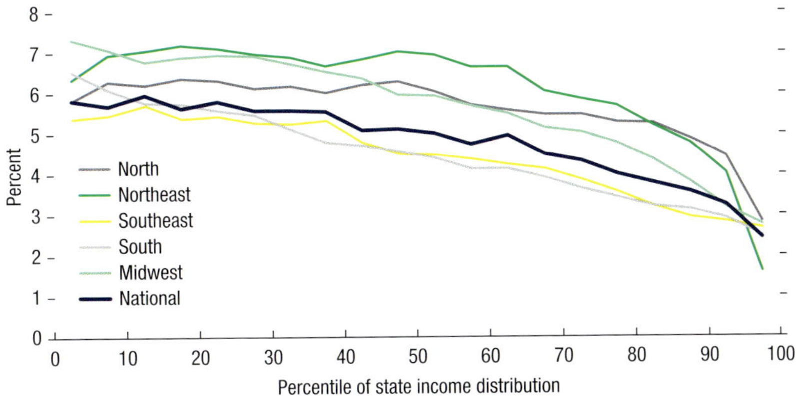

Sources: PNAD microdata; and IMF staff calculations.

sanitation, and quality infrastructure, is not examined. The estimates of inequality are based on *pretax* per capita income as reported in the PNAD, which includes data on labor income, retirement benefits, social security benefits, and income from financial and real assets.

Between-state inequality has decreased, given that real income per capita in the poorer regions of the north, northeast, and midwest grew faster than real income per capita in the richer regions of the south and southwest, possibly reflecting strong redistribution policies (Góes and Karpowicz 2017). The blue, green, and yellow lines in Figure 8.7 are above the national mean for each quantile of the regional income distribution adjusted for spatial-price differences at the state level. Real income growth was stronger for households belonging to the lower quantiles of the income distributions across all regions, although it was generally high at about the middle of the distribution in the poorer regions.

Within-state income distribution varies considerably from state to state. In 2014, the Gini coefficient of the most unequal state was 18 percent higher than the national Gini, whereas the Gini of the least unequal state was almost 20 percent lower than the national coefficient. These differences are, however, narrower than in the past because inequality within states also dropped. The standard deviation of state Gini coefficients declined from 0.035 to 0.033 between 2004 and 2014 (Figure 8.7).

Supported by schooling and labor formalization, household income in lower income deciles grew more than household income in the other deciles in nearly all states during the period, as indicated by the downward movement of the dots in Figure 8.8. However, inequality declined relatively more in the states with higher *initial* levels of inequality in 2004. This relationship is even stronger when

Figure 8.8. Brazil: Income Inequality in Brazilian States: Evidence of Convergence

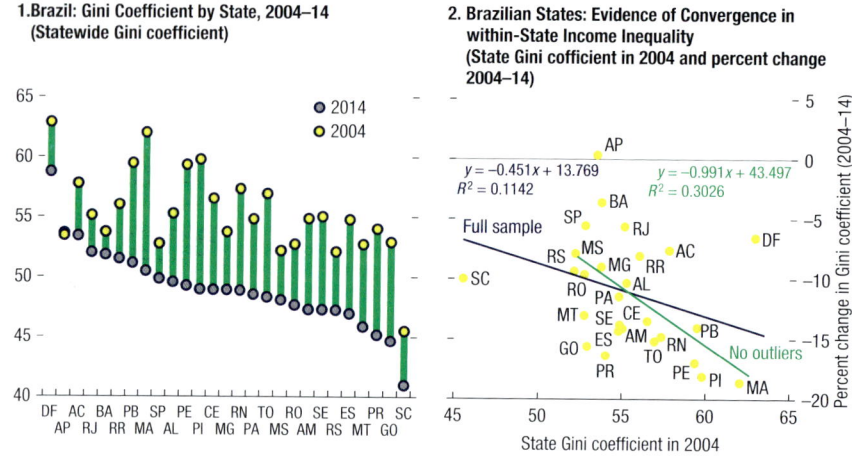

1. Brazil: Gini Coefficient by State, 2004–14
(Statewide Gini coefficient)

2. Brazilian States: Evidence of Convergence in within-State Income Inequality
(State Gini cofficient in 2004 and percent change 2004–14)

Sources: PNAD microdata; and IMF staff calculations.
Note: See Table 12.1 (Chapter 12) for state abbreviations.

excluding Santa Catarina (SC) and the Federal Distict (DF)—the most equal and the most unequal states, respectively.[5] This development illustrates convergence in within-state inequality indices across the country.

Figure 8.9 explores how within-region income distributions are related to the national income distribution.[6] Households that belong to the lowest and highest deciles of the regional income distribution also belong to the lowest and highest deciles of the national distribution. In other words, the very rich and the very poor have similar income levels across states. However, depending on the region, the regional median household income can fall anywhere between the 30th and 60th percentiles of the national distribution.

These differences have shrunk over time. For each percentile of the statewide income distribution depicted on the x-axis in Figure 8.10, the standard deviation in incomes from the national mean decreased between 2001 and 2014, as shown by the downward shift of the curve (black to green). The decrease in the deviation from the mean was more pronounced around the 30th to 70th percentiles, suggesting that most of the gains in equality were achieved through compression of income at about the middle of the distribution.

How has the recession affected inequality? The recession that hit Brazil between 2015 and 2017 may have reversed some equality gains. With the drop

---

[5] The percentage decline in the Gini in the figure was higher for states with the higher Gini in 2004, and the correlation is more negative when excluding the outliers.

[6] The lines in Figure 8.4 represent median household income per capita distributions of states that are located in the region.

Figure 8.9. Brazil: Income Inequality in Brazilian States: Dispersion of Median State Households' Incomes across Regions

Household Income per Capita Distribution, by State, 2014
(Percentiles of region-wide and nationwide household income distribution, RPI adjusted)

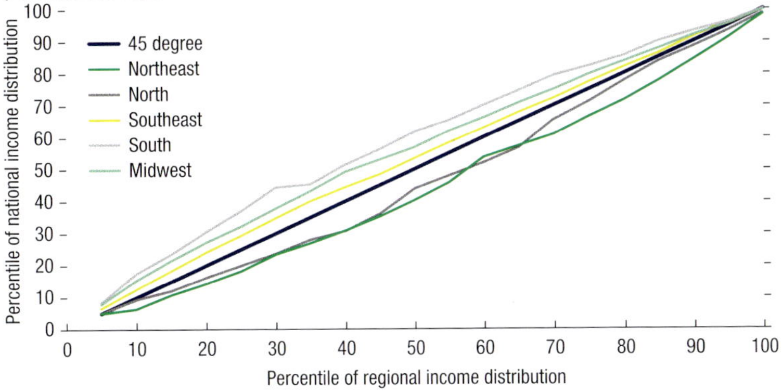

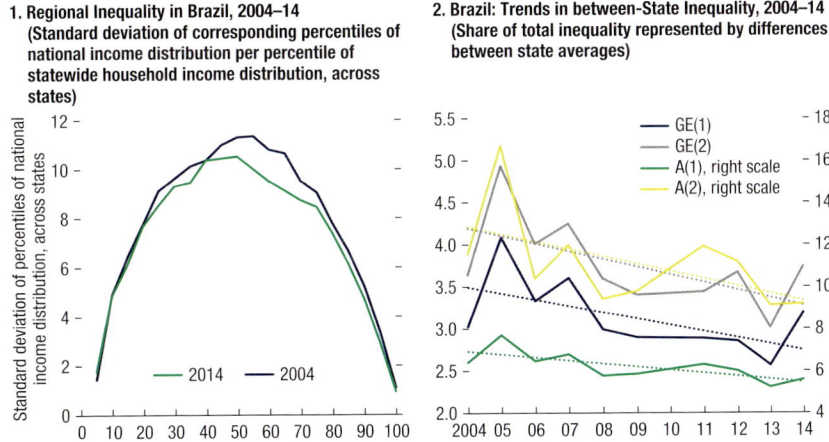

Sources: PNAD microdata; and IMF staff calculations.
Note: RPI = Rental Price Index.

in the employed population, real gross household earnings contracted in 2015 across all professions and for the first time in 11 years. However, earnings from work represent a higher share of total income in the survey and a higher share of the income of households in the lowest quartile. Job destruction and high inflation through 2016 may have affected relatively poor households more.

Figure 8.10. Brazil: Income Inequality in Brazilian States—Convergence in the Middle

1. Regional Inequality in Brazil, 2004–14
   (Standard deviation of corresponding percentiles of national income distribution per percentile of statewide household income distribution, across states)

2. Brazil: Trends in between-State Inequality, 2004–14
   (Share of total inequality represented by differences between state averages)

Sources: PNAD microdata; and IMF staff calculations.

The latest data indicate a slow-moving deterioration in income distribution. The 2015 PNAD showed no evidence of reversal of progress toward equality—although all real incomes declined, the higher incomes declined proportionally more, reducing inequality. The official (unadjusted) Gini index calculated for all income sources fell from 0.497 in 2014 to 0.491 in 2015. The Gini calculated for labor income fell from 0.490 to 0.485 and, for household income, from 0.494 to 0.493. But preliminary inequality estimates suggest that inequality widened slightly in 2016 for the first time in 22 years. The number of the poor in Brazil likely increased in the range of 2.5 million to 3.6 million by 2017, while the Gini index increased from 0.51 to 0.52–0.54 (World Bank 2017). Young, skilled workers in the services sector will probably represent the higher share of those falling below the poverty line because of the crisis.

CONCLUSIONS

This chapter documents a decline in inequality in Brazil during 2004–14, controlling for differences in state price levels. Inequality shrank both between and within the 27 Brazilian states. The decline in inequality can be attributed to the pronounced growth of incomes of poorer households and the convergence in household incomes in the middle of the distribution. Income convergence was stronger in states that were initially more unequal. The decline in inequality is also reflected in the consumption pattern dynamics of households that report increased consumption of durable goods by the poorer segments of the population compared with 10 years earlier.

REFERENCES

Almeida, A. N., and C. R. Azzoni. 2016. "Comparative Cost of Living of Brazilian Metropolitan Regions: 1996–2014." *Economic Studies* 46(1): 253–76.

Azevedo, J. P., A. C. David, F. Rodrigues Bastos, and E. Pineda. 2014. "Fiscal Adjustment and Income Inequality: Sub-national Evidence from Brazil." IMF Working Paper WP/14/85, International Monetary Fund, Washington, DC.

Deaton, A., and O. Dupriez. 2011. "Spatial Price Differences Within Large Countries." Unpublished Manuscript, Princeton University.

Dollar, D., T. Kleinberg, and A. Kraay. 2013. "Growth Still Is Good for Poor." Policy Research Working Paper 6568, World Bank, Washington, DC.

Góes, C., and I. Karpowicz. 2017. Inequality in Brazil: A Regional Perspective. Working Paper 17/225, Washington, DC.

Góes, C., and T. Matheson. 2017. "Domestic Market Integration and the Law of One Price in Brazil." *Applied Economics Letters* 24(5): 84–288.

Lakner, C., and B. Milanović. 2015. "Global Income Distribution: From the Fall of the Berlin Wall to the Great Recession." *The World Bank Economic Review* 30(2): 203–32.

Li, C., and J. Gibson. 2014. "Spatial Price Differences and Inequality in the People's Republic of China: Housing Market Evidence." *Asian Development Review* 31(1): 92–120.

Lustig, N., C. Pessino, and J. Scott. 2014. "The Impact of Taxes and Social Spending on Inequality and Poverty in Argentina, Bolivia, Brazil, Mexico, Peru, and Uruguay." *Public Finance Review* 42(3): 287–303.

Maurizio, R. 2014. "The Distributive Impact of the Minimum Wage in Argentina, Brazil, Chile and Uruguay." CEPAL, *Social Policy Series* 194 (LC/L 3825).

Menezes-Filho, N. A., and A. P. de Oliveira. 2014. "The Contribution of Education to the Fall in Inequality of Income per Capita in Brazil." Policy Paper No. 4, Public Policy Center— Insper, São Paulo.

Neri, M. 2010. *Tackling Inequalities in Brazil, China, India and South Africa—The Role of Labour Market and Social Policies.* Paris: OECD Publishing.

Neri, M. C., F. M. Vaz, and P. Souza. 2013. "Macroeconomic Effects of the Bolsa Família Program: A Comparative Analysis of Social Transfers." In *Bolsa Família Program: A Decade of Inclusion and Citizenship.* pp. 193–206. Brasília: Institute of Applied Economic Research.

Paes de Barros, R., M. de Carvalho, S. Franco, and R. Mendonça. 2010. "Determinants of the Fall in Inequality of Income in Brazil." IPEA Texto Para Discussão, Institute of Applied Economic Research, Brasilia.

Silveira-Neto, R. M., and C. Azzoni. 2012. "Social Policy as Regional Policy: Market and Nonmarket Factors Determining Regional Inequality." *Journal of Regional Science* 52(3).

Soares, F. V., S. Soares, M. Medeiros, and R. G. Osorio. 2006. "Programa de Transferência de Renda no Brazil: Impactos Sobre a Desigualdade, Texto para Discussão," No. 1228, Institute for Applied Economic Research, IPEA.

World Bank. 2017. "Safeguarding Against the Reversal in Social Gains During the Economic Crisis in Brazil. Poverty and Inequality Monitoring Note: Latin America and the Caribbean." Washington, DC.

CHAPTER 9

Poverty and Inequality in Brazil and Latin America

Ravi Balakrishnan, Frederik Toscani, and Mauricio Vargas

Brazil, and Latin America more broadly, have made impressive progress in reducing inequality and poverty since the turn of the century, although they remain highly unequal. Similar to other commodity exporters in the region, much of the progress in Brazil reflected real labor income gains for lower-skilled workers as well as higher government transfers. With the commodity boom over, a tighter fiscal envelope, and poverty rates already edging up, policies will have to be carefully recalibrated to sustain social progress. Better targeting of social transfers and reforms to decentralization frameworks also have an important role to play.

INTRODUCTION

Historically, Brazil has been one of the most unequal countries in the world. Even around the turn of this century, about 35 percent of the population lived below the poverty line. Since then, however, Brazil has made tremendous progress in reducing poverty and inequality. The poverty rate fell by more than 20 percentage points, and income inequality, as measured by the Gini coefficient, dropped from 0.60 to 0.52 during the commodity boom period.[1,2]

Previous analysis has shown that strong labor income growth in the lower-income segments was crucial for the reduction of inequality and poverty in Brazil. Average real income growth was high for all but the top decile of the income distribution, mirroring results in Latin America more broadly. Góes and Karpowicz (2017) find that most of the change in the Gini in Brazil can be explained by labor income growth, higher schooling levels, and labor

---

[1]The source for poverty and inequality data here is Institute of Applied Economic Research (IPEA). Several different measures of poverty exist. The one referred to here is based on the number of people who have income per capita that is insufficient to satisfy calorific necessities. The poverty line is defined by IPEA as twice the extreme poverty line, and calculations are based on household survey data (PNAD). The cross-country analysis presented later in this chapter uses internationally comparable poverty measures, most notably the share of people living on less than US$3.1 per day in purchasing-power-parity terms. Although the exact numbers differ depending on the poverty measure used, the trend is the same for all.

[2]In this chapter, the boom period is defined as the period 2000–14.

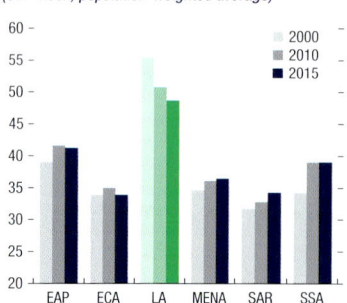

Figure 9.1. Gini Coefficient
(Gini index; population-weighted average)

Sources: World Bank, PovcalNet database; and World Bank, World Development Indicators (WDI) database.
Note: For 2015, Latin America (LA) is the average of available values from WDI. Countries include Bolivia, Brazil, Chile, Colombia, Costa Rica, the Dominican Republic, Ecuador, El Salvador, Honduras, Panama, Paraguay, Peru, and Uruguay. EAP = East Asia and Pacific; ECA = Europe and Central Asia; LA = Latin America; MENA = Middle East and North Africa; SAR = South Asia; SSA = sub-Saharan Africa.

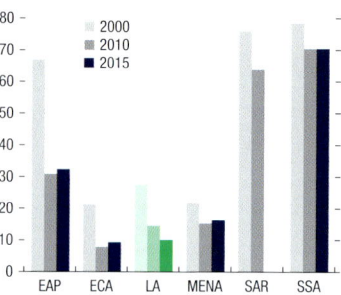

Figure 9.2. Poverty Rate
(Percent; headcount ratio at US$3.20 a day; 2011 PPP)

Sources: World Bank, World Development Indicators (WDI) database.
Note: For 2015, Latin America (LA) is the average of available values from WDI. Countries include Bolivia, Brazil, Chile, Colombia, Costa Rica, the Dominican Republic, Ecuador, El Salvador, Honduras, Panama, Paraguay, Peru, and Uruguay. No data are available for SAR in 2015. EAP = East Asia Pacific; ECA = Europe and Central Asia; LA = Latin America; MENA = Middle East and North Africa; PPP = purchasing power parity; SAR = South Asia; SSA = sub-Saharan Africa.

formalization. The targeted social program, Bolsa Família, also contributed to income convergence.

Against this backdrop, this chapter puts inequality and poverty developments in Brazil into regional perspective. It shows that the whole of Latin America did well, but improvements were particularly pronounced in commodity-exporting countries. The chapter then asks why and explores the channels through which commodity cycles affect social progress by using a microdata case study for Brazil, which the chapter compares with case studies for Bolivia and Peru.

Of great concern is the recent reversal in poverty and inequality gains. Although similar reversals have occurred in several other countries in the region, the deterioration in Brazil, in the context of a deep economic recession, has been particularly stark. This chapter concludes with a discussion of policies that can help maintain progress in the current period of lower commodity prices. The correct policy mix will be crucial to guaranteeing that Brazil can continue to move toward the twin goals of eradicating poverty and reducing inequality.

SOCIAL GAINS IN BRAZIL AND LATIN AMERICA DURING THE COMMODITY BOOM

Throughout the 20th century Latin America was associated with some of the highest levels of inequality in the world; but since 2000 it has been the only region to have seen a significant reduction in inequality (Figure 9.1). Poverty has also fallen significantly, although it has also dropped in other regions, and Latin America started from a relatively low base (Figure 9.2).

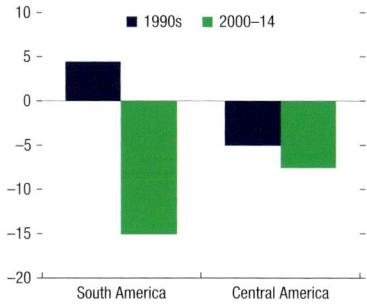

Figure 9.3. Change in Poverty Headcount Ratio
(Percentage points; US$3.10 a day)

Source: Inter-American Development Bank, SIMS database.
Note: South America comprises Argentina, Bolivia, Brazil, Chile, Colombia, Ecuador, Paraguay, Peru, and Uruguay. Central America comprises Belize, Costa Rica, El Salvador, Guatemala, Honduras, Mexico, Nicaragua, and Panama.

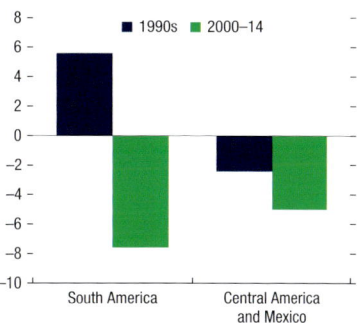

Figure 9.4. Change in Average Gini Coefficient
(Percentage points)

Sources: World Bank, World Development Indicators database; and IMF staff calculations.
Note: South America comprises Argentina, Bolivia, Brazil, Chile, Colombia, Ecuador, Paraguay, Peru, and Uruguay. Central America comprises Belize, Costa Rica, El Salvador, Guatemala, Honduras, Nicaragua, and Panama.

Overall, poverty reduction was strong across the region during the commodity boom, especially in South America (Figure 9.3).[3] Inequality as measured by the Gini coefficient declined in both Central and South America, but significantly more in South America (Figure 9.4).[4] In South America, the difference between the 1990s (when poverty and inequality increased) and the boom period was particularly stark.

A large literature has shown that the widespread decline in inequality across the region during the 2000s was caused by a reduction in hourly labor income inequality and by more robust and progressive government transfers (Azevedo, Saavedra, and Winkler 2012; Cornia and Martorano 2013; de la Torre, Messina, and Pienknagura 2012; López-Calva and Lustig 2010; Lustig, López-Calva, and Ortiz-Juarez 2013). For poverty reduction, and, to some degree, for inequality declines, an obvious hypothesis is that higher growth across Latin America during the boom period might have been the key driver. Relative to the 1990s, Figure 9.5 shows that during the commodity boom, growth did indeed increase in South America (where poverty fell the most), while in Central America growth was lower but remained high. Figure 9.6 shows that the association between GDP

---

[3]Given data availability, country coverage includes Argentina, Belize, Bolivia, Brazil, Chile, Colombia, Costa Rica, the Dominican Republic, Ecuador, El Salvador, Guatemala, Honduras, Mexico, Nicaragua, Panama, Paraguay, Peru, and Uruguay. Commodity exporters are determined according to whether net commodity exports surpassed 10 percent of total exports plus imports at the time of the October 2015 *World Economic Outlook*. Brazil does not fulfill that criterion, but it has the largest estimated natural resource reserves in the region. Hence, the full list of commodity exporters is Argentina, Bolivia, Brazil, Chile, Colombia, Ecuador, Honduras, Paraguay, and Peru.

[4]This chapter examines income inequality (income Gini) rather than wealth inequality.

Figure 9.5. Average Real GDP Growth
(Percent)

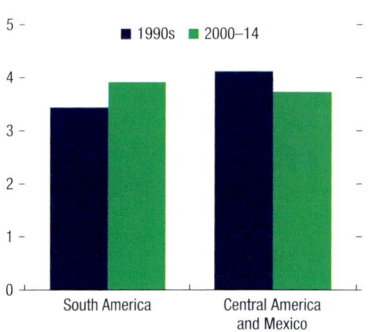

Sources: IMF, World Economic Outlook database; and IMF staff calculations.
Note: South America comprises Argentina, Bolivia, Brazil, Chile, Colombia, Ecuador, Paraguay, Peru, and Uruguay. Central America comprises Belize, Costa Rica, El Salvador, Guatemala, Honduras, Nicaragua, and Panama.

Figure 9.6. Average GDP Growth and Change in Poverty Headcount Ratio (2000–14)
(US$3.10 a day, PPP)

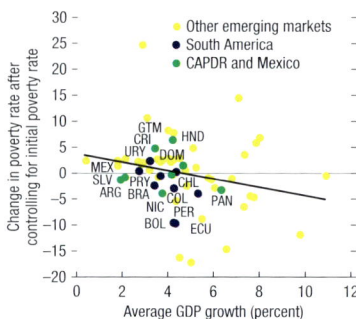

Sources: IMF, World Economic Outlook database; Inter-American Development Bank, SIMS database; and IMF staff calculations.
Note: South America comprises Argentina, Bolivia, Brazil, Chile, Colombia, Ecuador, Paraguay, Peru, and Uruguay. Central America comprises Belize, Costa Rica, El Salvador, Guatemala, Honduras, Nicaragua, and Panama. CAPDR = Central America, Panama, and the Dominican Republic; PPP = purchasing power parity. The figure controls for convergence effects. Specifically, the variable on the *y*-axis is the residual of a regression of the change in poverty on the initial poverty rate. Data labels in the figure use International Organization for Standardization (ISO) country codes.

growth and poverty reduction for individual countries across emerging market regions during the boom was positive.[5] South American countries, however, are generally below the fitted line, meaning that for every additional percentage point of growth, they reduced poverty by more than other countries. This outcome suggests that factors beyond high growth have been behind the remarkable turnaround in poverty reduction in South America in the 2000s.

A key question then is, why were the social gains greater in South America during the boom relative to other regions? Figure 9.7 provides a potential link: South America is home to many commodity exporters that experienced a significant boost in their terms of trade relative to other countries. Figures 9.8 and 9.9 zoom in on the differences in inequality and poverty reduction between individual commodity exporters and non–commodity exporters. The largest gains on both fronts were made in two countries highly dependent on commodity exports, Bolivia and Ecuador. Indeed, commodity exporters made larger gains in poverty reduction across the board except for Chile and Honduras, which experienced smaller gains than some non–commodity exporters such as Nicaragua and Panama.[6] For inequality, the same pattern holds but the picture is more mixed,

---

[5]To control for the initial level of poverty, the variable on the *y*-axis is the residual of a regression of the change in poverty on the initial poverty ratio.

[6] That poverty fell less in Chile than in other commodity exporters largely reflects Chile's relatively low poverty rates before the boom: poverty in 2000 stood at 10.3 percent and fell to 2.6 percent by 2013.

**Figure 9.7. Average Commodity Terms of
Trade Growth during Boom (2000–14)**
(Percent)

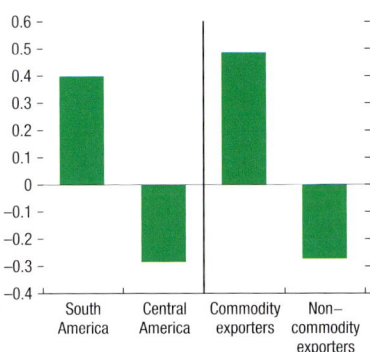

Source: IMF staff calculations.
Note: Terms of trade is the commodity net export price
index weighted by GDP (see Gruss 2014). All countries in
South America are commodity exporters except Uruguay.
All Central American countries are non–commodity
exporters except Honduras.

Figure 9.8. Change in Gini Coefficient
(Gini units)

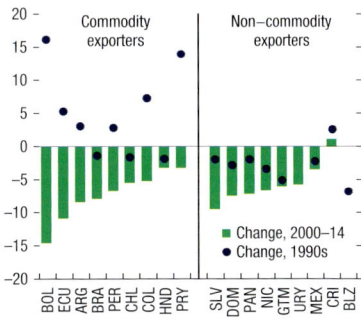

Sources: Inter-American Development Bank, SIMS
database; World Bank, World Development Indicators
database; and IMF staff calculations.
Note: Colombia uses 2003 and Brazil uses 2001 values for
2000, given data availability. Data labels in the figure use
International Organization for Standardization (ISO) country
codes.

with El Salvador and the Dominican
Republic seeing bigger reductions in
inequality than several commodity
exporters (Chile, Colombia, Paraguay,
Honduras).[7] For both poverty and
inequality, progress in Brazil was similar to that in comparator countries,
with improvements of similar magnitude to those in Peru, for example.

The significant progress in many
non–commodity exporters underscores the various factors that drive
social progress, of which commodity
cycles is only one. Indeed, Messina
and Silva (2018) argue that supply
factors, such as an increasing supply
of skilled workers, were likely the key
drivers of lower inequality in Central
America and Mexico and played an
important role across the region.

**Figure 9.9. Change in Poverty Headcount
Ratio**
(Percentage points; US$3.10 a day)

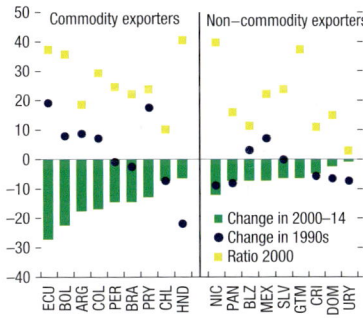

Source: Inter-American Development Bank, SIMS database.
Note: Colombia uses 2003 and Brazil uses 2001 values for
2000, given data availability. Data labels in the figure use
International Organization for Standardization (ISO) country
codes.

---

[7]The mean reduction in poverty during the boom period was statistically significantly larger in
commodity exporters than in non–commodity exporters. For inequality, the mean reduction is also
larger, but the result is not statistically significant.

Figure 9.10. Commodity Terms of Trade, Poverty, and Gini Coefficient

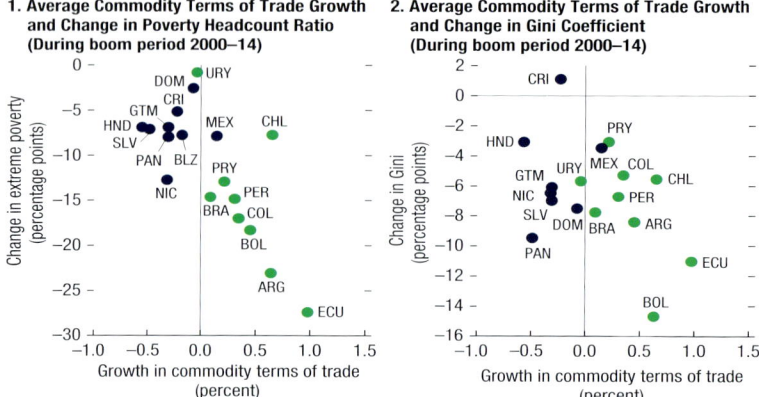

Sources: Inter-American Development Bank, SIMS database; World Bank, World Development Indicators database; and IMF staff calculations.
Note: Dark blue dots correspond to CAPDR and Mexico and green dots to South America. CAPDR comprises Central America, Panama, and the Dominican Republic. Chile uses 2013 values for the 2014 poverty headcount ratio due to data availability. Data labels in the figure use International Organization for Standardization (ISO) country codes.

Lustig, López-Calva, and Ortiz-Juarez (2012) also point to the expansion of cash transfers in Mexico and Brazil, while IMF (2017) highlights the role of government policies in boosting low wages in Uruguay.

COMMODITY CYCLES, POVERTY, AND INEQUALITY

Is There a Statistical Association?

What is the relationship between social indicators and the commodity cycle? The correlation between the reduction in poverty and inequality during the boom and the change in commodity terms of trade points to an interesting story (Figure 9.10).[8] For non–commodity exporters, no clear association is evident between changes in commodity terms of trade and changes in poverty and inequality. For commodity exporters, however, the relationship is strong, particularly for poverty. The size of poverty reduction is directly proportional to the growth rate of the commodity terms of trade in commodity exporters.[9] For

---

[8]The commodity terms of trade capture the income gain or loss a country experienced during the period owing to commodity price movements (Gruss 2014).

[9]Although Honduras is classified as a commodity exporter given its high net commodity exports, its commodity terms of trade declined because it exports nonextractive commodities and imports extractive ones whose prices increased by more. Consequently, commodity price changes led to a negative wealth effect for Honduras, and poverty fell significantly less than in most other Latin American countries.

inequality, the relationship for commodity exporters is not as strong as for poverty but is still clearly visible. A closer relationship between the commodity cycle and poverty (rather than inequality) is an empirical regularity found throughout this chapter.

Table 9.1 reports regressions of the share of income by decile on commodity terms of trade as well as several control variables.[10] Income shares of the second to eighth deciles increased significantly, while the share of the top decile declined. Because both low-income and medium-to-high-income segments gained, the poverty result is stronger than the inequality result. Nevertheless, inequality did tend to fall because the share of income going to the highest decile fell substantially, on average.[11] Interestingly, the bottom income decile did not see its share rise in a statistically significant way in response to higher commodity terms of trade, although its absolute income increased. As expected, and consistent with Figure 9.9, poverty reduction was driven more by developments closer to the poverty line, namely in the second to fourth decile, depending on the country.[12]

What Are the Channels?

The statistical relationship naturally leads to the question, through which channels does the commodity cycle influence social indicators? Essentially, a commodity boom is a positive wealth shock that propagates through the economy via various channels, as described in the sections that follow.[13]

Market and Private Sector Channels

The positive wealth shock has a direct impact on the commodity sector and creates spillovers to the rest of the economy, many of them transmitted via the labor market:

- First, the booming commodity sector expands. The expansion draws in labor and other resources. Higher labor demand pushes up real wages or employment, or both. It can also reduce or increase the skills premium, depending on the relative labor intensity of the commodity sector.[14]

---

[10]Because there is no statistical association for non–commodity exporters, the sample here includes only commodity exporters. The regression includes country fixed effects and lagged GDP per capita as a control variable.

[11]It is not possible to infer what happened to the income level of the top decile from these income-share regressions. Nonetheless, Figure 9.13 shows that real wages grew across all skill levels in commodity exporters, on average, during the boom, suggesting that in most countries the result in Table 9.1 reflects a relative rather than an absolute loss for the top decile.

[12]For example, in Bolivia nearly 40 percent of the population was below the poverty line in 2000.

[13]On the larger question of the long-term impact of natural resource abundance on GDP growth and development, there is no consensus. Van der Ploeg (2011), for example, shows that results supporting "the natural resource curse" are sensitive to sample periods and countries.

[14]Oil and gas production, for example, is substantially less labor intensive than agriculture but is more intensive in skilled labor.

Table 9.1. Commodity Terms of Trade and Income Share by Decile in Commodity Exporters

Variables	(1) Decile 1	(2) Decile 2	(3) Decile 3	(4) Decile 4	(5) Decile 5	(6) Decile 6	(7) Decile 7	(8) Decile 8	(9) Decile 9	(10) Decile 10
(Log) Net Commodity Price Index	0.151	0.395**	0.392*	0.405*	0.476**	0.575**	0.716***	0.790***	0.436	−4.310**
	(0.120)	(0.191)	(0.207)	(0.226)	(0.236)	(0.255)	(0.267)	(0.259)	(0.301)	(1.735)
Country fixed effects	Yes	Yes	Yes	Yes	Yes	Yes	Yes	Yes	Yes	Yes
Controls	GDP per capita	GDP per capita	GDP per capita	GDP per capita	GDP per capita	GDP per capita	GDP per capita	GDP per capita	GDP per capita	GDP per capita
Period	2000–14	2000–14	2000–14	2000–14	2000–14	2000–14	2000–14	2000–14	2000–14	2000–14
Observations	114	114	114	114	114	114	114	114	114	114
R^2	0.608	0.627	0.664	0.674	0.685	0.658	0.604	0.488	0.020	0.638
Number of countries	9	9	9	9	9	9	9	9	9	9

Sources: Socio-Economic Database for Latin America and Caribbean (CEDLAS and World Bank); and IMF staff calculations.

$*p < 0.10$; $**p < 0.05$; $***p < 0.01$.

- Second, improved terms of trade and the expansion of the commodity sector create spillovers to other sectors. Higher wealth and incomes cause domestic demand to increase, benefiting the nontradables sector. Higher investment by the commodity sector can lead, for example, to more construction, which is another way the positive wealth shock feeds into the economy, again expanding the nontradables sector.

- Third, changes in relative wages (a compression in the skills premium if the commodity sector and the nontradables sector are intensive in unskilled labor) will benefit more skill-intensive sectors and lead to further reallocation (Benguria, Saffie, and Urzua 2017).

Overall, the above channels should lead to more employment in the commodity and nontradables sectors. The impact on the non–commodity tradables sector is not immediately clear. On the one hand, the classic natural resource curse (Dutch disease) could be operating—higher demand expands the nontradables sector but crowds out the non–commodity sector because of a more appreciated real exchange rate (Harding and Venables 2016). On the other hand, if key tradables inputs are provided locally, positive spillovers can occur from the commodity sector to the manufacturing sector, as has been shown for the United States.[15] Given the relatively narrow initial manufacturing base in most Latin American countries, both effects might be modest, but commodity booms are likely to hamper export diversification to some degree.

For social outcomes, the expansion of the commodity and nontradables sectors, and the related increase in wages, should reduce poverty if those sectors employ workers from the lower end of the income distribution. Additionally, inequality will fall if the expanding sectors are intensive in low-skilled labor, causing the skills premium to decline.

Fiscal Channels

The positive wealth shock is also transmitted via higher fiscal revenues and expenditures:

- Higher government investment operates in a manner similar to higher commodity sector investment. It leads to more domestic demand, for example, via increased construction, with a resulting impact on wages and thus on poverty and inequality.[16]

- Larger transfers will have a direct impact on poverty and inequality, especially if the transfers are targeted to lower-income individuals.

---

[15]Allcott and Keniston (2018) demonstrate positive spillovers of the oil and gas sector to manufacturing in the United States. Michaels (2011) finds a similar positive result for the United States.

[16]Of course, public and private investment can also expand supply, not just demand.

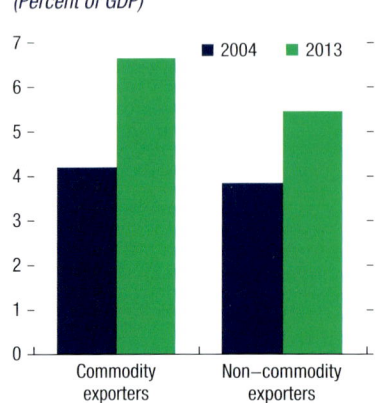

Figure 9.11. Public Investment in Latin America
(Percent of GDP)

Sources: IMF, World Economic Outlook database; and IMF staff calculations.

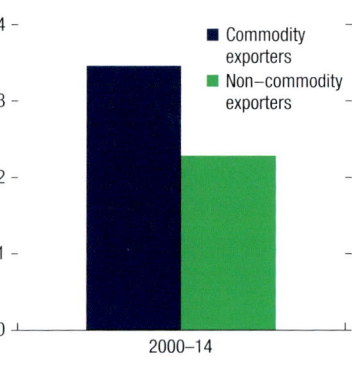

Figure 9.12. Total Employment Growth
(Percent)

Source: Inter-American Development Bank, SIMS database.

Other General Equilibrium Effects

While not a focus in the remainder of this chapter, the wealth shock can be transmitted via other general equilibrium effects, for example, via migration or the financial system.[17]

Regional Macroeconomic Evidence and Key Data for Brazil

In aggregate, then, commodity booms should reduce poverty and inequality through labor market developments and fiscal transfers.[18] Indeed, these mechanisms seem to have played out in the region. Public investment and employment growth were higher in commodity exporters than in non–commodity exporters (Figures 9.11 and 9.12). In line with the results of de la Torre and others (2015), commodity exporters also experienced significantly larger real labor income gains than non–commodity exporters across all skill levels (Figure 9.13). Low-skilled workers gained the most, compressing the skills premium and reducing inequality in both commodity exporters and non–commodity exporters (Figure 9.14) but because of different underlying wage dynamics. Specifically, as Messina and Silva (2018) note, the skills premium reduction reflects not just demand factors tied to the commodity boom but also an increase in the supply of high-skilled labor. In addition to labor income, government transfers also increased more in

---

[17]See, for example, Alberola and Benigno (2017).

[18]Note that the vast majority of households in Latin America outside the highest-income segments do not receive any capital income, so transfers and labor income account for the overwhelming share of their total income.

Figure 9.13. Real Labor Income Growth by Educational Level
(Percent)

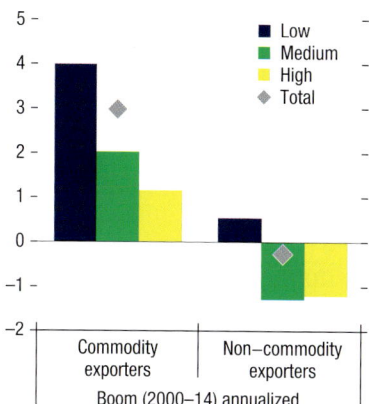

Source: Inter-American Development Bank, SIMS database.

Figure 9.14. Skills Premium Change in the 2000s
(Percentage point change in the ratio of hourly wage; high to low education)

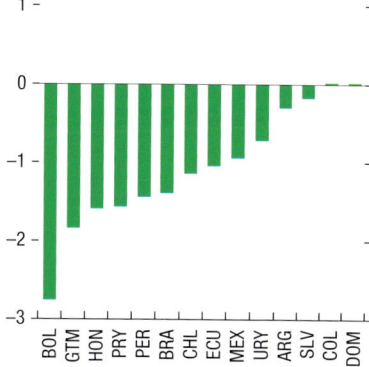

Sources: Socio-Economic Database for Latin America and the Caribbean (CEDLAS and World Bank); and IMF staff calculations.
Note: Data labels in the figure use International Organization for Standardization (ISO) country codes.

commodity exporters than in non–commodity exporters, further contributing to greater poverty and inequality declines in commodity exporters (Figure 9.15).

Looking more specifically at Brazil, the same patterns hold. Real labor income gains were strong, and they were strongest for lower-skilled workers, resulting in a substantial compression of the skills premium. The expansion of government transfers was more pronounced in Brazil than in most other countries, with the conditional cash transfer program Bolsa Família playing an important role (Barros and others 2010).

Figure 9.15. Average Government Transfers in Latin America
(Percent of GDP)

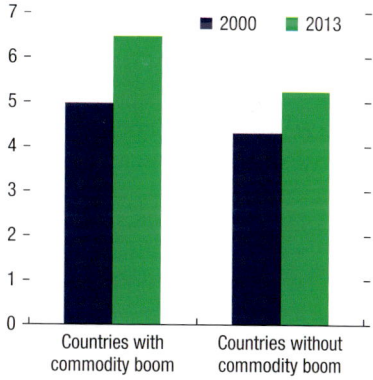

Sources: IMF, World Economic Outlook database; and IMF staff calculations.

Microdata Case Studies: Brazil and Comparison with Bolivia and Peru

This section examines Brazil, Bolivia, and Peru, all of which experienced significant reductions in poverty and inequality. They are also all commodity exporters, although Brazil is more diversified. The analysis first uses Shapley decompositions of household survey data to analyze the drivers of the decline in national inequality and poverty. This exercise helps identify whether labor income or transfer income played a larger role.[19] Within-country studies are then conducted for Brazil and Bolivia to disentangle the impact of a fiscal windfall from the pure market impact associated with a commodity boom.

The Fall in Poverty and Inequality in Brazil during the Commodity Boom, according to the Literature

Several authors have exploited household income data to try to understand the drivers of the fall in poverty and inequality in Brazil. Barros and others (2010) estimate that the drop in inequality between 2001 and 2007 was driven by both an expansion in government transfers and a compression in the ratio of labor income of better-educated workers to that of less-educated ones. They explain the latter by an expansion in the supply of educated workers.

Azevedo, Inchauste, and Sanfelice (2013) use Shapley decompositions to explain the roles of different factors in reducing inequality in several Latin American countries, while Azevedo and others (2013) use the same approach to explain the reduction in poverty. For Brazil, the former paper finds that the largest contributor to lower income inequality was higher labor income (contribution of 45 percent), but government transfers (contribution of 20 percent) and pensions (contribution of 18 percent) also played an important role. Similarly, for poverty, employment and earnings growth was the largest single factor, but nonlabor income (notably government transfers) played an important role, more so than in several other Latin American countries. The importance of transfers in Brazil can be noted by observing that the share of transfers in total household income of the bottom 20 percent of the distribution went from 3 percent to 24 percent between 2000 and 2010 (Azevedo, Inchauste, and Sanfelice 2013).

What Household Survey Data Show regarding Wage, Employment, and Government Transfer Developments in Bolivia and Peru[20]

In Bolivia during the boom, real labor income increased for all skills segments except for the highest one. Workers with intermediate levels of education

---

[19]Broadly speaking, a Shapley decomposition is a rigorous way to calculate how much any one factor contributed to changes in the income distribution. It isolates the contribution of one specific factor (for example, an increase in wages in the agricultural sector) by calculating a counterfactual distribution, holding all other factors constant. See Azevedo, Inchauste, and Sanfelice (2013) for more details.

[20]Official household survey data are used. For Bolivia, 2013 data are compared with 2007 data, while in Peru the comparison is between 2011 and 2007. For both countries, the official poverty lines are used to define poverty thresholds.

experienced the largest gains (Figure 9.16), a finding consistent with the cross-country regression results on changes in income share by decile.

Figure 9.17 looks at real per capita labor income and employment by sector for Bolivia (panel 1) and Peru (panel 2). The biggest winners in employment growth were construction and the extractive sector in Peru, and the extractive sector and commerce in Bolivia, in line with the previous discussion on channels. The broad services sector created the most jobs in both countries, in part reflecting the sector's size. Overall, employment growth came from the extractive and nontradables sectors.

The picture is more mixed for real wage growth. Average wages in the extractive sector fell in Bolivia, likely reflecting a compositional effect, with the number of informal (poorly paid)

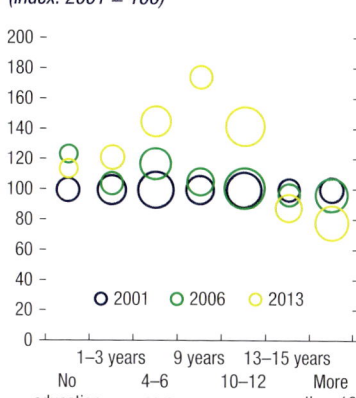

Figure 9.16. Bolivia: Index of Monthly Real Labor Income by Educational Level
(Index: 2001 = 100)

Sources: Improving the measurement of living conditions (MECOVI) household survey; and IMF staff calculations.
Note: The size of the bubble corresponds to the relative number of workers in each category.

miners increasing faster than employees in larger, capital-intensive mines. Manufacturing did poorly in both countries, especially in employment growth, again in line with a standard crowding-out story as well as with global trends.[21]

Finally, Table 9.2 reports the share of labor versus transfers in gross income (which includes transfers from the government and from family members or others). In Bolivia, government transfers increased markedly during the boom, partly reflecting the introduction of a noncontributory pension scheme. In Peru, transfers from the government did not increase substantially. In both countries, however, transfers account for a much smaller share of income than labor income, mechanically limiting their scope for lowering poverty and inequality.

Shapley Decompositions

The formal Shapley decompositions largely confirm the earlier conclusions. For both Bolivia and Peru, labor income played a larger role than nonlabor income in reducing inequality and poverty. Across sectors, changes in labor income of the nontradables (services) sector explain much of the social progress (Figure 9.18).[22]

---

[21] A decline in manufacturing employment has been a phenomenon not only in commodity exporters (see Chapter 3 of the April 2018 *World Economic Outlook*).

[22] See Vargas and Garriga (2015) for more details on the Shapley decomposition for Bolivia.

Figure 9.17. Real Labor per Capita and Sectoral Employment in Bolivia and Peru

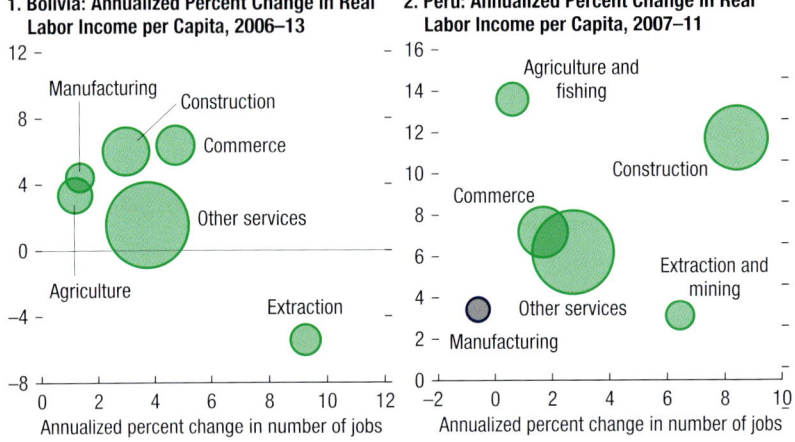

1. Bolivia: Annualized Percent Change in Real Labor Income per Capita, 2006–13
2. Peru: Annualized Percent Change in Real Labor Income per Capita, 2007–11

Annualized percent change in number of jobs

Sources: National household surveys (ENAHO) for Peru; improving the measurement of living conditions (MECOVI) household surveys for Bolivia; and IMF staff calculations.
Note: The size of the bubble corresponds to the absolute change between 2006 and 2013 in the number of workers in each sector whose income depends on each of the sectors for Bolivia, and the absolute change between 2007 and 2011 in the number of workers in each sector whose income depends on each of the sectors for Peru. Darker blue means a negative change.

Across skill levels, changes at the lower end of the distribution were important for understanding changes in social indicators. Specifically, low-skilled workers—defined as having complete primary or incomplete secondary education—were one of the biggest contributors to the drop in poverty and inequality. Interestingly, skilled workers in both countries (with complete secondary or tertiary education) were also important contributors to poverty reduction, even though they have the

Table 9.2. Composition of Households' Total Income

		2006	2007	2011	2012	2013
Bolivia	Labor	82.8	82.4	81.8	80.9	79.1
	Nonlabor	16.4	17.0	17.9	18.4	20.4
	Of which: Transfers from government	5.7	5.4	9.8	11.2	. . .
		2007	**2008**	**2009**	**2010**	**2011**
Peru	Labor	83.6	84.2	84.9	84.8	85.8
	Nonlabor	16.4	15.8	15.1	15.2	14.2
	Of which: Current transfers[1]	9.4	9.0	9.0	8.6	8.3
	Of which: JUNTOS program	0.5	0.7	0.3	0.3	0.3

Sources: National household surveys (ENAHO) for Peru; improving the measurement of living conditions (MECOVI) household surveys for Bolivia; and IMF staff calculations.
Note: Figures for Bolivia do not sum exactly to 100 percent because extraordinary retirement benefits, scholarships, and insurance compensation are not included. . . . = not available.
[1]Includes transfers within the country: pensions and transfers from individuals and institutions, public and private.

Figure 9.18. Shapley Decompositions of Poverty and Inequality by Employment Sector and Skill Level for Bolivia and Peru

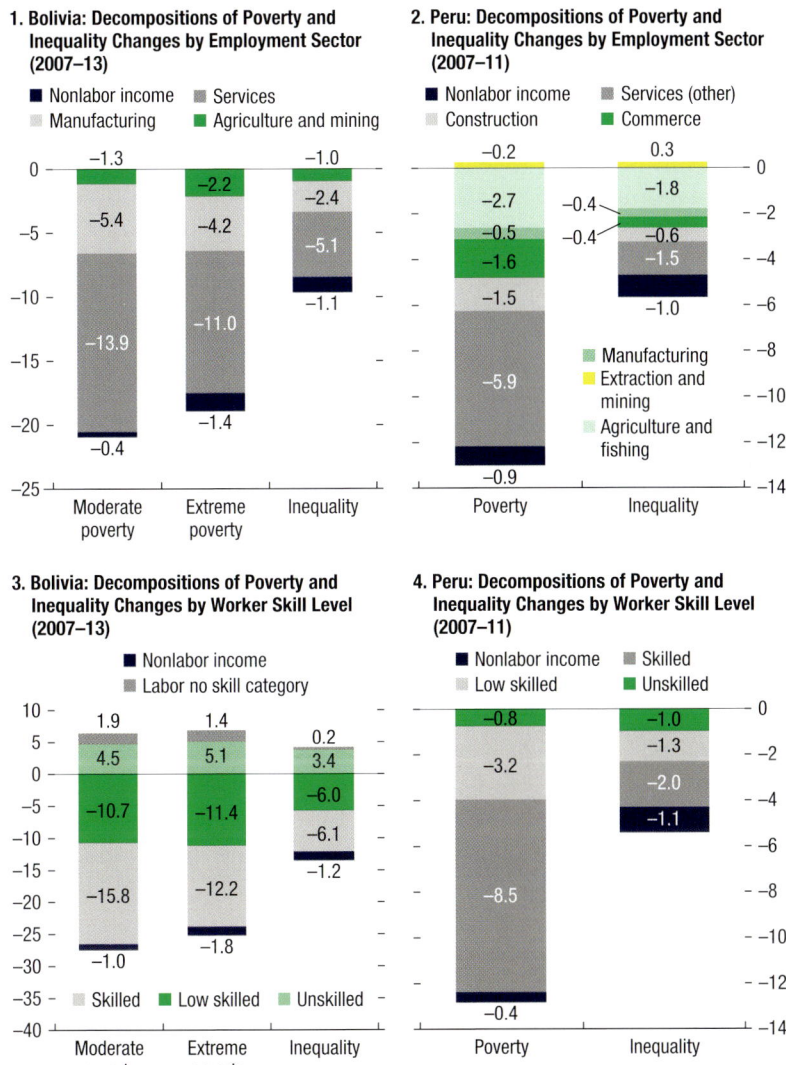

Sources: National household surveys (ENAHO) for Peru; improving the measurement of living conditions (MECOVI) household surveys for Bolivia; and IMF staff calculations.

Note: Gini coefficient change based on rescaled Gini coefficients in the range (0–100); poverty changes in percentage points. Unskilled (never attended school or incomplete primary education); low skilled (complete primary or incomplete secondary education); skilled (complete secondary, incomplete tertiary, or complete tertiary education).

highest wages, on average, and their wages grew the least. Although average income did not increase for skilled workers, wages at the lower end of their wage distribution moved up during the boom. This allowed a nontrivial fraction of skilled workers to exit poverty.[23]

Municipal-Level Analysis

This section studies the differences between commodity-producing and non-commodity-producing regions within Brazil and Bolivia. Both Brazil and Bolivia produce commodities with a range of labor intensity and redistribute a large share of the commodity windfall to producing regions.

Did Poverty Fall across the Whole Country or Only in Certain Regions?

Based on census data, poverty reduction was broad based in Brazil, with the entire municipal poverty distribution shifting toward less poverty during the boom period (left shift in Figure 9.19).[24] Indeed, poverty fell in 99 percent of Brazilian municipalities between the two census rounds and, on average, poverty fell by an impressive 18 percentage points.[25] In addition to the fall in poverty, the whole municipal inequality distribution also shifted left, indicating lower inequality throughout the country. Last, labor formality increased in most municipalities, a testament to the strong labor market. Results are similar for Bolivia, where poverty fell in 97 percent of the municipalities.

Did Municipalities That Produce Natural Resources Improve More than Others?

For Brazil, information from the national oil and gas regulator (National Agency of Petroleum, Natural Gas and Biofuels) and the Ministry of Mining was combined to construct the real value of natural resource production per capita for each municipality (Figure 9.20). Data at this level of precision were not available for Bolivia. Instead, a list of all municipalities that produce either hydrocarbons or minerals was constructed, without obtaining the precise volume or value of production.

In both countries, many municipalities produce natural resources, but value and volume of production are both regionally concentrated, creating a relatively

---

[23]For example, in Peru skilled workers make up about a third of the poor, with many close to the national poverty line.

[24]Population census data are used because household survey data are generally not representative at the municipal level. Typically, such data are available only at one-decade intervals (2001 and 2012 for Bolivia; 2000 and 2010 for Brazil). Importantly, poverty measures from the Brazilian and Bolivian censuses are not directly comparable. Specifically, the Bolivian population census does not provide data on monetary income, so it is not possible to calculate inequality or a standard income-based poverty measure. To capture poverty, measures of access to basic necessities were used (sanitation, water, electricity, adequate living space, and so on). See Feres and Mancero (2001).

[25]The "hump-shape" in the Brazilian distribution mostly reflects large regional differences.

Figure 9.19. Density Distributions by Municipality in Brazil

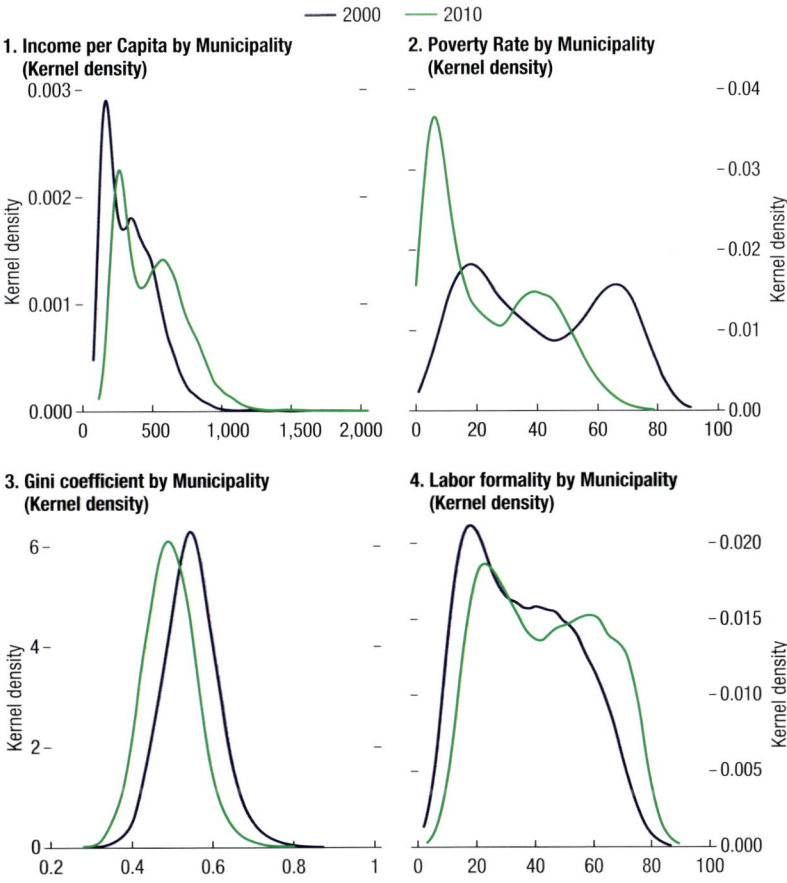

Source: Brazilian Institute of Geography and Statistics (IBGE).
Note: Figures show density of the municipal-level social outcomes.

small group of municipalities with high per capita natural resource production. For example, out of Brazil's more than 5,500 municipalities, the top 20 producers account for 75 percent of total production. In Bolivia, the region of Tarija produced about 70 percent of total natural gas in 2012.

To study the impact of natural resources, the change in poverty in producer municipalities is compared with the change in poverty in other municipalities, controlling for other factors (see Annex 9.1 for details of the identification strategy).

Poverty fell by more in natural resource municipalities (Table 9.3). For Brazil, higher real values of natural resource production are associated with larger declines in poverty, with producer municipalities reducing poverty by

1.4 percentage points, on average, relative to nonproducer ones.[26] For Bolivia, the natural resource municipalities reduced poverty by 2.7 percentage points more than other municipalities. Regarding inequality, the results are mixed for Brazil, with statistical significance dependent on which technique is used.

In summary, the social gains in Brazil and Bolivia were broad-based across municipalities, but natural resource producers experienced larger gains.

What within-Country Analysis Can Show about the Channels through Which the Commodity Boom Affected Poverty and Inequality

To isolate the fiscal impact from other channels, natural resources can be divided into offshore oil and gas production and domestic mineral mining for Brazil, and into onshore gas megacampos[27] and mineral mining for Bolivia.[28] Mineral mining tends to yield smaller fiscal windfalls but generates substantial labor demand in the local extractive sector. Offshore oil and gas has a minimal labor demand effect (and labor may not even be located in the municipality closest to the rig), but it generates important fiscal windfalls for municipalities closest to the oil field. Hence, for Brazil, the impact of offshore oil and gas production is a proxy for the pure fiscal channel, while mining picks up the combined impact (as seen in Table 9.4). Similar logic applies to the distinction between gas megacampos and mineral mining in Bolivia, although the analysis is less precise because

Figure 9.20. Value of Natural Resource Production per Capita by Municipalities, 2010

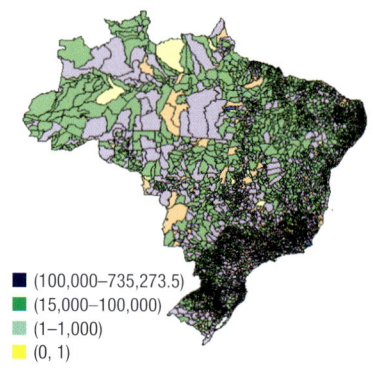

- ■ (100,000–735,273.5)
- ■ (15,000–100,000)
- ■ (1–1,000)
- ■ (0, 1)

Sources: National Agency of Petroleum, Natural Gas and Biofuels (ANP); Brazilian Mining Ministry; Brazilian Institute of Geography and Statistics (IBGE) (2010); and IMF staff calculations.
Note: The map shows natural resource (hydrocarbons + minerals) production per capita in 2010 for 5,565 Brazilian municipalities. Population data are from the 2010 population census. Data on hydrocarbon production volumes by field are from ANP. These data are assigned to municipalities based on geographic information and are valuated according to annual price data by state, also from ANP. Mineral production values data are from the Brazilian Mining Ministry. Values are in constant 2010 Brazilian reais.

---

[26]To construct the natural resource producer dummy variable in Brazil, a municipality is defined as a producer if it produces more than the mean amount of natural resources per capita (this essentially captures larger producers as opposed to municipalities with only, for example, very small-scale mining).

[27]So-called gas megacampos are the largest gas fields in Bolivia.

[28]For each country there is an additional category (onshore oil and gas production for Brazil and non-megacampo onshore oil and gas production for Bolivia) for which no impact is found (production is significantly smaller), so that category for each country is omitted from the discussion.

Table 9.3. Impact of Natural Resource Boom on Producer Municipalities in Brazil and Bolivia

	Brazil		Bolivia
	Poverty	Gini Coefficient	Poverty
Impact of Increase in Real per Capita Natural Resource Production (range for top 20 increases)	−0.39*** to −9.1***	0 to −0.05**	N/A
Impact of Being a Natural Resource Producer Municipality (dummy variable analysis)	−1.44***	0	−2.75*

Source: IMF staff calculations.
Note: N/A = not applicable.
*$p < 0.10$; **$p < 0.05$; ***$p < 0.01$.

neither the value or volume of production nor exact fiscal windfalls at the municipal level are known.

In Brazil, the pure fiscal impact (as measured by the impact of offshore oil and gas production) leads to some reduction in poverty and a marginal increase in labor formality (Figure 9.21).[29] It also leads to a shift of labor out of agriculture and into nontradables, essentially services and construction, because the increased

Table 9.4. Impact of Mineral and Offshore Hydrocarbon Production on Municipal Revenues and Extractive Sector Employment

	(1) Natural Resource Royalties per Capita	(2) Current Revenues per Capita	(3) Share of Workers in Extractive Industries
Change in Mineral Production per Capita	0.0174***	0.0241***	1.33e−05***
	(0.000922)	(0.006010)	(0.000004)
Change in Offshore Oil and Gas Production per Capita	0.0209***	0.0248***	−2.56E−06
	(0.001300)	(0.002640)	(0.000002)
Geographic Controls	Yes	Yes	Yes
Dependent Variable in 2000	Yes	Yes	Yes
Change in Dependent Variable between 1991 and 2000	No	No	No
State Fixed Effects	Yes	Yes	Yes
Observations	5,507	4,982	5,507
R^2	0.886	0.834	0.223

Source: IMF staff calculations.
*$p < 0.10$; **$p < 0.05$; ***$p < 0.01$.

---

[29]All coefficients shown in Figures 5.21 and 5.22 are statistically significant. When a coefficient is not statistically significant, the corresponding bar chart is zero (for example, public employment in Brazilian mineral municipalities).

fiscal resources are partly used for public investment.[30] Additionally, part of the fiscal windfall is used to increase public sector employment. In mineral municipalities, the labor market effects are much larger. Labor formality increased significantly and labor shifted from agriculture and manufacturing into construction and services. The results thus point to an important role for both fiscal and market channels, but especially the latter, in reducing poverty.[31]

Similarly, in Bolivia, while poverty was reduced more in gas megacampo municipalities, the labor market impact was greater in mining municipalities because the fraction of agricultural employment decreased significantly and net migration increased (Figure 9.22). In megacampo municipalities, public sector employment increased significantly, in line with the Brazilian results, and pointing to the fiscal windfall being used for public employment. Indeed, the increase in public employment is notable considering the small share of public sector workers in the average Bolivian municipality—the increase of about 2 percentage points in public sector employment in gas megacampo municipalities is greater than one standard deviation.

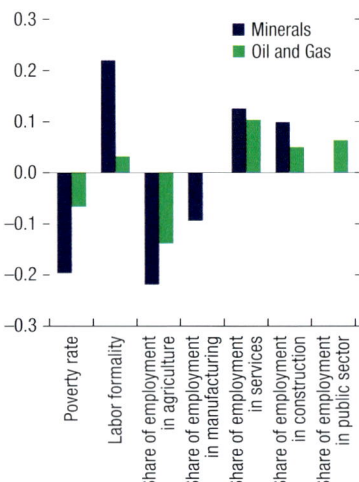

Figure 9.21. Brazil: Impact of a One Standard Deviation Increase in Natural Resource Extraction at the Municipal Level
(Percentage points)

Sources: Brazilian Institute of Geography and Statistics (IBGE); and IMF staff calculations.
Note: The change between the 1991 and 2000 censuses is included in the regressions as a control variable when available. Standard errors are clustered at the state level. Estimated coefficients are set to zero when they are not significant at least at the 10 percent level. When they are significantly different from zero, the figure shows the impact of a one standard deviation increase in the value of natural resource production per capita between 2000 and 2010.

---

[30]From regressions with local budget data, fiscal windfalls mainly tend to increase capital expenditure but also current expenditure, including wages.

[31]The effects are small for most municipalities—a one standard deviation increase in the value of mineral production per capita reduces the poverty rate by only 0.2 percentage point. For the big producers, however, the impact is economically significant, with an estimated reduction in poverty of between 3 and 9 percentage points for the top five producers.

Figure 9.22. Bolivia: Impact of Gas and Mineral Production at the Municipal Level
(Percentage points)

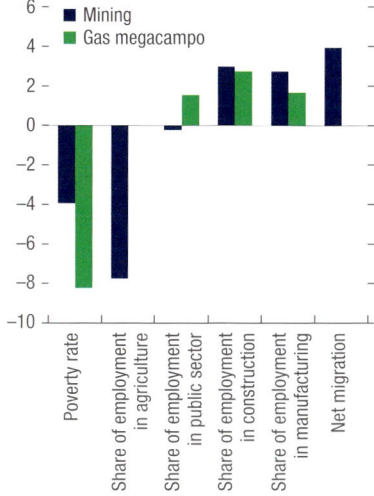

Sources: National Statistics Office (INE); and IMF staff calculations.

Overall, the results for Brazil and Bolivia are in line with growing evidence from other within-country studies in Latin America.[32] For Brazil, Cavalcanti, Da Mata, and Toscani (2016) find that the direct market effect (abstracting from the fiscal channel) of having an oil sector is beneficial for municipalities and leads to structural transformation away from subsistence agriculture and toward the services sector over the long term. Benguria, Saffia, and Urzua (2017) corroborate these findings for Brazil over the recent boom period by showing a compression in the wage premium as well as significant employment gains in the commodity and nontradables sector, combined with employment losses in the tradables sector in regions affected by the positive price shock.

FISCAL DECENTRALIZATION IN THE CONTEXT OF LARGE COMMODITY WINDFALLS

In Latin America, Bolivia, Brazil, and Peru redistribute large parts of the fiscal windfalls from natural resource extraction back to the subnational-level governments in producing regions. Colombia also redistributes royalties to subnationals, but with less focus on producer regions since a reform was enacted in 2012 (see Annex 9.2 for further details, including on the frameworks in advanced economies such as Canada and Norway).

Although fiscal windfalls do have some beneficial effects for producer regions, sharing large amounts of natural resource revenues with subnational producers has several conceptual drawbacks. First, it is unclear whether geographic and geological differences between regions should determine fiscal envelopes given the large horizontal inequities that result. Second, the volatile nature of natural resource revenues calls for careful intertemporal planning, which is even harder to achieve at the local level than at the national level. Third, resource revenues are essentially transfer revenues from a local government's perspective; thus, they do

---

[32]See Pellandra (2015) and Alvarez, Garcia, and Ilabaca (2017) on Chile; and Aragon and Rud (2013) and Loayza and Rigolini (2016) on Peru. Cust and Poelhekke (2015) provide a review of the literature.

nothing to encourage accountability and the building of own-revenue bases. Fourth, in per capita terms, large fiscal windfalls can lead to problems with absorptive capacity as well as governance (IMF 2009). Of course, the environmental impact of mining activity needs to be considered and creates a case for an additional transfer to producing regions.

Consider the departmental budget breakdown of Bolivia for 2012 (Figure 9.23). The main gas region (Tarija) has a population share of about 5 percent. Yet its budget accounted for more than a third of all departmental revenues and wages, and nearly half of all departmental capital expenditure. In Peru in the same year, the main natural-resource-producing departments (Moquegua and Cusco) received more than 2,000 nuevos soles (S/.) per capita in commodity-related transfers (*canons*), while some other departments received less than S/.1 per capita. Indeed, 12 of the 183 provinces in Peru receive about 50 percent of canon revenues (Santos and Werner 2015). In Brazil, most mineral royalties go to producing states and municipalities. For oil and gas, the formulas are complicated, but, in some cases, royalties can account for more than 50 percent of a municipality's revenues.

For Brazil, Caselli and Michaels (2013) find that large fiscal windfalls at the subnational level have not translated into substantial improvements in living standards, suggesting serious governance or capacity constraints at the local level. In both Peru and Bolivia, some local governments with the biggest windfalls per capita began to accumulate large deposits during the boom, while acute investment needs existed in other regions (Santos and Werner 2015, Chapter 10). Since the boom, the most important commodity-producing regions in Bolivia and Brazil, Tarija and Rio de Janeiro, respectively, have suffered severe fiscal sustainability problems. This issue is consistent with the drawbacks noted above, and several papers provide evidence that governance problems and capacity constraints at the subnational level often limit the effectiveness of public spending, especially in the context of high per capita natural resource revenues.[33]

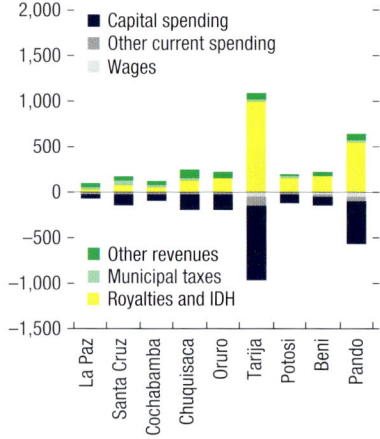

Figure 9.23. Bolivia: Departmental Budgets, 2012
(US dollars per capita)

Sources: National authorities; and IMF staff calculations.
Note: IDH = direct tax on hydrocarbons.

---

[33]See Caselli and Michaels (2013) for Brazil, Arellano-Yanguas (2011) for Peru, and Perry and Olivera (2009) for Colombia.

Given this problem, when the opportunity for substantive reforms to decentralization frameworks is present, those reforms should aim to minimize horizontal inequities, avoid boom-bust revenue cycles at the local level, and, crucially, clarify the goals of the revenue-sharing agreement. To help avoid boom-bust cycles that lead to large spending shocks, further use could be made of precautionary stabilization funds, such as in Chile, Colombia, and Norway. The reform of royalty-sharing arrangements in Colombia in 2012 is a good example of what can be done to reduce horizontal inequities.[34]

Notwithstanding the Colombian example, achieving consensus on larger reforms to revenue-sharing arrangements is difficult. Other actions can still play an important role, including building capacity at the subnational level and encouraging local governments to build their own-revenue bases to reduce reliance on transfers (for example, via property taxes). Transfer arrangements should also be made as transparent as possible to facilitate planning and oversight. Such measures will increase ownership and accountability and reduce revenue volatility. Finally, nonresource transfers can potentially be used to offset some of the horizontal inequities by using measurable criteria of local needs in some of the allocation formulas (for example, the equalization scheme in Canada).

CAN SOCIAL PROGRESS BE SUSTAINED WITH LOWER COMMODITY PRICES?

To sum up, Brazil and Latin America in general made tremendous progress in reducing inequality and poverty in the 2000s, especially in commodity-exporting countries. Much of the decline in poverty and the Gini coefficient occurred because labor income inequality fell, linked to a declining skills premium and the expansion of services and lower-skill jobs. But increasing social transfers also played a role.

Because commodity prices have been significantly lower since the end of the boom in 2014, there are concerns that social progress is threatened, especially in commodity exporters. Indeed, since 2014, employment growth has slowed much more in commodity exporters than in non–commodity exporters, while real wage growth has been negative for all skill groups (Figures 9.24 and 9.25). The poverty cycle has also turned in some commodity exporters, with increases in poverty rates in Brazil and Paraguay. As discussed earlier, the impact of commodity cycles on inequality is not as strong as on poverty. Nonetheless, inequality in commodity exporters has largely moved sideways since 2014 following the tremendous reduction in the boom years. At the same time, fiscal space in many commodity exporters has fallen, given a decline in commodity-related revenues and slowing growth. All these factors suggest that, absent policy measures, lower commodity

---

[34]Colombia's royalty-sharing arrangements are not fully integrated into the annual budget. A unified budget would be a preferable option for most countries.

Figure 9.24. Total Employment Growth
(Percent)

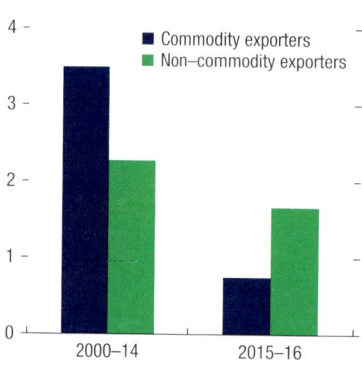

Figure 9.25. Real Labor Income Growth by Educational Level
(Percent)

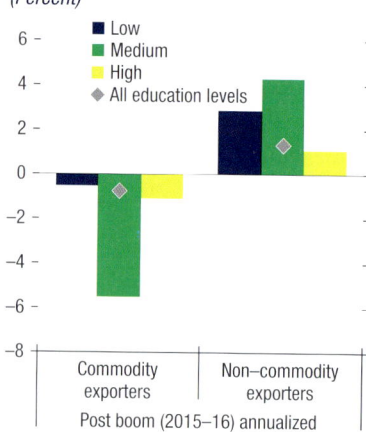

Source: Inter-American Development Bank, SIMS database.

Source: Inter-American Development Bank, SIMS database.

prices carry with them a significant risk of slower poverty reduction and possibly higher inequality in commodity exporters in the coming years.

How should commodity exporters respond to this challenge? While the channels by which commodity prices affected inequality and poverty during the boom will also be present in reverse during the postboom period, they need not be symmetric. For example, many commodity exporters saw significant migration to urban areas from rural areas. This experience may not reverse in the postboom period, owing to the high costs associated with moving. Moreover, countries that built up fiscal cushions during the boom can use the buffers in the postboom period to smooth the adjustment to lower commodity prices. Some countries, such as Bolivia and Peru, have been using their buffers, while the adjustment in countries without fiscal buffers (such as Ecuador) has been more difficult. And as shown in the social progress made in many non–commodity exporters in Latin America despite a negative commodity terms-of-trade shock, other policies still have a clear role to play in mitigating the impact of lower commodity prices on social progress:

- Central governments, especially in countries with limited fiscal buffers, still could maintain the quality of social and infrastructure spending by increasing revenues and reprioritizing spending.[35] Indeed, on the social protection side, Latin America already spends significantly less than

---

[35]Latin American tax and transfer systems are substantially less progressive than such systems in Organisation for Economic Co-operation and Development countries (Lustig 2012; Hanni, Martner, and Podesta 2015; OECD 2018). Lustig (2012) finds that in some Latin American

Figure 9.26. Composition of Social Spending, 2010
(Percent of GDP)

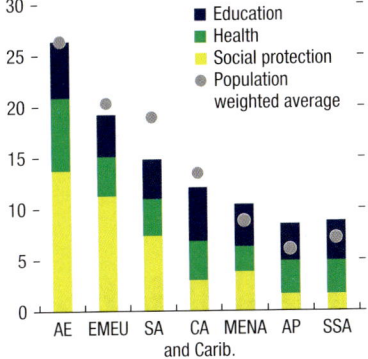

Sources: IMF, Fiscal Affairs Department database; and IMF staff calculations.
Note: AE = advanced economies; EMEU = emerging Europe; SA = South America; CA and Carib. = Central America and the Caribbean; MENA = Middle East and North Africa; AP = Asia and Pacific; SSA = sub-Saharan Africa.

Figure 9.27. Global Revenue Mix by Region, 2015
(Percent of GDP)

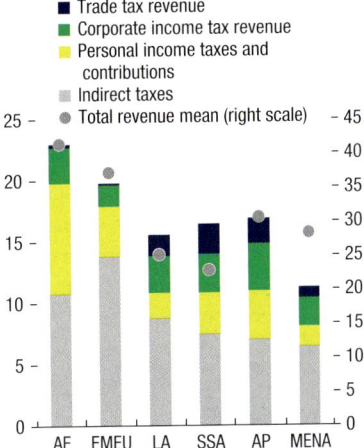

Sources: IMF, Fiscal Affairs Department database; and IMF staff calculations.
Note: AE = advanced economies; EMEU = emerging Europe; LA = Latin America; SSA = sub-Saharan Africa; AP = Asia and Pacific; MENA = Middle East and North Africa.

emerging Europe or advanced economies (Figure 9.26). Space to maintain such spending levels could be created by, for example, (1) increasing revenues from progressive personal income taxes, which, as Figure 9.27 shows, tend to be less in Latin America compared with other regions;[36] and (2) reducing universal price subsidies (such as energy subsidies), which are present in Latin America and typically highly regressive, although at lower levels than in other emerging market regions (Figure 9.28). Increasing the efficiency of spending could also play a role. For example, existing social transfers could be better targeted in many countries by making further use

countries, the net income of the poor and near-poor can be lower than it was before taxes and cash transfers. In-kind transfers in education and health, however, are progressive throughout the region.

[36]Hanni, Martner, and Podesta (2015) find that although maximum legal personal income tax rates in Latin America range from 25 to 40 percent, the effective tax rates tend to be substantially lower, with the effective rate for the top decile only 5.4 percent, on average. Consequently, the redistributive impact of personal income taxes in Latin America is very limited, achieving a reduction of just 2 percent in income inequality, which contrasts markedly with the countries of the European Union, whose distribution improves more than 12 percent after income taxes (OECD 2018). IMF (2014) recommends progressive personal income taxes as an important tool for achieving fiscal redistribution.

of means testing where feasible (IMF 2014).

- The allocation of revenue-capacity and spending responsibilities at different levels of government could be improved. Enhancing capacity at the local level is essential. Apart from reforming formulas for revenue sharing to take greater account of spending needs (for example, population size and poverty levels), thought should be given to greater use of stabilization funds, with clear rules and governance arrangements, in commodity exporters.

- Increasing the flexibility of labor markets and deploying policies aimed at retooling workers would help smooth the necessary adjustment to the rebalancing of demand caused by lower commodity prices. And while always challenging, continuing structural reforms to help diversify the production base would increase the resilience of commodity exporters to commodity price shocks.

- Given that better education was an important structural factor that helped reduce inequality and lift people out of poverty during the boom, pushing for further improvements in the quality of education should remain a priority, although gains from any policy measures will take time to be realized and will accrue only in the longer term.

South America faces an important challenge in managing the impact of lower commodity prices on social progress, especially their impact on inequality and poverty reduction since the turn of the century. Implementing the right policies will be key to meeting this challenge.

Figure 9.28. Composition of Social Spending
(Percent of GDP)

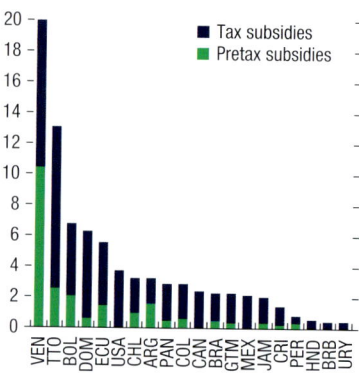

Sources: IMF, Fiscal Affairs Department database; and IMF staff calculations.
Note: Data labels in the figure use International Organization for Standardization (ISO) country codes.

REFERENCES

Alberola, E., and G. Benigno. 2017. "Revisiting the Commodity Curse: A Financial Perspective." *Journal of International Economics* 108.

Allcott, H., and D. Keniston. 2018. "Dutch Disease or Agglomeration? The Local Economic Effects of Natural Resource Booms in Modern America." *Review of Economic Studies* 85(2): 596–731.

Alvarez, R., A. Garcia, and S. Ilabaca. 2017. "Commodity Prices Shocks and Poverty in Chile." Unpublished.

Aragon, F. M., and J. P. Rud. 2013. "Natural Resources and Local Communities: Evidence from a Peruvian Gold Mine." *American Economic Journal: Economic Policy* 5(2): 1–25.

Arellano-Yanguas, J. 2011. "Aggravating the Resource Curse: Decentralisation, Mining and Conflict in Peru." *The Journal of Development Studies* 47(4): 617–38.

Azevedo, J. P., G. Inchauste, and V. Sanfelice. 2013. "Decomposing the Recent Inequality Decline in Latin America." Policy Research Working Paper 6315, World Bank, Washington, DC.

Azevedo, J. P., G. Inchauste, S. Olivieri, J. Saavedra, and V. Sanfelice. 2013. "Is Labor Income Responsible for Poverty Reduction? A Decomposition Approach." Policy Research Working Paper 6414, World Bank, Washington, DC.

Azevedo, J. P., J. Saavedra, and H. Winkler. 2012. "When Job Earnings Are Behind Poverty Reduction." Operational Studies Paper No. 97, World Bank, Washington, DC.

Barros, R., M. De Carvalho, S. Franco, and R. Mendonça. 2010. "Markets, the State and the Dynamics of Inequality in Brazil." In *Declining Inequality in Latin America: A Decade of Progress?* Washington, DC: Brookings Institution and UNDP.

Benguria, F., F. Saffie, and S. Urzua. 2017. "Commodity Shocks, Firm-level Responses and Labor Market Dynamics." Unpublished.

Caselli. F., and G. Michaels. 2013. "Do Oil Windfalls Improve Living Standards? Evidence from Brazil." *American Economic Journal: Applied Economics* 51: 208–38.

Cavalcanti, T., D. Da Mata, and F. Toscani. 2016. "Winning the Oil Lottery: The Impact of Natural Resource Discoveries on Growth." IMF Working Paper 16/61, International Monetary Fund, Washington, DC.

Cornia, G., and B. Martorano. 2013. "Development Policies and Income Inequality in Selected Developing Regions, 1980–2010." Economic Working Paper. University of Florence, Department of Economics and Business Sciences, Florence.

Cust, J., and S. Poelhekke. 2015. "The Local Economic Impacts of Natural Resource Extraction." *Annual Review of Resource Economics* 7(5): 215–68.

de la Torre, Augusto, A. Ize, G. R. Beylis, and D. Lederman. 2015. "Jobs, Wages, and the Latin American Slowdown." Washington, DC: World Bank Group.

de la Torre, Augusto, J. Messina, and S. Pienknagura. 2012. "The Labor Market Story Behind Latin America's Transformation." LAC Semiannual Report (October). World Bank, Washington, DC.

Feres, J. C., and X. Mancero. 2001. "The Unmet Basic Needs Method (NBI) and Its Applications in Latin America." Economic Commission for Latin America and the Caribbean, Santiago.

Goes, C., and I. Karpowicz. 2017. "Inequality in Brazil: A Micro-Data Analysis." Special Issues Paper. International Monetary Fund, Washington, DC.

Gruss, B. 2014. "After the Boom – Commodity Prices and Economic Growth in Latin America and the Caribbean." IMF Working Paper No. 14/154, International Monetary Fund, Washington, DC.

Hainmueller, J., and Y. Xu. 2013. "ebalance: A Stata Package for Entropy Balancing." *Journal of Statistical Software* 54(7).

Hanni, M., R. Martner, and A. Podesta. 2015. "The Redistributive Potential of Taxation in Latin America." *CEPAL Review* 116: 8–26.

Harding, T., and A. J. Venables. 2016. "The Implications of Natural Resource Exports for Nonresource Trade." *IMF Economic Review* 64 (2).

Inter-American Development Bank (IDB). 2015. *Decentralizing Revenue in Latin America: Why and How.* Washington, DC.

International Monetary Fund (IMF). 2009. "Macro Policy Lessons for a Sound Design of Fiscal Decentralization." Washington, DC.

————. 2014. "Fiscal Policy and Income Inequality." IMF Fiscal Affairs Department. Washington, DC.

————. 2017. "Uruguay: Selected Issues." Washington, DC.

Loayza, N., and J. Rigolini. 2016. "The Local Impact of Mining on Poverty and Inequality: Evidence from the Commodity Boom in Peru." Peruvian Economic Association Working Paper No. 33.

López-Calva, L., and N. Lustig. 2010. *Declining Inequality in Latin America: A Decade of Progress?* Washington, DC: Brookings Institution Press.

Lustig, N. 2012. "Taxes, Transfers, and Income Redistribution in Latin America." *Inequality in Focus* 1 (2).

Lustig, N., L. F. López-Calva, and E. Ortiz-Juarez. 2012. "Declining Inequality in Latin America in the 2000s: The Cases of Argentina, Brazil, and Mexico." Working Paper No. 266, Society for the Study of Economic Inequality, Palma de Mallorca.

————. 2013. "Deconstructing the Decline in Inequality in Latin America." Policy Research Working Paper No. 6552, World Bank, Washington, DC.

Messina, J., and J. Silva. 2018. *Wage Inequality in Latin America: Understanding the Past to Prepare for the Future.* Washington, DC: World Bank.

Michaels, G. 2011. "The Long-Term Consequences of Resource-Based Specialization." *Economic Journal* 121 (551): 31–57.

Organisation for Economic Co-operation and Development (OECD). 2018. *Revenue Statistics in Latin America and the Caribbean 2018.* Paris: OECD Publishing.

Pellandra, A. 2015. "The Commodity Price Boom and Regional Workers in Chile: A Natural Resources Blessing?" Unpublished.

Perry, G., and M. Olivera. 2009. "The Impact of Oil and Mining on Regional and Local Development in Colombia." CAF Working Paper 2009/06, CAF Development Bank of Latin America, Caracas.

Santos, A., and A. Werner (eds). 2015. *Peru: Staying the Course of Economic Success.* Washington, DC: International Monetary Fund.

Toscani, F. 2017. "The Impact of Natural Resource Discoveries in Latin America and the Caribbean: A Closer Look at the Case of Bolivia." IMF Working Paper No. 17/27, International Monetary Fund, Washington, DC.

van der Ploeg, F. 2011. "Natural Resources: Curse or Blessing?" *Journal of Economic Literature* 49 (2): 366–420.

Vargas, J.P.M., and S. Garriga. 2015. "Explaining Inequality and Poverty Reduction in Bolivia." IMF Working Paper No. 15/265, International Monetary Fund, Washington, DC.

Viale, C. 2015. "Distribution of Extractive Industries Income to Subnational Governments in Latin America: Comparative and Trend Analysis." Pontifical Catholic University of Peru, Lima.

ANNEX 9.1. THE LOCAL IMPACT OF NATURAL RESOURCE BOOMS IN LATIN AMERICA: METHODOLOGY

Brazil: The following equation is estimated to capture the local impact of the resource boom:

$$\Delta y_{i,\,2010} = \alpha + \beta \Delta x_{i,\,2010} + \gamma \Delta y_{i,\,2000} + \delta y_{i,2000} + \theta_{s} + \rho Z_{i} + \epsilon_{i},$$

in which $\Delta y_{i,2010}$ is the change in the dependent variable between 2000 and 2010 in municipality i and $\Delta x_{i,2010}$ is the change in the explanatory variable (natural resource production per capita measured in constant 2010 Brazilian reais) in municipality i. β is the coefficient of interest. The equation includes both the level of the dependent variable in 2000 ($y_{i,2000}$) to capture convergence effects and the change in the dependent variable between the previous census rounds (1991 to 2000, $\Delta y_{i,2000}$) to control for municipality-specific pretreatment trends. Additionally, the analysis includes state fixed effects θ_s to account for regional dynamics and a vector of geographic controls Z_i that measure, for example, whether a municipality is located on the coast. Standard errors are clustered at the state level.

Bolivia: The following simple difference-in-differences regression model is estimated using data from the 2001 and 2012 population censuses:[37]

$$y_{it} = \alpha + \gamma\, EM_i + \theta\, T_t + \rho\left(EM_i {}^* T_t\right) + X_{it}^{'}\beta + \varepsilon_{it},$$

in which y_{it} is the dependent variable, EM_i is a dummy variable equal to 1 for extractive sector municipalities, T_t is a time dummy equal to 1 in 2012, and the interaction $D_{it} = \left(EM_i {}^* T_t\right)$ is the treatment variable, so that ρ is the coefficient of interest. $X_{it}^{'}$ is a vector of municipality and time-varying covariates. A differentiation is made between mineral producers—"small" oil and gas producers, and the natural gas megacampo producers.

Because data from before 2001 are not available for Bolivia, the parallel trend assumption or control for pretreatment trends in the estimation cannot be explicitly tested. To improve identification, the control group is limited to those municipalities that have the best covariate overlap with the treatment group. In other words, the aim is to compare extractive sector municipalities to municipalities that looked very similar to them before the resource boom. To do this, an entropy balancing technique is used (Hainmueller and Xu 2013). The method assigns weights between 0 and 1 to municipalities in the control group to achieve optimal covariance overlap and is well suited to the setup with many more control municipalities than treatment municipalities.[38]

ANNEX 9.2. DETAILS OF NATURAL RESOURCE REVENUE SHARING IN LATIN AMERICA AND ELSEWHERE

Natural resource revenues are largely centralized in Chile, Ecuador, Mexico, Norway, Trinidad and Tobago, and Venezuela, with either very limited or no redistribution to subnational-level governments in producing regions. In the three case study countries and Colombia, significant revenue amounts go to subnational governments (see Viale 2015 for an overview). In Canada, provinces manage nonrenewable natural resources.

---

[37]See Toscani (2017) for more details.

[38]Entropy balancing achieves virtually perfect overlap both for the first and the second moment of the distribution. Like the now-popular synthetic control method, however, entropy balancing implicitly makes a strong linearity assumption.

Bolivia: A hydrocarbon royalty of 18 percent of revenues is levied in Bolivia. Of those, 11 percentage points go to producing departments, 6 percentage points stay with the central government, and 1 percentage point goes to the lightly populated departments of Pando and Beni. Additionally, a 32 percent hydrocarbon tax (*impuesto directo a los hidrocarburos*, or IDH) is levied and is allocated in a more complicated way. It goes to both producing and nonproducing departments as well as to municipalities, with 20 percentage points remaining with the central government. Mining royalties are distributed only to producing departments and municipalities, with an 85–15 split between the two. For more details, see IDB (2015).

Brazil: Most mineral royalties go to producing states and municipalities. For oil and gas, the allocation formula is complicated, but since the 1997 royalties law, substantial amounts of oil and gas revenues have been distributed to municipalities that either host an onshore oil and gas field or face an offshore oil and gas field. In some cases, royalties can account for more than 50 percent of a municipality's revenues.

Canada: In addition to being subject to federal and provincial corporate income taxes, natural resource income is subject to mining taxes, royalties, and land taxes at the provincial level. A fiscal stabilization program also enables the federal government to provide financial assistance to any province faced with a year-over-year decline in nonresource revenues greater than 5 percent and caused by an economic downturn. Finally, Canada has an equalization program to reduce fiscal disparities between provinces. The equalization transfers are unconditional and are determined by measuring provinces' ability to raise revenues.

Colombia: Before the 2012 reform, roughly 80 percent of royalties went directly to producer departments and municipalities, which had only 17 percent of the population. Following the 2012 reform, this amount was reduced to roughly 10 percent, with the remainder of the resources assigned to several central funds with specific goals. About 30 percent is saved in a stabilization fund, 10 percent goes to a science and innovation fund, 10 percent goes to a regional pension fund, and the remainder is allocated to subnational investment projects using a relatively complex distribution formula based on poverty levels and other factors. As a result, 1,089 municipalities received a share of commodity royalties in 2012 compared with 522 in 2011.

Norway: Government revenues from petroleum activities are transferred to the Government Pension Fund Global. Under the fiscal rule, petroleum revenues are phased into the economy gradually. Specifically, over time, government spending must not use any of the fund's capital, only its expected real return, which is currently estimated to be 3 percent. The fiscal rule also provides for petroleum revenue spending to be increased during economic downturns and decreased during economic upturns.

Peru: Overall, about 60 percent of fiscal revenues from the mining sector go to subnational governments, mainly consisting of mining sector corporate income taxes (*canon minero*) and mining royalties. There are various canons and they are only transferred to the department where production of the natural resource takes place. Resources are then further distributed within producing departments; consequently, producing provinces and municipalities receive a large share of the pie. See Santos and Werner (2015, Chapter 10) for more details.

PART IV

Strengthening the Fiscal Framework

Modernizing Fiscal Institutions

PAULO MEDAS

Improving Brazil's short- and long-term prospects depends critically on curing the fiscal malaise and restoring debt sustainability, notably by addressing structural fiscal idiosyncrasies and modernizing fiscal institutions. Brazil's fiscal framework is complex. Budgetary rigidity resulting from many competing constitutional and legal mandates and rules, including excessive revenue earmarking and mandatory spending, limits the fiscal policy's ability to adjust to shocks or changes in priorities, and promotes procyclicality and a deficit bias. Although politically difficult, a revamp of the institutional framework is necessary to limit the deficit bias, improve spending efficiency, and increase accountability. Particularly important would be the introduction of a medium-term expenditure framework based on a deep transformation of the annual budget process, including substantially reducing its rigidity, modernizing the public financial management framework, and designing new fiscal rules anchored by a debt target.

AN OVERVIEW OF HOW INSTITUTIONS EVOLVED IN BRAZIL

As part of Brazil's transition from military dictatorship to democracy, in 1988 the country introduced a new constitution that represented a major institutional change and affected many areas of public policy. The 1988 Constitution introduced significant social mandates, including a requirement that a share of tax revenue be earmarked for health, education, and social security.[1] The universalization of social rights, particularly social security, created large entitlement expenditures. Between 1988 and 2004, social security spending increased from 2.5 percent of GDP to 7.2 percent of GDP because of measures that broadened coverage and increased the system's generosity. Expenditure on pensions has sharply increased because of demographics and minimum wage increases.[2]

---

[1]Over the years, several changes were made to the constitution regarding the precise legal mechanism to ensure a minimum of spending, either via a minimum share of GDP or via earmarking of revenue.

[2]Welfare spending increased significantly with the enactment of the Social Assistance Organic Law in 1993 and the creation of the antipoverty fund in 2001.

The 1988 Constitution also significantly deepened the decentralization process. For the first time, municipalities were recognized as separate members of the federation. The constitution devolved significant expenditure responsibilities to states and municipalities and provided funding through transfers from the federal government—including a substantial share of income tax and industrial production tax revenues. Important tax bases were devolved to subnational governments, and the country's revenue-sharing system was reformed. At the same time, the constitution introduced expenditure requirements (education, health) for subnational levels of government. The 27 states (including the Federal District) and more than 5,000 municipalities together account for more than one-third of total government spending and revenue collection. Revenue-mobilization capacity is concentrated in the more prosperous states and municipalities of the south and southeast, and some equalization of expenditure capacity has been pursued through mandated revenue sharing. Political and administrative decentralization are also sizable. Each subnational jurisdiction has its own directly elected legislative and executive branches, as well as an independent judiciary.

A deep economic crisis and fiscal distress at all levels of government in the 1990s led to calls for further institutional reforms. The early 1990s was a period of hyperinflation, out-of-control fiscal accounts, and economic contraction. The fiscal imbalances were reflected at all levels of government. The central government had to bail out the subnational governments several times.[3] These imbalances led to a demand for significant changes to policies and institutions. In the second half of the 1990s and early 2000s, Brazil moved toward a new set of macro policies centered on three pillars: fiscal responsibility, inflation targeting, and exchange rate flexibility. These policies required fiscal reforms to achieve a necessary large fiscal adjustment and ensure fiscal discipline at all levels of government, a condition for macroeconomic stability.

A key pillar of the new framework was the introduction of the Fiscal Responsibility Law (FRL) in 2000. The FRL was created to change the way fiscal policy is made and to promote fiscal transparency and accountability. It requires a qualified majority for approval and modification, and it is binding for all entities of the public sector at all levels of government. The FRL is mainly based on procedural rules and involved significant changes to budget preparation, implementation, and reporting.

Fiscal targets were introduced at all levels of government. To meet the objective of containing fiscal deficits and rising debt, the FRL introduced overall targets and limits on the wage bill, debt, and guarantees for all levels of government.[4] In practice, the primary surplus for the public sector and the inflation targets have

---

[3]Relations between the federal government and the states are marked by a history of bailouts until the late 1990s. The largest rescue operations by the federal government include bailouts in 1989, 1993, 1994, and the last one in the late 1990s (Law 9496 of 1997). See Bevilaqua (2000) and Mora (2002).

[4]The FRL does not specify quantitative targets or limits for all items, but it does require that they be specified in separate legislation and regulations. For example, the primary surplus targets

become the key anchors of macro-fiscal policy. In addition, the FRL and other legislation include procedures to monitor implementation of targets and respective sanctions. The law also set restrictions on relations between government agencies and levels of government to prevent bailouts, monetization of deficits, and misuses of public financial institutions. In particular, it prohibits direct deficit financing by the central bank, and state-owned financial institutions are prohibited from lending money to their controlling agencies.

The FRL also promoted stronger controls and transparency at all levels of government. The specific institutional framework for budget planning, execution, and reporting required by the FRL also improved reporting, accounting, and transparency in more general terms. Reporting on fiscal developments is more robust and frequent, and the public has better access to fiscal data. This information includes bimonthly reports on budgetary implementation and an ongoing effort to improve and standardize public accounting and fiscal statistics for all levels of government.

The annual budget process also evolved. The Annual Budget Guidelines Law (Lei de Diretrizes Orçamentárias, or LDO), applicable to all levels of government, sets fiscal targets for the year and indicative targets for another two years. It includes a fiscal risks annex and actuarial evaluations of public programs (like social security). It also incorporates budgetary procedures that compensate for the lack of a modern organic budget law. However, because the LDO is approved annually, some legal uncertainty arises, as budgetary rules can change every year. The FRL also introduced several rules to increase the transparency of the annual budget law (for all levels of government) and improve controls.

FISCAL FRAMEWORK UNDER PRESSURE

In 2014–16, Brazil experienced one of its worst economic recessions in history. This recession was unlike past crises because it did not include high inflation or an external current account crisis. Brazil is now facing recovery. The public sector has accumulated large fiscal deficits, and public debt has risen close to historically high levels. A question is, to what degree did weaknesses in institutions contribute to policies that led to or intensified the crisis? Although fiscal institutions cannot guarantee good policies, there is a realization that the institutional framework was not solid enough and further improvements can be made.[5] This recovery period

---

are set every year at the beginning of the budget process. Congress sets debt limits for all levels of government.

[5]Sound fiscal institutions can help achieve better policies and ensure greater accountability of policymakers. North (1990) defines institutions as the rules of the game in society, or more formally, as the humanly devised constraints that shape human interaction. They can be either formal (for example, rules) or informal (for example, conventions and codes of behavior). There is widespread recognition that fiscal institutions have important effects on fiscal policy outcomes (for example, Poterba and von Hagen 1999). A well-known example is the role of budgetary institutions in preventing large and persistent deficits.

Box 10.1. Budgetary Rigidities

Because of its many rigidities, Brazil's budget process is markedly complex. This complexity has been exacerbated by the continuous creation of additional mandatory spending and revenue earmarking during booms (Figure 10.1.1).

Mandatory spending has averaged more than 80 percent of total federal spending. However, about half of so-called discretionary spending is inflexible. Social benefits represent the largest share. The education and health sectors also benefit from mandatory spending. Because mandatory spending continues to expand at a fast pace while discretionary spending is curtailed, the situation has deteriorated.

Revenue earmarking is also prevalent in the federal budget. Almost 80 percent of all revenue is earmarked, including contributions for the payment of pensions and transfers to subnational governments (Figure 10.1.2). For example, the constitution (Article 212) provides that at least 18 percent of tax revenue is to be allocated to education at the federal level (and 25 percent at the subnational level). A 2008 study found almost 400 norms that earmarked revenues to specific spending items (about 30 are in the constitution).

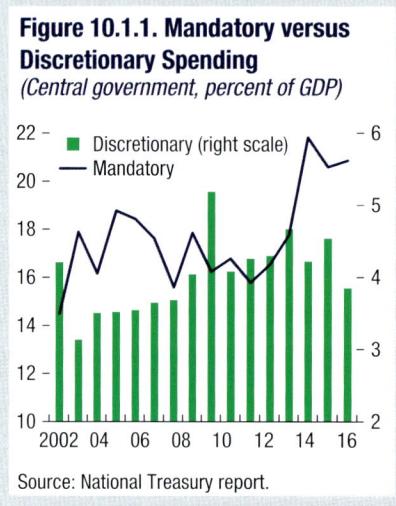

Figure 10.1.1. Mandatory versus Discretionary Spending
(Central government, percent of GDP)

Source: National Treasury report.

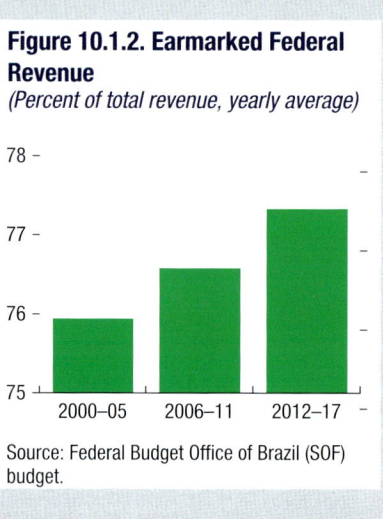

Figure 10.1.2. Earmarked Federal Revenue
(Percent of total revenue, yearly average)

Source: Federal Budget Office of Brazil (SOF) budget.

is an opportune time to assess possible weaknesses and determine how to further enhance the institutional framework. This process has already started, as discussed later in this chapter.

The current fiscal framework is complex and rigid. One of its main problems is the high degree of budgetary rigidities that result from the proliferation of competing constitutional and legal mandates and rules. The budget process is highly constrained by excessive revenue earmarking and mandatory spending, and the share of discretionary spending within the budget has become limited (Box 10.1). While these mandates may have policy and social objectives, they significantly constrain the flexibility of fiscal policy to adjust to shocks or changes in priorities. They also contribute to procyclical policies and a deficit bias. Public investment also becomes a victim of these rigidities because it is the main category

Box 10.1. Budgetary Rigidities   *(continued)*

Part of the rigidities comes from indexation. The most important item is pensions (Figure 10.1.3). Many pensions (about 70 percent) are linked to the minimum wage, and the remaining are linked to inflation. The minimum wage itself is indexed to inflation and real GDP growth, except the minimum wage cannot fall. The rise in the minimum wage also has important impacts on wages at the subnational government level.

All these rigidities tend to contribute to a deficit bias because they promote rising spending during upswings (including creating new earmarking) that is difficult to undo when revenue growth falters.

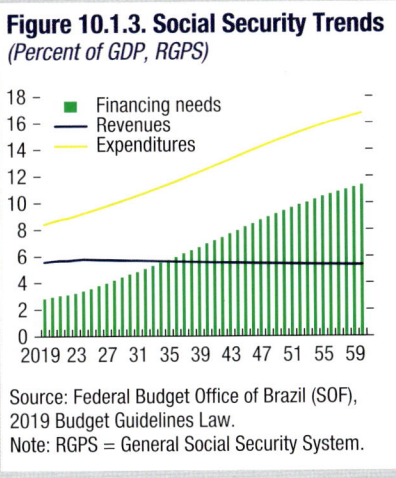

Figure 10.1.3. Social Security Trends
(Percent of GDP, RGPS)

Source: Federal Budget Office of Brazil (SOF), 2019 Budget Guidelines Law.
Note: RGPS = General Social Security System.

of expenditure that can be quickly cut when mandatory spending grows faster than revenues.

The effectiveness and credibility of the rules-based fiscal framework have been undermined by its uneven implementation and a series of ad hoc adjustments to the rules themselves. The existence of many rules at the national and subnational levels, together with the budgetary rigidities, make the system excessively complex. This situation has led to either the outright breach of and ad hoc changes to the rules, or attempts to evade them by taking advantage of lack of clarity in statistical or accounting standards and weak monitoring. Because of such practices, the effectiveness and credibility of the institutional framework have weakened, which in turn has put Brazil's public sector in a vulnerable position.

The rules were undermined by an expansion of government activities outside the framework. Coverage of the fiscal target was reduced by the exclusion of spending items and the largest state-owned enterprises. An investment adjustor was used to exclude part of the investment spending from the target. The two largest state-owned enterprises, Petrobras and Eletrobras, were also excluded from the fiscal targets and statistics beginning in 2009, just as they embarked on ambitious borrowing plans. In addition, public banks were used to conduct fiscal policy outside the fiscal rules perimeter. The government started to issue debt directly to the Brazilian Development Bank (Banco Nacional de Desenvolvimento Econômico e Social) to boost its lending capacity, significantly expanding quasi-fiscal operations. This policy, although successful in helping manage the 2008–09 global financial crisis, remained in place and contributed to rising public debt.

Lack of fiscal transparency, weak monitoring, and delays in recognizing spending also contributed to the problems. The Federal Court of Accounts identified arrears arising from delays in reimbursing public banks for the payment of social security benefits and the accrual of interest subsidies by banks. In addition, increases in floating debt (*restos a pagar*) also undermined the effectiveness of the target. Implementation of the rules at the subnational level has also been uneven. As the IMF's 2016 Fiscal Transparency Evaluation notes, it has been difficult to assess whether subnational governments have met the FRL rules, especially on wages. Similarly, the rules and regulations did not prevent some states from borrowing considerably during the boom years, leaving them in a fragile position for managing the latest economic recession. The mismanagement of public money, including widespread corruption in some public enterprises, has also brought to the fore weaknesses in governance and accountability, which is particularly important in some key areas where the information is opaque or large natural resources are involved.

Medium-term fiscal planning remains a key weakness. The budget process is fragmented and characterized by a strong focus on managing its implementation in the short term. The medium-term implications of today's policies or potential risks receive little consideration; some of the FRL requirements are met formally, but not in substance. Efforts have been made to strengthen medium-term planning through the multiyear plans intended to provide guidance for the annual budget laws. In practice, however, the key elements of sound medium-term fiscal planning are missing. There are no clear medium-term fiscal goals (for example, size of public debt). The planning and budget processes are not based on realistic assessments of medium-term financial constraints and spending plans. Finally, the management of fiscal risks, and their implications for fiscal policy, is limited, contributing to the accumulation of insufficient fiscal buffers during booms and the need for a procyclical fiscal contraction in the most recent period.

AN AGENDA FOR THE FUTURE

This section discusses how the institutional framework could be improved to help deliver better policies and greater accountability and reduce risks. While it is not possible to cover all the issues in one chapter given the many complexities involved, proposals are presented for some of the main areas. Among the core objectives are (1) reducing the strong deficit bias, (2) promoting more efficient spending, and (3) increasing government accountability. Given the large vulnerabilities, this section also discusses how to develop a framework more robust to economic cycles and large shocks; that is, how to reduce risks that can have large economic costs.

Budget Process: Reduce Rigidities and Strengthen Medium-Term Focus

Enhancing the budget process needs to involve increasing flexibility, improving the medium-term perspective, and strengthening accountability. At present, preparation of the annual budget is focusing on allocating the limited share of discretionary expenditure, because most expenditures are driven by revenue earmarking and spending mandates. In practice, the budget process is heavily influenced by short-term considerations, with all attention on bimonthly spending authorizations issued by the executive based on the latest revenue developments. This leaves little room for strategic management of the budget and its medium-term implications.[6] These weaknesses can be hidden during times of economic and tax revenue buoyancy, but they become evident when the economic cycle turns and budget revenues fall short of expectations.

Reducing the degree of budget rigidities would yield substantial benefits. Some of the revenue earmarking and spending mandates may have sound objectives, such as protecting education and health spending, but they have major shortcomings. Even when well-intended, they can have a significant detrimental impact on fiscal outcomes—including leading to excessive deficits—as discussed earlier. Reducing budget rigidities would also help improve the quality of policies by allowing greater flexibility to adjust policies to changing priorities and economic conditions. In addition, increasing competition for resources would create greater incentives to spend efficiently. In particular, the heavy focus on inputs distracts from assessing whether the resources are being used efficiently; for example, is higher spending on education leading to better education outcomes? Better options are available for ensuring appropriate funding of priorities that at the same time foster greater transparency and accountability. A crucial aspect explored next is the need to develop a medium-term approach to the budget process that incorporates a regular review of spending priorities and efficiency.

Developing a medium-term expenditure framework (MTEF) is a critical step toward improving fiscal management and supporting the fiscal rules. MTEFs have been introduced by many countries to address the shortcomings of annual budgeting (Box 10.2). Implementation will require formalization of the strategic phase of the budget preparation process. The baseline scenario and a set of new measures should be presented to decision makers ahead of setting the annual fiscal

---

[6]This lack of space is especially problematic because the extensive use of mandatory and indexed expenditures implies significant pressures on future budgets. Moreover, investments do not always acknowledge the operating costs they will generate in the future. Ongoing efforts aim to build up institutional capacity to provide strategic inputs to the overall budget process and develop medium-term fiscal planning.

Box 10.2. Medium-Term Expenditure Frameworks

Medium-term expenditure frameworks (MTEFs) have been introduced to mitigate the shortcomings of annual budgeting. Since Australia first published its "Report on the Forward Estimates of Budget Outlays" in 1983, more than 60 countries have introduced some sort of MTEF to enforce fiscal discipline, strengthen the strategic allocation of resources, and enhance resource predictability for line ministries by providing decision makers with an assessment of the full cost of potential decisions. Annual budgeting often leads to short-term incremental decision making, which fails to assess the full cost of policy decisions. By providing a medium-term assessment of current and new policies, MTEFs can help mitigate those shortcomings.

An MTEF is both a technical and an institutional tool for managing fiscal policy. An MTEF is not merely a technical instrument designed to forecast fiscal aggregates in the medium term; it is an institutional framework for setting multiyear fiscal objectives and ensuring they are respected in budget formulation, approval, and execution. To play a significant role in policymaking, MTEF preparation should involve cabinet-level decision making. Implementation of an MTEF will gradually transform the budget process and—for the most sophisticated models—ultimately lead to multiyear budgeting, as in France and the United Kingdom.

In times of economic crisis and fiscal distress, MTEFs are a powerful tool for setting a new fiscal path and defining the measures to achieve it. Preparing an MTEF allows for a reassessment of the current fiscal outlook and the design of a plan that can be implemented and monitored into the medium term. Evidence from the global financial crisis suggests that countries with strong fiscal planning institutions such as MTEFs—but also fiscal rules and efficiency management tools such as spending reviews—have (1) generally been quicker to formulate and adopt comprehensive fiscal adjustment strategies, (2) tended to protect public investment to a greater degree during the fiscal consolidation process, and (3) maintained their original fiscal adjustment plans despite additional negative shocks.[7]

Separating current policies from new policies is a cornerstone of MTEF preparation. This process always entails development of a baseline, which is based on the projected revenues and costs of policies and programs already approved, before new policy options are discussed. This sequence requires significant knowledge of the cost drivers of each public policy. Even though the general concept of a baseline appears intuitive, technical challenges can be significant. Each country has developed its own standards for defining current policies. In Sweden, a strict set of methodological rules has been formulated for each public policy, with the intention of avoiding inappropriate manipulation in calculating the baseline.

To be effective, an MTEF must influence the decision-making process. Integrating a medium-term approach into the preparation of the annual budget inevitably triggers some changes in existing processes. Countries that have fully implemented detailed MTEFs have transformed the traditional annual budgeting dialogue with ministries into a full debate about the medium-term cost of public policies. In the case of a fixed and binding framework, such as in France or the United Kingdom, the MTEF even sets detailed expenditure targets for more than a year.

---

[7]IMF (2014).

target in the LDO. New and corrective measures should be costed over the medium term to estimate their potential fiscal impact. This approach emphasizes the merits of measures that produce effects in the medium to long term. Decisions should be made not only on the target itself but also on the fiscal strategy that supports it, including the main measures required. This process would provide greater credibility to the targets and rules.

Publication of the fiscal strategy would also increase government accountability. Many countries publish their fiscal strategy in a dedicated macro-fiscal policy statement that presents (1) medium-term economic forecasts and their underlying assumptions, (2) fiscal projections, and (3) a qualitative discussion of the fiscal targets and strategies adopted by the government, including measures needed to achieve the objectives. Some countries complement this publication with additional information. For example, Sweden includes a quantitative discussion of new measures (with detailed medium-term costs) and Australia includes a fiscal risk statement. In Brazil, additional information could involve improving the supporting documentation attached to the LDO by including a fiscal policy statement.

Over time, moving to an MTEF will require deeper reorganization of the existing framework. Countries that have fully implemented an MTEF have gone as far as discussing resource allocations with ministries into the medium term. International experience suggests Brazil has two main options. The first involves an indicative and rolling framework (Australia, Sweden) in which the budget is discussed annually but decision making is based on medium-term costing. The second option involves a fixed and binding framework (France, United Kingdom) in which resource allocation for future years is determined on a periodic basis. Such options would entail a deep transformation of Brazil's annual budget process, including substantially reducing budget rigidities and adapting Brazil's legal framework.

One important step would be to modernize the Public Financial Management framework to generate flexibility, accountability, and efficiency. Brazil's volatile macroeconomic environment calls for a more flexible and modern framework. At the same time, improved mechanisms will be needed to ensure accountability, transparency, and the overall performance of public policies. This route would provide an opportunity to revisit the core processes of budgeting and expenditure management. In recent years, many emerging markets have focused on strengthening macro-fiscal institutions, such as fiscal rules, medium-term fiscal frameworks, and management of fiscal risks. Although such reforms are of great use for fiscal policy design and management, they cannot come to full fruition as long as they are built on outdated budgeting and expenditure management institutions. Most advanced economies have adopted second-generation institutions after deeply revising their basic budgeting frameworks.

New institutions should focus on improving the efficiency of public spending, including by introducing regular review of public expenditures. The medium-term approach to budgeting entails building institutions focused on delivering good-quality public spending. In the United Kingdom, MTEF preparation is fully integrated with a review process—the Spending Review—that covers all public policies. Setting a regular review of spending priorities in Brazil could ensure that key priorities are protected while providing flexibility to adjust as circumstances change. Governments could announce at the beginning of their mandates the priorities for the next years within the context of a full-fledged medium-term fiscal framework. Such an approach would promote accountability because governments would need to abide by the stated goals and mandates (for example, improve school enrollment or health standards). At the same time, the priorities would be revised at the beginning of each government mandate and funding changed accordingly. Modifications should be based on expenditure reviews and be linked to strategies to improve spending efficiency.[8]

The development of a detailed MTEF is also an opportunity to revisit the role of the planning function. Ensuring consistency between the qualitative and economic assessment of investment projects and the identification of available funds through the MTEF process is important. Greater attention could be given to public investment management given the limited fiscal space and the many infrastructure needs. As in other areas, the existing framework seems strong in theory, but practices are weak. The medium-term framework would allow for more realistic alignment between planning, budgeting, and the availability of public funding. Other improvements include (1) providing better coordination between federal and subnational governments in investment planning and review of funding mechanisms; (2) building subnational public investment management capacity and reducing the fragmentation of federal funding; (3) strengthening and standardizing procedures for project preparation, appraisal, and selection; and (4) enhancing project management capacity and accountability.

A Rules-Based Framework: Adjusting to the New Expenditure Rule

Brazil's rules-based framework did not fully deliver the intended results for several reasons. Fiscal rules are generally used to achieve two key policy objectives. One is to reduce the known "deficit bias" and ensure long-term debt sustainability. This means preventing governments from defaulting on their debts or running payment arrears (for example, not paying wages or suppliers on time). Another key objective is to contribute to macroeconomic stability. Fiscal policy should help smooth economic cycles—that is, promote stable economic growth—and avoid abrupt changes in the provision of public services. In Brazil, the dominant motivation for the rules seems to have been to constrain the deficit bias. Indeed, the introduction of the FRL was part of a significant effort to restore public debt to a declining trend. However, gross public debt has remained

---

[8]Spending reviews have been developed in several countries (for example, Australia, Canada, France, the Netherlands, and the United Kingdom). Such reviews can support the setting of priorities as they look at the effectiveness and efficiency of programs under current and alternative funding levels. The Ministry of Finance holds final responsibility for the spending review.

Figure 10.1. Brazil: Public Gross Debt
(Percent of GDP)

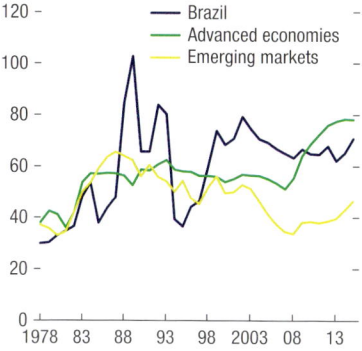

Source: IMF, Historical Public Database.

Figure 10.2. Policy Lending and Overall Balances
(Percent of GDP)

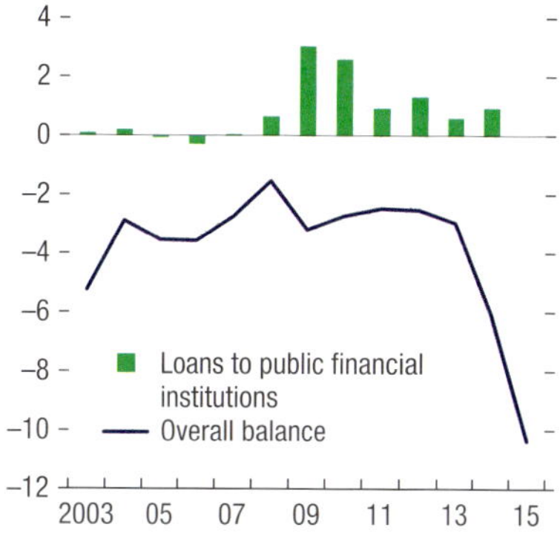

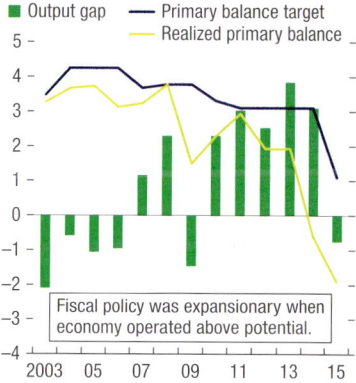

Source: IMF, Historical Public Database.

Figure 10.3. Primary Balance Target and the Economic Cycle
(Percent of GDP)

Sources: IMF, *World Economic Outlook*; Federal Budget Office of Brazil (SOF), Budget Guidelines Law.

relatively high when compared with other emerging markets. More recently, debt has been rising at a fast pace, reflecting a reduction in the primary surplus target and other factors as previously discussed (Figures 10.1 and 10.2).

The rules-based fiscal framework also did not prevent procyclical policies from being enacted. Fiscal policy tended to be tighter in periods of lower growth or when the output gap was negative (actual output below potential; Figure 10.3), except in 2009, when it was loosened. Afterward, as the economy rebounded, fiscal policy remained loose. This deficit bias was partly related to budgetary rigidities but also likely reflected the perception that the increase in revenues (during the commodity boom) would be permanent. This bias exacerbated the economic cycles and left Brazil vulnerable to recent economic shocks. Because of the lack of buffers, and with the overall deficit and debt rising fast, Brazil is now forced to adopt procyclical fiscal contraction to bring debt back to a sustainable path. Although necessary given the unsustainable debt dynamics, it is highly undesirable from the perspective of promoting stable economic growth.

The latest fiscal crisis has led to a renewed effort to improve the fiscal rules, starting with the introduction of an expenditure ceiling. This new rule was introduced to reverse the large deterioration in the public accounts in previous years. Robust expenditure growth has been a key driver of tensions and has contributed to a significant increase in public debt. Under the new fiscal rule, central government primary expenditures cannot grow faster than inflation. The rule will last for 20 years, but it can be revised to some degree after 10 years. This implies that primary expenditure as a share of GDP will have to be reduced significantly over the next two decades. This approach is necessary to improve the public accounts and put debt dynamics on a more sustainable path. However, implementation will be enormously challenging given the pressures from spending mandates (including pensions) and revenue earmarking.[9]

The chapter now turns to a proposal for strengthening the framework on a more permanent basis. As discussed, the two key objectives for fiscal rules are to ensure (1) long-term fiscal and debt sustainability; and (2) that fiscal policy contributes to macroeconomic stability, that is, reduces policy-driven volatility. A well-designed rules-based framework can help achieve these policy objectives. International experience shows that the rules should be simple and easy to monitor. Simplicity would mean reducing the number of rules and avoiding complexities that undermine their effectiveness and credibility. A specific proposal is presented here (although other variations are possible) that builds on the existing legal framework. First, a debt anchor for the public sector should be set that would help stabilize medium-term policies and ensure sustainability. Second, an operational rule should be introduced to ensure that the debt anchor is met and that procyclicality of fiscal policy is reduced. This could be done by making the expenditure rule permanent in a revised form. The framework could be made simpler by reducing the number of existing rules or restrictions on fiscal policy (Table 10.1).

A debt anchor is easy to monitor and would provide greater ability to manage shocks. The focus on the annual primary surplus has proved to be insufficient for controlling the growth of gross public debt.[10] Adopting a debt ceiling would strengthen the fiscal framework because a ceiling is a simple rule that is linked to debt-sustainability objectives. However, because the future is uncertain—countries can face large shocks—it would be wise to set a lower (prudent or safe) debt ceiling. The objective should be to keep debt below a "distress" level beyond which debt dynamics become difficult to control because it would require an unrealistically large fiscal effort to revert. Such a level would permit a gradual

---

[9]The new expenditure rule has already involved changing the minimum spending levels for health and education.

[10]This issue is common to other countries. In the euro area, for example, recent reforms strengthened the role of the debt ceiling because the initial heavy focus on fiscal deficits proved unsuccessful for containing debt (Eyraud and Wu 2015). Debt dynamics can be heavily influenced by factors other than the fiscal balance, such as stock-flow adjustments (for example, valuation changes) and off-budget operations, as has been the experience in Brazil.

Table 10.1. Fiscal Rules and Other Restrictions on Fiscal Management

Expenditure ceiling	Primary expenditures (with some exceptions) at the federal level can only grow with inflation (no real growth) until 2036.
"Golden rule"	Intended to contain indebtedness by the government by only allowing borrowing to fund capital expenditures. However, the definition of the rule in Brazil allows for borrowing above capital expenditures.
Primary surplus	Set every year in the budget guidelines law (LDO). It applies to all nonfinancial public sector entities with the exception of the two largest state-owned enterprises.
Debt limits at all levels of government	Never implemented at the federal level.
Wage bill limits	Sets limits on size of wage bill at all levels of government as a percentage of certain revenues.
Limits to guarantees	Applies to all levels of government.
Contracts between the federal government and some subnational governments	These "financial programs" were established at the time of the latest restructuring of subnational debt. The contracts set limits on debt and can involve other restrictions until subnational governments repay the federal government.

Source: Authors' research.

adjustment to shocks and the adoption of countercyclical policies. If the debt level breaches the safe debt ceiling, there would be time to take measures (mandated by law) to gradually reduce debt, avoiding the need for disruptive fiscal tightening.[11]

A multiyear expenditure ceiling rule, with periodic revisions, could supplement the debt anchor. For example, setting a stable path for an expenditure growth ceiling over three to four years, consistent with the debt target, would help preserve debt sustainability and add a stabilizing component to fiscal policy. Expenditures would follow a smooth and predictable path because they would not need to adjust to yearly shocks. However, to be effective and credible, such a rule will require that medium-term fiscal management be strengthened, rigidities be reduced, and fiscal buffers be rebuilt. In particular, development of a more sophisticated MTEF should be coordinated with the fiscal rules since they reinforce each other. Sweden provides a good example of an MTEF that was specifically designed to accompany a rule. It sets the total expenditure ceilings two years in advance. To ensure they are met, the estimated cost of existing policies must not breach any yearly ceiling and must also accommodate growing safety margins.

Brazil's high degree of decentralization also requires that fiscal policy be coordinated and that consistent rules be in place at the different levels of government.

---

[11]A prudent or safe debt ceiling should be set to ensure that even under adverse scenarios for debt dynamics, fiscal policy can stabilize or reduce debt with a high probability in a reasonable time. Because the likelihood of losing control of debt dynamics rises with debt itself, the upper bound of the safe debt zone must be sufficiently low to accommodate large adverse shocks without calling into question the government's capacity to generate the surpluses required to bring debt back to some long-term average level within a reasonable time. See Debrun (2015) and Fall and Fournier (2015).

This has been a thorny challenge in Brazil. Important advances have been made on the budget process and fiscal reporting at the subnational level, partly driven by the FRL. In addition, several rules (wages, debt, guarantees) and financial agreements (bailout contracts) between the federal government and states should facilitate overall coordination and prevent the buildup of fiscal imbalances. However, uneven implementation of the framework and weaknesses in transparency have led to several acute problems that emerged in the recent crises. Some states were allowed to build up large debt during the economic and commodity price upswing despite the existing restrictions on borrowing and constant monitoring by the federal government. In addition, subnational rules, especially the limits on wages, were not effectively monitored, including by external auditors. The institutions were not strong enough to withstand pressures to increase spending.

The rules-based institutional framework for the subnational level can be improved, especially by strengthening transparency and effectively implementing and monitoring the rules. The federal government and Congress have the tools to contain the accumulation of fiscal and debt imbalances at the subnational level—quantitative and procedural rules allow it.[12] The challenge is to build greater safeguards against political pressures for more spending. One important aspect is to give greater emphasis to risk management, which would help promote lower levels of debt and more stable fiscal policy. In that context, it would be important to review whether the debt limits are too lax and could let states become vulnerable to shocks. As discussed above, defining safe debt levels would help, particularly at the subnational level, where governments may have less capacity to manage volatility. A more intricate issue is whether the existing assignment of revenue sources and spending responsibilities creates structural imbalances or exposes subnationals to too much risk that they cannot manage alone. This issue would require reviewing existing intergovernmental relations, which is beyond the scope of this chapter.

Fiscal Transparency and Accountability

Fiscal transparency is a critical element of effective fiscal management. IMF (2012) defines fiscal transparency as "the clarity, reliability, frequency, timeliness, and relevance of public fiscal reporting and the openness to the public of the government's fiscal policy-making process."[13] Fiscal transparency helps ensure that governments' economic decisions are informed by a shared and accurate assess-

---

[12]These rules include limits on the debt level and external contracts that need to be approved by Congress. Most subnational governments are also not able to borrow without guarantees by the federal government. In addition, the bailout contracts between the federal level and states are another mechanism for coordinating annual budgets.

[13]*Clarity* refers to the ease with which these reports can be understood by users; *reliability* refers to the extent to which these reports reflect the government's true financial position; *frequency* refers to the regularity with which reports are published; *timeliness* refers to the time lag involved in the dissemination of these reports; *relevance* refers to the extent to which these reports provide users with the information they need to make effective decisions; and *openness* refers to the ease with

ment of the current fiscal position, the costs and benefits of any policy changes, and the potential risks to the fiscal outlook. Fiscal transparency also provides legislatures and citizens with the information they need to hold governments accountable for their fiscal performance and the use of public resources.

Brazil has a high degree of transparency in many areas. Its debt management office scores highly in evaluations of openness toward investors, and the country ranks seventh in the world in the International Budget Partnership's latest survey of budgetary openness, placing it above several advanced economies. It is one of the founders of the Global Initiative for Fiscal Transparency. The Fiscal Transparency Evaluation performed by the IMF in 2016 also highlighted several strengths, including efforts to produce data for all levels of government.[14] Fiscal statistics encompass the general government sector and recognize most of its assets and liabilities. Fiscal reports are published in a frequent and timely manner, and annual financial statements are audited. Extensive budgetary information is made available to the public through websites and online databases.

Notwithstanding the advances made in past decades, significant weaknesses have undermined the quality of the government's fiscal reporting and accountability. The information on public sector accounts is not complete or fully transparent, contributing to the loss of credibility of the rules-based framework as noted previously.[15] Information on the role of Brazil's public banks and nonfinancial state-owned enterprises (SOEs) in implementing public policies is lacking. This shortcoming is important in Brazil given the complex and opaque interactions among the different levels of government, large public banks, and SOEs. These relationships often involve large fiscal risks that are not well understood or widely disseminated. Widespread corruption scandals have occurred in SOEs. Some of the problems go beyond fiscal transparency and will require efforts to strengthen governance more generally, including reducing the impunity for mismanagement of public resources.

A central objective should be to better communicate the key elements of fiscal policy and fiscal risks. Although Brazil provides a wealth of fiscal information, it does not systematically provide summary documents that explain developments across the entire public sector, the main risks to the budget, and how they relate to the government's priorities. Relatedly, information on medium-term fiscal policy goals and challenges is lacking. Budget documents do not provide a clear

---

which the public can understand, influence, and hold governments accountable for their fiscal policy decisions.

[14]See Fiscal Transparency section, IMF.org.

[15]For example, although full accounting balance sheets are published by the federal and other governments, the published balance sheet for general government includes only debt and financial assets. Among the missing items are accounts payable, including floating debt (*restos a pagar*), and civil service pensions. Given the importance of SOEs and public banks, it would also be important to publish fiscal statistics for the entire nonfinancial public sector (that is, including Eletrobras and Petrobras) and for the entire public sector (including Banco Nacional de Desenvolvimento Econômico e Social, Caixa Econômica Federal, and Banco do Brasil).

picture of the objectives of fiscal policy over the medium term, including for key fiscal aggregates like public debt, and information on medium- to long-term fiscal challenges is limited. Publication of the medium-term fiscal strategy, as discussed earlier, would be a positive step. Another important element to building transparency would be to adopt international standards on macroeconomic and fiscal statistics and mechanisms to ensure they are followed. This effort would include setting up a permanent interagency committee for harmonized classifications in macroeconomic statistics. The credibility of statistics would be increased and understanding by the public in general would be enhanced.

Strengthening external oversight of fiscal accounts and policies would also improve accountability. There have been positive developments in these areas. The Court of Accounts is providing greater scrutiny, and an independent fiscal institution was created in late 2016, under the federal Senate, to promote greater fiscal transparency at the central government level. However, further action is needed to ensure that external audit agencies have enough capacity to fulfill their mandates at the different levels of government. Many of the efforts underway to strengthen governance and reduce corruption need to be consolidated. This agenda will have to go beyond the fiscal area. Nevertheless, it will be important to ensure greater governance in several key areas that have been vulnerable, including procurement processes and governance of SOEs and public banks. More effective monitoring and reduction of impunity, for example through Comptroller General audits of the use of federal funds by municipalities, can have a positive impact.[16]

Improving Management of Fiscal Risks

The analysis of fiscal risks helps in the design of prudent fiscal policy. The greater the risks faced by the government, the larger the buffers it needs. Once the medium-term fiscal plans have been made, risks must be identified, monitored, and mitigated so that the government can meet its fiscal targets, despite a variety of small shocks. The analysis of risks can also help authorities prepare in advance for how to respond to large shocks (for example, if the recovery is much slower than forecast). The reforms of the 1990s and 2000s improved the management of risks. As noted above, the FRL improved fiscal control and transparency at all levels of government. Public debt management was improved to reduce risks. Tight regulations also ensured Brazil entered the recession with a broadly sound financial sector.

The management of fiscal risks, nevertheless, could be enhanced to better prepare Brazil for large shocks and improve fiscal management. Several vulnerabilities were not addressed and policies were enacted that involve large fiscal risks.

---

[16]Avis, Ferraz, and Finan (2018) find that being audited reduces future corruption by 8 percent while also increasing by 20 percent the likelihood of experiencing a subsequent legal action. The reduction in corruption occurs mostly because audits increase the perceived nonelectoral costs of engaging in corruption.

For example, gross public debt remained high. Repeated loosening of the financial restrictions on subnational governments late in the first decade of the 2000s allowed some states and municipalities to enter the recession with weak finances.[17] Public banks and SOEs greatly expanded their operations and their liabilities. Moreover, insufficient attention was paid to monitoring the government's overall exposure to risk, taking account of the interdependencies between the many different sources of risk. Finally, published fiscal information suffered from several shortcomings. The absence of fully developed medium- and long-term fiscal projections meant that tax and spending decisions were made in the absence of good information about the implications beyond the budget year. In addition, although the government disclosed information on fiscal risks every year in the LDO, the reported information did not provide policymakers or the public with a clear and comprehensive view of the risks to which public finances were exposed.

Ultimately, the goal of risk management is to improve the disclosure, monitoring, and management of fiscal risks throughout the public sector. These improvements will help the government achieve its fiscal targets and policy objectives in a volatile environment, and better understand the implications from the highly complex relationship between the federal government, states, public banks, and SOEs. But the most important goals of risk management are to avoid major shocks and, if they do occur, to manage them. Because the risks can never be eliminated, the safe debt level discussed above is critical.

Individual fiscal risks are generally monitored, but no group adequately monitors aggregate fiscal risks. There is no "risk unit" responsible for assessing the magnitude of the government's overall exposure to risk, determining the major sources of risk, considering the interdependencies between the risks, and judging whether the risks are being adequately managed. But such a risk unit could be responsible for the central oversight of risk and could boost risk management. This group would be able to critically assess the main risks, inform the decision-making process, and propose mitigation strategies as needed (or alert the responsible agency to do so).[18] But the success of such a unit would also depend on strengthening the capacity to monitor individual risks. Although some areas of the institutional framework for managing risks are well developed, like the debt management unit, further strengthening is needed in other areas, for example, greater coordination and capacity in managing and mitigating risks posed by large public companies and public banks.

Improving risk-related information on public finances would allow for more informed decisions by policymakers and public debate. Efforts to enhance the disclosure of fiscal risks, including an improved fiscal risks statement (in an annex to the LDO), are already ongoing. Having a more robust medium-term fiscal

---

[17]The rules also seem to have been unable to contain within limits the rise of the wage bill at the subnational level.

[18]For example, such a unit could review the finances of subnational governments and recommend actions. Jointly with the central bank, to take another example, it could promote coordination in macroprudential policy and review the soundness of the financial sector.

framework with improved medium-term fiscal projections would improve the identification and analysis of fiscal risks. Long-term fiscal projections should also be developed to include not only pensions but also the government's overall finances (deficit and debt). Such projections would help assess the long-term risks related, for example, to the (possibly) rising cost of health care.[19] Fiscal statistics should be made more comprehensive, as discussed earlier. A clear and comprehensive view of all parts of the public sector could ultimately give the government and the public a "fiscal dashboard." The production of these statistics would help reveal the buildup of risks in the broader public sector. They would also reveal the accumulation of nondebt liabilities, even when debt might be contained.

REFERENCES

Avis, Eric, Claudio Ferraz, and Frederico Finan. 2018. "Do Government Audits Reduce Corruption? Estimating the Impacts of Exposing Corrupt Politicians." *Journal of Political Economy* 126 (5): 1912–61.

Bevilaqua, Afonso. 2000. "State Government Bailouts in Brazil." Department of Economics Working Paper No. 421, Pontifica Universidade Catolica, Rio de Janeiro.

Debrun, Xavier. 2015. "Safe Public Debt: Towards an Operational Definition." *Romanian Journal of Fiscal Policy* 6 (1): 1–16.

Eyraud, Luc, and Tao Wu. 2015. "Playing by the Rules: Reforming Fiscal Governance in Europe." IMF Working Paper 15/67, International Monetary Fund, Washington, DC.

Fall, F., and J.-M. Fournier. 2015. "Macroeconomic Uncertainties, Prudent Debt Targets and Fiscal Rules." OECD Economics Department Working Papers 1230, OECD Publishing, Paris.

Ferraz, Claudio, and Frederico Finan. 2008. "Exposing Corrupt Politicians: The Effects of Brazil's Publicly Released Audits on Electoral Outcomes." *The Quarterly Journal of Economics* 123 (2): 703–45.

International Monetary Fund (IMF). 2012. "Fiscal Transparency, Accountability, and Risk." IMF Fiscal Affairs Department, Washington, DC.

———. "G20 Countries: An Update." IMF Policy Paper, Washington, DC.

Mora, Monica. 2002. "Federalism and State Debt in Brazil." IPEA Discussion Paper No. 866, Institute of Applied Economic Research, Brasilia.

North, Douglas. 1990. *Institutions, Institutional Change and Economic Performance*. Cambridge, UK: Cambridge University Press.

Poterba, James M., and Jurgen von Hagen, eds. 1999. *Fiscal Institutions and Fiscal Performance*. Chicago: The University of Chicago Press.

---

[19]Most advanced economies now publish such projections; for example, the Office for Budget Responsibility's *Financial Sustainability Reports* in the United Kingdom and the Congressional Budget Office's *Long-Term Budget Outlook* in the United States.

CHAPTER 11

Fiscal Challenges of Population Aging in Brazil

ALFREDO CUEVAS, IZABELA KARPOWICZ, CARLOS MULAS-GRANADOS, MAURICIO SOTO, MARINA MENDES TAVARES, AND VIVIAN MALTA

Brazil's population is aging. Declining fertility rates and increasing life expectancy are important drivers of demographic changes in Brazil and Latin America, contributing to slower population growth and a rising share of the elderly in the population. Over the past half century, the fertility rate in Brazil has halved and is now in line with that of more advanced economies. Annual population growth has declined sharply. Meanwhile, thanks to income growth, redistribution policies, and health reforms, life expectancy has increased in Brazil, contributing to an increase in the dependency ratio. People ages 65 and older now constitute about 7½ percent of the total population, 2 percentage points more than a decade ago.

INTRODUCTION

Brazil's demographic trends are set to continue over the long term, raising the old-age dependency ratio—the ratio of people ages 65 and older to the population ages 15 to 64. Because of falling fertility rates, Brazil's population will start to decline in absolute terms by midcentury. According to the United Nations (UN), by 2050 Brazil's old-age dependency ratio will reach close to 37 percent, and by 2100 it will surpass that of more advanced economies. Brazil's statistical institute (Instituto Brasileiro de Geografia e Estatistica, or IBGE) projects a similar trend, with old-age dependency reaching 36 percent by 2050 (Figure 11.1).

However, an aging population will pose fiscal challenges in Brazil much earlier than 2050. Unlike in other countries, where demographic disequilibria point to difficult times sometime in the future, the Brazilian pension[1] system is already in deficit. This deficit was 2.8 percent of GDP in 2017, reflecting structurally high spending that has been exacerbated by a decline in contributing revenues caused by the high levels of unemployment in recent years. Public age-related spending

---

[1]Brazilian usage typically requires calling retirement programs by the term *aposentadorias* while reserving the term *pensões* for other specific benefits, such as survivors' or disability benefits. This chapter treats the terms *pensions* and *social security* as broadly synonymous, encompassing all of these various social security programs, unless explicitly indicated otherwise.

Figure 11.1. Old-Age Dependency
(Percentage point increase)

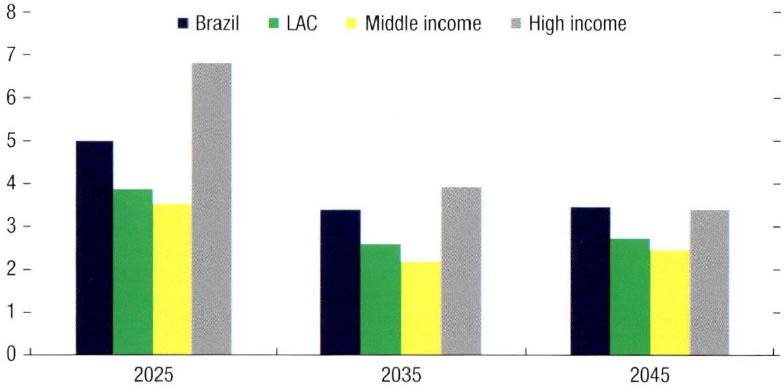

Source: United Nations estimates.
Note: Figure shows ratio of population ages 65 and over to population ages 15–64. LAC = Latin America and the Caribbean.

(on retirement and other pensions) is projected to reach levels incompatible with fiscal sustainability within the next decade. Pension expenditures already represent a large share of total public spending (12 percent of GDP in 2015) and, in the absence of reforms, are projected to increase to 16 percent of GDP in 2025. Beyond that, these spending needs will continue to rise, reaching 26 percent of GDP by 2050 as the elderly share of the population more than triples over today's levels.

Past reforms moderated pension deficits for a time, but urgent attention to aging-related spending is needed once again. The 1998 pension reform had a limited impact on deficits, and in 2003 parametric changes were introduced in the mandatory public sector pension regime. In 2012 a defined-contribution pillar for the public regime was established that reduced replacement rates for higher earners and enhanced progressivity and equity for private pensions at a relatively low transition cost. The macroeconomic impact of the reform was expected to be positive for Brazil (IMF 2012). However, these reforms were insufficient and will not contain the pension-spending growth that lies ahead.

This chapter explores several reform options. A combination of reforms to revise benefits eligibility is considered that might contain future deficits in the least distortionary way for labor incentives. Delaying retirement would generate significant fiscal savings but is not sufficient on its own. Changing the benefits indexation formula and removing existing payroll tax exemptions are also potentially useful measures. Reforms to pension spending programs should start now so that changes can be implemented gradually.

BRAZIL'S PENSION SYSTEM

The Brazilian social security system offers a full menu of benefits, including old-age, disability, and survivors' insurance. The system comprises two main schemes: the Regime Geral de Previdência Social (RGPS) is the "general regime" for private sector workers, and the Regimes Próprios de Previdência Social (RPPS) is the set of special regimes for various categories of public sector workers. The institutions that offer retirement pensions also provide maternity benefits and worker's compensation, without requiring individuals to make separate contributions.[2]

When compared with other countries, the large size of Brazil's pension system is evident. Total pension expenditure (public and private) as a share of GDP is very high, especially considering that Brazil, although aging, is still a relatively young country. Given the demographic structure of the country, estimated spending on pensions in Brazil in 2015 was among the highest in a sample of about 100 countries (Figure 11.2; Table 11.1) and similar to spending in countries with much older populations.[3]

Gross and net replacement rates are higher than the Organisation for Economic Co-operation and Development (OECD) average, for both male and female pensioners (at 70 percent and 76 percent of the average wage for men, respectively). Combined employer and employee pension contribution rates are extremely high and exacerbated by additional payroll levies, and contribute to high informality levels (contributors represent only 46 percent of the working-age population compared with 86 percent in advanced economies). Pension coverage, expressed as the share of pensioners to the population ages 65 and older, is high at 93 percent and close to the advanced economy average, reflecting the low effective (or average) retirement age for men and women and noncontributory pensions for certain classes of individuals meeting some qualifying criteria. The minimum retirement age with full contributory history in the man-

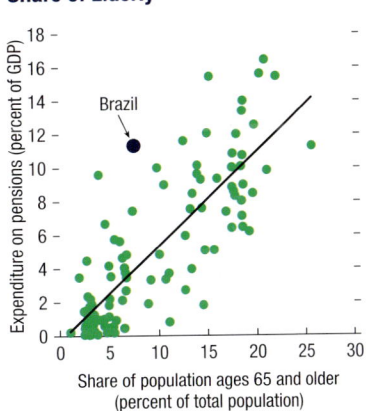

Figure 11.2. Pension Expenditure and Share of Elderly

Sources: World Bank, World Development Indicators; and IMF staff estimates based on a sample of about 100 countries.
Note: Figure shows data for 2014 or latest available estimate.

---

[2]For a description of the social security system, see Cuevas and others (2017).

[3]In Brazil, some of the pension system benefits have social assistance features, which complicates cross-country comparisons. Social benefits in other countries may be included in different expense categories.

Table 11.1. Benchmarks of Key Indicators

Pension spending (percent of GDP)	
Brazil	11.3
Advanced Average	8.7
Emerging Average	5.0
Developing Average	1.8

Statutory retirement age - male		Statutory retirement age - female	
Brazil	65	Brazil	60
Advanced Average	64	Advanced Average	63
Emerging Average	61	Emerging Average	59
Developing Average	59	Developing Average	58

Old-age dependency ratio (pop. 65+/pop. 15–64)		Avg. spend. per pensioner (% GDP per pop. 15–64)	
Brazil	12	Brazil	105%
Advanced Average	26	Advanced Average	32%
Emerging Average	11	Emerging Average	57%
Developing Average	6	Developing Average	85%

Contribution Rate, Pensions		Coverage (Pensioners to pop. 65 and older)	
Brazil	28%	Brazil	93%
Advanced Average	20%	Advanced Average	106%
Emerging Average	15%	Emerging Average	77%
Developing Average	13%	Developing Average	34%

Source: IMF, International Financial Statistics; IMF, *World Economic Outlook*; Organisation for Economic Co-operation and Development; and actuarial reports from national statistical agencies.

datory public regime is 48 for women and 53 for men, and the average retirement age in the RGPS is 58 for "age" pensions and 55 for "contributory" pensions, compared with 64 for OECD countries. At close to 4 percent, the (real) internal rate of return, that is, the difference between what an average retiree (a person who enters the labor market at 25 years old and retires at 65) receives from the pension system and what the retiree contributed during his/her working years, is also high from an international perspective (Cuevas and others 2017).

There is a benefit within the RGPS called Previdência Rural (rural pension) for males/females ages 60/55 or older, who have completed at least 180 months of work in rural areas. The benefit is equal to the minimum wage, and the program represents about 20 percent of the government's pension expenditures. The RGPS has been running deficits, mainly driven by rural pensions. RGPS revenues increased from 4.7 percent of GDP in 2003 to 6.1 percent in 2014. During the same period, expenditures increased from 6.2 percent to 7.5 percent of GDP because the number of pension recipients increased by 40 percent (Caetano 2015). However, "urban" pension balances have been in positive territory in recent years, and overall deficits were driven by limited contributions in rural areas. In 2015–16, reflecting declining revenues caused by rising unemployment, the overall deficit in the RGPS reached 2.3 percent of GDP and continued to grow in 2017 to 2.8 percent of GDP.[4] Growing deficits in the pension system require growing subsidies by the Treasury to finance the gap.

Over the past two decades, Brazil has adjusted some pension plans to reduce outlays. These adjustments include the 2003 reform of the RPPS for new entrants; the introduction of the *fator previdenciário* for RGPS beneficiaries in 1999, and its subsequent replacement with a progressive 85/95 formula in 2015; and the tightening of the criteria for survivor benefits in 2015 (Cuevas and others 2017).[5] Past reforms have been insufficient to contain pension spending growth, however, and have left important challenges unaddressed, such as the following:

- The average retirement age is low by international standards—54 in Brazil compared with 64 on average in the OECD (Queiroz and Figoli 2010).

- Spending on pensions as a percentage of GDP is high relative to the share of the elderly in the population (Table 11.1).

- Benefits are growing faster than revenues because of an aging population, limited incremental gains from labor formalization, and the connection between the value of pensions and the minimum wage formula, which pushes pension spending growth above GDP growth.

- The multiplicity of pension systems, with their differentiated degrees of "generosity," increases inequities, and the duplication of benefits puts pressure on overall pension spending.

CHALLENGES FROM POPULATION AGING

Demographic Outlook

Brazil's population is one of the world's fastest aging.[6] A continued but gradual decline in fertility rates is projected to take place in less-developed economies, including Brazil (Figure 11.3). Because these estimates are surrounded by considerable uncertainty, the UN illustrates two scenarios: the "medium fertility" projection for less-developed economies assumes a continuous decline to about two children per woman by 2100 from 2.6 in 2015, while the "low fertility" scenario implies an immediate drop of about 0.5 children per woman.

The decreasing trend in fertility rates is coupled with increasing longevity. Longevity improvement is expected to slow in more-developed economies;

---

[4]A similar deficit was recorded in 2015 in the RPPS, where the number of beneficiaries is substantially lower because contribution rates are extremely low.

[5]The *fator previdenciário* is a penalty for taking early retirement based on actuarial calculations. The 85/95 rule refers to the sum of age and time of service necessary for women/men to obtain full retirement pension benefits.

[6]Based on demographic projections in the *2015 Revision of the UN World Population Prospects*. The assumptions behind the projections of fertility and mortality rates and migration are described in Clements and others (2015). In Figure 11.3, "more developed economies" are Australia, Canada, European countries, Japan, New Zealand, and the United States, while "less developed countries" include the rest of the world.

Figure 11.3. Projected Fertility and Mortality Rates

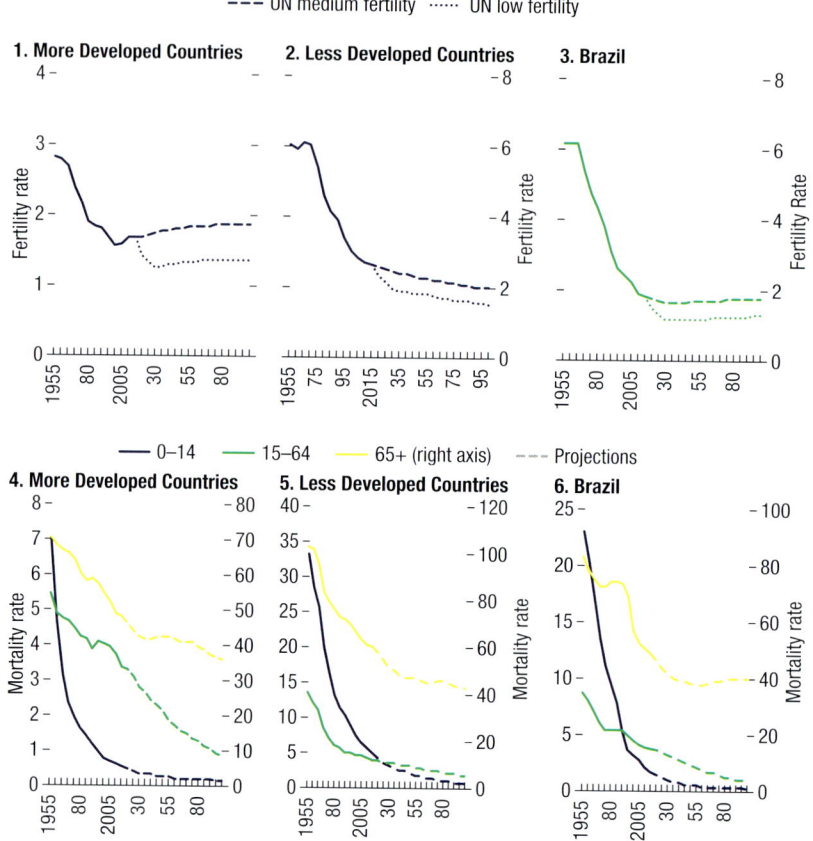

Sources: United Nations; and IMF staff estimates.

however, for the less-developed economies and Brazil, the projections suggest continued increases in life expectancy, as both old-age mortality and under-five mortality decrease owing to increasing health care coverage. As the share of the youth and working-age populations declines, the ratio of those ages 65 and older to those ages 15 to 64 is expected to reach 40 percent by 2100 in Brazil. Using these population projections, Figure 11.4 plots the old-age dependency ratio for the population ages 65 (alternatively, 55) and older. These ratios will increase from about 17 percent (28 percent) in 2016 to 56 percent (88 percent) in 2060 according to the IBGE. Figure 11.4 shows that, under the young retirement age prevalent in the current system, not only does the system exhibit a larger dependency ratio today, but it also shows a faster rate of aging over time (measured by the increase in the dependency ratio). In other words, the financial imbalances

Figure 11.4. Population Projections

1. Old-Age Dependency Ratios
(Ratio of elderly population to working-age population, percent)

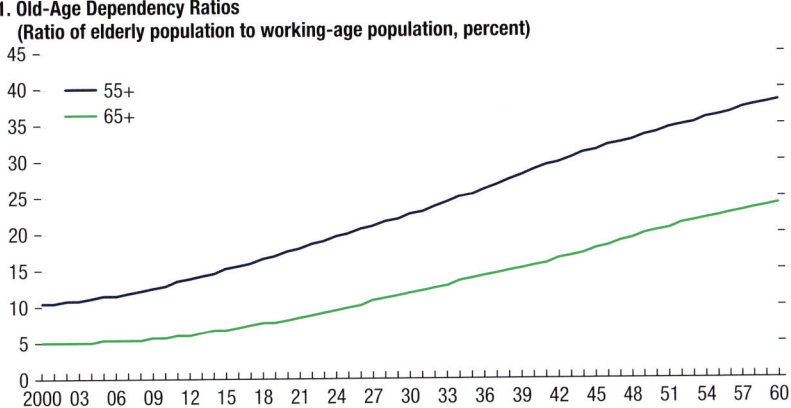

2. Age Pyramid, 2010–16
(Share of population in each age cohort and sex, in percent of total population)

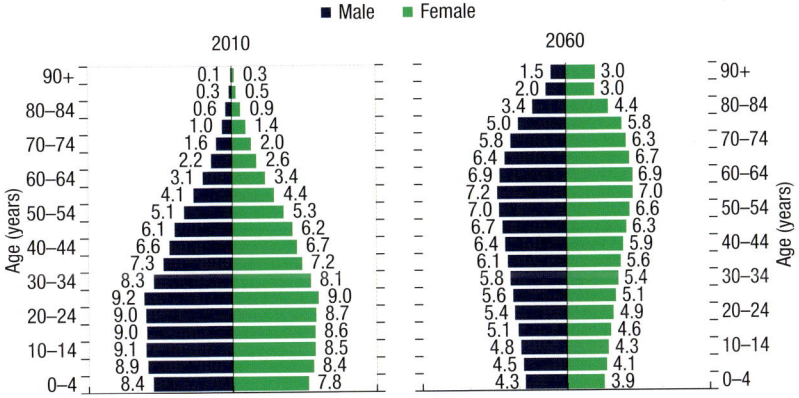

Sources: Brazilian Institute of Geography and Statistics; and IMF staff estimates.

arising from population aging are disproportionately larger when the retirement age is relatively low.

Fiscal Impact

Population aging has been an important driver of pension spending in Brazil. The growth in pension expenditure as a share of GDP can be decomposed into four distinct factors or drivers: the growth of average replacement rates, the increase in benefit coverage, the impact of demographic changes on the old-age dependency ratio, and the change of the inverse of the employment rate. Figure 11.5 shows that the worsening age profile in Brazil and increasing

Figure 11.5. Pension Expenditure

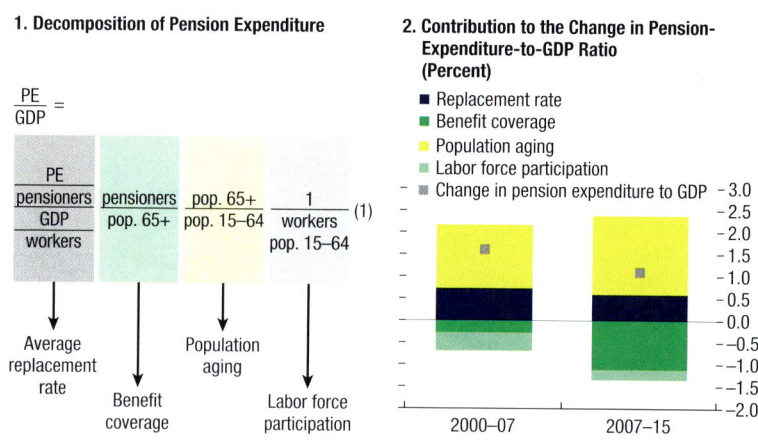

Sources: National Institute of Social Security (INPS); Organisation for Economic Co-operation and Development; United Nations; World Bank, World Development Indicators; and IMF staff estimates.

replacement rates have strongly affected pension expenditure growth over the past decade and a half. Higher replacement rates have been the main driver of increasing pension spending in other emerging market economies since the 1990s, but the declining labor force and population aging have also played a role in emerging Europe (Clements and others 2013). The *fator previdenciário,* in effect since 1999, may have helped reduce the ratio of pensioners to the elderly population (that is, the "benefit coverage" ratio; see Cuevas and others 2017).

Reflecting its rapidly aging population, Brazil's spending on pensions is projected to reach unsustainable levels in the next decade. In an inertial baseline projection without reforms, pension spending rises to 14 percent of GDP by 2021 (Figure 11.6), 18 percent of GDP by 2030, and 29 percent of GDP by 2050. This projection reflects the decline in real GDP over 2015–16 and the rise in the real value of the minimum wage (affecting some 70 percent of pensioners), and uses the Treasury's growth projections for the retiree population, which is subject to larger-than-usual uncertainty because of the 85/95 rule introduced in mid-2015.

Long-term pension spending trends are substantially worse in Brazil than in advanced and other less-developed economies.[7] If policies remain unchanged, spending on pensions would reach 21.5 percent of GDP by 2050 in Brazil. The net present value of the funding gap for the social security system has been

---

[7]The demographic estimation uses baseline population projections from the UN under the "medium variant" scenario, which uses probabilistic models to extract projections of fertility and mortality rates for individual countries. Beyond 2065, pensions are projected to grow in line with demographic developments.

Figure 11.6. Pension Expenditure Projections, 2015–21
(Percent of GDP)

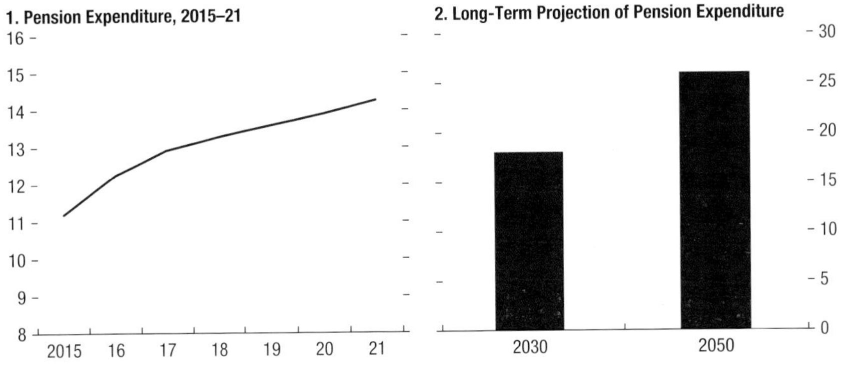

1. Pension Expenditure, 2015–21

2. Long-Term Projection of Pension Expenditure

Sources: General Social Security Regime (RGPS) and Pension Regimes for Government Workers (RPPS) actuarial reports; and IMF staff estimates.

estimated to be 25 percent of GDP over the next two decades (IMF 2012). However, since the time that estimation was made, Brazil's potential growth has been revised downward, adversely affecting revenues and contributing to an even larger funding gap.

A sensitivity analysis illustrates the effect of different aging scenarios on long-term pension spending and the effect of reforms. Holding everything else constant in expression (1) shown in panel 1 of Figure 11.5, an increase in the share of the population ages 65 and older translates into an increase in the ratio of pension spending to GDP. In the short term, the effects of different assumptions on growth should be small, given that current pensions are determined by past growth and wage realizations. However, pension spending can exceed the model's outcome if pensions are indexed to minimum wage growth and minimum wages grow faster than average productivity, as is the case in the "no reform" scenario in Brazil.[8]

The impact of lower fertility and higher longevity on pension spending could be significant. Compared with the baseline projections shown in Figure 11.6, two risk scenarios are estimated that consider potential shocks on fertility and longevity assumptions. For example, under the "low fertility" scenario, spending on pensions would increase by 2 percentage points of GDP by 2050 (18 percentage points by 2100). Under the "longevity risk" scenario, assuming that mortality rates for those ages 65 and older decline 50 percent faster than at the baseline, pension spending would be 1.3 percentage points of GDP higher by 2050 (3.7 percentage points higher by 2100).

---

[8]Second-order interactions are not considered in the model.

REFORM OPTIONS

Policies available to address fiscal pressures from pensions belong to two broad groups: policies that affect labor force participation and policies that directly affect features of these spending programs. Broadly speaking, policies directed at pension programs aim to increase financing of these programs or lower the generosity of benefits, or both.

Labor Force Participation

Policies that increase labor force participation for women and the elderly can partially offset the impact of aging. As in other developing economies in Latin America, female labor force participation in Brazil is substantially lower than male participation: 65 percent versus 85 percent of the population ages 15–64 in 2014. Absent a decline in average productivity per worker, halving that gap would boost GDP and increase financing for pension spending, so that the ratio of such spending to GDP would fall by 1 percentage point by 2050.

Brazil's labor force participation rate for the population ages 55 to 64 is low (56 percent in 2014 compared with 81 percent for those ages 25–54).[9] Even though this gap is common in other Latin American countries, halving it would reduce the ratio of pension spending to GDP by 1 percentage point by 2050.

Pension System Reforms

Although countries may opt for a variety of policies to reform their pension systems, efforts generally aim to contain eligibility, increase revenues, and lower replacement rates. The combination of policies will depend on the country's objectives and will reflect different social, political, and economic preferences.

- **Raising retirement ages:** This option is especially attractive because it helps complement efforts to boost the labor force participation of older workers. To be effective over time, the raising of retirement ages needs to be accompanied by reforms that reduce actuarial imbalances. In other words, if retirement age is delayed but retirees earn substantial additional benefits because of that delay, the deficit might be pushed back for some time, but it will not be eliminated. Delaying the retirement age while simultaneously adjusting the rate of benefit accrual will reduce actuarial imbalances, which is paramount, and will smooth the trajectory of spending over time. (See the third bullet under this paragraph.)

- **Increasing revenues:** Revenues can be increased by *increasing taxes on pensions* for upper-income groups or *increasing payroll contributions*, or both.

- **Reducing replacement rates:** Replacement rates at the time of retirement can be moderated by lengthening the period over which the pensionable wage is estimated or by modifying benefit calculation formulas (accrual

---

[9]International Labour Organization, based on Pesquisa Mensal de Emprego.

Figure 11.7. Reform Options to Stabilize Pension Spending, 2015–30

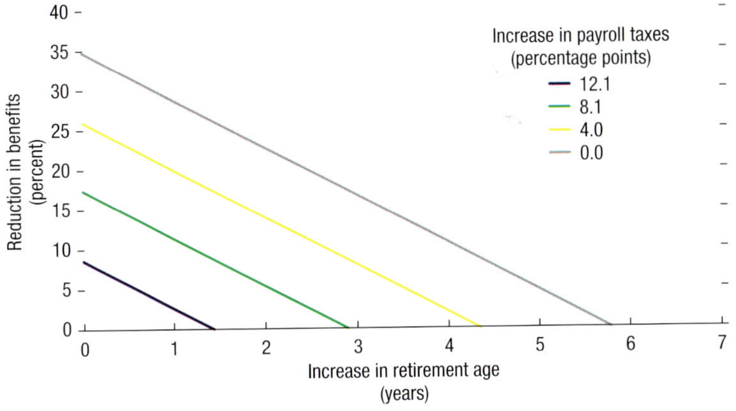

Source: IMF staff estimates.

rates). In addition, growth of the average ratio of pensions to wages in the system can be reduced by abandoning the indexation of benefits to the minimum wage (or modifying the formula for indexing the minimum wage, which in the past several years has caused the minimum wage to grow faster than average productivity).

Brazil faces several policy alternatives to stabilize, and eventually reduce, pension deficits. With a pension system deficit equivalent to 1.5 percent of GDP in 2015 (projected to reach 4.2 percent in 2025 in the authorities' scenario),[10] the minimum objective of any pension reform should be to stabilize the financing gap. By introducing reforms that prevent pension imbalances from growing, the government can stabilize the amount of the subsidy that needs to be transferred every year from the federal budget to the social security system. This would be a major step forward in addressing fiscal sustainability problems in Brazil.[11]

Options for containing spending include some combination of the three main policy instruments mentioned previously (raising the retirement age, increasing contributions, managing the size of benefits). These trade-offs are illustrated in Figure 11.7. In Brazil's case, pension contributions are already high and need to be reduced over time to reduce market disincentives, so increasing them is especially difficult. To stabilize pension spending over 15 years without increasing payroll taxes, Brazil would have to, for instance, reduce average benefits by almost 35 percent or increase the retirement age (without raising individual pensions

---

[10]Tesouro Nacional (2015), includes RGPS and RPPS of the federal government.

[11]Under the proposed constitutional amendment to cap the ratio of nominal expenditures to GDP over the next 20 years, the objective is even tougher because it implies that federal social security spending must fit under the cap.

Figure 11.8. Estimated Impact of Various Pension Reform Options
(Percent of GDP)

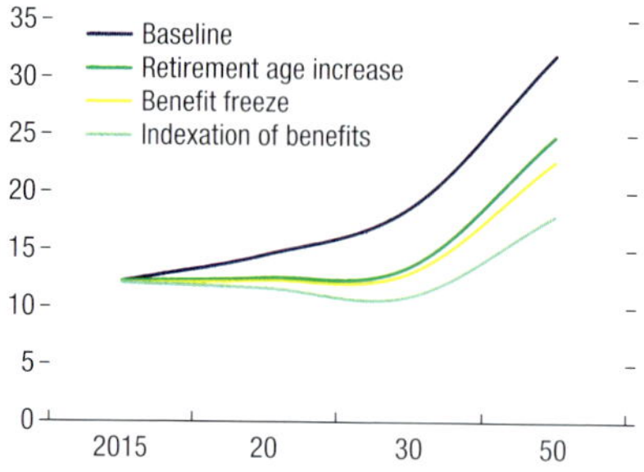

Expenditure Increase (2015–30) (Percentage points of GDP)	
Projected Spending Increase	**5.9**
Impact of Reforms	**−7.1**
Retirement Age Increase	−4.7
Indexation of Benefits	−2.6
Benefit Freeze	−0.8
Decrease in Social Contributions	1.0
Net Change	**−1.2**

Source: IMF staff estimates.

because of the postponement of retirement) by almost six years. Any combination of options along the green line in Figure 11.7 would achieve the same result.

Gradually raising retirement ages is an attractive policy option for Brazil, but it is not sufficient. Increasing the retirement age would also boost labor force participation and growth, and would avoid the need for larger benefit cuts. It would also be desirable given that the retirement age in Brazil is comparatively low. Increasing the retirement age by five years over the next five years would generate savings in pension spending equivalent to 4.7 percentage points of GDP by 2030 compared with the "no reform" baseline. However, this overestimates the potential contribution of the retirement age increase to savings because the model from which those calculations are derived is based on macroeconomic data and assumes that individual pension payments remain unchanged (that is, the replacement rate at retirement does not rise despite the retirement date being postponed), which is not the typical case when the contributory history is longer. In the model, pension spending would be higher than the 2015 level by about 1 percentage point of GDP (Figure 11.8).

Another source of pressure is the growth in real benefits to existing pensioners. Removing the automatic link between pensions and the minimum wage (or changing the minimum wage formula) is a useful way to address this issue. This approach would reduce pension expenditure by about 2.6 percentage points in 2030 (6.1 percentage points of GDP in 2050). Front-loading the rescue of the pension system by removing existing payroll tax exemptions would be advisable. A levy of 10 percent on nominal benefits could also be considered as part of a package aimed at creating space to gradually lower the currently high payroll contributions. After 2050, the system would stabilize by linking the increase in the retirement age to gains in life expectancy.

DISTRIBUTIONAL EFFECTS OF THE REFORM

Brazil's Congress received a government proposal for social security reform in December 2016; the reform proposal was, after some modification, approved in committee, but has never been taken to the floor. This proposal addresses many of the main sources of financial imbalance under the present system. The proposal introduces a minimum retirement age for women and men, with some transitional arrangements; extends the minimum contribution period; and adjusts the benefit payable at retirement. In addition, the reform would, over time, reduce differences between the regimes for private and public sector employees. The reform would also limit the scope for accumulation of benefits, such as both a retirement benefit and a survivors' pension, and would lower the rural pension subsidy.

At present, there are large differences in the benefits received by private sector and public sector employees. Public sector workers enjoy higher wages during their productive life, at all points in their career and across most professions (Góes and Karpowicz 2017). Moreover, public sector workers generally retire earlier than private sector employees under existing rules and have higher average post-retirement incomes, and their retirement benefits are often subject to larger annual revisions than those of their counterparts in the private sector.

The pension system seems to reinforce other sources of inequality. Pension benefits are unequal in part because the option to retire by length of contribution is most easily exercised by earners with stable, formal sector jobs. Moreover, many high-income workers retire by length of contribution at a relatively early age, and then continue to work in the private sector while they draw a pension. The highest net benefit (public transfer), defined as the difference between total benefits received after retirement and total contributions paid during a person's working life, accrues to better-off individuals—public sector workers and high-skilled private sector workers—under the current system. In fact, the World Bank (2017) estimates that about half of all pension "subsidies" in Brazil accrue to the top income quintile of the population, while only 4 percent accrue to the bottom 20 percent.

Inequalities also persist within the RGPS between the urban and rural levels. Skilled workers in urban areas, especially men, have sufficiently long contribution histories to retire by length of contribution. In rural areas, workers retire according to age (men age 60 and women age 55 who have completed at least 180 months of work in family agriculture) and receive a benefit equal to one times minimum wage, hereafter called the "rural pension." The number of beneficiaries of rural pensions is higher than estimates of the rural population older than age 55, across all states, suggesting that there may be abuse in the system (Figure 11.9).

In the transition to the new system, the proposed reform would affect currently employed formal workers, especially those who are further away from retirement. By bringing the various parameters of the private and public pension systems closer, the reform would do much to narrow inequalities over time. But because the reform aims to modify various parameters in the private system too,

Figure 11.9. Retirement Benefits and Monthly Earnings

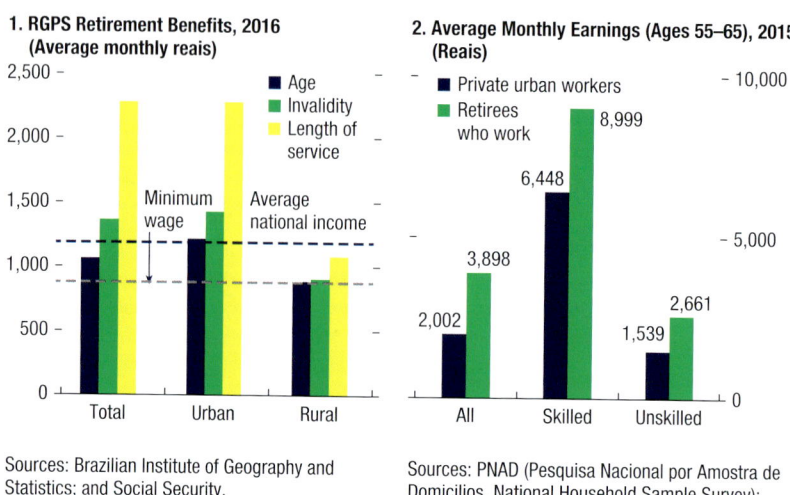

Sources: Brazilian Institute of Geography and Statistics; and Social Security.

Sources: PNAD (Pesquisa Nacional por Amostra de Domicilios, National Household Sample Survey); and IMF staff calculations.

including contributions, retirement incentives, and the value of benefits, it would affect not only the pension system's sustainability but also the distribution of income across various categories of workers. In the new steady state, once the transition period ends, the proposed reform would affect the lifetime incomes of private unskilled, public, and rural workers only marginally, while skilled urban workers would earn more because they would be required to work longer. Nevertheless, the proposed reform has an important component of progressivity: it would significantly reduce the high net transfers that currently flow to higher-income workers (and their survivors).

The new rules governing minimum retirement age and benefits would not only generate fiscal savings but also reduce inequities in a social security system that currently disproportionately benefits a small share of the population already enjoying higher wages—public employees. Figure 11.10, panel 1, shows net cumulative transfers to four types of workers from the social security system, before and after the proposed reform. This is the difference between all retirement and survivors' benefits, on the one hand, and all contributions paid by or on behalf of the employee, on the other hand. The calculation shows that the present discounted value of net transfers would be lower after the reform for all four types of workers, but the reduction would be greater for the public sector worker and the private sector skilled worker (Figure 11.10, panel 2).

Figure 11.10. Pension Reform Outcomes

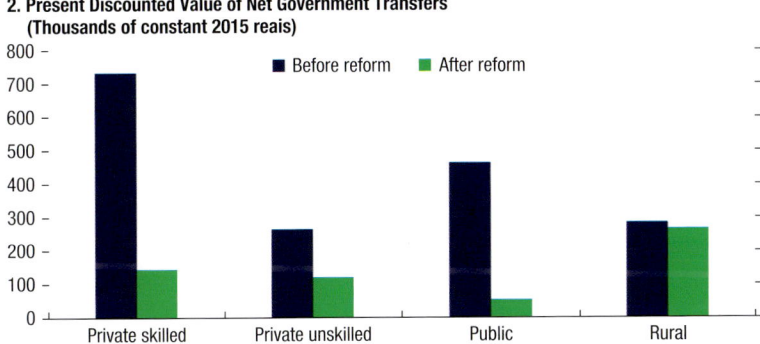

1. Change in Lifetime Income after Reform
(Thousands of constant 2015 reais)

■ Gross ■ Net[1]

Sources: PNAD (Pesquisa Nacional por Amostra de Domicilios, National Household Sample Survey); and IMF staff calculations.
[1]Earnings minus taxes and social security contributions paid by the worker.

2. Present Discounted Value of Net Government Transfers
(Thousands of constant 2015 reais)

■ Before reform ■ After reform

Sources: PNAD (Pesquisa Nacional por Amostra de Domicilios, National Household Sample Survey); and IMF staff calculations.

CONCLUSIONS

Brazil's population is aging rapidly, and fiscal pressures are set to rise over time under the current framework of benefits and contributions. The demographic profile of the country and the already extensive benefits system will put finances under considerable strain over the next decades. As the dependency ratio climbs, spending on pensions could surpass 30 percent of GDP by 2050 if the existing system is not reformed. Although labor market interventions to boost labor force participation can provide some temporary respite, reforms that directly address high replacement rates and early retirement ages cannot be avoided.

This chapter discusses some possible pension reform options at a very general level, without detailing transitional arrangements. But several of these ideas have been under discussion in Brazil for a long time; in fact, some are consistent with specific aspects of the ambitious social security reform proposal sent to Congress by the government in December 2016—and still awaiting a vote. It is worth repeating that the combination of an adverse demographic trend and the characteristics of the current benefits system are driving up pension spending. Because demographic trends in Brazil are unlikely to change (given that they follow patterns that are broadly common to the vast majority of nations), social security reform is of utmost importance. To preserve the social security system's ability to carry out its functions in the future, reforms should start as soon as possible.

REFERENCES

Caetano, M. 2015. "Social Security." Unpublished manuscript.

Clements, B., D. Coady, F. Eich, S. Gupta, A. Kangur, B. Shang, and M. Soto. 2013. "The Challenge of Public Pension Reform in Advanced and Emerging Economies." Occasional Paper No. 275, International Monetary Fund, Washington, DC.

Clements, B., K. Dybczak, V. Gaspar, S. Gupta, and M. Soto. 2015. "The Fiscal Consequences of Shrinking Populations." IMF Staff Discussion Note, SDN/15/21, International Monetary Fund, Washington, DC.

Credit Suisse. 2016. *Brazil Economic Digest*. June 21.

Cuevas, A., I. Karpowicz, C. Mulas-Granados, and M. Soto. 2017. "Fiscal Challenges of Population Aging in Brazil." IMF Working Paper 17/99, International Monetary Fund, Washington, DC.

Góes, C., and I. Karpowicz. 2017. "Inequality in Brazil: A Regional Perspective." IMF Working Paper 17/225, Washington, DC.

Gragnolati, M., O. H. Jorgensen, R. Rocha, and A. Fruttero. 2011. *Growing Old and Older in Brazil*. Washington, DC: World Bank.

International Monetary Fund (IMF). 2012. Selected Issues Paper for the 2012 Article IV Consultation, Washington, DC.

Ministry of Finance. 2015. "Macroeconomic Scenario 2016−19." October 27.

Ocké-Reis, C. O. 2013. "Measurement of Tax Expenditures: The Case of Health Insurance, 2003−11." Technical Note N. 5, Institute of Applied Economic Research, Brasilia.

Organisation for Economic Co-operation and Development (OECD). 2015a. *Pensions at a Glance*. Paris.

———. 2015b. *Economic Survey Brazil*. Paris.

Pereira, E. S. 2013. "Evolution of the Average Age of Receipt and the Average Contribution Period for Pensions between 1999 and 2012." Social Security Ministry report, Brazil.

Queiroz, B. L., and M. G. B. Figoli. 2010. "The Social Protection System for the Elderly in Brazil." Background paper prepared for the Workshop on Aging in Brazil, The World Bank, Brasília, April 6–7.

Receita Federal. 2016. Demonstration of Tax Expenditures, Estimates, Effective Bases—2013. Ministério da Fazenda.

Schmidt, M. I., B. B. Duncan, G. Azevedo e Silva, A. M. Menezes, C. A. Monteiro, M. I. Schmidt, S. M. Barreto, D. Chor, and P. R. Menezes. 2011. "Chronic, N on-Communicable Diseases in Brazil: Burden and Current Challenges." The Lancet Series, No. 9781, Vol. 377.

Tafner, P., C. Botelho, and R. Erbisti. 2015. "Pension Reform—A Visit from an Old Lady." Ed. Gestão Pública. 2015.

Tesouro Nacional. 2015. "Summary Report on Budget Execution and Other Statements." December 2015.

Valdés-Prieto, S. 2007. "Pension Reform and the Development of Pension Systems: An Evaluation of World Bank Assistance." The World Bank Country Study, No. 56343.

CHAPTER 12

The Subnational Fiscal Crisis

Fabian Bornhorst, Guilherme Mercês, and Nayara Freire

This chapter discusses the impact of the 2015–16 recession on the public finances of Brazilian states and reviews recent modifications to the subnational fiscal framework. A history of subnational bailouts by the federal government since the 1980s has shaped today's intergovernmental relationships and fiscal responsibility legislation. Although only a few—but important—states face high indebtedness, the recession brought to the fore structural fiscal problems that are similar across all states, primarily related to high and rigid personnel and social security expenditures. In the absence of financing, liquidity problems emerged as revenues collapsed, which, in turn, caused an increase in committed but unpaid expenditures. In Rio de Janeiro, the state affected the worst, civil servant wages were delayed and public service provision suffered. The Fiscal Recovery Regime is a vehicle for overcoming liquidity problems, but implementation of structural fiscal reforms at the state level needs to advance to secure the sustainability of subnational fiscal accounts.

INTRODUCTION

Fiscal imbalances and the need to adjust public accounts at all levels of government have been a central aspect of the Brazilian economic debate. At the federal level, the rapid increase in public debt has prompted the government to limit the growth of federal primary expenditure by enshrining a fiscal rule in the constitution, and it has helped bring about an earnest discussion of wide-ranging reforms to ensure fiscal sustainability, first and foremost by reforming the social security system.

Similar in many respects to the federal level, the fiscal challenge is even more immediate in many of Brazil's 27 states and 5,570 municipalities. In some cases, civil servants' pay is being delayed, and arrears with suppliers are hampering the provision of public services. In fact, a closer look reveals that a substantial number of subnational entities are on the verge of insolvency, already failing to comply with limits established by the Fiscal Responsibility Law (FRL). In addition to fiscal risks, dissatisfaction with public services, many of which are provided by lower-level government entities, runs deep and leads to social and political-institutional risks.

The case of the state of Rio de Janeiro is emblematic. Rio was disproportionately affected by the 2015–16 recession, which hit the pillars of the state's economy: oil and gas, the car industry, and the construction sector. Almost half a million jobs were lost between 2014 and 2016, a 10 percent decline. Rio's total revenue fell by 35 percent owing to lower tax collection and lower royalties. Faced with collapsing revenue but ever-growing mandatory expenses in the context of a highly rigid budget, Rio de Janeiro declared financial calamity over public accounts in June 2016, on the eve of the 2016 Olympic Games, and began negotiations with the federal government for a new bailout. High rates of crime and deteriorating fiscal and social conditions prompted the federal government to declare a federal intervention to improve public security in the state (Box 12.1).

A similar fiscal challenge is found in other states, and the difficulties extend to thousands of Brazil's municipalities. According to the FIRJAN Fiscal Management Index, more than 85 percent of 4,544 Brazilian municipalities surveyed are in a difficult or critical fiscal situation. Moreover, the diagnosis of the structural fiscal challenge is strikingly similar across the three levels of government: a high and growing share of budgets is committed to mandatory expenditures, notably expenses for salaries and pensions. Given the mandatory nature of the expenditure, in times of falling revenue expenditures cannot be reduced, leaving public accounts vulnerable to the economic cycle. At the subnational level (states and municipalities), this situation is exacerbated by high dependence on transfers from the federal government, with little or no access to financing. As a result, states and municipalities are increasingly relying on the postponement of expenditure and are accumulating unpaid commitments, exacerbating the fiscal challenge today and in the future. The challenge is twofold: to help subnational entities regain their financial footing—while ensuring the provision of public services and avoiding moral hazard—and, more broadly, to bolster the system of intergovernmental finances.

This chapter begins by tracing the evolution of the subnational fiscal framework and reviews how it was modified to respond to the crisis. The framework is key to understanding the budgetary, institutional, and legal constraints that states face, and is a determinant of the fiscal indicators that are used to evaluate subnational fiscal performance. Finally, the challenges for states, and the subnational fiscal framework more generally, are discussed.

THE SUBNATIONAL FRAMEWORK BEFORE THE CRISIS

A Long History of Subnational Bailouts[1]

The history of subnational fiscal challenges can be traced back to the 1960s and the ensuing decades. The 1966 tax reform concentrated taxes at the federal level, reducing the tax autonomy of states. With increasingly easy access to

---

[1]For a detailed discussion, see Bevilaqua (2002), Mora (2002), and Dillinger (1997).

financial markets and no expenditure restraint, states' indebtedness grew quickly. Public banks at the state level played an important role in this process, not only by promoting external financing for states, but also by facilitating debt rollovers and leveraging state government revenues. Absent any subnational controls or limits imposed by a national framework, the indebtedness of many subnational entities reached unsustainable levels in the 1980s.

The 1988 Constitution promoted the decentralization of tax competency in favor of subnational governments, especially municipalities, and the establishment of a system of intergovernmental transfers. However, spending mandates in the constitution were ample and formulated in the context of a high-inflation environment. Clarity about the assignment of spending responsibility was lacking, and subnational policies were in large part determined by decisions made at the federal government level (see Ter-Minassian and de Mello 2016). Borrowing restrictions were not strictly enforced, causing debt to increase in the early 1990s. Several rounds of subnational-debt-rescheduling initiatives became necessary to address the debt stock, which initially accumulated in hard currency. At the end of the process, the federal government emerged as the main creditor of Brazilian states. Ever since, the renegotiation of debt-repayment terms and associated conditionality has become a defining feature of intergovernmental relations and discussions in Brazil.

- An early attempt in 1989 (Federal Law 7,976) provided the framework for the federal government to refinance states' and municipalities' external debt and extend its maturities to 20 years. However, the law was insufficient to solve the problem of indebtedness because it did not include refinancing of domestic debt securities, and domestic financing continued. For Rio de Janeiro, for example, data from the state Treasury show this represented more than half of the total debt at the time.

- In 1993 a further renegotiation of terms (Federal Law 8,727) introduced a mechanism that would link states' debt service to their revenue capacity in an effort to reduce the debt burden. In addition, beginning in 1994, in the wake of the macroeconomic stabilization plans and the Plano Real, the federal government began to focus its efforts on imposing greater fiscal discipline on federal entities. States' adjustment to the new low-inflation environment and high real rates proved difficult.

- In 1997 a milestone was reached (Federal Law 9,496) that allowed the federal government to refinance all state and municipality debt instruments, including states' obligations arising from credit operations. In addition, public state-level banks were privatized and states were prohibited from issuing debt securities. Refinancing agreements had a 30-year maturity profile, and the real interest rate was fixed at 6 percent (9 percent in some cases), plus the annual variation of a price index (the IGP-DI, General Price Index-Internal Availability). At the time, these were generous refinancing conditions, and the program was taken up by all states with two exceptions (Amapá and Tocantins).

From Fiscal Adjustment Programs to the Fiscal Responsibility Law

Joining the 1997 debt-refinancing program with the federal government was linked to states' implementation of Restructuring and Fiscal Adjustment Programs (Programas de Reestruturação e de Ajuste Fiscal, or PAFs). The PAFs are contracts between the federal government (creditor) and states (debtors) that provide a framework for the fiscal adjustment, with numerical fiscal targets for the primary balance and limits for the wage bill and for debt service for three-year periods. In addition to serving as an instrument for monitoring and controlling a state's fiscal policy, the near-universal take-up of the PAFs by states also served as a fiscal policy coordination tool in the federation, facilitating the general government's formulation and implementation of fiscal policy. As such, the subnational fiscal policy articulated in the PAFs in coordination with the National Treasury was an important tool for ensuring compliance with fiscal targets for the entire nonfinancial public sector, an important leg of the macroeconomic tripod[2] that emerged in the late 1990s.

A key feature of the 1997 refinancing agreement was a numerical limit on debt service to avoid crowding out other expenditure, in an attempt to address an important shortcoming of previous debt-rescheduling arrangements. Specifically, payment on interest and amortization by states to the federal government was limited to 12 percent of state revenue in 1999, and the ratio gradually increased to 13 percent in 2001 and beyond. Whenever the debt service due was higher than this limit, the difference was capitalized with the still-outstanding debt stock. Although it provided important flexibility in the annual budget, the limit also resulted in an ever-growing debt burden for those states that had entered the agreement with a high level of debt relative to revenues. As a result, highly indebted states and municipalities faced an ever-increasing debt burden almost by design.

In 2001 the Fiscal Responsibility Law (FRL, Complementary Law 101/2000) enshrined into primary law the bailout terms of the 1997 debt rescheduling and the key features and indicators introduced by the PAFs. In addition to establishing limits to debt and personnel expenditure (at 200 percent and 60 percent of net current revenue, respectively), the FRL provisions also prohibit incumbents in the last four months of a term of office from committing expenditures for which there are insufficient financial resources. The FRL applies to all levels and all branches of government, and establishes sanctions for noncompliance ranging from corrective mechanisms to individual penalties. The FRL quickly became a cornerstone of the fiscal policy framework in Brazil even as the PAFs remained an important tool by which subnational fiscal policy was determined in practice.

During the boom years of 2002–08, the FRL provided a solid fiscal framework for the federal government and subnational entities. The procyclical nature of some of its provisions—ratios expressed as a share of revenues—facilitated

---

[2] The tripod comprises the fiscal primary surplus, the inflation-targeting regime, and the floating exchange rate regime.

compliance. But challenges began to emerge when growth began to falter in the aftermath of the global financial crisis, and in 2011 the commodity cycle began to turn. At the subnational level, as revenues fell, demand for financing—credit operations for states require National Treasury approval—increased, including from international financial institutions. To allocate the financing, the National Treasury instituted an internal rating mechanism based on the states' repayment capacity (Capacidade de Pagamento, or CAPAG) designed to assess states' fiscal repayment capacity. But, naturally, the states with more vulnerable fiscal accounts required more financing, and decision making was not free from political considerations. According to data from the National Treasury, between 2012 and 2014, the federal government guaranteed more loans to states and municipalities with lower fiscal capacity (classified as C and D) than for entities classified as A or B. In other words, the federal government helped states that were already facing fiscal imbalances to finance their deficits without pursuing structural reforms, often by providing sovereign guarantees to international lenders. In practice, new credit operations allowed states to continue to finance investment, while state revenues were increasingly used to finance recurrent expenses, notably personnel expenditures (see Rossi and Aguiar 2018).

THE SUBNATIONAL FRAMEWORK AFTER THE CRISIS

The 2015–16 recession exposed not only structural fiscal problems in subnational finances but also the limits and shortcomings of the subnational framework more generally. Before the crisis, the combination of PAFs, the FRL, and a tight although discretionary lid on subnational external borrowing managed by the National Treasury kept subnational finances under control. But with the recession, the states' debt-to-revenue ratios increased, arrears accumulated, and three states were forced to declare "public calamity" over public finances.[3] With spending on public services (health, education, security) growing, civil servants' wages fell into arrears and political pressure on the federal government to help troubled states increased. The challenge was to reform the subnational framework in a way that enabled the worst-hit states to regain their financial footing while avoiding moral hazard within the federation, and creating incentives for much-needed fiscal reforms.

Retroactive Debt Relief

Since 2014 the subnational framework has evolved in several steps. In 2014 the states' interpretation of a controversial law[4] allowed for the *retroactive* application of a lower interest rate to states' debt. The new rate was the lower of either

---

[3]Declaring public calamity over public finances is a decision made by subnational governments that has largely symbolic consequences. Several municipalities have followed suit.

[4]Complementary Law 148/2014 modified the FRL to allow for a modification of the terms agreed to in the 1997 debt rescheduling.

consumer price inflation plus 4 percent a year or the central bank's policy rate, replacing the original charges. The retroactive debt relief was implemented in 2015, bringing debt relief to states and several municipalities. In addition to the retroactive debt relief, in June 2016, at the height of the recession and soon after the impeachment of President Dilma Rousseff, states reached an agreement with the federal government to suspend debt-service payments for six months, after which debt-service payments would gradually resume until reaching the regular payments in July 2018, capitalizing any delayed debt service. That agreement also foresaw lengthening the repayment schedule for another 20 years.

The Fiscal Recovery Regime and Strengthened Control over States

The measures helped alleviate cash flow pressures for states during the recession. But they proved insufficient for addressing the structural fiscal gap in some states, notably Rio de Janeiro, and in other rapidly aging states, such as Rio Grande do Sul. To this end, a Fiscal Recovery Regime (Regime de Recuperação Fiscal, or RRF) law was approved in late 2016 that provides the framework for federal assistance to states in fiscal distress. Specifically, the RRF outlines the eligibility criteria states have to meet to participate[5] and provides a framework for states to negotiate individual agreements with the federal government that can lead to the suspension of debt repayments for up to three years, in return for a fiscal adjustment program.[6] A specific program is negotiated and agreed on by each participating state and the federal government and is overseen by the Fiscal Recovery Council, with representatives from the Ministry of Finance, the Court of Accounts, and the participating state.

In addition, the federal government significantly strengthened control over state finances. To address the shortcomings in the mechanism that provided financing for states, the National Treasury further reviewed the process by which states contracted debt, in many instances from international partners and with a sovereign guarantee. The internal rating system CAPAG was revised to strengthen objective criteria for assessing the states' repayment capacity and to limit the discretionary influence in overwriting the ratings. The National Treasury also improved transparency in subnational finances by moving to harmonize accounting standards and publishing aggregate and state-level data (Ministry of Finance 2016). This measure includes enforcing the timely submission of data and common classification of expenditure lines, in particular in personnel, according to criteria agreed on with the Court of Accounts.

---

[5]The qualifying fiscal situation was determined as net debt exceeding net current revenues, personnel and debt-service payments exceeding 70 percent of net current revenue, and total payment obligations exceeding cash holdings.

[6]The RRF (Complementary Law 159/2017) is specific about the necessary elements of a fiscal recovery plan and specifies tools for implementing the fiscal adjustment.

STATES' RECENT FISCAL PERFORMANCE

Budget Restrictions on Subnational Entities

State budget constraints are a useful starting point for understanding the mechanics and limitations imposed by the subnational framework on states' fiscal policy. The analysis of subnational public accounts in Brazil should, however, not be restricted to the evolution of deficits and debt. States and municipalities are prohibited from issuing debt securities and are therefore prevented from financing budget deficits. Hence, the widely used below-the-line measure for determining the fiscal position of the nonfinancial public sector, developed in the 1980s and tracked monthly by the Central Bank of Brazil, is not the only, or best, fiscal indicator for subnational governments. An extended analysis of above-the-line flows provides important insights into revenue and expenditure trends and shows the growing importance of unpaid commitments (*restos a pagar,* or RAP).[7] The cash flow budget constraint faced by states is as follows:

$$Revenue = Expenses. \tag{12.1}$$

The funds available to pay for expenses are current revenue (CR), composed of the state's own revenues and transfers from the federal government; financing, or changes in indebtedness (ΔD); and the postponement of expenses due, represented as the change in accounts payable (ΔRAP). On the expenses side, states need to pay for primary current expenditure (CE), which includes personnel costs and other operating costs; debt-service costs (amortization and interest); and investments (I). Substituting into equation (12.1) yields the following:

$$CR + \Delta D + \Delta RAP = CE + (Amort + i) + I. \tag{12.2}$$

Equation (12.2) shows the budget constraint of Brazilian subnational governments. The equation shows that a subnational entity's fiscal space for investment depends on the relationship between its revenue collection capacity (CR) and its mandatory expenditure ($CE + Amort + i$), the precommitment of the current year's budget for expenses from previous years (RAP), and new debt. But, as outlined earlier, financing is subject to strict approval by the National Treasury, and debt service is capped by the FRL. Hence, states' fiscal results, as measured only below the line, are predictable and controllable, but they may not reflect fiscal performance in a broader economic sense because unpaid commitments ("between the lines") and investment are the variables that balance the accounts.

The budget constraint also provides the conceptual basis for a set of fiscal indicators used to assess subnational fiscal performance in Brazil. Specifically, it allows the following indicators to be defined:[8]

---

[7] *Restos a pagar* (RAP) include arrears, unpaid accrued expenditure, and budgetary carryovers yet to be accrued; in other words, budgetary commitments at early stages of the budgetary process that have not been fully processed, executed, and paid.

[8] The fiscal aggregates are defined in the FRL and by state legislation and are reported annually by the Ministry of Finance and the National Treasury.

Indebtedness: The ratio of (net) debt to (net current) revenues is the preferred measure of state indebtedness, and the FRL mandates that no state can have a ratio greater than 200 percent.

Personnel expenditure: The ratio of personnel expenditure to (net current) revenues highlights the share of revenues committed to payroll expenses. The FRL allows some adjustments to total personnel expenditure.[9]

Commitments payable: The ratio of cash balances, net of any outstanding but unpaid commitments (RAP), to (net current) revenue. The indicator shows to what extent available cash at the end of a period is compromised by already committed but not yet executed expenditures. At the end of an electoral term, the FRL further prohibits this indicator from becoming negative; that is, cash resources need to be greater than the volume of commitments payable before an elected term ends.

Investment capacity: The ratio of investment expenditure to (net current) revenue.

Only a Few States Face a Large Debt Burden

States' aggregate indebtedness in Brazil fell by 52 percentage points between 2000 and 2017 (Figure 12.1), but heterogeneity is large. The picture is favorable for most states, with 23 of 27 states having indices below 100 percent of revenues, and 14 not even reaching 50 percent, all well below the established limits. But debt in four large states is markedly higher, and in Rio de Janeiro (270 percent) and Rio Grande do Sul (219 percent) indebtedness surpassed the 200 percent limit established in the FRL. Although only four states display these issues, these states produce nearly 60 percent of Brazil's GDP and are home to about 45 percent of Brazil's population.

High Personnel Expenditure

High mandatory expenses, notably for payroll and pensions, is a defining characteristic of all subnational entities (see also Afonso and Pinto 2016). The contractionary effect of the recession on revenues brought to the fore a structural problem that had been growing for years (Mercês and Freire 2017). Given the mandatory nature and high rigidity of these expense items, a drop in revenue automatically translates into higher financing needs, a reality for the majority of Brazilian states (Figure 12.2). On average, the ratio of personnel expenditures to net current revenue was 56 percent in 2017. The FRL mandates a maximum threshold of 60 percent; at 54 percent the Court of Accounts is alerted to the problem, and at 57 percent the entity is subjected to restrictions that limit further personnel expense increases, such as the granting of additional benefits, pay

---

[9]Total personnel expenditure includes active and inactive personnel and pensioners as well as personnel costs that arise from the outsourcing of contracts. To arrive at a comparable indicator across states, the FRL permits deductions for legal indemnities and judicial deposits in connection with payroll expenditure, expenses in relation to commitments from previous years, and personnel expenses covered by revenues that are earmarked solely for paying pensions.

Figure 12.1. Aggregate State Indebtedness
(Net debt as percent of net current revenue)

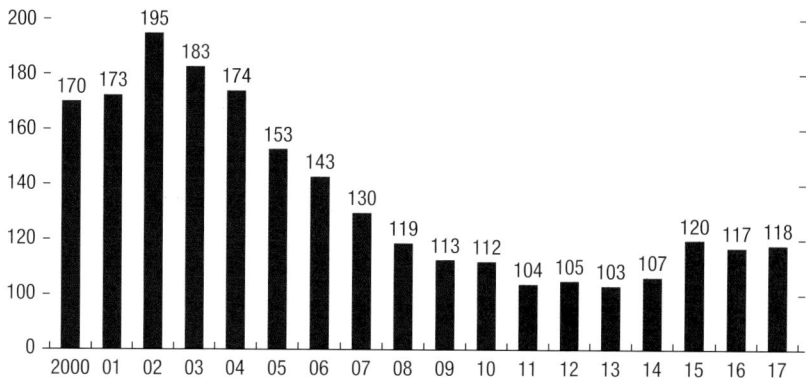

Source: National Treasury.

increases, and other adjustments. In 2017, 16 Brazilian states exceeded the alert limit (54 percent); of these, eight were within the prudential limit (expenditure between 57 and 60 percent of revenues) and four had already exceeded the legal ceiling (Figure 12.2).

As in the federal government, the biggest driver of subnational expenditure is social security, given that benefits outweigh contributions. In 2017, the shortfall of subnational social security systems was 1.3 percent of GDP (88.8 billion reais). In 25 of 27 states, the social security system recorded a deficit that required, on average, 11.4 percent of revenues to cover the shortfall to pay beneficiaries in

Figure 12.2. Personnel Expenditure
(Net personnel expenditure as percent of net current revenue, 2017)

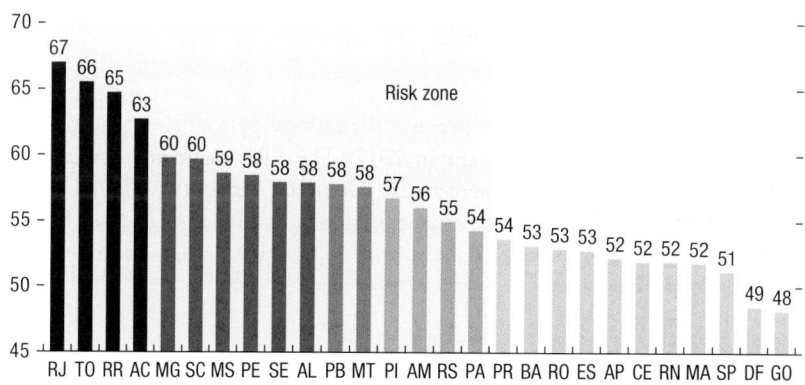

Source: National Treasury.
Note: See Table 12.1 for state abbreviations.

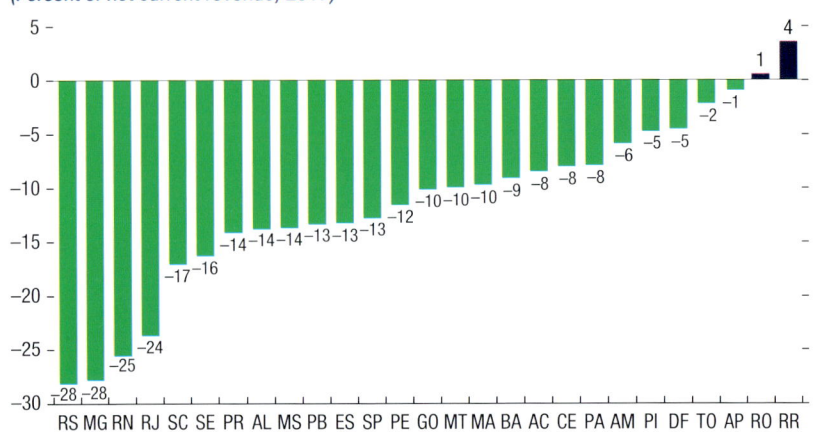

Figure 12.3. Social Security Deficit
(Percent of net current revenue, 2017)

Source: National Treasury.
Note: See Table 12.1 for state abbreviations.

excess of the system's contributions (Figure 12.3). The deficits were larger in states whose demographic structures are older, for example, in Rio Grande do Sul.

Low Investment and Accumulation of Unpaid Commitments

Unsurprisingly, these trends leave little to no room for investment in infra-structure, public safety, health, education, and transportation. Compared with 2014, the year before the recession, states reduced their investments by 52 per-cent in real terms, while their reduction in revenue was only about 4 percent, which reduced investment to below 6 percent of net revenue (Figure 12.4). Only the state of Ceará has invested more than 10 percent of revenues; the states with the largest fiscal problems—Rio de Janeiro, Minas Gerais, and Rio Grande do Sul—have investment rates at or below 2 percent of revenues.

In a context of falling revenues, the inability to issue debt and high budgetary rigidity led the postponement of expenses—accumulating unpaid commitments—to become an important source of financing. All states increased their unpaid commitments during 2015–16, reaching about ½ percent of GDP per year for all states combined, a significantly weaker fiscal position when compared with a below-the-line measurement. Not surprisingly, five states closed 2017 with unpaid commitments that were higher than available cash resources (Figure 12.5).

CHALLENGES GOING FORWARD

The 2015–16 recession exposed states' structural fiscal problems—mostly related to pension and personnel expenditures—that, in large part, remain

Figure 12.4. Investment Capacity
(Investment as percent of net current revenue, aggregate for all states)

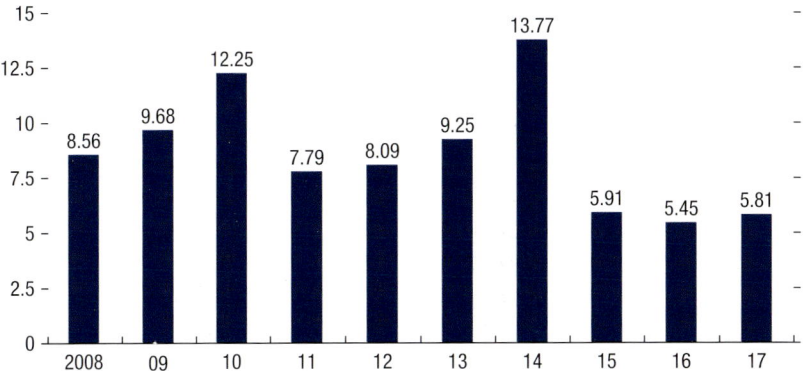

Source: National Treasury.

Figure 12.5. Cash Balances Net of Commitments
(Percent of net current revenue, 2017)

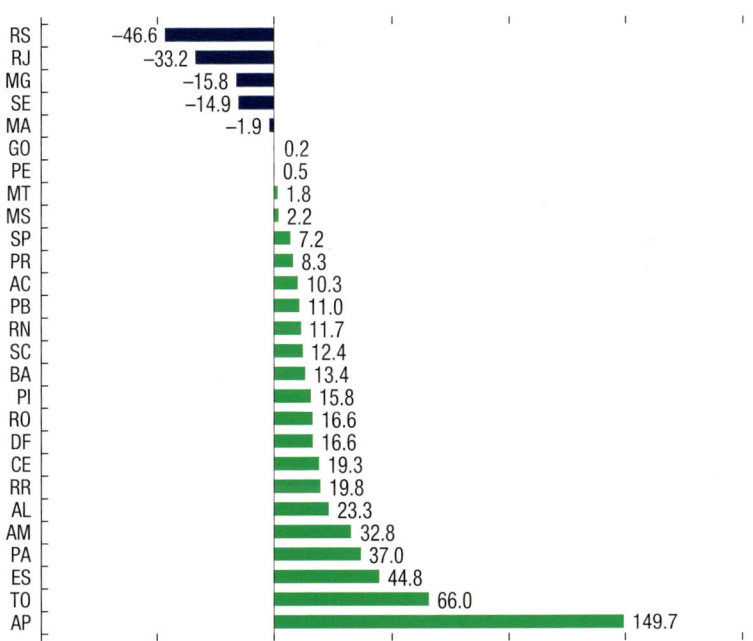

Source: National Treasury.
Note: See Table 12.1 for state abbreviations.

Box 12.1. Rio de Janeiro

The fiscal situation of the state of Rio de Janeiro is the most critical in Brazil. It reflects structural fiscal problems as well as the state economy's turning fortunes. Rio was disproportionately affected by the 2015–16 recession because of its dependence on the oil and gas industry at a time when oil prices collapsed and Petrobras, the state-owned company, found itself in the midst of the Lava Jato ("Car Wash") corruption scandal.

Between 2013 and 2016 Rio's net current revenue collapsed by more than 20 percent, sending it back to levels last seen in 2009. The fall in oil prices triggered a collapse in royalties from oil production, which alone contributed to more than half of the revenue decline. Tax revenue, primarily state turnover taxes, contracted with economic activity, contributing the remainder. Rio's debt-to-revenue ratio is the highest among states; it jumped from an already-high 154 percent of GDP in 2013 to 270 percent in 2017, well exceeding Fiscal Responsibility Law (FRL) thresholds. The explosive debt trajectory was a consequence of untenable starting conditions, since Rio's debt was already high at the time of the 1997 debt renegotiation, and the FRL limit to annual debt-service payments caused the debt stock to increase through capitalization of residual debt service. In addition, six successive years of budget deficits pressed fiscal accounts, exacerbated by the large and growing stock of unpaid commitments, which stood at 33 percent of current revenue in 2017.

In 2016 the state was unable to pay civil servants on time, was forced to reduce public services, and defaulted on external loans from international financial institutions, triggering sovereign guarantees. Federal government support became inevitable, and an emergency operation was undertaken on the eve of the 2016 Olympic Games. Subsequently, the Fiscal Recovery Regime was put in place, and Rio became the first state to sign an agreement with the federal government.

The agreement suspends debt service for three years and allows the state to borrow to cope with liquidity problems while putting state assets up for sale. The agreement also projects a balanced budget from 2022 onward, but one year after the agreement part of the required adjustment measures was delayed. The payroll contribution to pensions was increased from 11 to 14 percent; however, this increase is not sufficient to close the deficit in the pension plan. Personnel expenditure continues to be greater than the legal threshold because the measures that have been taken are not sufficient to contain payroll growth. Priority expenditure is squeezed, hampering the provision of public services. And as the end of the recession and rising oil prices provide temporary relief to fiscal accounts, the pressure to implement structural measures has faded, and whether state finances will be on a structurally sustainable footing at the end of the program horizon is still uncertain.

The revenue collapse not only exposed the large and growing share of personnel expenses in overall expenditure, it also brought to light poor accounting practices and the need to harmonize and review data provision in states more generally. For example, in 2005 a state decree authorized the use of oil royalties to cover the state's social security deficit. Hence, higher royalty revenues would reduce the personnel-to-current-revenue indicator on two accounts: in the numerator, by reducing the social security deficit, and by increasing the denominator. When royalties fell with falling oil prices from 2014 onward, the indicator rapidly increased beyond the critical thresholds (Figure 12.1.1). Between 2015 and 2016, personnel spending increased by almost 30 percentage points of net current revenue. Correcting for the impact of royalties (and other extraordinary revenues, for example, property sale income), the state would have already breached the critical threshold of 60 percent in 2014.

Box 12.1. Rio de Janeiro   *(continued)*

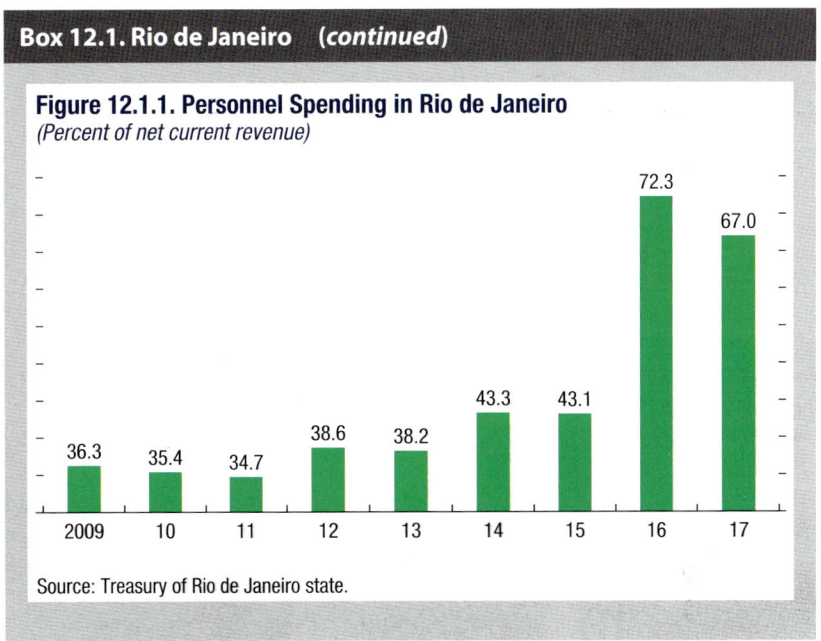

Figure 12.1.1. Personnel Spending in Rio de Janeiro
(Percent of net current revenue)

Source: Treasury of Rio de Janeiro state.

unresolved. The well-known federal-government-level spending rigidities also pressure state finances, although to varying degrees. However, without easy access to financing and bound by legal limits, those states that were hit hard by the crisis had little choice but to incur arrears, becoming noncompliant with fiscal responsibility legislation. Investment has fallen across the board and, in a few but important cases, public service provision in health and security has been impaired. Within these spending rigidities, expenditure on social security is high and unsustainable, in particular where the population is aging faster. States can take—and have been taking—measures to reduce social security deficits, including by raising contributions and proposing temporary surcharges. But there is a limit, legally and politically, to social security reforms that can be undertaken by states alone, putting a premium on comprehensive social security reform led by the federal government. A federal reform designed to tackle unsustainable entitlements, including by addressing high replacement rates and unifying systems across service categories (see Cuevas and others 2017, and World Bank 2017), could be emulated in large part by the states.

On the revenue side, competition between states in setting turnover taxes to attract businesses, often granting generous tax incentives, has contributed to states' forgoing significant amounts of revenue, often in return for questionable benefits. Harmonization of state-level tax rates, timely sunset clauses on exemptions, and cooperation on tax administration would reduce not only tax expenditures but also the cost of doing business across states. More broadly, and in the context of broader reforms, a review of tax-sharing arrangements and better alignment of taxation authority and expenditure responsibilities between and across levels of government could improve coordination in the federation (see Ter-Minassian 2012).

The federal government has rightly identified the provision of accurate, timely, and comparable subnational data as a priority area for improvement. Important progress, even if uneven across states, has been made, including by the National Treasury's accessible publication of state-level data (for example, Ministry of Finance 2016). However, state-level data standards differ, and the enforcement of standards is uneven. State-level courts of accounts have an important role to play in leveling accounting standards and enforcing comprehensive, accurate, and timely fiscal reporting. Some states have also undertaken external fiscal transparency assessments (IDB and IMF 2016).

The history of subnational bailouts in Brazil will continue to be a defining feature in the relationship between states and the federal government. The federal government is the states' main creditor and debt guarantor, and market discipline to enforce subnational fiscal discipline is not an immediate option for

Table 12.1. Brazilian States and the Federal District, 2015

	Abbreviation	GDP	Population
Acre	AC	0.2	0.4
Alagoas	AL	0.8	1.6
Amazonas	AM	1.4	1.9
Amapá	AP	0.2	0.4
Bahia	BA	4.1	7.4
Ceará	CE	2.2	4.4
Distrito Federal	DF	3.6	1.4
Espírito Santo	ES	2.0	1.9
Goiás	GO	2.9	3.2
Maranhão	MA	1.3	3.4
Minas Gerais	MG	8.7	10.2
Mato Grosso do Sul	MS	1.4	1.3
Mato Grosso	MT	1.8	1.6
Pará	PA	2.2	4.0
Paraíba	PB	0.9	1.9
Pernambuco	PE	2.6	4.6
Piauí	PI	0.7	1.6
Paraná	PR	6.3	5.5
Rio de Janeiro	RJ	11.0	8.1
Rio Grande do Norte	RN	1.0	1.7
Rondônia	RO	0.6	0.9
Roraima	RR	0.2	0.2
Rio Grande do Sul	RS	6.4	5.5
Santa Catarina	SC	4.2	3.4
Sergipe	SE	0.6	1.1
São Paulo	SP	32.4	21.7
Tocantins	TO	0.5	0.7

Source: IBGE (Brazilian Institute of Geography and Statistics).

strengthening commitment to fiscal discipline. Thus, the challenge will remain to develop the subnational framework to support subnational fiscal adjustment programs through structural fiscal reforms while avoiding moral hazard.

REFERENCES

Afonso, Jose Roberto, and Vilma da Conceição Pinto. 2016. "State Expenditures with Executive Active Personnel: A Comparison between Federated Units." IDP–Virtual Notebooks, 21/10/2016.

Bevilaqua, Afonso S. 2002. "State Government Bailouts in Brazil." IDB Working Paper No. 153, Inter-American Development Bank, Washington, DC.

Cuevas, Alfredo, Izabela Karpowicz, Carlos Mulas-Granados, and Mauricio Soto. 2017. "Fiscal Challenges of Population Aging in Brazil." IMF Working Paper No. 17/99, International Monetary Fund, Washington DC.

Dillinger, W. 1997. "Brazil's State Debt Crisis: Lessons Learned." The World Bank, Country Department 1–Latin American and the Caribbean Region, Economic Notes 14, September.

FIRJAN—Federation of Industries of the State of Rio de Janeiro. 2018. FIRJAN Fiscal Management Index: Base Year 2016.

Inter-American Development Bank (IDB) and International Monetary Fund (IMF). 2016. "Sao Paulo: Evaluating Fiscal Transparency." Washington, DC.

Mercês, Guilherme, and Nayara Freire. 2017. "Fiscal Crisis of the States and the Case of Rio de Janeiro." Revista GEO UERJ.

Ministry of Finance. 2016. "Public Finances Bulletin of Subnational Institutions." Brasília.

Mora, Mônica. 2002. "Federalism and State Debt in Brazil." Institute of Applied Economic Research, Text for Discussion No. 866, March.

Rossi Júnior, Jose Luiz, and Fernando Aguiar. 2018. "Understanding the Evolution of the Fiscal Situation of the Brazilian States: 2006–2015." *Economia* 19: 105–131.

Ter-Minassian, Teresa. 2012. "Reform Priorities for Subnational Revenues in Brazil." Policy Brief IDB-PB-157, Inter-American Development Bank, Washington, DC.

Ter-Minassian, Teresa, and Luiz de Mello. 2016. "Intergovernmental Fiscal Cooperation–International Experiences and Possible Lessons for Brazil." Technical Note No. IDB-TN-1048, Inter-American Development Bank, Washington, DC.

World Bank. 2013. "Federative Republic of Brazil, BR Intergovernmental Finance. DLW–Impact and Implications of Recent and Potential Changes to Brazil's Subnational Fiscal Framework." Latin American and Caribbean, Report No. ACS5885, Washington, DC.

———. 2017. *A Fair Adjustment: Efficiency and Equity of Public Spending in Brazil: Volume 1–Overview*. Washington, DC: World Bank Group.

CHAPTER 13

Rightsizing the Public Sector Wage Bill

Izabela Karpowicz and Mauricio Soto

Brazil's public sector wage bill is comparatively high and competes with other spending. Rightsizing the wage bill is necessary to comply with the federal government expenditure ceiling, stimulate administrative efficiency, and bring more equity into the system. A reform should include subnational governments, where most of the public employment is concentrated and where the wage bill has grown pronouncedly in recent years. Brazil's wage bill grows inertially owing to automatic progression rules. To contain its growth, therefore, it is necessary to reduce salaries in real terms and shrink employment through attrition. In the medium term, a review of the compensation structure should simplify the wage grids, merge allowances into the base wage, and align government pay to private wages in low-skill professions.

Rightsizing personnel expenditure—in this chapter denoted as the wage bill—is coming to the fore of the reform agenda in Brazil. As the government strives to meet multiple goals—regain fiscal sustainability, comply with fiscal rules, and improve income distribution—taking a closer look at the wage bill across all government levels becomes necessary.

To comply with fiscal rules and ensure fiscal sustainability, Brazil must contain the wage bill. A 2016 constitutional amendment limits the federal government's primary expenditure growth to the rate of inflation. Meeting this rule requires a break from historical trends: on average, the federal wage bill increased by about 4 percent a year in real terms during 2000–16. In subnational governments, containing the wage bill is fundamental to maintaining personnel expenditures below 60 percent of the net revenues ratio (at least two states are already surpassing this level), as mandated by the Fiscal Responsibility Law.

Reviewing government compensation can have productivity spillovers. Growth of wages in the public sector may put pressure on economy-wide wages because, across many professions, public wages can be used as benchmarks for private sector compensation. Evidence suggests that Brazil's wages have grown above productivity in recent years and may be hindering job creation and growth (Lipinsky 2015). In addition, high compensation levels in the public sector can crowd out available skills that are much needed to support private sector competitiveness and job creation.

Moderating civil servants' wage growth would be equitable. Over the past decade, labor formalization, income growth, the government social welfare program Bolsa Família, and schooling have contributed to declining inequality (Góes and Karpowicz 2017). But growth of civil servants' incomes has affected equality negatively. To the extent that wages are higher in the public sector than in the private sector, systematic government wage increases have undermined the success of redistribution policies and slowed equality gains in Brazil.

The Brazilian experience in managing the wage bill can provide lessons to other countries that might also need to evaluate government compensation and employment practices in the context of broader reforms. International experiences suggest that increases in the wage bill tend to be associated with worse fiscal outcomes and can have adverse implications for private sector employment (IMF 2016). In some countries, wage bill policies have had limited success in achieving their objectives while exacerbating fiscal pressures and constraining inclusive growth (Tamirisa and Duenwald 2018). The literature suggests that blunt responses such as wage and hiring freezes can provide temporary relief. Structural reforms that target sectors with excessive employment and wage levels, supported by strong institutions, are required for more sustained wage bill adjustment while protecting service delivery.

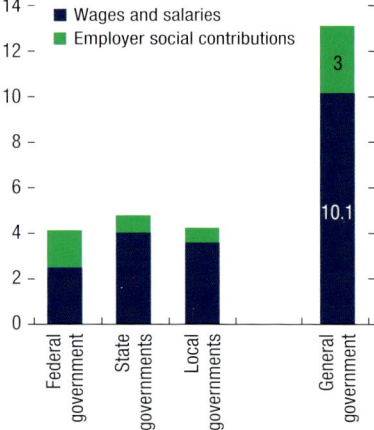

Figure 13.1. Compensation of Employees, 2016
(Percent of GDP)

Source: IMF, Government Finance Statistics.

In the general government, expenditure on compensation of employees reached 13 percent of GDP in 2016 (Figure 13.1). The wage bill includes spending on wages and salaries (10 percent of GDP) and the government's social contributions as an employer (3 percent of GDP). The wage bill accounts for a substantial portion of government expenditure. In the federal government, the wage bill is the second-largest primary spending item after social security benefits. In state and municipal governments, it is nearly half of primary expenditure.

Subnational governments account for a large share of the general government wage bill. Nearly 75 percent of the wage bill and 85 percent of government jobs are in state and municipal governments. This approach reflects the division of responsibilities: about 55 percent of employees in state and municipal governments work in health, education, and security, compared with 35 percent in the federal government (Figure 13.2). The federal government including the judiciary accounts for 8 and 17 percent of federal government employment and the wage

Figure 13.2. Government Employment, 2015
(Percent of working-age population)

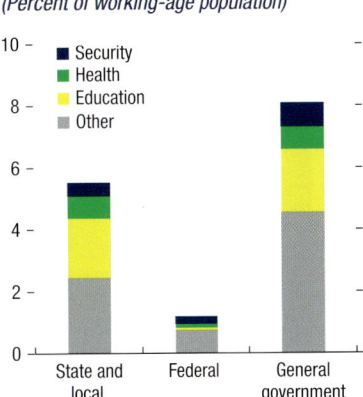

Source: PNAD (Pesquisa Nacional por Amostra de Domicílios, National Household Sample Survey).

Figure 13.3. Government Monthly Pay, 2015

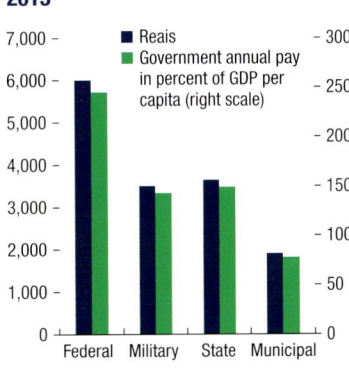

Source: PNAD (Pesquisa Nacional por Amostra de Domicílios, National Household Sample Survey).

bill, respectively, and the military accounts for 28 percent and 13 percent of federal government employment and the wage bill, respectively.

Substantial pay disparities occur across the different levels of government. Average compensation levels are considerably higher for civilians in the federal government (about to R$6,000 per month in 2015) than for military (about R$3,500), state officials (about R$3,500), and municipal employees (about R$1,900; Figure 13.3). While federal government employees tend to be better educated (Figure 13.4), the differences in pay across governments remain controlling for schooling, with wider differences for those with high school or more.

The wage bill varies considerably across states. As a share of their own GDP, states spend between 4 (São Paulo) and 20 (Roraima) percent of GDP (Figure 13.5). Poorer, smaller states in the north and northeast tend to spend more on the wage bill (as a share of their economy and per capita) and have higher government employment (as a share of the state population). An exception is the federal district (DF), where the central government administration is located, which has the highest per capita wage bill. The government wage bill in the education sector follows a similar pattern—higher in poorer states and dispersed (between 0.8 and 4.5 percent of state GDP). Public health wage bills are substantially smaller.

THE NEED FOR GOVERNMENT WAGE AND EMPLOYMENT REFORM

The wage bill has been increasing, particularly in subnational governments, raising concerns about fiscal sustainability. Spending on employee compensation increased by 1 percentage point of GDP in 2010–16, largely reflecting higher wage expenditure in state and municipal governments. In the federal government, although the wage bill increased in real terms over the six years, it has remained broadly constant in percent of GDP. This is the case for employee compensation in the federal executive, judiciary, and legislative branches.

The wage bill is at a high level relative to peers. At 13 percent of GDP, the wage bill is substantially above comparators, including advanced economies (where the average compensation of government employees is 10 percent of GDP), emerging market economies (9 percent of GDP), and

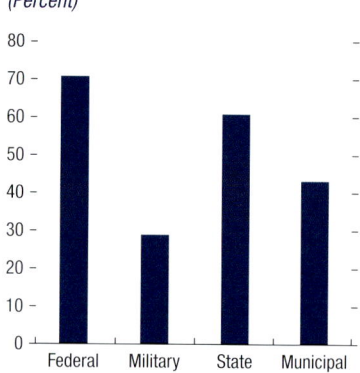

Figure 13.4. Share of Employees with Education beyond High School
(Percent)

Source: PNAD (Pesquisa Nacional por Amostra de Domicílios, National Household Sample Survey).

Latin America (8 percent of GDP; Figure 13.6). This is true even considering only spending on wages and salaries (see Karpowicz and Soto 2018 for a discussion of measurement issues and cross-country comparisons). Employee compensation stands at nearly 45 percent of general government revenue, a much higher share than in advanced and emerging market economies (Figure 13.7). Brazil also spends more on compensation of public employees in per capita terms than other emerging markets do. Adjusted for purchasing power parity, Brazil's wage bill per

Figure 13.5. Government Wage Bill and Employment
(By state, 2015)

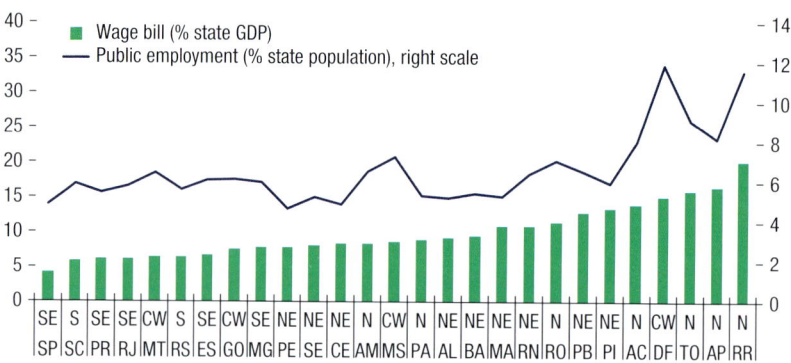

Source: PNAD (Pesquisa Nacional por Amostra de Domicilios, National Household Sample Survey).
Note: Data labels correspond to the five geographical regions of Brazil: N for North, NE for Northeast, CW for Central West, SE for Southeast, and S for South.

Figure 13.6. Compensation of Employees, 2016
(Percent of GDP)

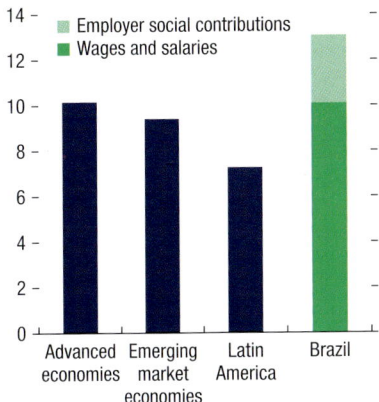

Source: IMF staff calculations using World Economic Outlook and Government Finance Statistics data.

Figure 13.7. Compensation of Employees, 2016
(Percent of government revenue)

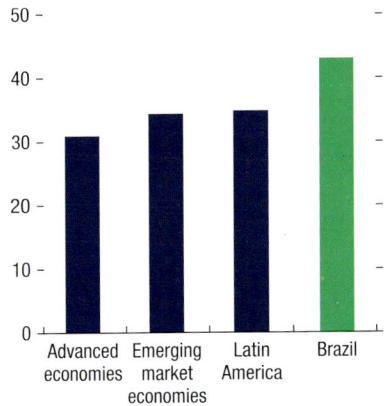

Source: IMF staff calculations using World Economic Outlook and Government Finance Statistics data.

capita is higher than the average observed in LA5 countries (Brazil, Chile, Colombia, Mexico, Peru), Latin America and the Caribbean, emerging market economies, and the entire sample of 158 countries.

Curtailing the federal government wage bill is crucial to compliance with the constitutional expenditure ceiling. A constitutional rule caps the federal government's primary expenditure growth at the rate of inflation. To comply with this rule, federal government expenditure must be reduced by 2.5 percentage points of GDP (from about 20 to 17.5 percent of GDP in 2017–23). This will require pension reform (to offset the projected growth in pension spending), substantial reductions in other expenditure items, and a reduction in federal government expenditure on personnel by at least 1 percentage point of GDP (Figure 13.8). Such adjustment in the wage bill requires a break from historical trends—the federal wage bill has traditionally increased in real terms, and complying with the rule will imply real reductions. In state governments, reducing the wage bill is important to compliance with the Fiscal Responsibility Law.

The considerable space taken by the wage bill limits other productive spending. Brazil's wage bill is six times greater than public investment. This reflects a very low public investment level in Brazil and high spending on personnel (Figure 13.9). Furthermore, the wage bill is procyclical. In real terms, the wage bill has displayed some procyclicality over the past three decades, increasing on average 0.47 percentage point for a 1 percent increase in the output gap, above the emerging market average (IMF 2016).

Figure 13.8. Federal Government Expenditure, 2017–23
(Percent of GDP)

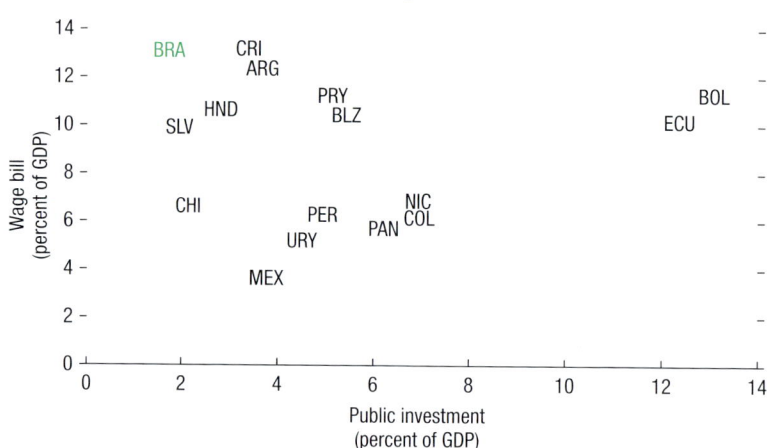

Source: IMF staff calculations.

In the past decade, government wages have outpaced those in the private sector—public wages increased by nearly 45 percent in real terms, while those in the private sector increased by about 25 percent. Such growth puts pressure on economy-wide wages as, across many professions, public wages can be used as benchmarks for private sector compensation. This can also crowd out available skills that are much needed to support private sector competitiveness and job creation.

Figure 13.9. Public Investment and Wage Bill in Latin America

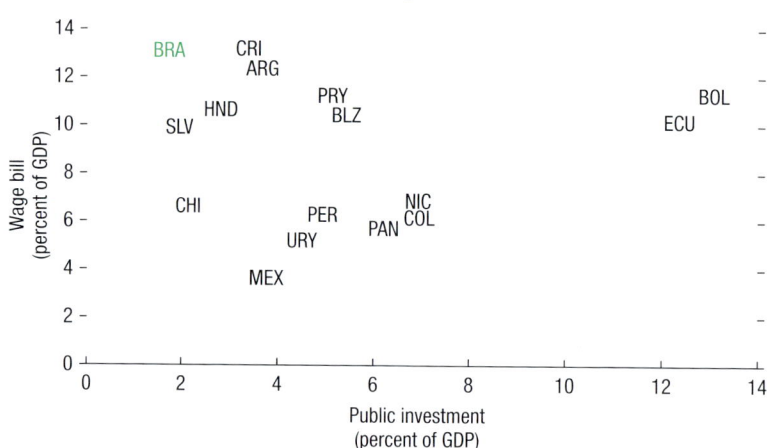

Source: IMF staff calculations.
Note: Data labels in the figure use International Organization for Standardization (ISO) country codes.

The level of pay is the main factor explaining the relatively high wage bill. Brazil's general government *employment* is about in line with that observed in other emerging market and developing economies (below 9 percent of the working-age population), albeit slightly higher than in other Latin American economies (Figure 13.10). In contrast, relative to other countries, Brazil's government workers command a substantially higher pay premium than those in the private sector. Controlling for observable characteristics (including age, education, and gender), public pay is about 30 percent higher than pay in the formal private sector. This markup is substantially higher than the average markup (9 percent) for countries in the Luxembourg Income Study data set (Figure 13.11). This is

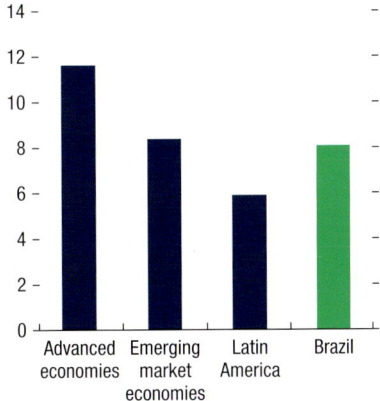

Figure 13.10. Government Employment
(Percent of working-age population)

Source: IMF staff calculations using World Economic Outlook and Government Finance Statistics data.

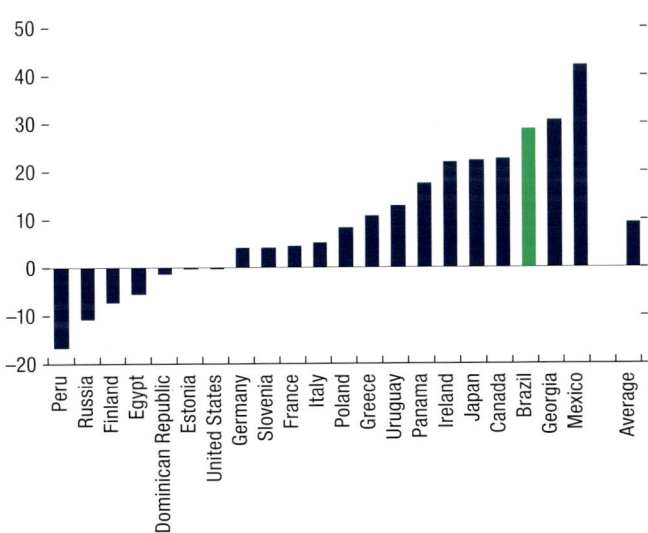

Figure 13.11. Public Wage Premiums, by Country
(Percent)

Source: IMF staff calculations using Luxembourg Income Study data.

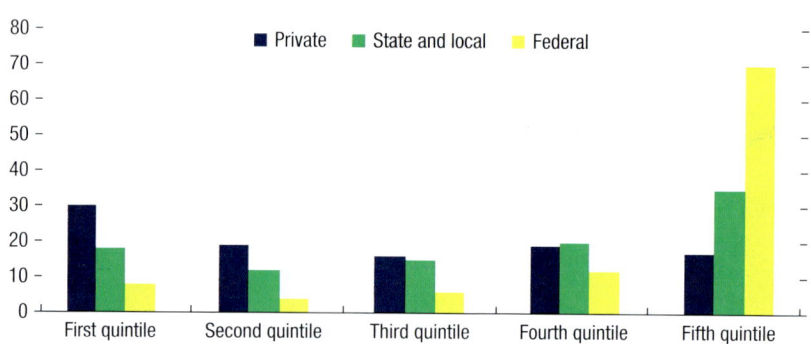

Figure 13.12. Distribution of Employment, by Sector and Earnings Quintile
(Percent of total)

Sources: Monthly Employment Survey (PME)/Brazilian Institute for Geography and Statistics (IBGE); and IMF staff calculations.

consistent with recent work that shows that, controlling for observable characteristics, public sector wages are as much as 50 percent higher than private wages for those with fewer years of education, but the premium decreases somewhat at higher educational levels (Góes and Karpowicz 2017).

The wage gaps would be even higher from the perspective of lifetime income. Lifetime net pension benefits are also higher in the public sector. The net transfer received by the government (the difference between all retirement and survivor benefits, on the one hand, and all contributions paid by or on behalf of the employee, on the other hand) is particularly high for public workers, implying a high internal rate of return on their pensions (see Chapter 11). When controlling for the more generous retirement benefits, public-private cumulative lifetime pay differentials are even higher.

Government workers, particularly those in the federal government, are among those better off in the earnings distribution. Most government workers are in the top two quintiles of the earnings distribution (80 percent of federal government workers and 55 percent of state and local government workers; Figure 13.12). To the extent that wages are higher in the public sector than in the private sector, systematic government wage increases might have undermined the success of redistribution policies and slowed equality gains in Brazil.

THE FEDERAL GOVERNMENT IN FOCUS

At the federal government level, timely payroll data are publicly available from the Transparency Portal. The monthly payroll data for more than 580,000 civilian employees include name, position, total earnings, terms of contract, and tenure (Table 13.1). Mean federal earnings are about R$9,600 (the median is R$7,700). Earnings at the 90th percentile are 5.4 times those at the 10th percentile, with

Table 13.1. Summary of Civilian Federal Payroll, October 2017

	Gross Monthly Salary[1]			Contractual (percent)	Tenure (years)	Employees (thousands)	Percent of	
	Mean	Median	P90–P10				Employment	Wage Bill
Lower Skills	5,685	5,115	3.0	7.3	19.5	273	47	28
Clerical	5,364	4,974	2.7	7.3	19.5	209	36	20
Technical	6,733	6,272	2.8	1.1	19.8	64	11	8
Higher Skills	11,641	11,324	3.2	2.6	14.3	274	47	57
Professional	9,541	8,630	2.6	0.9	14.6	19	3	3
Professor	12,012	11,630	3.2	0.9	11.2	131	22	28
Health Care	13,907	13,849	4.1	1.1	17.2	20	3	5
Analyst	14,004	13,397	3.2	1.2	12.1	34	6	8
Management	23,872	24,943	1.5	0.4	15.9	36	6	15
All	9,611	7,647	5.4	4.2	16.3	583	100	100

Source: Brazilian Transparency Portal.

[1]Reais.

Table 13.2. Coefficients of Log Earning Regressions

	All	All	Lower Skills	Higher Skills
Lower Skills		−68		
Management		65		62
Contractual	−26	−65	−17	−139
Tenure 0–20 Years	2.8	2.9	2.0	3.3
Tenure 20+ Years	−0.3	−0.4	−0.1	−0.7
Entity Controls	Yes	Yes	Yes	Yes
State Controls	Yes	Yes	Yes	Yes
Job Description Controls	Yes	No	No	No
Number of Observations (thousands)	567	567	262	306
R^2	0.68	0.62	0.28	0.61

Source: IMF staff calculations.
Note: All coefficients shown are significant at the 99 percent level.

more compression by skills (the ratio is about 3 within lower- and higher-skill positions). More than 95 percent of those on the payroll have permanent contracts. The average tenure is 16 years, with higher tenure for those in lower-skill positions.

The civilian federal workforce includes a diverse range of skills and pay. Clerical, administrative, and technical employees account for 47 percent of employment and 28 percent of the federal government wage bill. The rest corresponds to professionals (including higher-education professors, management and high-ranking government officers, health and social security professionals, and police). The different shares of employment and compensation reflect pay differentials largely related to levels of education and responsibility: the average monthly pay of clerical and administrative employees is about R$5,700, while professionals earn R$11,600 a month and high-ranking officers R$23,900 a month.

The compensation structure depends on multiple career streams that reward seniority and complicate wage bill management. More than 130 career streams (*carreira*) set specific rank and pay progression and allowances for government employees, defined across occupational and professional job categories (OECD 2010). These streams are often entity-specific, preventing mobility across ministries. Only about one-quarter of the federal workforce is under "job groups" that allow for mobility across different entities.

Higher-skill positions command higher earnings. In a log-earnings specification, controlling for entity and geographical location, lower-skilled workers earn about 68 percent less, while those in managerial positions earn 65 percent more, relative to workers in professional positions (Table 13.2).

Seniority is an important determinant of earnings. Each additional year of tenure up to 20 increases earnings by 2 percent in low-skill positions and 3.3 in high-skill positions. However, the premium for additional years of tenure disappears after 20 years. This reflects the typical wage profile associated with many careers, with automatic increases of 3–4 percent for the first 10–20 years of service in professional posts (in other words, pay would be about 30–40 percent higher for those

Figure 13.13. Wage Differentials by Federal Entity
(Percent)

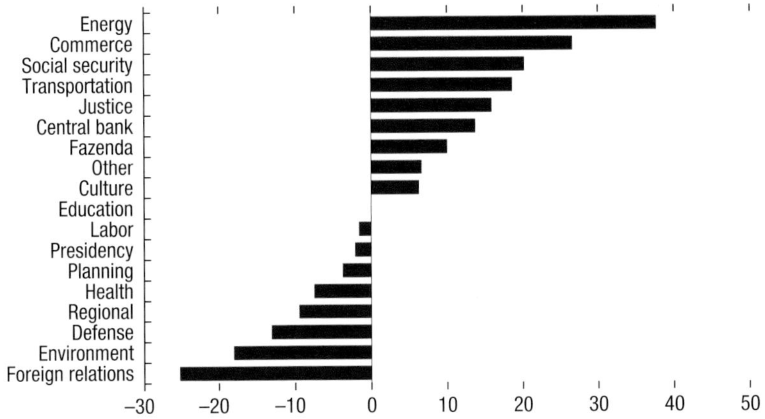

Source: IMF staff calculations.
Note: Coefficients of entity in log-earnings regressions controlling for job position, tenure, and state. The excluded entity is the Ministry of Education, which has average earnings slightly below the average for the federal government. Wage differentials are similar for low-skilled workers.

with 10 years of tenure compared with new entrants in comparable positions) and 1–2 percent in clerical positions.

Pay also includes a performance component. Federal government pay also includes a performance-based bonus (*gratificações e bônus de desempenho*) that reflects the attainment of institutional (80 percent) and personal goals (20 percent). However, these bonuses can only be weakly related to performance: nearly 80 percent of the government workforce received the bonus in 2017.

The multitude of careers and wage grids introduces disparities in earnings for similar positions *across* different entities. Controlling for position, terms of contract, tenure, and state, federal government earnings vary substantially across entities (Figure 13.13). These differences can be striking and seem to contradict the principle of equal pay for equal work. On average, a motorist in the Ministry of Energy earns about 30 percent more than in the rest of the federal government, and a telephone operator in the Ministry of Transportation earns 53 percent more than in the rest of the federal government.

The wage structure is relatively compressed, introducing some distortions. More than 90 percent of federal government civilian employees receive earnings above R$3,500 (R$3,100 after tax withholding and deductions). This is more than 3.5 times the minimum wage and nearly equal to the average earnings a *professional* could expect to earn in the private sector. The combination of relatively high government wages for low-skilled workers, the high returns to seniority, and the disparate compensation by entity explain why workers in clerical, administrative, and technical positions often earn higher wages than those in entry-level professions. For example, an *auxiliar* (assistant) with 10–20 years of service can earn a salary higher than an entry-level engineer.

The wage scales are updated periodically through agreements between the federal government and the different categories of workers. Agreements can cover different groups under different careers and wage structures, such as the police, teachers, and doctors, as well as the Ministry of Finance and the Treasury. For example, in the 2015 salary accord, the government and employee representatives agreed to a salary increase in two steps: 5.5 percent to be effective August 2016 and 5 percent to be effective January 2017. This was originally agreed to with about 70 percent of workers representing different career streams and entities, and later extended to the wider federal sector. However, these adjustments were delayed during the crisis, and the first adjustment took place only in January 2018.

REFORM OPTIONS

Government wage bills are inertial. The constitution provides job stability to government workers after three years of service (Article 41). Thus, meaningful employment reductions can be achieved only by attrition (replacing fewer workers than those who retire). The constitution also states that government remuneration cannot be reduced in nominal terms (Article 37. XV). Thus, pay adjustments can generally be made only by limiting wage increases. And even in the absence of negotiated pay increases, nominal wages tend to increase automatically with the seniority premium that applies to most careers.

To achieve fiscal savings in the near term, wages would have to fall in real terms and the employment-to-population ratio would have to decrease. In a baseline where annual negotiated wage increases are above the rate of inflation (consistent with recent experience) and government employment grows in line with population growth, the wage bill would remain roughly stable in percent of GDP. Achieving fiscal savings would require substantial adjustments to remuneration and hiring. For example, achieving total savings of 0.5 percentage point of GDP would require freezing average remuneration in nominal terms (that is, no negotiated wage increase) and halting new hiring for the next five years (Table 13.3). This illustrates the magnitude of measures that are likely required to comply with the constitutional expenditure ceiling. In state and municipal governments, a similar adjustment would achieve savings of nearly 2 percentage points of GDP.

Containing remuneration growth: The relatively high government wage premium relative to the private sector indicates room for saving without affecting service delivery (freezing average wages for about five years would be necessary to realign pay to that of the private sector). The government should consider a multiyear agreement with employees to maintain wage increases below the rate of inflation. An alternative would be to differentiate negotiated increases by performance while maintaining the average increase under the rate of inflation. In addition, the government should review nonsalary pay, including existing bonuses and allowances (*auxílios*). This should be done for both the federal government

Table 13.3. Illustrative Options for Containing the Wage Bill

	2017	2018	2019	2020	2021	2022
Federal Government						
Wages and Salaries Spending (baseline)	2.5	2.5	2.5	2.5	2.5	2.5
Impact of Freezing Wages		−0.1	−0.2	−0.3	−0.4	−0.5
Impact of Halting New Hiring		0.0	−0.1	−0.1	−0.1	−0.2
Wage Bill (after measures)		2.4	2.2	2.1	2.0	1.9
State and Local Governments						
Wages and Salaries Spending (baseline)	7.6	7.6	7.7	7.7	7.7	7.7
Impact of Freezing Wages		−0.3	−0.6	−0.9	−1.2	−1.5
Impact of Halting New Hiring		−0.1	−0.2	−0.3	−0.4	−0.5
Wages and Salaries Spending (baseline)		7.2	6.8	6.5	6.1	5.7

Source: IMF staff calculations.

(including the legislative and judiciary) and the subnational governments, where the compensation structure of health-care professionals should introduce incentives to increase productivity (World Bank 2017).

Containing employment growth: Because employment levels do not seem high relative to other countries, initial efforts should be made to enhance workforce flexibility. There might be room to curtail employment growth, particularly for low-skilled individuals in the federal government, where one-third of employment comprises clerical positions. Nevertheless, any curtailment in hiring should be well targeted to entities and positions with identified overemployment and supported by measures to better allow for job movement across the different entities of the federal government. In state and municipal governments—where most of the growth in employment has occurred in the past decade (World Bank 2017)—any employment adjustments would need to be carefully targeted to ensure adequate service delivery. For example, in education, attrition-based policies should target school districts with relatively low student-to-teacher ratios (World Bank 2017).

In the medium term, it is necessary to rethink the compensation structure. Structural adjustments require a review of the legal framework that regulates pay and employment. Multiple wage grids must be simplified, starting by merging careers for which the wage structure overlaps. Wages should be gradually realigned with the private sector, particularly for low-skilled individuals, for whom the wage premium seems to be the highest. The seniority increases should be either eliminated or greatly reduced (an average increase of 3 percent per year of seniority is excessive in an environment of 4 percent inflation) and linked to performance and job responsibility. However, structural reforms to the wage structure will take time and carry risks—unifying salary structures tends to push personnel costs up; in a transition, setting different compensation levels for the same job can complicate human resource management; legal risks can mitigate the savings—and thus should be considered carefully. There might be scope for improving wage composition and transparency by limiting the number and size of allowances, including by setting a limit on the weight of these in total remuneration by individual and entity. In light of the high wage bill, a review of employment and compensation in the judiciary could be considered, but it would need to satisfy the peculiarities imposed by the legal framework and ensure continued trust in the system.

Particularly for state and municipal governments, long-term workforce planning should reflect demographic developments. Assuming a constant ratio of public employment in total population, as in the 2015 National Household Sample Survey, and population aging, as projected in national statistics per the Brazilian Institute of Geography and Statistics, the ratio of teachers to students through tertiary education will grow from 38 per 1,000 students in 2016 to 44 per 1,000 students over the next decade. To maintain a constant ratio of teachers to student-age population over this period, the teachers' population would have to decline by about 10 percent of total employment in education (nearly 250,000 teachers). Estimated savings on the wage bill from such a decrease are in the order of 0.15 percent of GDP and, given the retirement profile of teachers, could be achieved easily through attrition.

Brazil urgently needs to enhance its oversight and fiscal transparency of subnational government wage bills. Real-time payroll information—such as that available in the Transparency Portal for the federal government—should be available for subnational government employment and remuneration, following common standards. This effort would support the monitoring of fiscal rules and inform measures needed to comply with efficiency and sustainability objectives. Moving toward a medium-term budget approach should help improve human resource management.

REFERENCES

Clements, Benedict, Sanjeev Gupta, Izabela Karpowicz, and Tareq Shamsuddin. 2010. "Evaluating Government Employment and Compensation." Technical Notes and Manuals 10/15, International Monetary Fund, Washington, DC.

Da Ros, Luciano. 2015. "The Cost of Justice in Brazil: An Exploratory Comparative Analysis." *The Observatory of Social and Political Elites* 2 (9): Federal University of Paraná.

Góes, Carlos, and Izabela Karpowicz. 2017. "Inequality in Brazil: A Regional Perspective." IMF Working Paper 17/225, International Monetary Fund, Washington, DC.

Hamilton Matos dos Santos, Cláudio, Carolina Valani Cavalcante, Felipe dos Santos Martins, Luciana Pacheco Trindade Lacerda, and Bernardo Patta Schettini. 2016. "Evolution of Public Employment in Brazilian Subnational Governments in the Period 2004–14." IPEA Technical Note Carta del Conjuntura, Institute of Applied Economic Research, Brasilia.

International Monetary Fund (IMF). 2016. "Managing Government Compensation and Employment—Institutions, Policies, and Reform Challenges." IMF Staff Report to the Executive Board, Washington, DC.

Justice in Numbers. 2017. National Council of Justice, Brazil.

Karpowicz, Izabela, and Mauricio Soto. Forthcoming. "Rightsizing Brazil's Public sector Wage Bill." IMF Working Paper, International Monetary Fund, Washington, DC.

Lipinski, Fabian. 2015. "Macroeconomic Implications of Minimum Wage Increases in Brazil." IMF Country Report No. 15/122, International Monetary Fund, Washington, DC.

Mulas-Granados, Carlos, and Izabela Karpowicz. 2016. "Stretching the Limits: Evolution of Subnational Public Finances in Brazil." Brazil Selected Issues Paper, International Monetary Fund, Washington, DC.

Nemer Tenoury, Gabriel, and Naercio Menezes-Filho. 2017. "The Evolution of the Public-Private Wage Differential in Brazil." Insper Policy Paper No. 29, Insper, São Paulo.

Organisation for Economic Co-operation and Development (OECD). 2010. *OECD Reviews of Human Resource Management in Government—Brazil Federal Government.* Paris.

———. 2013. "Judicial Performance and Its Determinants: A Cross-Country Perspective." OECD Economic Policy Papers N. 05, Paris.

Tamirisa, Natalia, and Christoph Duenwald. 2018. "Public Wage Bills in the Middle East and Central Asia Region." IMF Departmental Paper, Washington, DC.

World Bank. 2017. "A Fair Adjustment: Analysis of the Efficiency and Equity of Public Expenditure in Brazil." *The World Bank Public Expenditure Review* 1.

PART V

Challenges to the Monetary and Financial Framework

CHAPTER 14

The Conquest of Lower Interest Rates in Brazil—Where Does Neutral Stand?

ROBERTO ACCIOLY PERRELLI AND SHAUN K. ROACHE

This chapter examines the connections between macroeconomic fundamentals and the neutral real interest rate in Brazil. The analysis finds that acclaimed theoretical frameworks, such as Ramsey structural consumption models, are informative but cannot fully explain the trends in Brazil's neutral rate over the past two decades. Brazil's inflation gaps, financial deepening, public debt, and sovereign risk are among the key drivers of its neutral rate. The models also gauge the procyclical role of public sector lending—via the Banco Nacional de Desenvolvimento Econômico e Social, or BNDES—in the determination of the neutral interest rate.

INTRODUCTION

Since the global financial crisis, emerging markets have experienced sizable declines in their neutral real interest rates, reflecting both a decline in the rates of interest and output growth in advanced economies (Holston, Laubach, and Williams 2017) and improved domestic fundamentals (Perrelli and Roache 2014; Rachel and Smith 2017). Brazil is not different from others in this regard. However, the country still features one of the highest real interest rates among its peers. This chapter uses a combination of theoretical models and various econometric techniques to identify the main factors that have contributed to Brazil's high neutral real interest rate.

These findings suggest that domestic factors, including policy choices, account for the bulk of the changes in Brazil's neutral interest rate since the inception of the inflation-targeting regime. Brazil's inflation gaps, financial deepening, public debt, and sovereign risk are among the key drivers of its neutral rate. The results gauge the procyclical role of public sector lending—via Brazil's national development bank, BNDES—in determining the neutral interest rate.

A RAMSEY MODEL FOR BRAZIL'S NEUTRAL RATE

The Ramsey model of optimal saving provides an important, albeit simplistic, starting point for the analysis of neutral rates. In Ramsey-type models an economy's neutral rate is linked to its per capita income growth and consumer preferences toward saving and risk. High neutral rates correspond to fast expected income growth unless behavioral changes provide offsetting effects. Behavioral parameters related to households' risk aversion and future consumption discount rate, hardly observed in typical macroeconomic data, play an important role in this framework. The solution to the Ramsey model sheds light on a country's saving and investment decisions—neutral rates in low-saving countries are typically higher than in high-saving peers. Therefore, increasing household saving contributes to a lower neutral rate.

The Ramsey model is calibrated for Brazil by computing average estimates of the neutral real interest rate for three equally spaced subperiods since Brazil adopted an inflation-targeting regime: 2000–05, 2006–11, and 2012–17. The first period was marked by domestic and external crises that led to high volatility in inflation, growth, and exchange rates. In contrast, during the second period Brazil enjoyed a commodity-led boom, with lower inflation, an appreciating currency, and high growth rates. The latest period was marked by political crisis and a profound, long-lasting economic recession. In each of these periods, the neutral rate estimates are compared with the average annual growth rate of Brazil's real GDP per capita and contrasted with the average ex ante real policy rate.[1] The real policy rate is defined as the nominal policy rate (Special Settlement and Custody System—Sistema Especial de Liquidação e Custódia, or SELIC) deflated by one-year-ahead expected inflation based on the Brazilian central bank's *Focus* survey. The results are plotted in Figure 14.1.

The results suggest ranges for the neutral rate that vary dramatically over time. Figure 14.1 shows a clear downward trend in the ex ante real policy rate, from an average of 12 percent in 2000–05 to about 7 percent in 2006–11, and to 5 percent in 2012–17. Meanwhile, Ramsey-model estimates more closely tracked developments in per capita income growth, starting at an average of 5 percent, rising toward 7 percent, and collapsing toward zero in the latter years. In all cases, a high degree of uncertainty seems to be built into the Ramsey estimates, as indicated by the green whiskers in Figure 14.1 that reflect the grids of behavioral parameters used in the calibration of that model.[2]

---

[1] The use of the ex ante real interest rate has been adopted in the recent literature (for example, Hamilton and others 2015). The use of survey data on inflation expectations recognizes that there is a maturity mismatch between short-term rates and inflation expectations that are often expressed for the coming 12 months.

[2] An extension of the Ramsey model considers the possibility that consumers will develop habit persistence (see Fuhrer 2000). If consumption rises in tandem with per capita income, the real interest rate needs to increase sufficiently to encourage households to postpone consumption. This may be particularly relevant for Brazil, where historically high real interest rates would imply implausibly impatient or very risk averse households (or both). Perrelli (2012) and Perrelli and

Figure 14.1. Brazil: Ex Ante Real Policy Rate, Neutral Rate from Ramsey Model, and per Capita Income Growth Rate, 2000–17
(Annual averages, percent)

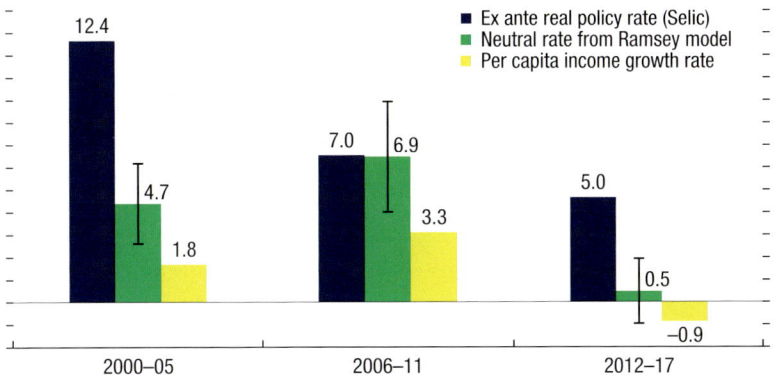

Sources: Central Bank of Brazil; Haver Analytics; and authors' calculations.

Yield Curves and Inflation Gaps

Structural models are informative for developing a view about the neutral rate, but this complex subject often requires further statistical examination. For instance, differences between Brazil's ex ante real policy rate and the results from the Ramsey framework might be explained by policy choices and economic factors beyond those included in the structural consumption models. This section sheds light on some of the possible factors, with special emphasis on inflation expectations.

Statistical Filters and Yield Curves

To start, it is instructive to detrend Brazil's ex ante real policy rate using a set of statistical filters to eliminate possible business cycle distortions to the estimates. Figure 14.2 decomposes the ex ante real policy rate into a trend and a "gap" (that is, the difference between the rate and its trend).[3] This gap can be large at times, such as when Brazil's monetary policy responded to domestic shocks (for example, political crises in 2002–03 and 2015–16) and to external pressures (for

---

Roache (2014) calibrate a Ramsey model with habit formation for Brazil but find that Brazil's ex ante real policy rate can hardly be matched using habit-formation parameters typically suggested in the academic literature.

[3]A range of statistical filters was considered—including Hodrick-Prescott, Ravn-Uhlig, and Christiano-Fitzgerald—with time-varying parameters or multiple penalty factors. To attenuate the end-point bias common in some of these filters, in the computation of the trend the exercise used out-of-sample projections of the ex ante real policy rate based on market expectations recorded by the Brazilian central bank's *Focus* survey.

Figure 14.2. Brazil: Ex Ante Real Policy Rate—Statistical Trend and Interest Gaps, 2001–17
(Percent, gap equals actual minus trend real rate)

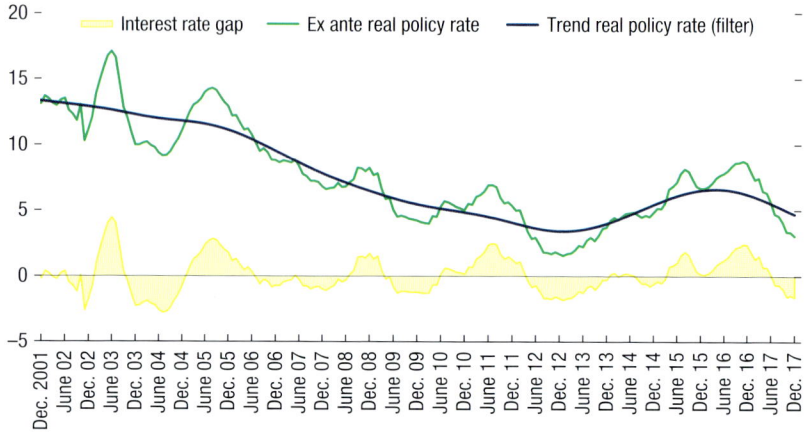

Sources: Central Bank of Brazil; and authors' calculations.

example, the global financial crisis in 2008–09). This approach suggests a sustained declining drift from the beginning of the inflation-targeting regime until 2012. The reversal in the interest rate trend from 2013 onward is the object of the analysis in the next sections.

One way to adjust policy rates for the cycle is to use information offered by financial markets on the dynamics of interest rates over time at different maturities across the sovereign bond yield curve. The reasoning is as follows: with well-anchored inflation expectations, the average slope of the yield curve (that is, the difference between short- and long-term interest rates on sovereign fixed-income instruments) should mainly reflect the term premium. Temporary deviations from this rule are common but, when computed over a sufficiently long horizon and between cyclically equivalent end points, the average term premium can be considered neutral with respect to the business cycle. Therefore, the neutral real interest rate can be gauged by adding the "excess" term premium—defined as the current term premium minus the sample average—to the trend real short-term interest rate.[4]

Figure 14.3 illustrates this approach. Yields on Brazil's long-term 10-year local currency sovereign bonds have traded in a range between 10 percent and 15 percent since 2006 (when data on these securities became consistently available). Meanwhile, Brazil's short-term, three-month interest rates (extracted from swap contracts), as expected, tracked the nominal policy rate (SELIC). As a result, the

---

[4]For further discussion, see, for example, Basdevant, Björksten, and Karagedikli (2004).

Figure 14.3. Brazil: Slope of the Yield Curve, 2005–17
(Percent, slope is the difference between long- and short-term yields)

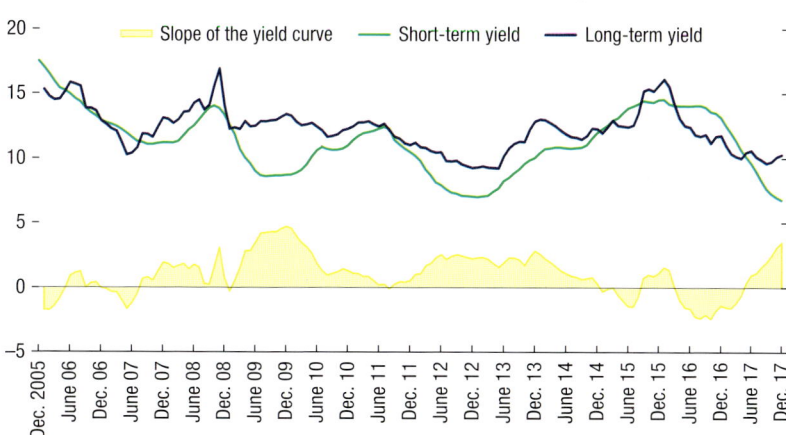

Sources: Central Bank of Brazil; Haver Analytics; Thomson Reuters Datastream; and authors' calculations.

yield curve sloped upward during most of 2006–17, with an average term premium (the difference between long- and short-term yields) of 100 basis points.

Considering that the filter-estimated trend real interest rate averaged 5¼ percent in 2017, when the average "excess" term premium was very low (it started large and negative early in the year and turned large and positive later), the yield curve model suggests an estimate for Brazil's neutral real interest rate of about 5¼ percent during 2017. Nevertheless, a wide confidence interval should be added to this estimate because the excess term premium is prone to significant cyclical variation, and the filter-based trend is often unable to reliably disentangle permanent (or very persistent) from temporary fluctuations.[5] For instance, the filtered trend may be identifying extended cyclical variation that may not be driven by an underlying structural shift in saving-investment balances, potential output growth, or consumer preferences. Additional information and structure may be required to identify such cases, including on the behavior of inflation.

Inflation Gaps and Surprises

To examine the possible impact of inflation outcomes on the neutral rate, this analysis focuses on two measurements of inflation deviations from expected outcomes: gaps and surprises. Inflation gaps, defined as the actual inflation rate minus the midpoint of the inflation target band in each year, have been

---

[5]This methodology relies on the identification of cyclically neutral positions to anchor the computation of the average term premium, which may be difficult to hold in short sample periods. Given Brazil's limited experience with the duration of business cycles under its inflation-targeting regime, the results are subject to high uncertainty.

Figure 14.4. Brazil: Inflation Gaps, 2000–17
(Percent, actual inflation minus the midpoint of the inflation target band)

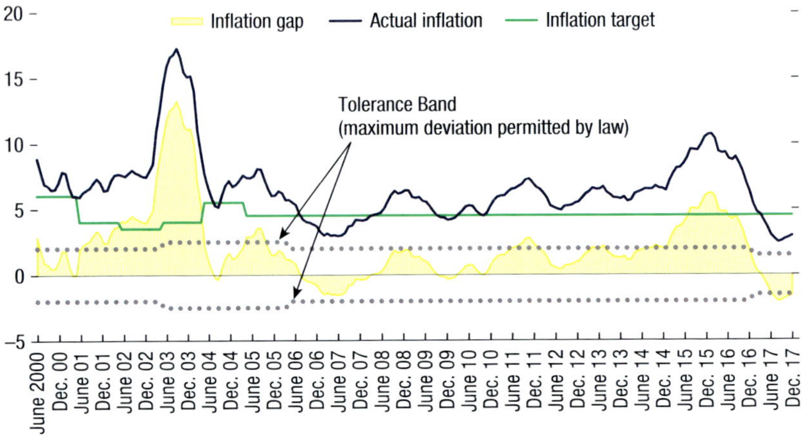

Sources: Central Bank of Brazil; Haver Analytics; and authors' calculations.

predominantly positive throughout the history of the inflation-targeting regime in Brazil. Whereas the Central Bank of Brazil (BCB) targets the annual inflation rate by the end of the year, this analysis finds that Brazil's 12-month inflation ran above the midpoint of the target band in more than 80 percent of the months since the inflation-targeting regime was established (Figure 14.4). In such situations, barring strong seasonal effects, private agents may expect further tightening of the policy rate so that the midpoint of the target range can be reached by the end of the year. Or they may simply give up on the monetary authority's intention to reach the midpoint of the target band that year. To the extent these deviations affect the credibility of monetary policy, larger inflation gaps can be expected to be positively associated with higher neutral rates over a long period. The rationale for this conjecture is as follows: poor inflation-targeting performance could lead private agents to doubt central bank credibility and to rely less on the inflation-targeting regime and more on past inflation outcomes when setting prices, thereby increasing inflation inertia. This hypothesis is tested in the next section.

Inflation surprises are defined as actual inflation outcomes versus what was expected by forecasters in previous periods. Of course, economic forecasters have tried to internalize these persistent deviations from the inflation target in their models. Notwithstanding their efforts, perhaps the most reliable survey of inflation expectations (the BCB's *Focus*) suggests that actual inflation posted above expected inflation in two-thirds of the period since the inception of the inflation-targeting regime. Interestingly, large inflation surprises tended to be accompanied by large movements in the diffusion index—the share of items in the inflation basket with price increases (Figure 14.5). This empirical evidence

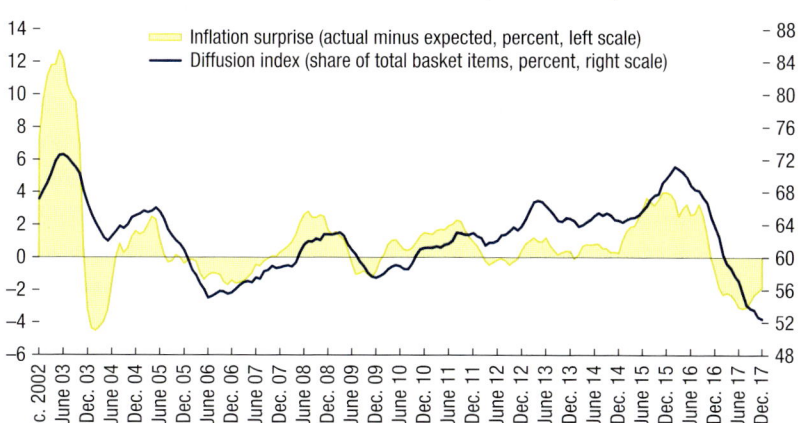

Figure 14.5. Brazil: Inflation Surprises and Diffusion Index, 2002–17
(Percent, surprise is actual inflation minus 12-month-ahead expected inflation; diffusion index is the share of inflation basket items with price increases)

Sources: Central Bank of Brazil; Haver Analytics; and authors' calculations.

suggests that forecasters have consistently failed to capture both the intensity of price changes and their dissemination across various economic sectors.

The conjecture is that persistent inflation gaps and surprises in Brazil may have affected the BCB's credibility and, as a result, weakened the monetary policy transmission mechanism, which in turn influenced changes in the neutral rate.[6] The roles of these and other fundamentals are explored in the next section.

CONNECTING CHANGES IN MACROECONOMIC FUNDAMENTALS TO THE NEUTRAL RATE

In the search for policy factors that may explain the behavior of Brazil's neutral rate, two parsimonious models are estimated—one for the long-term and another for the short-term equilibrium real interest rate—that try to decompose changes in the neutral rate by fundamental determinants. The approach follows Goldfajn and Bicalho (2011) in the sense that these estimates are used to obtain a possible range for the neutral rate.[7]

---

[6]Central bank credibility may affect the effectiveness of monetary policy in several ways. For a discussion applicable to Latin America, see Carrière-Swallow and others (2016).

[7]It is possible to think of the neutral rate as either a short- or a long-term concept (Archibald and Hunter 2001). The former is consistent with stable inflation over the period needed for the monetary policy transmission mechanism to fully operate. The latter is associated with an economy in a steady state. Bernhardsen and Gerdrup (2007) argue that neutral rates are affected not only by the determinants of long-term equilibrium real interest rates but also by temporary changes in consumption and investment demand.

Long-Term Equilibrium Real Interest Rate

The long-term equilibrium interest rate is estimated as a function of global interest rates along with Brazil-specific inflation gaps and surprises, financial deepening, public indebtedness, sovereign creditworthiness, and productivity growth. Specifically, the control variables are as follows:

- Global interest rates: Three-month "shadow" rates and 10-year yields on US Treasury securities
- Inflation gap: Difference between the actual 12-month consumer's inflation rate (IPCA—Broad National Consumer Price Index) and the center of the BCB's inflation target band
- Inflation surprise: Difference between one-year-ahead expected inflation (from the BCB's *Focus* survey) and the actual inflation outcome
- Financial deepening: Domestic credit to the private sector as a percent of GDP
- Public indebtedness: Ratio of net public debt to GDP
- Sovereign risk: Five-year credit default swap (CDS) spreads
- Productivity growth: Annual growth rate of output per employed person

Because of interest parity conditions, the coefficients on global interest rates are expected to be positive.[8] Wider inflation gaps and surprises are likely associated with higher neutral rates. Similarly, elevated public indebtedness and sovereign risk are expected to push the neutral rate up as lenders demand a premium for credit risk. On the other hand, to the extent that financial deepening reflects an increased supply of savings (whether foreign or domestic), higher provision of credit to the private sector should reduce the neutral rate. The econometric estimates are largely consistent with these priors, fit the data well, and pass the usual diagnostic tests (Table 14.1).[9]

The model suggests that, since the global financial crisis, lower global interest rates (Figure 14.6, blue bars) contributed almost 200 basis points to the decline in Brazil's long-term interest rate (although this contribution has recently fallen). Domestic variables accounted for most of the decline, however. During 2011–14, the long-term real interest rate estimated by the model averaged 4 percent, of which 3.7 percentage points were due to domestic factors. During 2015–16, at the peak of Brazil's recession, the contribution of domestic variables jumped to 6.3 percentage points when the long-term rate averaged 7.2 percent. Inflation gaps played a key role during that period.

Conversely, in 2017 the contribution of domestic factors dropped to 3 percentage points when the long-term interest rate averaged 4.8 percent. In that same year, three domestic indicators—financial deepening, public indebtedness, and sovereign risk—accounted for almost 400 basis points of the rate (Figure 14.6,

---

[8] The proxies for short-term global interest rates are the US "shadow" rates computed by Wu and Xia (2016), based on the seminal work of Black (1995).

[9] Interestingly, productivity growth turned out to be insignificant for Brazil.

Table 14.1. Brazil: Long-Term Equilibrium Real Interest Rate, 2003–17

	Dependent variable: Real policy rate deflated by 12-month-ahead expected inflation[1,2,3]									
	(A)	(B)	(C)	(D)	(E)	(F)	(G)	(H)	(I)	(J)
Linear trend	-0.137 (0.05)***			-0.083 (0.04)*	-0.081 (0.07)	-0.200 (0.21)	-0.153 (0.03)***	-0.157 (0.05)***	-0.104 (0.03)***	
Global short-term interest rate_t		1.131 (0.19)***								0.549 (0.08)***
Global long-term interest rate_t			2.294 (0.63)***							0.544 (0.15)***
Inflation gap				0.378						0.813
s.e.				(0.28)						(0.06)***
Inflation surprise					0.545 (0.460)					
Private credit/GDP_t-4						-0.321				-0.097
s.e.						(0.19)*				(0.03)***
Public debt/GDP_t-4							0.294 (0.08)***			0.100 (0.02)***
Productivity growth_t-4								-0.861 (0.35)**		
Sovereign risk_t-2									1.267 (0.390)***	0.188 (0.10)*
Constant	11.281 (1.19)***	6.361 (0.46)***	-0.024 (2.1)	8.167 (1.62)***	8.464 (2.44)***	19.526 (2.82)***	-7.985 (5.22)	12.180 (1.76)***	7.293 (1.56)***	
Adjusted R^2	0.47	0.37	0.39	0.47	0.41	0.63	0.51	0.33	0.54	0.83
Long-run variance	n.a.	11.68	24.96	32.04	80.00	4.92	9.18	29.29	13.92	0.40
Engle-Granger coint. test (prob)[4]	n.a.	0.00	0.00	0.72	0.62	0.07	0.14	0.02	0.01	0.05
Sample size	60	59	59	59	59	55	55	55	53	53

Source: Authors' calculations.

[1] Standard errors are in parentheses.

[2] Models B thru L are cointegrating regressions (fully modified least squares).

[3] Long-run covariance estimates use prewhitening with lags based on the Akaike information criterion, Bartlett kernel, and Newey-West automatic bandwidth selection.

[4] Probability of rejecting the null hypothesis of no cointegration when the null hypothesis is true.

*$p < .10$; **$p < .05$; ***$p < .01$.

Figure 14.6. Brazil: Long-Term Equilibrium Real Interest Rate, 2005–17
(Contributions to the equilibrium real interest rate, percentage points)

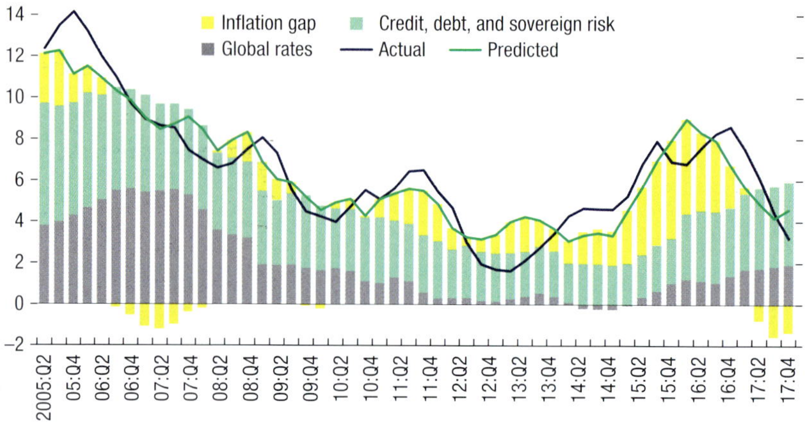

Sources: Central Bank of Brazil; Haver Analytics; and authors' calculations.

green bars) while better inflation perfomance reduced it by nearly 100 basis points (Figure 14.6, yellow bars). Although informative for policy discussions, these contributions require wide confidence intervals because of the limited sample size and inherent uncertainty in econometric models of this nature.

The Neutral Real Interest Rate in the Short Term

The short-term equilibrium interest rate can diverge substantially from the longer-term notion of the neutral rate, and this clearly should be taken into account by policymakers. Following Rudebusch and Svensson (1999), adapted by Bernhardsen and Gerdrup (2007) for Norway and by Goldfajn and Bicalho (2011) for Brazil, this analysis estimates a simple model that relates the output gap to the interest rate gap to help disentangle the short- and long-term dynamics of the neutral rate changes from movements from its long-term trajectory. The model incorporates the impact of the public sector on financial deepening and the cycle—via the BNDES—in the gap equation (see Annex 14.1).

The coefficients' signs are consistent with the priors, including the real interest rate gap and the exchange rate gap, which are both negative and significant (Table 14.2). The government consumption gap is not significant, but the effect of BNDES lending is positive and statistically significant, suggesting a procyclical role for public sector lending during the sample period. The estimated coefficient on the global output gap is positive but not statistically significant.

Table 14.2. Brazil: Determinants of the Short-Term Equilibrium Real Interest Rate, 2004–17

Dep. variable: Output gap	Lagged output gap	World output gap	Interest rate gap	Exchange rate gap	BNDES lending gap	Government consumption gap
Adj. $R^2 = 0.83$	α	β	γ	δ	ρ	θ
Point estimate	0.660	0.023	−0.441	−3.472	0.058	0.053
Std. error	(0.10)***	(0.11)	(0.11)***	(0.92)***	(0.03)*	(0.04)

Sources: Central Bank of Brazil; Haver Analytics; Thomson Reuters Datastream; and authors' calculations.

Note: Standard errors are in parentheses. HAC standard errors and covariance estimates use prewhitening with up to four lags from the Akaike information criterion, Bartlett kernel, and Newey-West automatic bandwidth selection with up to four lags. BNDES = Brazil's national development bank.

*$p < .10$; **$p < .05$; ***$p < .01$.

Using the results from Table 14.2, the neutral rate is estimated by finding the real interest rate consistent with the closing of all these gaps.[10] As a corollary, the short- and long-term equilibrium real interest rates are equal, suggesting a possible level for the neutral real interest rate. This situation is illustrated in Figure 14.7, which shows that early in 2015 both rates met at about 4½ percent, but increased to nearly 6½ percent two years later. Under current trends, Brazil's neutral real interest rate is expected to be about 4½ percent in 2018, when the short- and long-term curves cross again.

Figure 14.7. Brazil: Short- and Long-Term Equilibrium Real Interest Rates, 2005–17
(Percent)

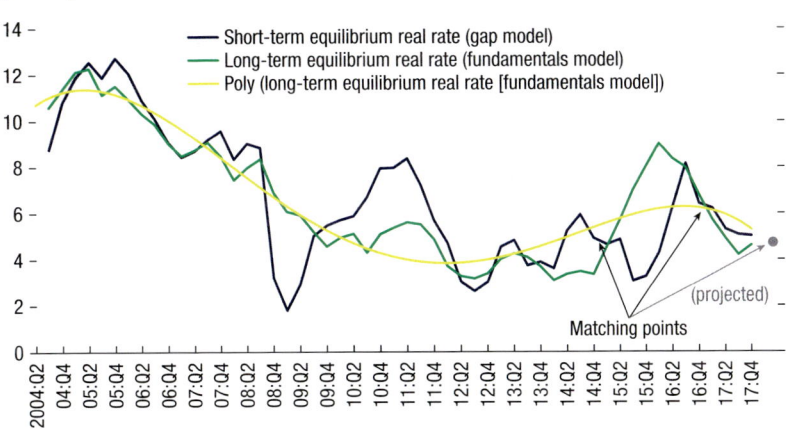

Sources: Central Bank of Brazil; Haver Analytics; Thomson Reuters Datastream; and authors' calculations.

---

[10]For that, the investment-saving model is rewritten such that the short-term equilibrium real interest rate equals the long-term equilibrium real interest rate plus the sum of all other gap variables at each time.

CONCLUSIONS

This chapter examines the connections between macroeconomic fundamentals and the neutral real interest rate in Brazil. The analysis finds that acclaimed theoretical frameworks, such as Ramsey structural consumption models, are informative but cannot fully explain the trends in Brazil's neutral rate over the past two decades. It shows that econometric analyses based on the slope of the yield curve, widely used by market participants, are subject to cyclical perturbations that often limit their applicability. This chapter uses a combination of two parsimonious regression models—a cointegration equation for the long-term equilibrium real interest rate and a gap equation for its short-term version—that usefully identify a range for the neutral rate while providing information about the contribution of domestic factors and global conditions. Brazil's inflation gaps, financial deepening, public debt, and sovereign risk are among the key drivers of its neutral rate. The models also gauge the procyclical role of public sector lending—via the BNDES—in determining the neutral interest rate.

REFERENCES

Archibald, Joanne, and Leni Hunter. 2001. "What Is the Neutral Real Interest Rate, and How Can We Use It?" *Reserve Bank of New Zealand Bulletin* 64: 15–28.

Basdevant, Olivier, Nils Björksten, and Özer Karagedikli. 2004. "Estimating a Time Varying Neutral Real Interest Rate for New Zealand." Reserve Bank of New Zealand Discussion Paper, Wellington.

Bernhardsen, Tom, and Karsten Gerdrup. 2007. "The Neutral Real Interest Rate." *Norges Bank Economic Bulletin* 2(78): 52–64.

Black, Fischer. 1995. "Interest Rates as Options." *The Journal of Finance* 50: 1371–76.

Carrière-Swallow, Yan, Luis Jácome, Nicolás Magud, and Alejandro Werner. 2016. "Central Banking in Latin America: The Way Forward." IMF Working Paper 16/197, International Monetary Fund, Washington, DC.

Fuhrer, J. C. 2000. "Habit Formation in Consumption and Its Implications for Monetary Policy Models." *American Economic Review* 90(3).

Goldfajn, Ilan, and Aurélio Bicalho. 2011. "The Long Crossing to Normality: The Real Interest in Brazil." In *New Dilemmas of Economic Policy—Essays in Homage to Dionisio Dias Carneiro*, edited by E. L. Bacha and M. B. de Bolle. Rio de Janeiro: Grupo Editorial Nacional.

Hamilton, James D., Ethan S. Harris, Jan Hatzius, and Kenneth D. West. 2015. "The Equilibrium Real Funds Rates: Past, Present, and Future." NBER Working Paper 21476, National Bureau of Economic Research, Cambridge, MA.

Holston, Kathryn, Thomas Laubach, and John C. Williams. 2017. "Measuring the Natural Rate of Interest: International Trends and Determinants." *Journal of International Economics* 108: 59–75.

Perrelli, Roberto Accioly. 2012. "The Neutral Real Interest Rate in Brazil." Brazil—Article IV Staff Report, IMF Country Report No. 12/191, International Monetary Fund, Washington, DC.

Perrelli, Roberto Accioly, and Shaun K. Roache. 2014. "Time-Varying Neutral Interest Rate—The Case of Brazil." IMF Working Paper 14/84, International Monetary Fund, Washington, DC.

Rachel, Lukasz, and Thomas D. Smith. 2017. "Are Low Real Interest Rates Here to Stay?" *International Journal of Central Banking* 13(3): 1–42.

Ramsey, Frank. 1928. "A Mathematical Theory of Saving." *The Economic Journal* 38: 543–59.

Rudebusch, Glenn D., and Lars E. O. Svensson. 1999. "Policy Rules for Inflation Targeting." In *Monetary Policy Rules*, edited by J. B. Taylor. Chicago: University of Chicago Press.

Wu, Jing Cynthia, and Fan Dora Xia. 2016. "Measuring the Macroeconomic Impact of Monetary Policy at the Zero Lower Bound." *Journal of Money, Credit and Banking* 48: 253–91.

ANNEX 14.1. AN ECONOMETRIC MODEL OF THE SHORT-TERM EQUILIBRIUM REAL INTEREST RATE FOR BRAZIL

To find the short-term equilibrium interest rate, the following gap equation is estimated (see Table 14.2):

$$Y_t - \breve{Y}_t = \alpha(Y_{t-1} - \breve{Y}_{t-1}) + \beta(Z_t - \breve{Z}_t) + \gamma(r_t - \bar{r}_t) + \delta(e_t - \bar{e}_t) + \rho(L_t - \breve{L}_t) + \theta(G_t - \breve{G}_t) + \varepsilon_t,$$

where

$Y_t - \breve{Y}_t$ is Brazil's output gap (actual minus potential output)

$Z_t - \breve{Z}_t$ is the world's output gap (actual minus potential output)

$r_t - \bar{r}_t$ is the real interest rate gap (actual minus the long-term neutral rate estimated by model J in Table 14.1)

$e_t - \bar{e}_t$ is the exchange rate gap (actual minus its long-term trend estimated by the authors using statistical filters)

$L_t - \breve{L}_t$ is the gap of BNDES lending (actual minus its long-term trend estimated by the authors using statistical filters)

$G_t - \breve{G}_t$ is the gap of central government consumption (actual minus its long-term trend estimated by the authors using statistical filters).

CHAPTER 15

Interest Rates and Inflation

Troy Matheson

The conventional view among economists is that higher interest rates reduce infla-tion. However, the prolonged period of low inflation and low interest rates in advanced economies following the global financial crisis appears to be inconsistent with this view. This situation has sparked a debate: do lower interest rates increase inflation (the conventional view), or do they lead to lower inflation (the so-called Neo-Fisherian view)? This chapter finds strong evidence in favor of the conventional view of mone-tary policy transmission in Brazil. While lower inflation and lower nominal interest rates can be achieved over the long term by targeting a lower level of inflation, this outcome is likely to come at the cost of lower output (and employment) in the short term—a cost that can be mitigated by enhancing monetary policy transparency and credibility. Monetary policy transmission could be made more efficient by reducing distortions and improving the allocation of resources in the financial sector.

INTRODUCTION

The conventional view among economists is that *higher* interest rates lead to *lower* inflation. The rationale behind this view is that higher interest rates increase the cost of borrowing and dampen demand across the economy, resulting in excess supply and lower inflation. In this context, higher interest rates reduce inflation through several channels, including the exchange rate channel, the credit channel, and the bank–balance sheet channel (see Mishkin 1996). A central bank facing the prospect of higher-than-targeted inflation would raise interest rates enough to increase the real (inflation-adjusted) cost of borrowing, thereby reduc-ing aggregate demand and returning inflation back toward the desired level.

Some debate has occurred about whether *lower* inflation can be achieved by setting *lower* policy interest rates, the so-called Neo-Fisherian effect. At the heart of the debate is a well-known equation in economics, the Fisher equation, that relates the nominal interest rate R_t to the real interest rate r_t and expected inflation $E_t \pi_{t+1}$ (all annualized):

$$R_t = r_t + E_t \pi_{t+1}.$$

Taken at face value, and assuming that the real interest rate is fixed in the long term, the equation implies that a lower long-term inflation rate can be achieved by permanently setting the nominal interest rate to a lower level (see Cochrane

Figure 15.1. Headline Inflation and Policy Rate

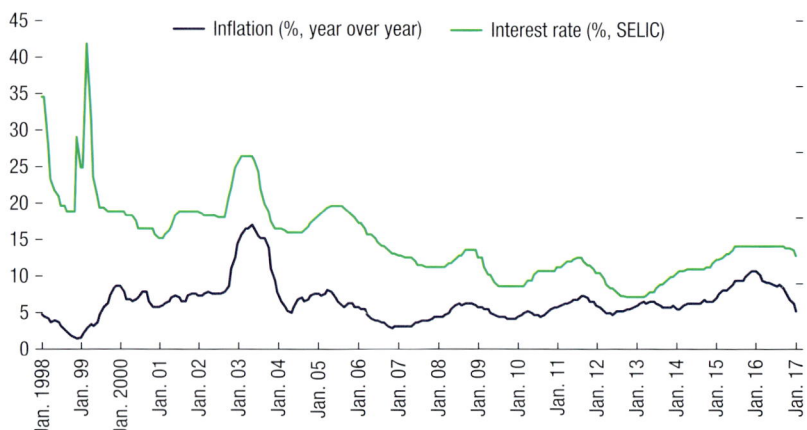

Source: Haver Analytics.
Note: SELIC = Sistema Especial de Liquidação e Custodia (Special Clearance and Escrow System).

2016). Indeed, proponents of this view often point to the positive relationship between nominal interest rates and inflation seen across many countries as evidence of Neo-Fisherian effects (see Figure 15.1).[1]

Would a commitment to fixing the policy interest rate to a lower level eventually lead to lower inflation? To answer this question, this chapter presents an empirical analysis conducted to assess the impact of changes in Brazil's policy rate on inflation. The chapter then evaluates a simple model with long-term Neo-Fisherian effects in the context of several countries' historical experiences in making the transition to lower levels of inflation. A summary of key findings and policy conclusions rounds out the chapter.

EMPIRICAL ANALYSIS

The empirical analysis is based on vector autoregressions (VARs). The baseline VAR is estimated using monthly data ranging from 2003 to 2016 and contains six variables: monthly headline inflation, the nominal interest rate (Sistema Especial de Liquidação e Custodia, or SELIC), the output gap, 12-month-ahead inflation expectations, monthly percentage changes of commodity prices, and monthly percentage changes of the real effective exchange rate. Inflation responses to the interest rate are likely to differ across different sectors of the economy, so in addition to the baseline VAR, five additional VARs are estimated as a robustness check, including inflation for different sectors of the economy. Overall, the

---

[1]Neo-Fisherian effects exist in standard models used by central banks under the assumption that economic agents have perfect foresight and do not base their decisions on past observations. See García-Schmidt and Woodford (2015) and Garín and Sims (2016).

Figure 15.2. Correlation: Headline Inflation and Interest Rate
(Correlation and 20th to 80th percentiles)

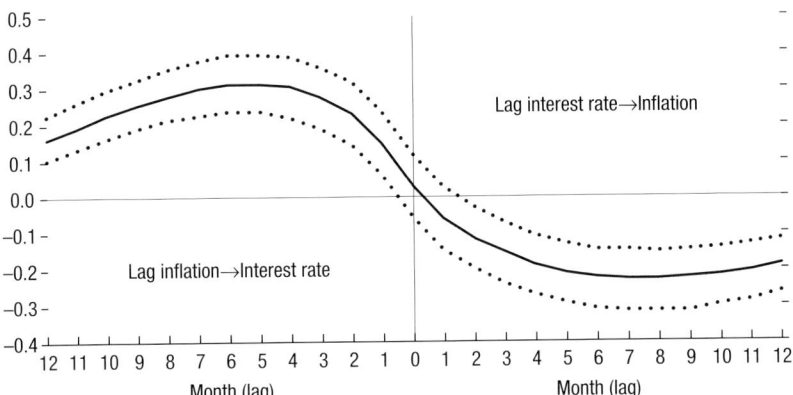

Source: IMF staff estimates.
Note: Dotted lines show 20th and 80th percentiles.

empirical analysis examines the impact of policy interest rate changes on headline inflation, non-regulated-price inflation, regulated-price inflation, service-price inflation, tradables inflation, and nontradables inflation.[2]

Cross-correlations show that *higher* inflation leads to *higher* interest rates and *higher* interest rates lead to *lower* inflation, consistent with the conventional view. The estimated cross-correlation function from the baseline VAR is displayed in Figure 15.2; the results for all inflation rates can be found in Annex 15.1. The results show a statistically significant positive relationship between past levels of inflation and the interest rate, and a statistically significant negative relationship between past levels of the interest rate and inflation. These results broadly reflect the standard view of the transmission of monetary policy to inflation. Because inflation tends to lead the policy interest rate, it appears that the central bank has responded to inflation developments over this sample, partly as the result of unanticipated demand and supply shocks (such as food and regulated-price shocks, and exchange rate shocks). The results also suggest a peak correlation between leads and lags of inflation and leads and lags of the interest rate of about six months.

Structural VARs also support the conventional view that an unexpected cut in the policy interest rate increases inflation in the short term. Responses of headline inflation to a 100 basis point cut in the policy interest rate are displayed in Figure 15.3; the results for all other inflation rates can be found in Annex 15.1.

---

[2]VAR lag lengths are selected using the Schwarz-Bayesian Inflation Criterion. Parameter uncertainty is captured in the analysis using bootstrapping methods, where for each VAR is resampled 1,000 times.

Figure 15.3. Headline Inflation after 100 Basis Point Cut in Policy Rate
(Percent, annualized)

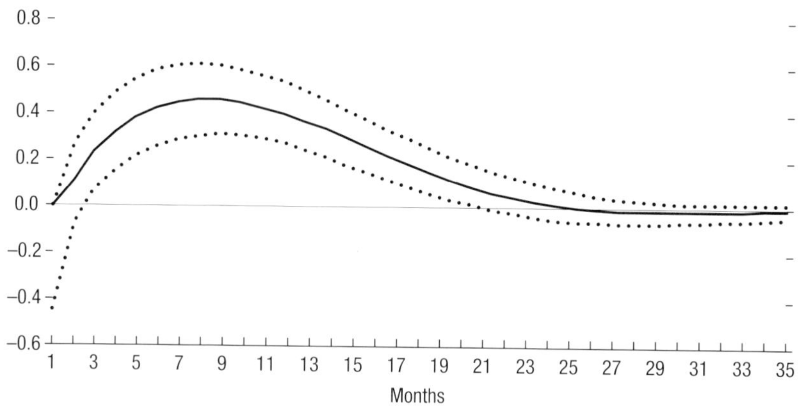

Source: IMF staff estimates.
Note: Dotted lines show 20th and 80th percentiles.

Here, the uncertainty about the responses relates both to uncertainty about the parameters of the VARs and to the recursive ordering used to identify the monetary policy shock.[3] Examining all possible recursive identification schemes allows the analysis to be indifferent to whether an interest rate shock has a contemporaneous or a lagged impact on inflation. The results show that an unexpected cut in the policy interest rate tends to increase inflation over time, with the magnitude of the impact dependent on the sector of the economy. The peak impact generally occurs about nine months after the shock. The short-term impact of a lower interest rate on inflation is less clear-cut, with identification schemes that allow for a cut in the interest rate to immediately affect inflation (within the same month) sometimes suggesting a positive relationship between inflation and interest rate shocks. Overall, however, the results from the structural VARs strongly support the standard view of monetary policy transmission.

HOW CAN LOWER INFLATION BE ACHIEVED OVER THE LONG TERM?

Although little evidence suggests that a lower interest rate leads to lower inflation in Brazil in the short term, the long-term Fisher equation can still help inform policy advice. The long-term Fisher equation is

---

[3]Each VAR contains six variables, so there are 720 different ways to order the variables to identify shocks; 69 of these orderings lead to unique inflation responses to an interest rate shock. Using bootstrapping methods, 1,000 parameterizations of each reduced-form model are simulated, leading to 69,000 different estimates of the response of inflation to an interest rate for each VAR examined.

Figure 15.4. Simulated Responses to a Change in the Inflation Target from 4.5 Percent to 2 Percent

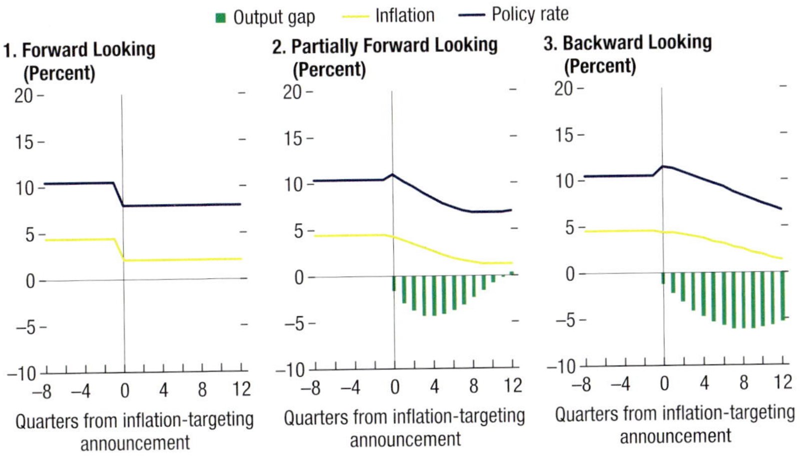

Source: IMF staff calculations.

$$R^* = r^* + \pi^*,$$

in which the steady-state nominal interest rate is equal to the steady-state real interest rate plus the inflation target. Assuming the long-term neutrality of money (that is, nominal variables do not affect real variables in the long term), the inflation target determines the steady-state nominal interest rate. This relationship can easily be inserted into a simple (and standard) New Keynesian model (see Annex 15.1).

Model-based simulations show that lower long-term inflation and nominal interest rates can be achieved by lowering the inflation target, but this strategy is likely to be costly in the short term when the central bank has limited policy credibility. The results show that a reduction in the inflation target reduces both the nominal interest rate and inflation in the long term (Figure 15.4). If households and firms in the economy have expectations that are either partially forward-looking or entirely backward-looking, the transition to the new inflation target requires lower output to move inflation expectations to the new target; the real interest rate must rise to reduce demand in the short term. On the other hand, in a purely forward-looking model the central bank is fully credible, and households and firms fully understand the future implications of monetary policy actions and immediately embed this knowledge in their expectations. In this case, the transition of inflation and nominal interest rates to the new target is instantaneous once the target is announced, and output is unaffected.

Disinflation episodes across countries show that inflation was slow to adjust to lower levels and the transition to lower inflation was costly to output, reflecting unanchored inflation expectations and limited monetary policy credibility before the disinflation. Figure 15.5 shows the behavior of inflation, interest rates, and the output gap in the two years before the adoption of inflation targeting in the first five countries that formally adopted the practice, in addition to the Volker disinflation episode in the United States, beginning in 1981.[4] The behavior of inflation, interest rates, and the output gap follow broadly similar trends across countries. Nominal interest rates and inflation rates were positively correlated and tended to decline together once the central bank formally adopted inflation targeting; output gaps generally moved into negative territory. These results are qualitatively (and quantitatively) very similar to the simulation results obtained when households' and firms' expectations for inflation and output are not assumed to be entirely forward-looking. The large output losses during disinflation across these countries likely reflect a high degree of inflation persistence and limited policy credibility before the adoption of inflation targeting. Changing the inflation target would likely be less costly if the central bank had more policy credibility and more-anchored inflation expectations before the target change.

CONCLUSIONS

There is strong evidence of the conventional view of monetary policy transmission in Brazil, suggesting that a cut in the policy interest rate leads to higher inflation in the short term. Cross-correlations show that higher inflation leads to higher nominal interest rates, and higher interest rates result in a reduction in inflation. Because inflation tends to lead the policy interest rate examined in the sample, it appears that the central bank has responded to inflation developments, partly as the result of unanticipated demand and supply shocks (such as food and regulated-price shocks, and exchange rate shocks). Structural VARs also suggest that an unexpected cut in the policy interest rate leads to a broad-based rise in inflation across the sectors examined, with the peak impact on inflation occurring about nine months after a monetary policy shock.

Model-based simulations and cross-country evidence suggest that lower inflation and lower nominal interest rates can be achieved over the longer term if the central bank commits to a lower inflation target. If households and firms base their output and inflation expectations on the past (even partially), the transition to the new inflation target comes at the cost of lower output in the short term, with larger output losses and more prolonged transition periods occurring when expectations are more backward-looking. An examination of disinflation episodes across several countries broadly supports the key findings from model simulations that assume that expectations were at least partially backward-looking before disinflation.

Although permanently lowering inflation in Brazil will not be easy, a lower inflation target could be achieved at less cost with enhanced monetary policy

---

[4]For each country, the output gap is defined as the percentage deviation of real GDP from a linear trend.

Figure 15.5. Disinflation Episodes across Countries

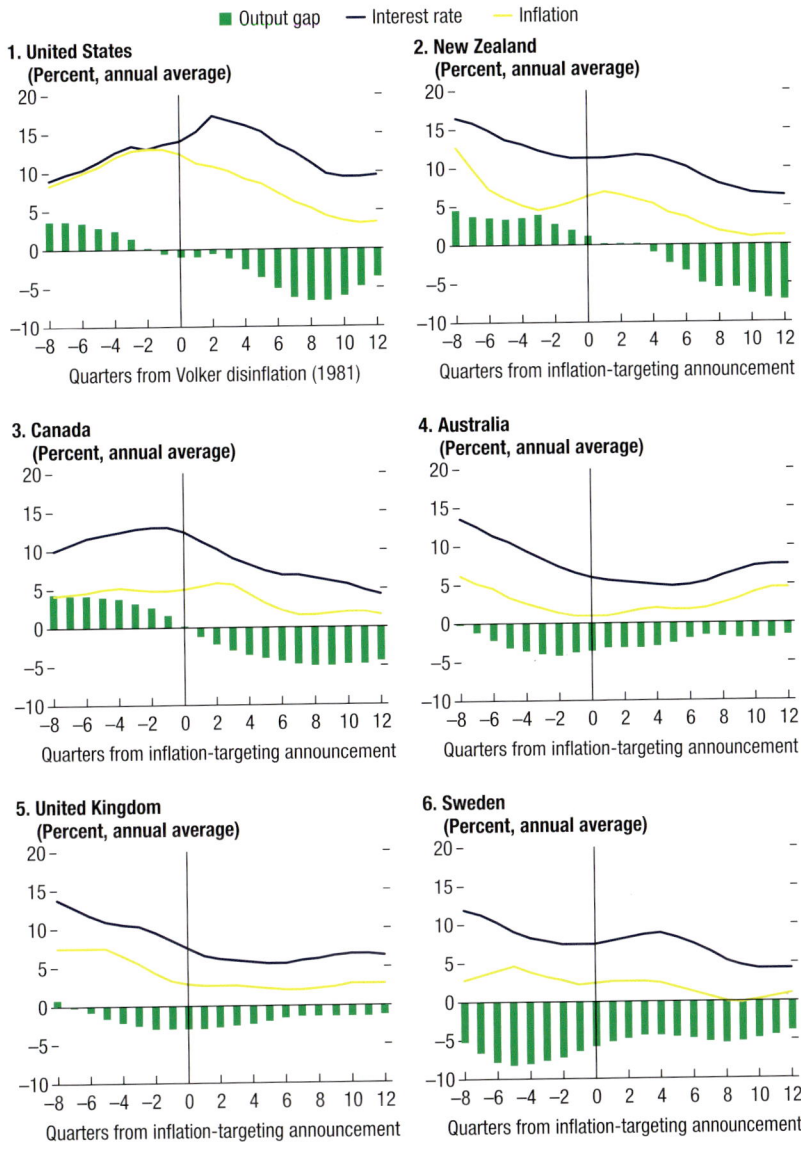

Source: IMF staff estimates.

transparency and credibility. Enhanced credibility can better anchor inflation expectations, reduce the persistence of inflation, improve the short-term trade-off between inflation and output, and mitigate the associated cost should a lower inflation target be desired over the medium term. As discussed in Domit and others (2016), there are several dimensions along which Brazil's inflation-targeting framework can be improved to enhance transparency and credibility, including increasing the autonomy of the central bank and changing the inflation target from a range that needs to be met at the end of each year to a longer-term point target. The National Monetary Council made a step in this direction in 2016 by narrowing the target range from 4.5 percent +/–2 percent to 4.5 percent +/–1.5 percent beginning in 2018. In 2017, it also announced that it would reduce the inflation target to 4.25 percent for 2019 and to 4 percent for 2020.

Monetary policy transmission could also be made more efficient by reducing distortions and improving resource allocation in the financial sector. There is general agreement that the effectiveness of monetary policy in Brazil could be improved by changing various credit policies that involve earmarking and credit subsidies. As already planned by the authorities, the gap between the subsidized interest rate on long-term lending (Taxa de Juros de Longo Prazo, or TJLP) and market interest rates will be reduced over time. Linking the TJLP more tightly to a market-determined rate will enhance the transmission of SELIC changes to longer-term interest rates, will increase the potency of a given change in the SELIC, and could contribute to lowering interest rate volatility over the business cycle. Improving the efficiency of resource allocation in the financial sector could also contribute to a lower long-term real interest rate in Brazil, allowing lower nominal interest rates for a given inflation target.[5]

REFERENCES

Cochrane, John. 2016. "Michelson-Morley, Occam and Fisher: The Radical Implications of Stable Inflation at Near-Zero Interest Rates?" Working Paper, Hoover Institution, Washington, DC.

Domit, Sílvia, Douglas Laxton, and Joannes Mongardini. 2016. "Upgrading Brazil's Inflation-Targeting Framework." IMF Country Report No. 16/349, Washington, DC.

García-Schmidt, Mariana, and Michael Woodford. 2015. "Are Low Interest Rates Deflationary? A Paradox of Perfect-Foresight Analysis." NBER Working Paper No. 21614, National Bureau of Economic Research, Cambridge, MA.

Garín Julio, Robert Lester, and Eric Sims. 2016. "Raise Rates to Raise Inflation? Neo-Fisherianism in the New Keynesian Model." NBER Working Paper No. 22177, National Bureau of Economic Research, Cambridge, MA.

International Monetary Fund (IMF). 2016. "Upgrading Brazil's Inflation-Targeting Framework." IMF Country Report No. 16/349, Washington, DC.

Mishkin, Frederic. 1996. "The Channels of Monetary Policy Transmission: Lessons for Monetary Policy." NBER Working Paper No. 5464, National Bureau of Economic Research, Cambridge, MA.

---

[5]See Minutes of the 205th Meeting of the Monetary Policy Committee of the Central Bank of Brazil for a discussion.

ANNEX 15.1. DATA AND ROBUSTNESS DATA

Annex Table 15.1.1. Data, Sources and Transforms

Series	Source	Transform*
Headline IPCA	IGBE	$\Delta\log(x)$*1200
Nontradable IPCA	IGBE	$\Delta\log(x)$*1200
Tradable IPCA	IGBE	$\Delta\log(x)$*1200
Services IPCA	IGBE	$\Delta\log(x)$*1200
Nonregulated IPCA	IGBE	$\Delta\log(x)$*1200
Regulated IPCA	IGBE	$\Delta\log(x)$*1200
Inflation expectations (12 months ahead)	BCB	x
Interest rate (SELIC)	BCB	x-hptrend(x)
Activity Index (IBC-BR)	BCB	$\log(x)$*100-hptrend($\log(x)$)*100
Commodity Price Index (IC-BR)	BCB	$\Delta\log(x)$*1200
Real Effective Exchange Rate (broad)	JP Morgan	$\Delta\log(x)$*1200

Source: IMF staff.

Note: *Δ = first difference; BCB = Central Bank of Brazil; hptrend = Hodrick-Prescott Filter; IGBE = Brazilian Institute of Geography and Statistics.

Empirical Results

See Figures 15.1.1 and 15.1.2.

Simple Model

The investment/saving (IS) curve relates the current level of the output gap, y_t, to the lagged output gap, expectations of the future output gap, and the real interest rate (deviation from the steady state):

$$y_t = \delta E_t y_{t+1} + (1 - \delta) y_{t-1} - \sigma(R_t - E_t \pi_{t+1} - r^*).$$

The Phillips curve relates the current level of inflation to inflation expectations, past inflation, and the output gap (where $0 \leq \alpha \leq 1$):

$$\pi_t = \alpha E_t \pi_{t+1} + (1 - \alpha) \pi_{t-1} + \gamma y_t.$$

The monetary policy rule relates the nominal interest rate to the steady-state nominal interest rate and the expected deviation of inflation from the inflation target:

$$R_t = R^* + \mu(E_t \pi_{t+1} - \pi^*),$$

where $\mu > 1$ to ensure a unique and stable solution, and the long-term Fisher equation is

$$R^* = r^* + \pi^*.$$

The parameter values are $\sigma = 1$, $\gamma = 0.05$, $\mu = 1.5$, and $r^* = 6$. The parameters in the Phillips and IS curves related to persistence are $\delta = \alpha = 1$ in the forward-looking model, $\delta = \alpha = 0.5$ in the partially forward-looking model, and $\delta = \alpha = 0$ in the backward-looking model.

Figure 15.1.1. Range of Cross-Correlations between the Interest and Inflation Rates
(Median and 20th and 80th percentiles)

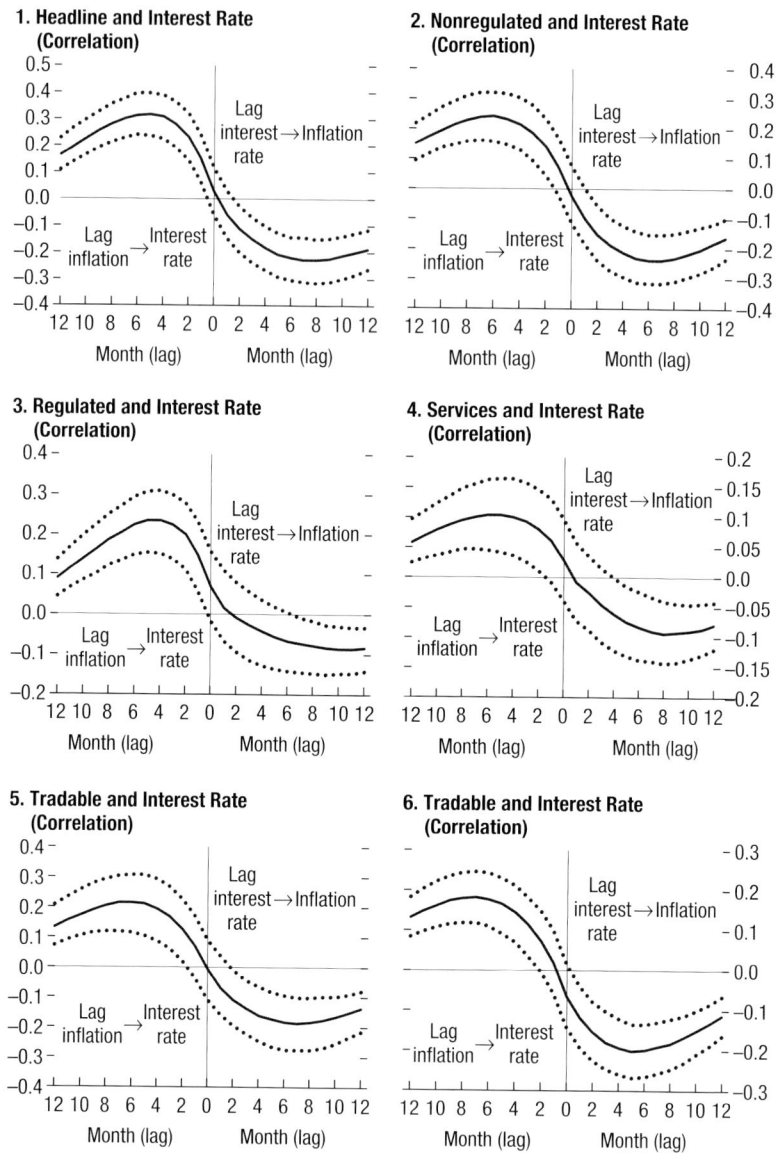

Source: IMF staff estimates.

Figure 15.1.2. Range of Inflation Responses to 100 Basis Point Cut in Policy Rate
(Median and 20th and 80th percentiles)

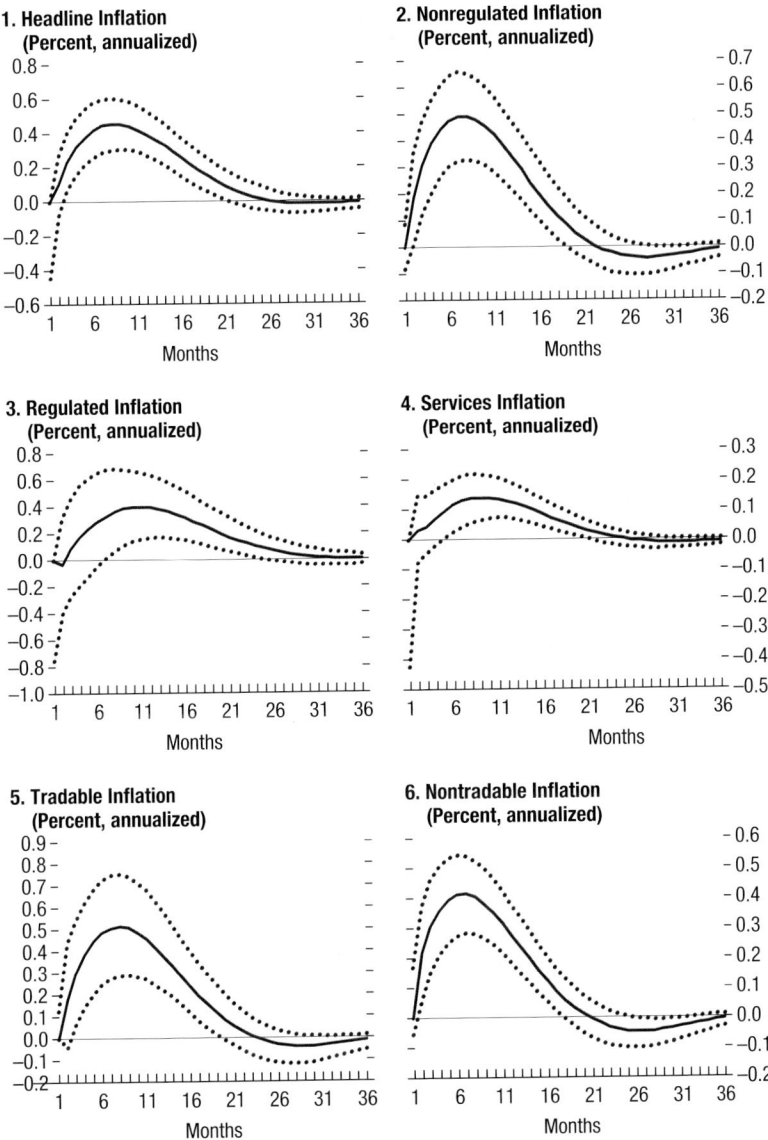

Source: IMF staff estimates.

CHAPTER 16

Earmarked Credit and Public Banks

Steen Byskov

Credit market interventions in Brazil have not delivered the economic benefits they were designed for and have led to high fiscal costs. Macro instability historically precluded the development of free market finance beyond short-term finance, which motivated policymakers to develop extensive interventions for longer-term finance. Directed credit makes up half of total credit and amounts to about a quarter of GDP. Among firms, directed credit tended to benefit older, lower-risk, and larger firms, and it was used to promote national champions. Subsidies, explicit and implicit, embedded in directed credit peaked at 2.1 percent of GDP in 2015. Directed lending is generally provided at regulated interest rates, which has impeded monetary policy transmission. As directed credit has expanded, monetary tightening has had to operate through a narrower credit channel—the free market half of the credit market—thus leading to greater volatility in free market interest rates. Recent reforms, most notably the long-term rate (TLP) reform,[1] address the pricing of directed credit, reducing the embedded subsidies. Reducing the subsidies will not only alleviate fiscal costs and improve monetary transmission but will also reduce the resistance to steering the credits away from powerful vested interests that receive them. Financial sector reforms are needed for both directed credit schemes and the free market, which continues to function poorly.

INTRODUCTION

Low savings, fiscal deficits, and inflation, along with elevated and volatile interest rates, have hindered the development of a well-functioning credit market in Brazil (Figure 16.1). The low level of savings, which has consistently been less than 20 percent of GDP, combined with fiscal financing needs that have absorbed financial savings, have deprived the financial sector of resources to allocate to productive use through the private credit market. Persistent inflation and elevated and volatile interest rates have limited private financial intermediation to mostly short-term transactions and made it costly, with Brazil having very high

---

[1]The Taxa de Longo Prazo (TLP) reform introduces market-based pricing to replace the regulated Taxa de Juros de Longo Prazo (TJLP) interest rate. The TJLP rate applies to about two-thirds of earmarked credit for firms and about one-third of all earmarked credit.

loan-to-deposit spreads of about 20 percent.

Poorly functioning financial markets have depressed productivity growth in Brazil. Not only is capital accumulation below that of most high-growth emerging markets (see, for example, Dutz and others, forthcoming), but the allocation of capital in the economy is inefficient. Estimated returns to capital across individual firms vary greatly in Brazil (see Vasconcelos 2017), reflecting inefficient competition and the failure to reallocate capital to where it could be most productively applied. Optimal allocation of capital within industries could raise productivity an estimated 40 percent in the manufacturing sector (see de Vries 2014).

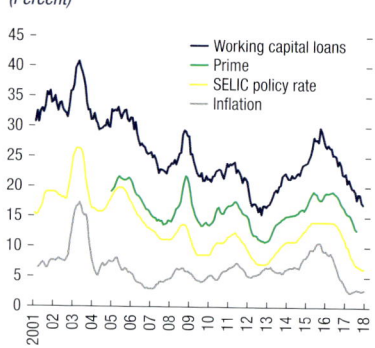

Figure 16.1. Interest Rates and Inflation in Brazil, 2001–18
(Percent)

Source: Central Bank of Brazil.
Note: SELIC = Sistema Especial de Liquidação e Custodia (Special Clearance and Escrow System).

To mitigate the lack of a functioning private credit market, over time Brazil has introduced a series of interventions to fill the gap in the market for medium- and long-term finance. To varying degrees, public banks serve policy objectives, and they account for half of bank credit. Moreover, a complex web of credit market interventions—often, but not always, implemented through public banks—shapes Brazil's credit market.

Subsidies embedded in credit have been a tool for promoting national champions and serving social objectives. Large industrial firms have received credit on preferential terms with the expectation that they could lead economic development. Moreover, credit was made easier during the global financial crisis to provide countercyclical stimulus. Programs for social housing and small farmers have benefited from low-cost public programs.

The interventions, however, have also had a variety of unintended consequences. The fiscal cost of credit market interventions peaked at an estimated 2.1 percent of GDP in 2015, and risks have accumulated in the public banks. Regulated interest rates that do not respond to monetary policy have impeded monetary transmission and led to elevated costs in the free market. In addition, long-term finance in Brazil has become almost exclusively intermediated through the federal government or various constitutional funds.[2]

A recent reform to earmarked credit, the introduction of the TLP as a new interest rate for the Brazilian Development Bank (Banco Nacional de

---

[2]Various funds are constitutionally established to serve social and development objectives; see Box 16.1.

Desenvolvimento Econômico e Social, or BNDES), aims to mitigate several of these effects. By converging to a market-based interest rate, the reform separates directed lending from embedded subsidies. This allows the BNDES to fill gaps in the market for long-term finance without imposing a cost on the government. It also mitigates the impact on monetary transmission, and it can help support the development of market-based long-term lending (see Byskov and Clavijo 2017).

This chapter summarizes findings on whether public banks and credit market interventions have achieved their objectives and discusses unintended consequences. It describes the interventions and discusses the effectiveness of the interventions in meeting their objectives. The fiscal costs and risks associated with the interventions are examined. The impact on monetary transmission and the free credit market is reviewed and directions for reform are described.

CREDIT MARKET INTERVENTIONS: PUBLIC BANKS AND EARMARKED CREDIT

Credit market interventions to address financing gaps in Brazil have evolved over many years, take many forms, and pursue multiple objectives. The free market has failed to provide medium- and long-term finance, and the interventions have generally aimed to fill this gap. Public banks and earmarked credit are the cornerstones of Brazilian credit market interventions.

Three large federal public banks and several smaller public banks make up almost half of the Brazilian credit market (Figure 16.2). The BNDES accounts for 11 percent of banking system assets and focuses on medium- and long-term finance for enterprises and on infrastructure investments. The BNDES is the largest provider of credit to the productive sector and accounts for about three-quarters of earmarked credit to firms or one-third of total credit to firms. Banco do Brasil, the country's largest commercial bank, with 17 percent of assets and more than 5,400 branches, focuses on rural areas and agriculture, where it has two-thirds of the market. Caixa Economia Federal (CEF), with 15 percent of assets, is the third-largest commercial bank and focuses on housing finance, with a 74 percent market share. It also manages the Severance Indemnity Fund (Fundo de Garantia do Tempo de Serviço, or FGTS, a constitutionally established fund), which provided 282 billion Brazilian reais in funding for financial intermediation. Banking assets are concentrated within the top six banks, which account for 82 percent of assets, and the remaining 129 banks make up just 18 percent of assets.

Figure 16.2. Banking Assets by Controlling Shareholder, 2018:Q1

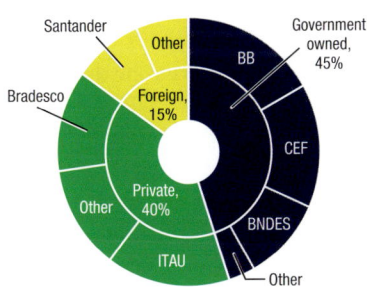

Source: Central Bank of Brazil.

Earmarked credit market interventions attempt to direct funds to priority areas, often with medium- and long-term funding and generally at regulated interest rates. Earmarked credit is partially funded by special funds that are often constitutionally established, through federal government lending, and through tax-exempt financial instruments and demand deposits. Box 16.1 summarizes the earmarked credit interventions.

Various funds, often constitutionally established, are leveraged to fund credit market interventions at low interest rates (Figure 16.3). A Workers' Support Fund (Fondo de Amparo al Trabajador, or FAT) funded with dedicated taxes allocates at least 40 percent of its assets to financial intermediation managed mostly by the BNDES. The FGTS provides the funding through CEF, and various other constitutional funds are managed by the BNDES and other development banks.

Figure 16.3. Funds Dedicated to Earmarked Lending, 2017

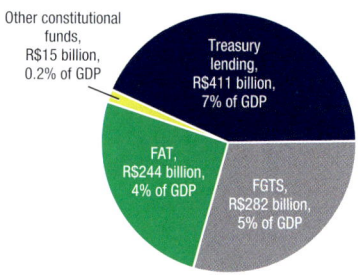

Source: Central Bank of Brazil.
Note: FAT = Fundo de Amparo ao Trabalhador (Workers Assistance Fund); FGTS = Fundo de Garantia do Tempo de Serviço (Employees' Severance Guarantee Fund); R$ = Brazilian reais.

After the global financial crisis, the federal government increased lending to the BNDES. To underpin investments during the crisis, the government expanded its lending to the BNDES, initially motivated by countercyclical credit provision considerations. The expansion, however, continued after the commodity boom helped Brazil emerge from the recession, and outstanding lending reached R$411 billion at the end of 2017. These funds were provided at the TJLP rate and thus include an important embedded subsidy.

Tax-exempt financing instruments and demand deposits are used to attract funds for earmarked credit. By waiving the 15 percent tax on interest income, the instruments allow banks to attract the funds at more favorable rates to onlend to the priority sectors. Real estate letters of credit (Letras de Credito Imobiliario) and agricultural letters of credit (Letras de Credito Agropecuario) are directed for real estate and agricultural lending, respectively. Rural savings deposits (Poupanca Rural) are directed for rural lending, and savings deposits (Poupanca) are directed for real estate lending. Regular demand deposits, although not tax exempt but normally collected at low cost, carry an obligation that 34 percent be directed to rural lending and 2 percent to microfinance.

Direct subsidies are provided for certain segments. Certain on-budget federal subsidies, referred to as interest rate equalization, allow lower interest rates to be charged for specific priorities, such as the Investment Support Program for enterprise investments and the Programa de Fortalecimento da Agricultura Familiar (PRONAF) program for small farmers. These subsidies amounted to R$9 billion in 2016.

Box 16.1. Earmarked Credit Interventions

Government Interventions

Workers' Support Fund (FAT), the Merchant Marine Fund, and PIS-PASEP (O Programa de Integração Social e o Programa de Formação do Patrimônio do Servidor Público)

FAT is a constitutionally established Workers' Support Fund. FAT is funded with a 0.65 percent tax on the gross revenues of companies, 1 percent on the payroll of nonprofits, and 1.65 percent on imports of goods and services. The constitution assigns at least 40 percent of FAT resources to economic development programs implemented by the Brazilian Development Bank (BNDES). FAT provides 27 percent of BNDES funding. The PIS-PASEP is a precursor to FAT, and the Merchant Marine Fund is directed to the naval industry and related infrastructure. These two funds account for 7 percent of the BNDES' total funding.

FAT funding of the BNDES amounted to R$244 billion in 2017 and was remunerated at the TJLP before 2018 and has been remunerated at the TLP since then.

Severance Indemnity Fund (FGTS)

The FGTS is a mandatory severance indemnity fund for employees. It collects 8 percent of an employee's salary to put into individual accounts at Caixa Economia Federal, a commercial public bank. The FGTS is managed by a trustee board composed of workers, entrepreneurs, and federal government representatives. Its resources are mostly directed to real estate credit at subsidized interest rates.

The fund totaled R$282 billion as of 2016 and is remunerated at 5.1 percent.

Regional Development Constitutional Funds

These constitutional funds are established to promote regional development in specific regions and include the Northeast Fund, the North Fund, and the Midwest Fund.

The funds totaled R$96 billion and were remunerated at TJLP before 2018 and have been remunerated at TLP since then.

Treasury lending at below-market interest rates

The federal government lends long-term funds for onlending mostly through the BNDES. The onlending is predominantly for long-term finance for enterprises.

The outstanding amount was R$411 billion at the end of 2017. Loans originated before 2018 are priced based on the TJLP, and loans originated since then are priced based on the TLP.

Direct subsidies

The government provides subsidies to reimburse banks for lending under certain programs at below-market interest rates. The largest such program was the Investment Support Program (PSI) Programa de Sustentação do Investimento operated by the BNDES, which offered loans at rates as low as 3 percent. Other subsidized credit programs include the Minha Casa Minha Vida (My House My Life) housing program and Programa de Fortalecimento da Agricultura Familiar program to strengthen family farming, both directed to low-income families.

Tax exemptions

Savings instruments such as savings accounts and real estate and agriculture letters of credit are exempt from income tax.[3] Certain credit operations are exempt from the financial

---

[3]Not all resources in letters of credit for agriculture seem to have been assigned to agriculture. See Normativo nb 4487/2016 from the Central Bank of Brazil.

> ### Box 16.1. Earmarked Credit Interventions (*continued*)
>
> transactions tax, such as infrastructure and development financing that fulfills certain criteria, all credit transactions that use Regional Development Constitutional Funds (Northeast Fund, North Fund, and Midwest Fund), and the Minha Casa Minha Vida housing program's infrastructure projects, among others.
>
> #### Central Bank Regulations
>
> ##### Deposit-collection-based earmarked lending
>
> Central bank regulations require that commercial banks lend for real estate, rural projects, and microfinance at below-market interest rates based on their deposit collection. Different types of deposits are subject to different earmarked lending requirements.
>
> ##### Differential reserve requirements for earmarked credit
>
> Loans to infrastructure projects offered at the public credit programs' contractual terms can be deducted from the central bank's reserve requirements.
>
> ##### Regulation of earmarked credit rates
>
> The TJLP rate is regulated by the National Monetary Council. The central bank sets the Taxa de Referência, a reference rate that remunerates savings accounts. The National Monetary Council also sets the agriculture earmarked credit rate.

Subsidies are thus embedded in earmarked lending through a variety of instruments. The simplest are direct subsidies through interest rate equalization programs. The onlending of government and constitutional funds at artificially low interest rates provides an implicit subsidy, which is sensitive to the movement of market interest rates. Finally, tax exemptions on savings instruments and the redirection of demand deposits provide a subsidy shared between the savers and the borrowers.

THE EFFECTIVENESS OF CREDIT MARKET INTERVENTIONS

The evidence in favor of credit market interventions is modest. A laudable initiative by the BNDES to publish at the contract level its lending operations has allowed for independent research, and the Central Bank of Brazil publishes extensive data on earmarked credit. Much of the research has not yet been peer reviewed, and the conclusions may evolve over time. The evidence does not offer much support for the effectiveness of the interventions.

During the global financial crisis, credit market interventions played a countercyclical role, but the expansion continued beyond the crisis (see Coleman and Feler 2015). In fact, even though Brazil, buoyed by higher global commodity prices, was recovering, earmarked credit continued to grow rapidly and accounted for all credit deepening between 2010 and 2016 (Figure 16.4). It appears that the expansion of earmarked credit has supressed free credit.

Figure 16.4. Earmarked and Free Credit
(Percent)

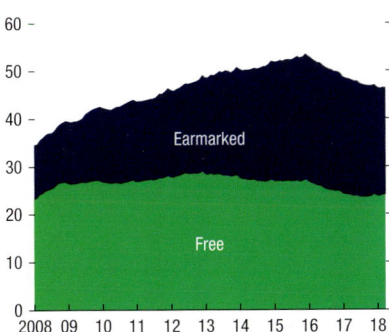

Source: Central Bank of Brazil.

The evidence on economic outcomes focuses on lending by the BNDES and offers little support for impact commensurate with the associated costs. Firms that borrowed from public banks or under earmarked programs were larger, older, and less risky than firms that borrowed only in the free market (Bonomo and Martins 2016). This pool of borrowers suggests that earmarked lending was not directed toward firms suffering credit constraints, and this finding is corroborated by the strong performance of the BNDES' credit portfolio. Some studies have found a modest impact on exports, investment, employment, and output (DeNegri and others 2011; Inoue, Lazzarini, and Musacchio 2013), in particular during the global financial crisis, when countercyclical provision of credit had some merit. The aggregate effect of BNDES lending on total factor productivity growth, however, cannot be established as significantly different from zero (Coelho and Lage de Sousa 2010; Ribeiro and DeNegri 2009). Meanwhile, a series of papers have suggested political influence in lending decisions by the BNDES. The high cost of earmarked credit is addressed in the next section.

The distributional impact of programs with social objectives needs further evaluation. The housing finance program My House My Life uses FGTS funds to offer low-cost credit for housing with a social objective and provides lower rates for more vulnerable groups. Similarly, PRONAF offers interest rate subsidies for small farms. These programs undoubtedly come at a high cost, but the evidence on the distributional and impact effects of these programs is inadequate.

FISCAL COSTS AND RISKS

The credit market interventions designed to offer credit at lower interest rates have resulted in large costs to the federal government and to publicly managed funds; these costs peaked at 2.1 percent of GDP in 2015 (Figure 16.5). The costs arise through a variety of channels discussed in Box 16.1. The costs directly to the federal government include on-budget subsidies, which amounted to R$9 billion in 2016, as well as the gap between the government's funding costs and the price at which it onlends the funds. In addition, the exemption from the 15 percent tax on savings deposits, as well as on the special real estate and agricultural letters of credit, represents forgone revenue estimated at R$7.4 billion.

Figure 16.5. Estimated Fiscal Cost of Credit Market Interventions

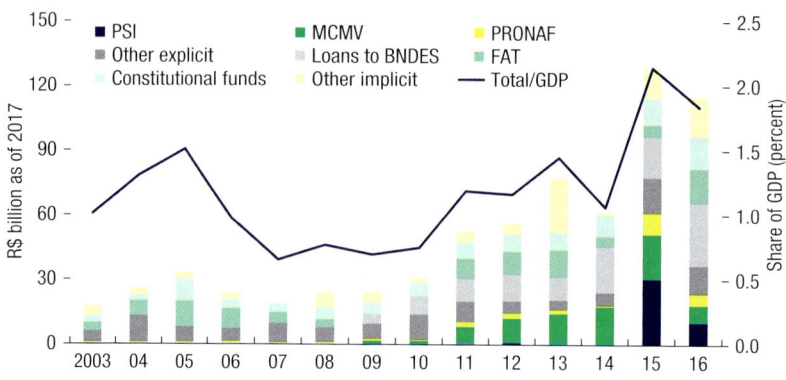

Source: Ministério da Fazenda/Ministry of Finance, Brazil.
Note: BNDES = Brazilian Development Bank; FAT = Fundo de Amparo ao Trabalhador (Workers Assistance Fund); MCMV = Minha Casa Minha Vida (Federal Housing Program); PSI = Programa de Sustentação do Investimento (Investment Support Program); PRONAF = National Program to Strengthen Family Farming.

Constitutionally established funds bear equally large costs from subsidies that are embedded in earmarked credit. The FGTS is used for onlending by the CEF and is remunerated at about 7 percent, and FAT and other constitutional funds are used for onlending by the BNDES and remunerated at the TJLP. Although these rates are for long-term finance, the returns have historically been well below the money market rate, Certificado de Depósito Interbancário (see Figure 16.6).

The fiscal cost of earmarked credit interventions is sensitive to market interest rate movements and is procyclical. As is evident in Figure 16.6, regulated rates are much more stable than the money market rate. If market interest rates, including fiscal funding costs, rise 5 percentage points relative to the regulated price at which the R$411 billion in Treasury funds are provided, all else being equal, the implicit fiscal subsidies rise by R$21 billion, or 0.3 percent of GDP. This estimate does not consider that the government's cost of funding may rise further as its credit quality deteriorates because it must meet higher expenditures for the credit subsidies, and the government's marginal cost of funding is likely to rise faster than its average cost of funding. An economic shock that leads to a tightening of monetary policy therefore also has an important negative impact on the fiscal sector through the earmarked credit interventions. As a corollary, it leads to pro-cyclicality in the subsidies embedded in the directed lending because the subsidies will grow when monetary policy tightens.

Fiscal risk can also arise from the need to recapitalize public banks, in particular when credit and market risks are poorly managed. Brazil has historically experienced large costs from recapitalizations. In the late 1990s several banks owned by Brazilian states were recapitalized, and in 1996 Banco do Brasil was recapitalized and the CEF was relieved of losses on unpaid mortgage debt. Then in 2001 the CEF, Banco do Brasil, and the regional development banks Banco do

Figure 16.6. Remuneration for Earmarked Credit Funding
(Percent)

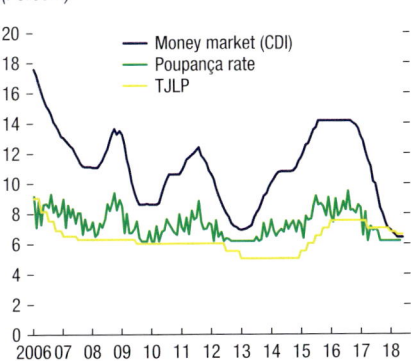

Source: Central Bank of Brazil.
Note: CDI = *certificado de deposito interbancário* (interbank money market rate); Poupança = savings account; TJLP = *taxa de juros de longo prazo* (long-term interest rate).

Nordeste and Banco da Amazonia all received capital contributions under the Programa de Fortalecimento das Instituições Financeiras Federais program. The CEF has been under solvency pressure because of poor profitability, strong lending growth, and tightening prudential requirements.

The high fiscal costs and their association with interest rates leave the country particularly exposed to financial crises. A shock to the economy that requires substantial monetary tightening would increase fiscal expenditures for earmarked credit at a time when the country can least afford it. Failure to meet these additional expenditures could reinforce a credit contraction.

The structure of the housing market, based as it is on savings deposits, creates a particular exposure to increasing interest rates. Regulated interest rates in the housing market are precluding the participation of capital markets in the funding of these long-term assets. Instead, the system continues to rely on savings deposits collection at regulated rates. Although these deposits are stable as long as the regulated rate is not too far below the market rate, a spike in market interest rates could cause a large outflow of deposits, creating a liquidity risk for the mortgage finance system. In 2015 the inflow of savings deposits was severely affected by the rise in market rates relative to the rate offered on savings deposits. Lenders could choose to attract funds at higher market rates, exposing the system to interest rate risk. This structure not only bears risks but is also curtailing the deepening of housing finance because capital market resources cannot be leveraged.

The interventions have led to the state's overwhelming dominance in long-term fixed income finance. Large fiscal debts have made the government the dominant issuer of long-term securities, and high interest rates have made these securities attractive to institutional investors. Mutual funds, pension funds, and insurance companies all predominantly invest in government securities or hold funds with the banks, which, in turn, are large holders of government securities. Meanwhile, the government provides funding for the BNDES and CEF through direct lending or through constitutional funds. In turn, the BNDES provides long-term finance for infrastructure and enterprises, and the CEF provides long-term finance primarily for housing but also for infrastructure. Effectively, the federal government has become a significant intermediary of long-term funding, which leaves it with the maturity risk and as the almost sole financier in the long-term finance market.

EFFECTS ON MONETARY POLICY TRANSMISSION AND FREE MARKET FOR CREDIT

The regulated interest rates associated with earmarked lending suppress the effectiveness of monetary policy. Because the supply of earmarked credit and interest rates are regulated, that part of the credit market does not respond as well to monetary policy. Estimates show that if earmarked loans responded to changes in the policy rate (Sistema Especial de Liquidação e Custodia, or SELIC) in the same way as non-earmarked loans, an increase of 0.84 percent would have the same effect as the current effect of a 1 percent SELIC increase (see Pazarbasioglu-Dutz and others 2017; Bonomo, Brito, and Martins 2015). As a consequence, changes in the SELIC must be larger to achieve monetary policy objectives.

Credit interest rates in the free market are raised by several effects associated with earmarked credit. Monetary tightening raises interest rates in the free credit market more than it otherwise would have, and the expansion of earmarked credit requires monetary tightening. The earmarked lending requirements associated with demand deposits, along with large, although recently reduced, reserve requirements, make financing free market credit through deposits an expensive practice. The requirements associated with deposit collection are illustrated in Figure 16.7. The fiscal cost of providing earmarked credit raises sovereign interest rates and competition for funds raised for the free credit market. These effects are complex to estimate and are not quantified in this chapter.

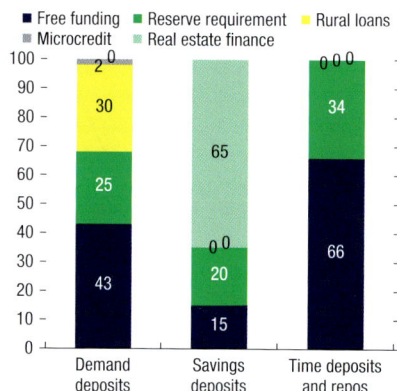

Figure 16.7. Deposit-Based Earmarked Credit and Reserve Requirements
(Percent)

Source: Central Bank of Brazil.

REFORM DIRECTIONS

The objectives for public banks and earmarked credit interventions must be regularly reviewed. The system has been built up over many years and now carries large fiscal expenditures, offers low returns to mandatory savings in constitutional funds, and contributes to high interest rates in the free market. The system needs to adjust so that interventions occur only when the benefits are expected to outweigh the costs. This strategy requires a clear and coordinated approach to monitoring and evaluation. The interventions today are varied and implemented by different means, and the costs are borne by several different actors. Objectives and policies are set by a range of participants, including different ministries, the central bank, the BNDES, and the other public banks. Thus, a coordinated effort is needed to monitor, evaluate, and revise objectives and to reform the public banks and earmarked credit.

The My House My Life and rural finance programs must be rigorously evaluated for their impact and distribution of subsidies. Because these programs do not aim to increase efficiency, they should be evaluated based on incidence, that is, the distribution of the subsidies and whether they reach their intended beneficiaries. The preferred solution for housing subsidies is to offer up-front subsidies to targeted beneficiaries to help them make a down payment, which, in turn, reduces the credit risk for housing finance lenders and thus provides better access to credit. For small farms, alternatives to credit subsidies include well-targeted income support and assistance with managing risks to crop yields and output prices, which would also help reduce credit risk and thus facilitate access to credit.

Disconnecting subsidies from credit decisions can improve transparency and outcomes. The TLP reform achieves the separation between subsidies and the direction of credit by tying the cost of finance in the earmarked system to the government's cost of funds. Subsidies, when needed, can then be better targeted to firms and projects with clear externalities. When offered independently, subsidies can also be better targeted based on externalities or social objectives regardless of whether the beneficiaries have a need for credit.

The earmarked housing credit market would benefit from a reform similar to the TLP reform, both to disconnect subsidies from directed credit and to enable a shift from the current short-term deposit funding to long-term capital market funding. As discussed, the short-term funding model for housing finance is risky when lending for 20- or 25-year mortgages. When interest rates rose in 2015, savings deposits dropped because they became uncompetitive despite their tax exemptions. Shifting the interest rate risk to the capital market would be preferable because it is a risk that will materialize when the government can least afford it.

Long-term finance should be mobilized from the private sector for enterprise investments, infrastructure, and housing. Several complementary actions can facilitate this shift. Lower interest rates on sovereign debt through macroeconomic policy will be important in directing private investors toward long-term nonsovereign investments. The BNDES can move out of lending to corporations that have the ability to issue securities in the market; instead, it can become a facilitator of market development, for example, by leading syndicated loans, providing credit enhancement rather than straight loans, and structuring the projects it is involved in to attract investors when feasible. Oversight of pension funds could also ensure that managers invest according to the long-term horizon of the funds' beneficiaries rather than pursue short-term instruments, as is currently the case.

The efficiency of free market financial intermediation needs to improve. Intermediation spreads in the free market remain too high to serve the economy's needs. The contracting environment can be enhanced through insolvency reform and secured transaction reforms, some of which are being contemplated. Credit-information sharing should be expanded to include positive information. Finally, competitive conduct in the financial industry should be evaluated to ensure that market conduct supports efficient financial intermediation.

REFERENCES

Bonomo, Marco, Ricardo D. Brito, and Bruno Martins. 2015. "The after Crisis Government-Driven Credit Expansion in Brazil: A Firm-Level Analysis." *Journal of International Money and Finance* 55(C): 111–34.

Bonomo, Marco, and Bruno Martins. 2016. "The Impact of Government-Driven Loans in the Monetary Transmission Mechanism: What Can We Learn from Firm-Level Data?" Working Papers Series 419, Research Department Central Bank of Brazil, Brasilia.

Byskov, Steen, and Mateo Clavijo. 2017. "Understanding the Effects of the Taxa de Longo Prazo (TLP) Reform in Brazil." World Bank, Washington, DC.

Coelho, D., and F. Lage de Sousa. 2010. "A Survey on BNDES Effects on Manufacturing Firms' Performance." In *Advanced and Integrated Productive Structure: Challenges of Brazilian Productive Development,* edited by Fernanda de Negri and Mansueto Almeida, 267–92. Brasília: Institute of Applied Economic Research.

Coleman, N., and L. Feler. 2015. "Bank Ownership, Lending, and Local Economic Performance during the 2008–2009 Financial Crisis." *Journal of Monetary Economics* 71(C): 50–66.

DeNegri, Joao Alberto, Alessandro Maffioli, Cesar M. Rodriguez, and Gonzalo Vázquez. 2011. "The Impact of Public Credit Programs on Brazilian Firms." Working Paper No. IDB-WP-293, Inter-American Development Bank, Washington, DC.

Dutz, M., and others. Forthcoming. "Brazil's Productivity Agenda." World Bank.

Inoue, Carlos F. K. V., Sergio G. Lazzarini, and Aldo Musacchio. 2013. "Leviathan as a Minority Shareholder: Firm-Level Implications of State Equity Purchases." *Academy of Management Journal* 56(6).

Pazarbasioglu-Dutz, Ceyla, Steen Byskov, Marco Antonio Cesar Bonomo, Igor Andre Carneiro, Bruno Martins, and Adriana Hernandez Perez Azevedo. 2017. "Brazil Financial Intermediation Costs and Credit Allocation." World Bank, Washington, DC.

Ribeiro, E., and F. DeNegri. 2009. "Public Credit Use and Productivity in Brazil." Presentation at 2009 LACEA/LAMES Meeting.

CHAPTER 17

In Pursuit of Anchored Inflation Expectations in Brazil: The Role of Transparency and Communication

YAN CARRIÈRE-SWALLOW AND JUAN YÉPEZ

Following several years of inflation expectations that exceeded the midpoint of the central bank's target, and amid a rapid disinflationary process that began in late 2016, inflation forecasts in Brazil are now broadly aligned with the central bank's target (Figure 17.1). These subdued inflation dynamics are the reflection of a large output gap; hence, they are cyclical in nature. Against this background, ensuring that inflation expectations remain well anchored is a policy priority. This chapter argues that strengthening the Central Bank of Brazil's (Banco Central do Brasil, BCB) transparency framework and communication strategies—that is, how openly and how well the central bank communicates in guiding markets—could make monetary policy decisions more predictable and keep medium-term inflation expectations firmly anchored. In particular, the BCB should continue its recent practice of providing clear public guidance about the conditional future direction of monetary policy and the balance of risks to inflation reaching the target within the policy horizon.

BRAZIL'S CENTRAL BANK TRANSPARENCY FRAMEWORK

The use of an inflation-targeting regime in Brazil over the past two decades has coincided with better-anchored inflation expectations, but there is still scope for improving this framework. An important aspect of this evolving framework has been the degree of central bank transparency that, despite significant improvements, falls below that of comparator countries (Figure 17.2).[1] Transparency provides the public with a better understanding of the central bank's objectives

---

[1]This chapter uses the Dincer and Eichengreen (2014) index of central bank transparency, which covers five categories: the political, economic, procedural, policy, and operational aspects of central bank transparency. This index does not control for the quality of central bank publications, which creates some degree of uncertainty around the reported transparency scores. In this context, rankings based on this index reflect relative (and not absolute) performance, and results are presented relative to the range of transparency scores across peers.

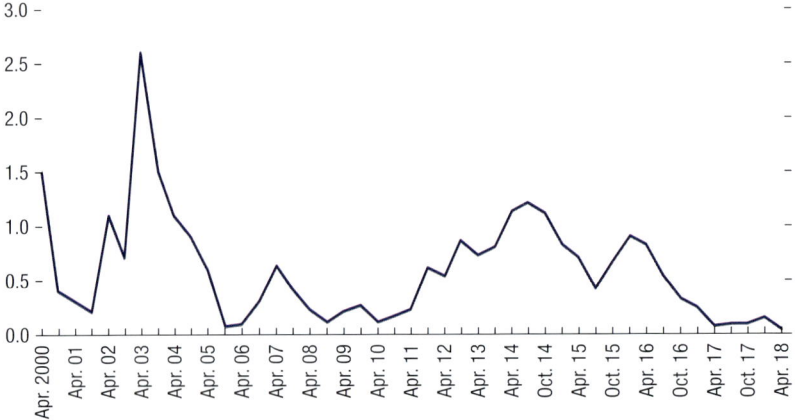

Figure 17.1. Absolute Deviation of Inflation Expectations from the Midpoint of the Central Bank of Brazil Target
(Percentage points; two years ahead)

Sources: Consensus Economics; Haver Analytics; and IMF staff calculations.

and the factors that motivate its monetary policy decisions. This, in turn, enables public accountability of independent central banks and greater credibility over time (Blattner and others 2008).

Although there is no agreement on what constitutes a best practice transparency framework, the following are thought to be the essential elements: (1) a formal policy objective such as price stability (including an explicit quantification of the objective), (2) an assessment of the current state of the economy, (3) an explanation of policy decisions, (4) a forward-looking analysis, and (5) publication of the economic data and forecasts used in the central bank's assessment.

The BCB's transparency framework is characterized by policy rate decisions accompanied by press releases that explain the decision and provide an assessment of the bal-

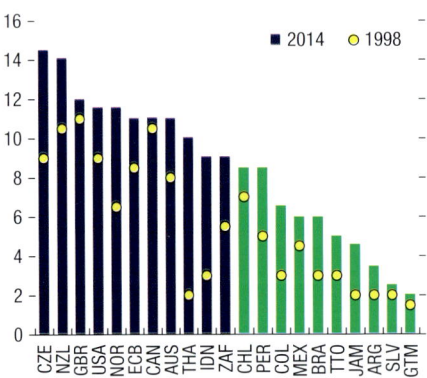

Figure 17.2. Central Bank Transparency Index
(Index)

Source: Dincer and Eichengreen (2014).
Note: Green bars refer to Latin America and Caribbean countries. Data labels in figure use International Organization for Standardization (ISO) country codes.

ance of risks for inflation.[2] In addition, the baseline scenarios and balance of risks are delineated in quarterly monetary policy reports. Alongside these reports, the BCB releases most of the data used for its monetary policy decisions (all but the output gap are available at high frequency in Excel format). As is common practice among established inflation-targeting central banks, the BCB releases minutes of its prior policy meetings before the subsequent meeting. Although names are not assigned to transcribed comments, the BCB is one of only a few central banks that identify how individual committee members voted. As part of the accountability component of the transparency framework, the central bank governor is periodically summoned to Parliament. Deficiencies in the framework arise from gaps in political transparency (Brazil has no central bank act that defines monetary policy and financial stability mandates) and operational transparency (from the lack of assessments of the central bank's forecasting and operational performance).

CENTRAL BANK TRANSPARENCY AND THE DEGREE OF ANCHORING OF INFLATION EXPECTATIONS

Transparency about monetary policy objectives, outlook, past policy misses, and possible future policy responses reduces policy uncertainty and enhances the ability of central banks to manage expectations (Blinder and others 2008). Central bank transparency has been found to be associated with better-anchored inflation expectations, including in the case of Brazil (Montes and others 2016). The degree of anchoring of medium-term inflation expectations and the policy response to a supply-side shock (akin to the terms-of-trade shock experienced by Brazil in 2015–16) can be examined within an interacted panel vector autoregression (IPVAR) framework. Conditional impulse responses are obtained by allowing the coefficients of the IPVAR to vary with the degree of central bank transparency.[3]

Although this framework admittedly does not allow for establishing a causal relationship between transparency and the degree of anchoring of inflation expectations, results point to a strong link between the two. Figure 17.3 (panel 1) displays the response of medium-term inflation expectation gaps conditional on central bank transparency. Among a sample of 20 inflation-targeting economies, lower transparency is associated with inflation expectation gaps that widen significantly in response to inflationary shocks. In line with the literature, the analysis finds that the gains from increasing central bank transparency display

---

[2]The informational content of these reports has significantly increased since 2016, with the central bank putting more emphasis on the balance of risks and providing more guidance on the monetary policy stance.

[3]See Annex 17.1 for details.

diminishing returns.[4] The largest benefits accrue mainly at low levels of transparency. This trend suggests that the BCB, characterized by lower levels of transparency, stands to benefit from expanding its transparency framework.

Do more transparent central banks enjoy greater room to maneuver interest rate policy in the face of transitory inflation shocks? The analysis here shows that the degree of transparency is associated with the procyclicality of monetary policy following a terms-of-trade bust (Figure 17.3, panel 2). Specifically, a more sizable and protracted policy rate tightening in reaction to the shock occurs in economies with less transparent central banks. A central bank with the BCB's current transparency score increased the policy rate by 50 basis points for each 100 basis point increase in inflation following the decline in the terms of trade. In contrast, a country with Australia's current level of transparency kept the policy rate unchanged.[5] This mone-

---

[4]Looking at a different measure of credibility allows for extending this analysis to a broader sample. Brito, Carrière-Swallow, and Gruss (2018), in a sample of 44 countries, demonstrate a strong relationship between central bank transparency and disagreement among professional forecasters of inflation—another common proxy for central bank credibility. Raising transparency from low levels was associated with large reductions in forecast disagreement even in countries that never adopted an inflation-targeting framework.

[5]Unless otherwise noted, transparency scores refer to 2014, the latest year for which the Dincer and Eichengreen (2014) augmented transparency score is available. This could provide an outdated view for some central banks and would not capture recent improvements in transparency frameworks.

Figure 17.3. Cumulative Response of 20 Inflation-Targeting Economies to a 20 Percent Reduction in the Terms of Trade, 2000–18

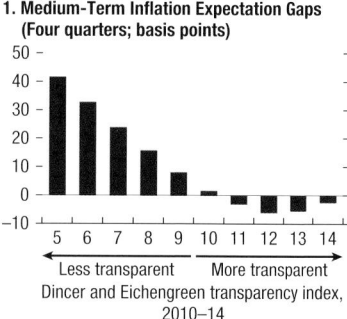

1. Medium-Term Inflation Expectation Gaps
   (Four quarters; basis points)

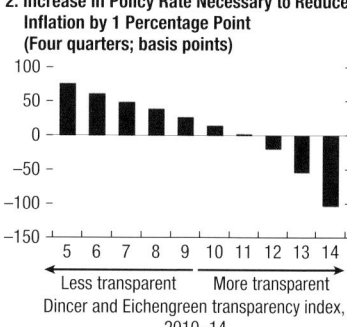

2. Increase in Policy Rate Necessary to Reduce Inflation by 1 Percentage Point
   (Four quarters; basis points)

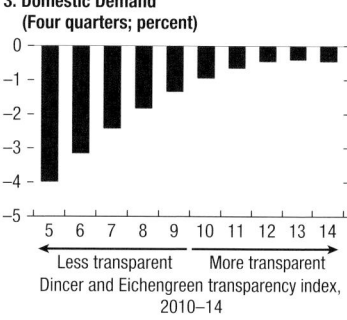

3. Domestic Demand
   (Four quarters; percent)

Sources: Consensus Economics; Dincer and Eichengreen 2014; Haver Analytics; IMF, International Financial Statistics database; national authorities; and IMF staff calculations.
Note: Dincer and Eichengreen transparency index ranges from 1 to 15, with 15 being the most transparent.

tary tightening increases macroeconomic volatility, because inflation and output move in opposite directions after a terms-of-trade decline (Figure 17.3, panel 3).

The BCB has scope to continue strengthening its transparency framework, and more may be gained by focusing on the quality of its communication rather than the quantity. The next section presents an analysis that tries to identify a causal relationship between transparency and credibility by focusing on the communication components of central bank transparency and measuring their impact on market expectations about the future path of interest rates and medium-term inflation.

CENTRAL BANK COMMUNICATION: FROM QUANTITY TO QUALITY

Within a given transparency framework, a sound communication strategy by the central bank should strengthen the signal-to-noise ratio. In this regard, how much information is disseminated is not as important as the quality of the information provided to the public. This section looks at the communication strategies pursued by the BCB and their effects on central bank predictability and credibility since 2010, a period characterized by a series of large terms-of-trade and other supply-side shocks.[6]

What constitutes an effective communication strategy? Blinder and others (2008) posits that "successful central bank communication efforts should make policy more predictable, and market expectations about future short-term rates more accurate." To examine this empirically, short-term central bank predictability can be measured using surveys of financial market analysts that are gathered the day before each monetary policy decision. Analysts are asked about their expectations regarding the outcome of the upcoming monetary policy decision. The difference between the expectation and the outcome could be viewed as a forecast error or monetary policy surprise; large forecast errors about future short-term rates could be a sign of deficiencies in the communication framework.[7]

Short-term predictability of interest rate decisions is low in Brazil (Figure 17.4, panel 1). Forecast errors for Brazil are among the largest in a sample of 17 inflation-targeting economies. Monetary policy surprises are also relatively frequent in Brazil. Since 2010 the BCB "surprised" markets almost once every five meetings (Figure 17.4, panel 2). Low policy predictability could reflect greater volatility of inflationary shocks affecting Brazil. However, unlike the rest of the central banks in Latin America, the frequency of monetary policy surprises has decreased in Brazil, partly reflecting the BCB's strategy of providing more

---

[6]More specifically, the section looks at the structure and content of press releases communicating policy decisions and the minutes of the monetary policy meeting.

[7]Although short-term predictability is important and certainly forms part of a central bank's objectives, predictability of monetary policy decisions should be seen in a broader context and over extended periods.

Figure 17.4. Monetary Policy Predictability

1. Size of Monetary Policy Surprises, 2010–18
(Root mean square error of monetary policy forecasts)

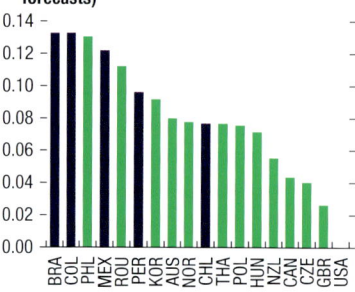

2. Frequency of Monetary Policy Surprises, 2010–18
(Percent of total monetary policy meetings)

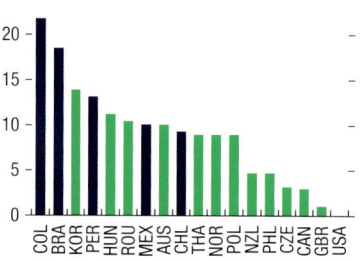

3. Evolution of Monetary Policy Surprises in Latin America
(Percent of total monetary policy meetings)

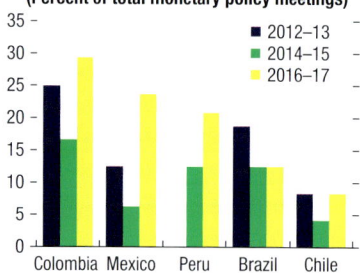

Sources: Bloomberg Finance L.P.; and IMF staff calculations.
Note: Data labels in panels 1 and 2 use International Organization for Standardization (ISO) country codes.

Figure 17.5. Text Length of Central Bank Press Releases, 2013–18
(Average word count)

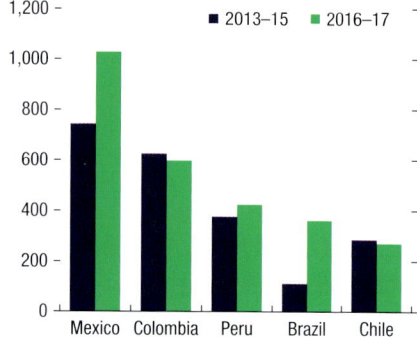

Source: IMF staff calculations.

guidance about the monetary policy stance during the recent loosening cycle (Figure 17.4, panel 3).

Press releases accompanying policy decisions are a key aspect of a central bank's communication toolkit. The length of central bank statements may reflect both the level of detail that it wants to transmit to the public and its efforts to increase procedural transparency (Taborda 2015). Figure 17.5 depicts recent trends in the length of press releases that accompany policy decisions in five Latin American economies. Brazil exhibits large changes, with the BCB devoting more text to the explanation of policy decisions and to the assessment of risks to the inflation outlook. These longer press releases are evidence of a push to improve policy transparency—statements before 2016 did not provide an explanation of the factors

Figure 17.6. Clarity of Central Bank Communication

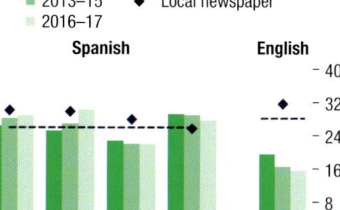

1. Readability Indices of Central Bank Press Releases[1]
(Index)

2. Correlation between Text Length and Readability Scores, 2010–18
(Correlation coefficients)

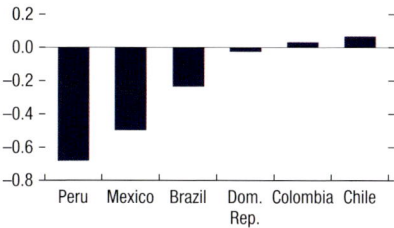

3. Clarity of Central Bank Communication and Monetary Policy Predictability[2]

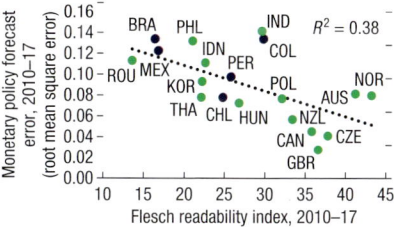

Sources: Bloomberg Finance L.P.; and IMF staff calculations.
Note: WHD REO = IMF Western Hemisphere Department *Regional Economic Outlook*. Data labels in panel 3 use International Organization for Standardization (ISO) country codes.
[1]Local newspapers correspond to the articles from the business section of *Folha International* (Brazil), *El Mercurio* (Chile), *El Espectador* (Colombia), *El Universal* (Mexico), and *El Comercio* (Peru).
[2]The chart shows the Flesch readability index for press releases in English. For Mexico, the English version of the monetary policy discussion of the inflation report was used.

influencing the Monetary Policy Committee's decisions.[8]

Of course, an increase in words does not necessarily mean clearer communication. Central banks could be verbose without providing any meaningful information. Language complexity can have a significant bearing on whether the text is readable or comprehensible. Figure 17.6 (panel 1) reports average readability scores for Latin American central bank press releases.[9] The press statement scores are shown against benchmarks to compare clarity of communication. These indices suggest that press statements in Brazil use more complicated language than the business sections of local newspapers.[10] A longer central bank statement is not only more diffi-

---

[8]The explanation of policy decisions was presented in the minutes of the monetary policy meetings, which are published with a two-week lag.

[9]The Spanish press releases for Chile, Colombia, Mexico, and Peru and the English translations for Brazil are used. The Flesch reading ease (RE) index is used for Brazil, which is defined as RE $= 206.835 - (1.015 \times ASL) - (84.6 \times ASW)$, in which ASL = average sentence length and ASW = average number of syllables per word. Following Taborda (2015), the Flesch-Szigriszt index for documents in Spanish is used for the other economies. That index is defined as RE $= 206.835 - (ASL) - (84.6 \times ASW)$.

[10]Minutes are also an important central bank communication tool for shaping market expectations. However, this analysis focuses on press releases because they tend to receive more media attention, allowing central banks to reach a wider audience, not just financial market participants (Berger, Ehrmann, and Fratzscher

Figure 17.7. Frequency of Explicit Policy Guidance in Central Bank Press Releases, 2011–18
(Percent of total press releases)

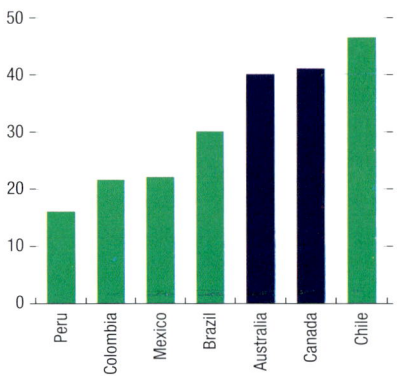

Sources: Central bank websites; and IMF staff calculations.

Figure 17.8. Effect of Unanticipated Increase in Policy Rate on Breakeven Inflation, 2011–18
(Basis points; one-day change in difference between yield on 10-year nominal and inflation-linked government bonds)

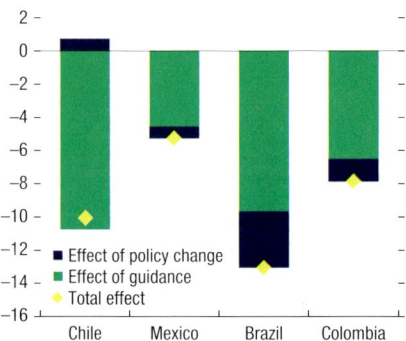

Sources: Bloomberg Finance L.P.; central bank websites; and IMF staff calculations.

cult to read, but also could reduce the ability of market participants to make informed judgments—highlighting the difference between the quantity and the quality of communication (Figure 17.6, panel 2). More readable press statements are also associated with lower monetary policy forecast errors (Figure 17.6, panel 3).

Central banks can also enhance the effectiveness of monetary policy by including forward-looking language in their communications. Figure 17.7 displays the frequency of press releases with explicit guidance on the likely future direction of monetary policy. During 2011–18 explicit policy guidance by the BCB was used infrequently. However, since late 2016 the BCB has included a policy "bias" at a rate of once every two meetings. The use of this forward-looking language appears to be associated with higher transmission from policy rates to inflation expectations. As Figure 17.8 reports, monetary policy decisions appear to have a larger effect on long-term inflation compensation measures when accompanied by announcements that contain an explicit policy bias. This analysis allows for a more direct identification strategy about the effects of transparency on credibility. Results suggest higher policy transparency helps anchor inflation expectations, confirming the results presented in the previous section.

Guiding market expectations requires not only forward-looking communication but also consistency between words and deeds. This track record of monetary policy communications and decisions supports the central bank's predictability and credibility. Using computational linguistic measures, first the tone in the

2011). In particular, it is the general public whose inflation expectations eventually feed into the actual evolution of inflation.

Figure 17.9. Correlation between Tone Index and Changes in Future Policy Rates, 2011–18
(One month ahead)

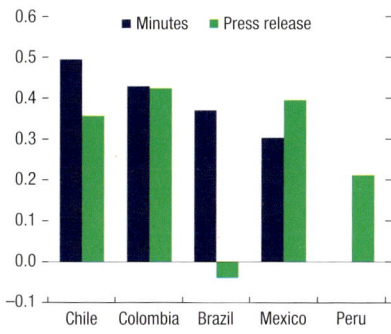

Sources: Central bank websites; and IMF staff calculations.

Figure 17.10. *R*-Squared from Regressions of Daily Changes in Market Rates and Tone Index, 2011–18
(Percent)

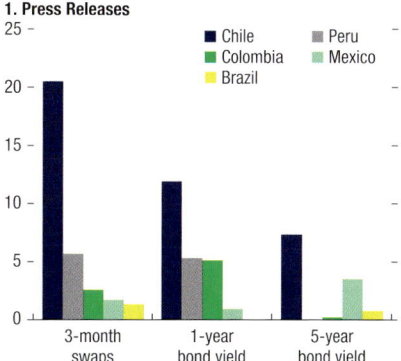

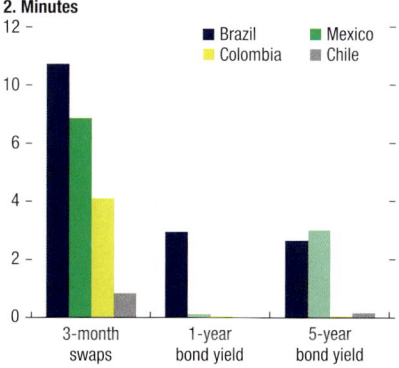

Sources: Haver Analytics; and IMF staff calculations.
Note: Panel 1 shows the difference in the adjusted *R*-squared between a regression of daily change in market rates on the unexpected monetary policy change and a regression in which the tone index of communication is included. Panel 2 shows the adjusted *R*-squared of a regression of the daily change in market rates on the tone index from minutes.

policy discussion section of the minutes can be summarized as being "hawkish" or "dovish," depending on word choice and context.[11] Second, the tone of communication can be compared with central bank policy action. Figure 17.9 displays the correlations between the tone indices and future policy rate changes. It should come as no surprise that central banks tend to back up their words with deeds. More hawkish (dovish) tones tend to result in a tightening (loosening) of the policy rate in subsequent meetings. The tone in the BCB's minutes is a reliable predictor of future policy changes. As mentioned, this reliability is particularly important when inflation expectations are not fully anchored.

Finally, markets appear to listen to the central bank, given that the tone of press releases and minutes affects not only the short end of the yield curve but also medium- and long-term interest rates (Figure 17.10). Except in the case of Chile, market sensitivity to the tone of central bank press releases is muted. However, market rates appear to be somewhat sensitive to the tone of Brazil's

---

[11]See Chapter 3 of the IMF's April 2018 *Regional Economic Outlook: Western Hemisphere* for a discussion of how this tone index is constructed.

minutes, as a result of the richness of their informational content compared with press releases (particularly before 2016). These results indicate that, given that inflation expectations are strongly anchored, effective use of communication can provide greater room to maneuver interest rate policy in the face of transitory inflation shocks.

POLICY INSIGHTS

The credibility of a central bank—as measured by the anchoring of medium-term inflation expectations—has significant implications for policy decisions in response to short-term inflationary shocks. Credibility, in turn, is strongly related to transparency and communication.

The BCB stands to benefit from further developing and strengthening its transparency framework and communication strategies. Greater transparency and communication would help the public better anticipate central bank decisions and align their medium-term inflation expectations with the central bank's objective—and thus strengthen the effects of monetary policy changes. These changes, in turn, could increase maneuvering room for monetary policy, particularly at times when policy space is constrained.

Communication strategy plays an important role in increasing predictability. What type of information central banks publish is important, but so too is how this information is communicated to the general public. The analysis presented in this chapter argues that central banks that communicate clearly and unambiguously also tend to be among the most predictable. In this context, central banks that provide policy guidance (for example, an easing or tightening bias) in the run-up to monetary policy decisions, with such statements explicitly conditional on current forecasts, considerably improve the transmission of policy rates to long-term inflation compensation measures.

Strengthening the transparency framework would entail filling current data gaps, for example, by increasing the horizon of survey-based expectations. The lag in the publication of minutes can also be reduced.[12] However, transparency and communication are not a panacea, and central banks have to tailor their strategies so that they align with their policy objectives.

REFERENCES

Berger, H., M. Ehrmann, and M. Fratzscher. 2011. "Monetary Policy in the Media." *Journal of Money Credit and Banking* 43 (4): 689–709.

Blattner, T., M. Catenaro, M. Ehrmann, R. Strauch, and J. Turunen. 2008. "The Predictability of Monetary Policy." ECB Occasional Paper 83, European Central Bank, Frankfurt.

Blinder A. 2009. "Talking about Monetary Policy: The Virtues (and Vices?) of Central Bank Communication." BIS Working Paper 274, Bank for International Settlements, Basel.

---

[12]Since August 2015 the Bank of England has published minutes alongside its interest rate decisions.

Blinder, A. S., M. Ehrmann, M. Fratzscher, J. D. Haan, and D. J. Jansen. 2008. "Central Bank Communication and Monetary Policy: A Survey of Theory and Evidence." *Journal of Economic Literature* 46 (4): 910–45.

Brito, S., Y. Carrière-Swallow, and B. Gruss. 2018. "Disagreement about Future Inflation: Understanding the Benefits of Inflation Targeting and Transparency." IMF Working Paper 18/24, International Monetary Fund, Washington, DC.

Dincer, N., and B. Eichengreen. 2014. "Central Bank Transparency and Independence: Updates and New Measures." *International Journal of Central Banking* 10 (1): 189–259.

Montes, G. C., L. V. Oliveira, A. Curi, and R. T. F. Nicolay. 2017. "Effects of Transparency, Monetary Policy Signalling and Clarity of Central Bank Communication on Disagreement about Inflation Expectations." *Applied Economics* 48 (7): 590–607.

Schmitt-Grohé, S., and M. Uribe. 2018. "How Important Are Terms-of-Trade Shocks?" *International Economic Review* 59: 85–111.

Taborda, R. 2015. "Procedural Transparency in Latin American Central Banks under Inflation Targeting Schemes: A Text Analysis of the Minutes of the Boards of Directors." *Ensayos Sobre Politica Economica* 33 (76): 76–92.

Towbin, P., and S. Weber. 2013. "Limits of Floating Exchange Rates: The Role of Foreign Currency Debt and Import Structure." *Journal of Development Economics* 101 (1): 189–94.

ANNEX 17.1. PANEL VECTOR AUTOREGRESSION MODEL AND METHODOLOGY

The empirical strategy used to estimate the effect of terms-of-trade shocks on inflation expectations and monetary policy procyclicality is based on an interacted panel vector autoregression (IPVAR) framework that captures the dynamic response of the policy interest rate, domestic demand, the nominal effective exchange rate, consumer price index (CPI) inflation, and two-year-ahead inflation expectation gaps to a terms-of-trade shock, akin to the one experienced by the region since 2012. Following Towbin and Weber (2013), the coefficients of the "domestic" variables are allowed to vary deterministically with the level of central bank transparency. This variable is lagged by two years to avoid endogeneity issues.

Simultaneity issues are addressed in the identification of the empirical model by assuming that countries in the chapter's sample take the terms of trade as exogenously given—that is, variations in the terms of trade can be regarded as an exogenous source of aggregate fluctuations. This assumption is common in the existing related literature (Schmitt-Grohé and Uribe 2018).

Denoting the vector of domestic variables as y_t and the vector of exogenously given variables as y_t^*, the model can be specified as follows:

$$\begin{pmatrix} y_t^* \\ y_t \end{pmatrix} = \begin{pmatrix} A_{11,i,t}(L) & 0 \\ B_{21,i,t}(L) & B_{22,i,t}(L) \end{pmatrix} \begin{pmatrix} y_{t-1}^* \\ y_{t-1} \end{pmatrix} + \begin{pmatrix} 0 & 0 \\ 0 & C_{22} \end{pmatrix} \begin{pmatrix} I_i \\ X_{i,t} \end{pmatrix} +$$

$$\begin{pmatrix} R_1 & 0 \\ R_2 & R_3 \end{pmatrix} \begin{pmatrix} \varepsilon_{i,t}^* \\ \varepsilon_{i,t} \end{pmatrix}. \tag{17.1}$$

$$B_{pq,i,t} = A_{pq,i,t} + D_{pq,i,t} X_{i,t}. \tag{17.2}$$

The coefficients for the domestic variables, B, can vary with country characteristics $X_{i,t}$ (that is, credibility and transparency). $\varepsilon_{i,t}^*$ and $\varepsilon_{i,t}$ are vectors of independent and identically distributed shocks. L is the number of lags. The matrix R is computed using a Cholesky factorization of the estimated covariance matrix of reduced-form VAR residuals. The block-zero restriction is imposed a priori, and external shocks are identified using a small open economy assumption. The assumption implies that the external variable does not depend on domestic conditions. Because the chapter's analysis focuses on the effects of terms-of-trade shocks, the ordering of the variables in the domestic variables vector, y_t, in the structural VAR is immaterial. The IPVAR is estimated using ordinary least squares and allows for country fixed effects. Two lags are chosen following the Schwarz criterion.

The dynamic response of inflation expectation gaps to terms-of-trade shocks is illustrated using cumulative, conditional impulse-response functions at a four-quarter horizon. To capture the strength of transmission of policy rates and the procyclicality of monetary policy, the cumulative impulse response of the policy rate is divided by the cumulative response of CPI inflation, both at the four-quarter horizon.

The vector y_t^* is given by

$$y_t^* = \left(ToT_{i,t} \right). \tag{17.3}$$

$ToT_{i,t}$ denotes the log first difference of terms of trade, defined as the relative price of exports in terms of imports.

The vector of domestic variables y_t is given by

$$y_t = \begin{pmatrix} MPR_{i,t} \\ DD_{i,t} \\ NEER_{i,t} \\ CPI_{i,t} \\ Gap_{i,t} \end{pmatrix}. \tag{17.4}$$

The variable MPR denotes the first difference of the monetary policy rate. The variables DD, $NEER$, and CPI denote the log first differences of real final domestic demand, the nominal effective exchange rate, and headline CPI for country i, respectively. Gap is the first difference of the absolute difference between the two-year-ahead inflation expectation gap and the central bank's target.[13] National accounts and financial data were obtained from Haver Analytics, the $NEER$ measure was obtained from the IMF's Information Notice System, and inflation expectation forecasts were obtained from Consensus Economics long-term forecasts. Central bank transparency is measured using the Dincer and Eichengreen (2014) augmented transparency index.

---

[13]The results from this exercise are robust to the use of forecasts at a five-year horizon, also from Consensus Economics.

The panel contains the following 20 economies under an inflation-targeting monetary policy framework: Australia, Brazil, Canada, Chile, Colombia, the Czech Republic, Hungary, India, Indonesia, the Republic of Korea, Mexico, New Zealand, Norway, Peru, the Philippines, Poland, Romania, Russia, Thailand, and Turkey. The panel covers the period 2000–18 at a quarterly frequency.

Selection of countries in the sample was based on whether a country was classified as being under an inflation-targeting framework, based on the IMF's 2016 *Annual Report on Exchange Arrangements and Exchange Restrictions* and on the availability of long-term inflation forecasts from Consensus Economics. Sweden was excluded because its policy rate has been negative since 2014.

PART VI

Fighting Corruption

CHAPTER 18

Corruption in Emerging Market Economies: How Does Brazil Fare?

CARLOS E. GONCALVES AND KRISHNA SRINIVASAN

Countries in Latin America compare unfavorably with advanced economies in terms of perceptions of corruption, but there is significant variation within the region. Brazil fares worse than expected given its level of development, whereas Chile and Uruguay are positive surprises. Corruption is a headwind to economic growth and development, but significant limitations impede the calculation of a precise estimate of the impact. Subject to this caveat, this chapter finds that improvements in percep- tions of corruption could boost a country's GDP per capita by anywhere from 12 per- cent to 35 percent, depending on the assumptions made. Getting rid of corruption will require an institutional "big push," one that revamps de facto law enforcement capa- bilities, under strong political leadership and with the support of society, including free and active media.

INTRODUCTION

Corruption in emerging market economies—and particularly in Latin America—has made headlines in recent years, notably in light of schemes to shelter assets. Leaked documents in Panama, and the Petrobras and Odebrecht scandals in Brazil, have had spillover implications for several countries in Latin America and the Caribbean. These incidents have led to economic and political fallout in several countries, marked by sharp declines in public and private invest- ment, policy paralysis, and a call for governments and elected representatives to tackle corruption more aggressively.

In response, many countries in Latin America, including Argentina, Brazil, Chile, Ecuador, Guatemala, Mexico, Paraguay, and Peru, have either upgraded or are in the process of upgrading their legal and judicial frameworks. In addition, several countries have introduced and enhanced asset declaration requirements and taken measures to augment fiscal transparency. Only time will tell whether these reforms are sufficient, but for now it is clear that corruption investigations are delving deeper, and anti-corruption forces appear to be more committed to the cause this time around. For instance, the Odebrecht probe and Brazil's Lava Jato ("Operation Car Wash") have resulted in the convictions of several public officials and heads of leading conglomerates; in Mexico eight former state governors are facing charges or have been convicted; and Guatemala has successfully unveiled cases of tax evasion, money laundering, and illegal funding through its International Commission against Impunity.

This chapter examines the economic aspects of corruption. It analyzes the theoretical underpinnings of how corruption (and its attendant distortions) affect the economy and takes a fresh look at the impact of corruption on economic development and growth. First, it provides a working definition of corruption and some theoretical reasoning for how competing views on corruption have evolved. It then discusses the data on corruption and how countries in Latin America, notably Brazil, stack up against their peers in the rest of the world. How corruption affects growth is addressed, followed by a review of the implications for economic development. Finally, the implications for policies are discussed, and some concluding remarks are provided.

THEORY

A Proper Definition

So, what is corruption? The term *corruption* may be broadly defined as "the abuse of public office for private gain" (IMF, forthcoming 2018, and Rose-Ackerman 2012). This characterization warrants two important observations. First, *public office* does not simply refer to politicians exercising power after winning competitive elections. Society also, albeit indirectly, entrusts power to unelected bureaucrats. Many instances have been found in which low-ranking public officials pass on part of the rents they extract to others in the system, notably at the higher echelons, reaching all the way to their political masters. Hence, corruption can occur at a "grand," or political, level and at a petty, or bureaucratic, level. Second, the definition excludes instances of foul play that may take place without the direct involvement of public officials or politicians. If two private firms strike a deal to the detriment of a third, say, via industrial espionage, then illegal harm ensues. This example fits better into the definition of private sector fraud.

Corruption is also sometimes placed into the two categories of *supply side* and *demand side*, according to which side initiated the talks—the private sector (briber) or the public sector (bribed). This distinction can be somewhat misleading because it does not really matter who makes the first phone call, the briber or the bribed; what really counts is the call itself and why both players expect to get away with their plans for stealing from the public purse.

The Old View: Grease in the Wheels

Interestingly, although there is now broad consensus that corruption is an important obstacle to economic development, not too long ago some social scientists espoused a different view. The competing—and now largely obsolete—view suggested that corruption could spur growth by acting as the economy's counterpart of the famous grease that helps the rusty wheel turn.

This idea was initially put forward by Leff (1964) and Huntington (1968), who argued that if the legal and regulatory policy framework was clogged with red tape, then finding (illicit) ways to circumvent such impediments would boost growth. In effect, bribes would play the role of a "market" against red tape.

At first blush, this reasoning looks plausible. For example, in many developing economies, retrieving an imported capital good from customs may take several months because of excessive red tape, which increases the effective cost incurred by the entrepreneur. But the port official in charge may be willing to sweep the maze of legal requirements under the rug and speed up the process in exchange for a bribe. Isn't the possibility of this type of exchange beneficial for the economy as whole?

For sure, yes, from a partial equilibrium and short-term perspective, but not from a general equilibrium, long-term point of view. The fundamental flaw in the grease-in-the-wheels theory is that inefficient policies and cumbersome regulations are neither inevitable hurdles nor exogenous and randomly distributed impediments. Instead, they may arise and persist precisely because they allow public officials and high-ranking politicians to extract rents, in disguise, from society.

To put it differently, the grease-in-the-wheels hypothesis does not resist one additional layer of strategic theorizing: the grease itself is endogenous! The wheels that turn the economy around will need no illicit greasing—and rents will not shuffle around—if corrupt deals are expected to be duly penalized.

The New View: Corruption as a Bad Nash Equilibrium

As in any type of social interaction, the way individuals form beliefs and expectations about each other's actions is crucial in understanding corruption. If people believe that most transactions involve an exchange of bribes, the individual payoff for acting honestly is greatly reduced, as in the problem of the prisoner's dilemma.

Of course, not every person is the same: different people face different personal costs of engaging in illicit activities (for some the cost may be so high that they would never offer or accept a bribe). But even those who dislike corruption may nevertheless end up engaging in it if society is stuck in a high-corruption equilibrium. It may be a matter of sheer survival. For example, if a family's only way to secure an appointment for a sick child with the local doctor is by paying a bribe (because everyone else does), a common practice in sub-Saharan Africa, chances are the family will pay.

But one does not need to rely on extreme scenarios to show that if corruption is endemic, few would deviate from paying a bribe. If a construction company is unlikely to secure a public project unless it pays a bribe to public officials and their patrons—regardless of its technical expertise and track record—refusing to "play by the rules" may result in the company's closure altogether. As in the Odebrecht example, in which the company spent considerable resources buying the support of key public officials in exchange for contracts in several Latin American countries, construction companies offering bribes are more likely to secure projects than those that do not—regardless of how much more efficient these firms may be. In sum, deviating from the practice of bribery may be too costly when you expect many others not to do likewise. Corruption is a Nash equilibrium that is not easily broken.

But is it possible to break the above-mentioned vicious cycle leading to the inferior Nash equilibrium? Is there a stable, Pareto-superior one, lurking in the corner? Fortunately, yes.

To understand why, let us resort to yet another thought experiment: suppose the expected costs of corruption increase following the adoption of a series of de facto actions and de jure measures. Pick the private agent that was close to refusing to offer a bribe. For this individual (or firm), the balance now tilts toward acting honestly: being arrested is a very costly proposition that has just become more probable. But—and this is crucial—it does not stop there: when the "swing corruptor" becomes honest, a chain of reinforcing beliefs is unleashed if there is common knowledge across large segments of society that these costs have increased. This occurs because a second (and third and so on) entrepreneur will anticipate the change in behavior of the briber-turned-honest-competitor and then possibly also conclude that paying bribes is not necessary anymore. The bigger the initial push, the larger the number of agents changing their behavior. Moreover, those who remain corrupt are now more easily detected, notably because they are fewer in number and hence more visible—and because the firms that no longer pay bribes now have huge stakes in the fight against corruption because it hampers their competitiveness, so they become collaborators.

The Hurdle of Collective Action

Why is weeding out corruption such a difficult challenge, often ending in failure and preservation of the status quo? The problem, as Mancur Olson (1971) would have put it, is that fighting corruption is itself a public good.

Essentially, the benefits of living in a corruption-free environment are shared among *everyone* in society; thus, these gains are not immensely large from the perspective of any one individual. Putting up a fight is, however, very costly from the perspective of any individual. Dispersed benefits and concentrated costs vitiate against collective action. In this environment, inertia usually ensues because the best strategy is to free-ride on the efforts of others who fight corruption—but of course, that being the case, in equilibrium little effort is exerted and corruption persists.

To make things worse, on the other side of the battlefield the exact opposite holds: for the members of organized interest groups benefiting from corruption under the status quo, losing the capacity to extract rents is individually very costly. Hence overcoming the collective action problem of supplying concerted effort is less difficult: special interests fight hard and usually defeat initiatives aimed at ending their rent-seeking activities.

All that said, the fact that there are some countries in the world where corruption is not systemic suggests that the hurdle of collective action is not impossible

Figure 18.1. Normalized Corruption Indices[1]

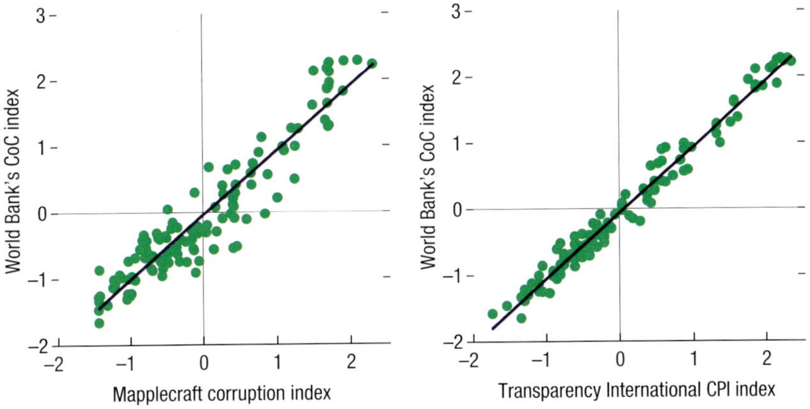

Sources: Mapplecraft; Transparency International; and World Bank.
Note: CoC = control of corruption; CPI = Corruption Perceptions Index.

to overcome and that a better equilibrium is achievable. But the fact that corruption is still so pervasive outside developed economies suggests that the battle is an uphill one.

MEASURING CORRUPTION

The Indices

Hard data on corruption are almost impossible to find for a large set of countries; therefore, most studies rely on survey data, such as Transparency International's Corruption Perceptions Index (CPI) or the World Bank's Control of Corruption (CoC) indicator. Corruption surveys can be based either on questions about "perceptions" or on actual "experience" with giving and taking bribes, but since data on the latter are more difficult to collect—notably because both bribe givers and takers are unlikely to come clean about their actions—empirical work has relied largely on surveys of perceptions. Although such data are more comprehensive in coverage, they come with their own share of problems: perceptions could be influenced by the state of the economy, the individual's well-being, and other factors.

Survey data should be used with caution, although it is somewhat reassuring that different survey measures of corruption are highly correlated (Figure 18.1). Moreover, greater care is needed in analyzing variations in corruption indices over time, notably because some indices (for example, the CPI) have undergone changes in methodology and because, as mentioned, survey responses based on perceptions could be influenced by the business cycle and other short-term factors without there being any fundamental change in corruption.

Figure 18.2. Cross-Country Distribution of Corruption

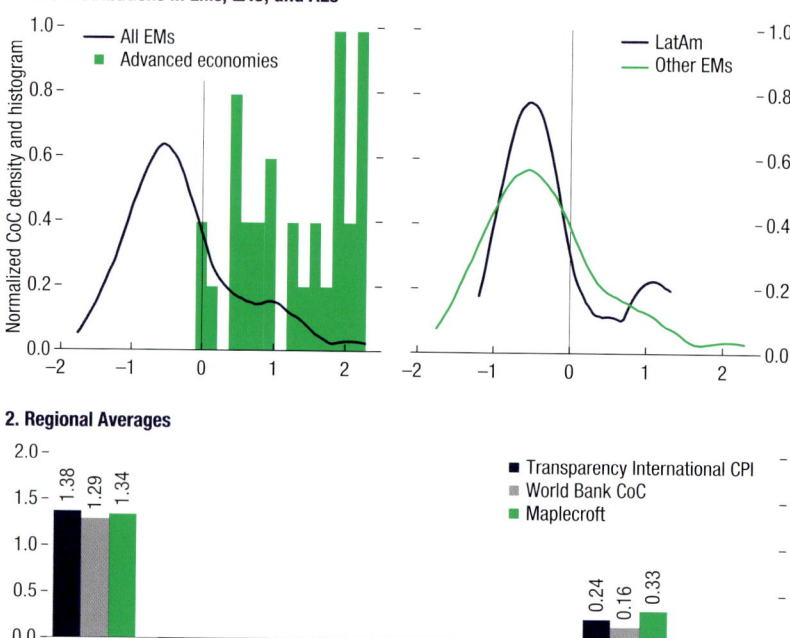

1. CoC Distributions in EMs, LAC, and AEs

2. Regional Averages

Sources: Transparency International; Verisk Maplecroft; and World Bank, World Governance Indicators database.

Note: The IMF does not construct these measures. Higher index means less corrupt. Emerging market and developing economies exclude Latin America and the Caribbean. CoC = control of corruption; CPI = corruption perception index; EMs = emerging markets; LAC = Latin America and the Caribbean; LatAm = Latin America.

Since by construction these indices have very different averages, the analysis in this chapter normalizes all of the indices by subtracting averages and dividing the outcome by each series' standard deviation. When it comes to CPI and CoC, the higher the index, the *less* corrupt the country.

Is Latin America an Outlier among Emerging Markets? Where Does Brazil Stand?

Latin Americans rightly condemn their political systems as highly corrupt. But are these countries outliers when compared with other emerging market economies? As Figure 18.2 suggests, advanced economies are indeed much less corrupt than emerging market economies. However, Latin America does not look like a clear outlier within the latter group (more on that later).

Regional averages mask a great deal of within-region variability. In Latin America, for instance, Chile and Uruguay present corruption indices similar to those found in advanced economies and diverge strongly from the region's average.

How does Brazil stack up? Surprisingly, not too badly—significantly worse than the top performers, Chile and Uruguay, but better than most other countries in the region.

But there is a catch.

A Measure of "Excess Corruption"

Realistically, corrupt practices can be expected to be more widespread in less-developed economies because they are likely to be at earlier stages in the process of institutional development, reflected by a combination of factors, including poor law enforcement, lack of fiscal transparency, weak contractual frameworks in public procurement, and weak governance in state-owned enterprises. For analytical purposes, then, it may be useful to assess the incidence of corruption controlling for a country's level of development—a measure of "excess corruption" given the country's income level. Put differently, Brazil is not Switzerland, so we should not expect it to be as corruption-free. But given Brazil's income per capita, how is it faring?

To answer that question, the World Bank's CoC indicator is regressed on income per capita and income per capita squared, and the residuals are used as a gauge of excess corruption, a measure of corruption not being in line with the country's level of development.[1,2]

Table 18.1 shows that higher GDP per capita is associated with lower perceived corruption (higher CoC), but there are decreasing returns—as a country gets richer and richer, more income does not buy less corruption (the squared term is negative and statistically significant).[3] This result is intuitive: a country with per capita GDP of US$10,000 has a level of institutional quality much lower than that of a developed economy with a per capita GDP of US$30,000. But between the latter and a richer nation with per capita GDP of US$50,000, the

---

[1]Results are basically the same if Transparency International's CPI is used instead.

[2]Corruption indicators do not change much over time, so whether averages or point estimates are used does not change the basic conclusion.

[3]Perhaps surprisingly, isolating the income levels effect, government consumption is associated with less corruption (higher indices) in this sample.

Table 18.1. Corruption and Income Levels

Variables	Average CoC 2002–16	
	(1)	(2)
Average GDP per Capita	4.40e-05*** (5.58e-06)	8.42e-05*** (7.97e-06)
(Average GDP per Capita)^2		−6.13e-10*** (1.23e-10)
Constant	−0.778*** (0.0790)	−1.060*** (0.0700)
Observations	134	134
R^2	0.614	0.698

Sources: World Bank; and authors' calculations.
Note: Exludes countries with populations of less than 500,000. CoC = control of corruption. Robust standard errors are in parentheses.
***$p < 0.01$.

corresponding gap in institutional quality should be less significant. Hence, mathematically speaking, the function linking GDP per capita to corruption should, in principle, be concave, which is corroborated empirically by the negative coefficient on the squared GDP term.

By construction, ordinary least squares estimators produce deviations from the fitted relationship that add up to zero in the whole sample. But, of course, the zero-sum property does not have to hold for a subsample of countries—say, Latin America. Indeed, most Latin American countries in the sample are by this measure more corrupt than expected—that is, they present negative residuals—albeit not dramatically so.

Using this measure, does Brazil's relative position change from the one depicted earlier, in Figure 18.3? Yes, and as Figure 18.5 shows, for the worse.

Corruption and Growth Correlations

Theory suggests that corruption is an impediment to socioeconomic progress (Figure 18.4). Corruption could lead to a misallocation and theft of public resources, create incentives for the private sector to invest in rent-seeking activities that do not yield any real productivity gains, give rise to adverse selection writ large in politics (honest people usually shy away from working in a corruption-ridden environment), increase uncertainty (unlike formal taxation, the corruption tax can change unexpectedly), and foster distrust, both among citizens and between citizens and their representatives in government.

The next two sections offer evidence that these obstacles are not just theoretical. The discussion shows that corruption and subpar growth performance in the past 20 years are, even if weakly, correlated. The chapter then shows that corruption also bears negatively on the level of GDP.

A note of caution is in order before the analysis begins. In particular, results from simple correlations or standard Barro-like growth regressions should be interpreted with much caution, since identifying true causal links using nonexperimental data is always challenging.[4] Disclaimer having been made, is there any discernible correlation between growth and corruption levels in a cross-section of

---

[4]Reverse causality and omitted variable bias are nearly insurmountable obstacles in empirical analysis of macro phenomena.

Figure 18.3. Quantiles of Average Control of Corruption, Latin America

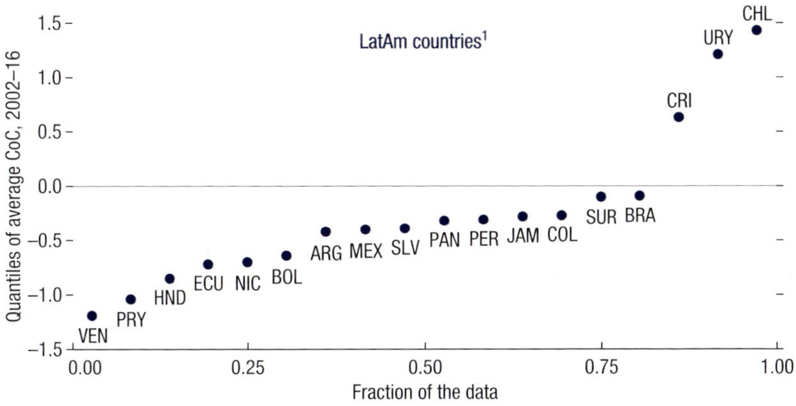

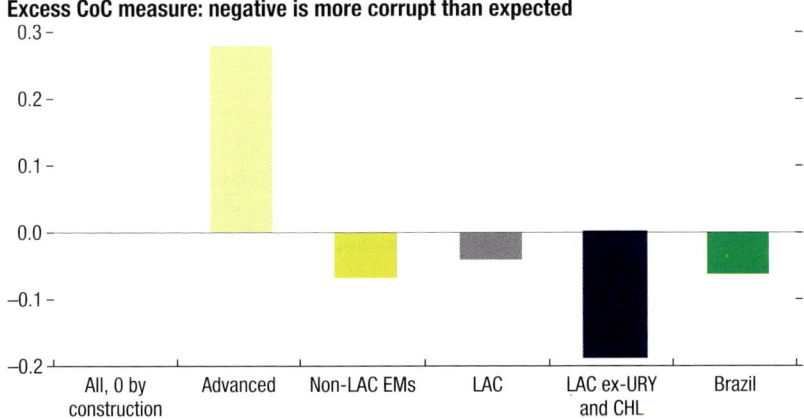

Sources: World Bank; and authors' calculations.
Note: CoC = control of corruption; LatAm = Latin America.
Data labels in the figure use International Organization for Standardization (ISO) country codes.
[1]Excluding countries with population of less than 500,000.

countries? Figure 18.6 plots the growth rates of 136 countries from 1996 to 2016 against their corruption indices in 1996.

Figure 18.6 suggests two ideas: (1) low-corruption countries (higher indices) grew, on average, *less* in the past 20 years; and (2) at the lower end of the corruption index distribution, growth volatility is astonishingly high. However, tracing correlations using nonparametric data like that in Figure 18.6 is fraught with problems: in this case, low-income countries both tend to grow more rapidly

Figure 18.4. Excess Corruption Measure

Excess CoC measure: negative is more corrupt than expected

Sources: World Bank; and authors' calculations.
Note: CoC = control of corruption; CHL = Chile; EMs = emerging markets; ex = except; LAC = Latin America and the Caribbean: URY = Uruguay.

Figure 18.5. Quantiles and "Excess Control of Corruption"

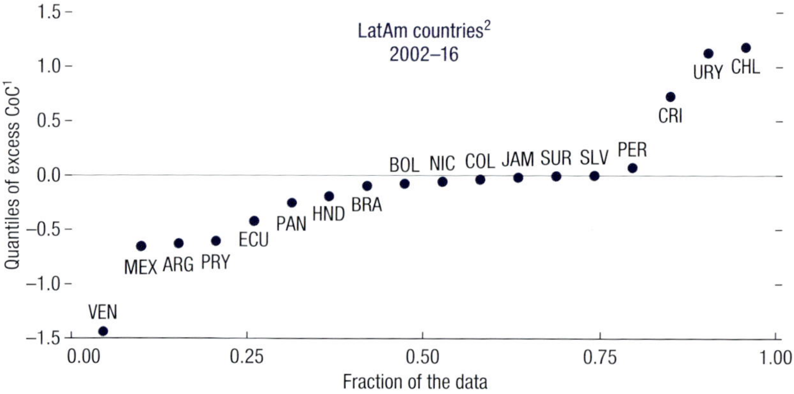

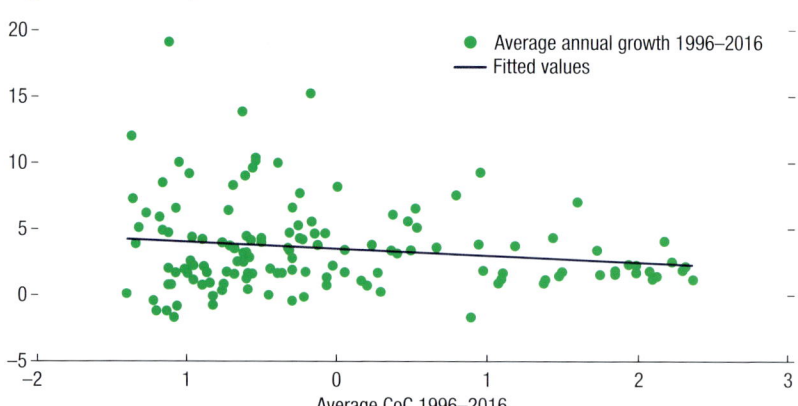

Sources: World Bank; and authors' calculations.
Note: CoC = control of corruption; LatAm = Latin America. Data labels in the figure use International Organization for Standardization (ISO) country codes.
[1]Higher means less corrupt.
[2]Excluding countries with population of less than 500,000.

(catching up with the frontier is easier than expanding it) *and* are more corrupt, thus rendering the correlation between these two indicators blatantly spurious—a classic case of omitted variable bias.

To overcome this specific source of endogeneity, Figure 18.7 shows instead the residuals of a growth regression on initial GDP per capita against the "excess corruption" index. That is, the influence of GDP levels both on growth and on

Figure 18.6. Corruption and Growth

Sources: World Bank; and authors' calculations.
Note: CoC = control of corruption.

Figure 18.7. Controlling for Initial GDP

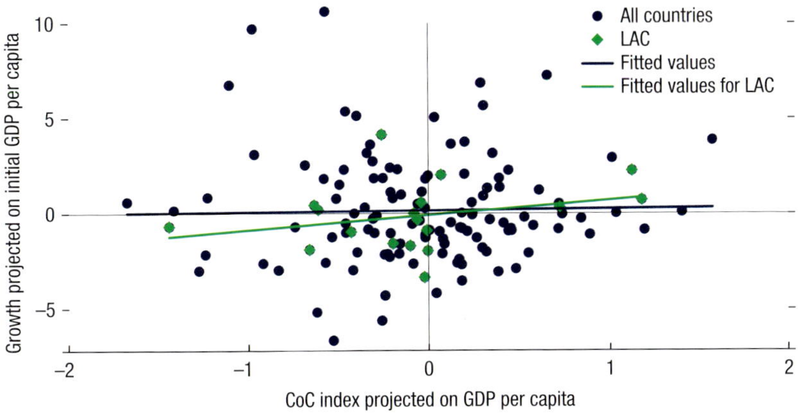

Sources: World Bank; and authors' calculations.
Note: CoC = control of corruption; LAC = Latin America and the Caribbean.

corruption is removed, rendering the correlation between these two free from influence of the level of GDP.

The slope of the relationship is now reversed, suggesting a slightly *negative* correlation between corruption and growth after controlling for initial GDP per capita (positive relationship with the index). Interestingly, this hinges on Latin American countries being included in the sample (as the dark blue fitted line suggests, in Figure 18.7, the correlation is stronger for this subset of countries). Take Latin America out and the overall correlation no longer differs statistically from zero.

Table 18.2. Corruption and Growth

Variables	All	Excluding LICs	Excluding LICs and AEs	LatAm only
	Annual Growth Rates 1996–2016			
Initial GDP per Capita	−6.18e-05***	−9.73e-05***	−0.000226***	−0.000160***
	(1.30e-05)	(1.87e-05)	(3.73e-05)	(4.63e-05)
Excess CoC Index	0.469	0.361	0.292	0.751*
	(0.511)	(0.512)	(0.558)	(0.360)
Constant	4.299***	5.526***	6.692***	3.934***
	(0.399)	(0.529)	(0.680)	(0.641)
Observations	135	98	79	21
R^2	0.083	0.204	0.250	0.258

Sources: Acemoglu and others (2001); and authors' calculations.
Note: Excludes countries with populations of less than 500,000. AEs = advanced economies; LatAm = Latin America; LICs = low-income countries. Robust standard errors are in parentheses.
***$p < 0.01$; **$p < 0.05$; *$p < 0.1$.

Figure 18.8. Variation in Control of Corruption

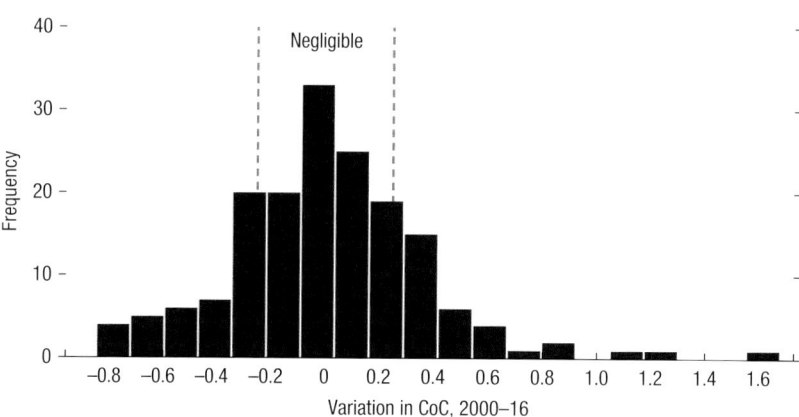

Sources: World Bank; and authors' calculations.
Note: CoC = control of corruption.

As a matter of fact, many other uncontrolled-for variables may affect both corruption and growth simultaneously, rendering the link between these variables spurious. Generally, to address such problems an analysis would resort to country dummy regressions (fixed effects estimations), which control for all nonobservable idiosyncratic factors that are time invariant. However, this method works nicely when explanatory variables display a good amount of variation over time, but if they do not, the country dummies will absorb everything. This is a crucial problem in this analysis, since corruption indices vary a lot *across* countries (Figure 18.8) but very little over time *within* countries.[5]

Table 18.3 suggests that, indeed, the lack of sufficient time variation in corruption makes it difficult to estimate its effect on growth in a panel regression setting with fixed effects. The coefficients of corruption on growth in the two versions of the model are statistically insignificant.[6]

Time variation in corruption indices is a noisy variable and subject to reverse causality. Nevertheless, "extreme variations" are seldom fortuitous, that is, they probably carry some credible information content, since only tangible real institutional changes explain dramatic shifts in perceptions of corruption. Figure 18.9 plots growth against *extreme* variations in perceived corruption only. The countries witnessing strong deterioration in perceptions of corruption between 1996

---

[5]Not only that, pure reverse causality may, in principle, be a problem. Because survey data are being used, it may well be that reported corruption is smaller (higher indices) in times of robust growth simply because when incomes rise, people become more optimistic.

[6]The first time period in the panel refers to 1996–2006; the second comprises the years 2007–16. Initial GDP is log of GDP per capita for 1995 and 2006, respectively.

Table 18.3. Panel Regressions

Variables	(1) GDP Growth	(2) GDP Growth
Log of Initial GDP	−12.54**	−20.32***
	(4.922)	(6.103)
Control of Corruption Index	0.507	1.163
	(1.183)	(1.368)
Constant	114.9*** (43.93)	180.9*** (53.51)
Fixed Effects	Yes	Yes
Time Effects	No	Yes
Observations	673	673
R^2	0.320	0.466
Number of id	170	170

Sources: World Bank; and authors' calculations.
Note: CoC = control of corruption. Robust standard errors are in parentheses.
***$p < 0.01$.

and 2016 experienced an average growth rate of –2.74 percent per year, while those in which corruption perceptions registered the strongest gains grew, on average, by 1.69 percent. The difference between these two groups is astoundingly large, approximately 4.5 percentage points each year. Again, because the analysis is addressing *growth residuals* from a regression on initial GDP per capita, average growth for the *whole* sample is zero.[7]

Figure 18.9. Extreme Variations in Corruption and Growth

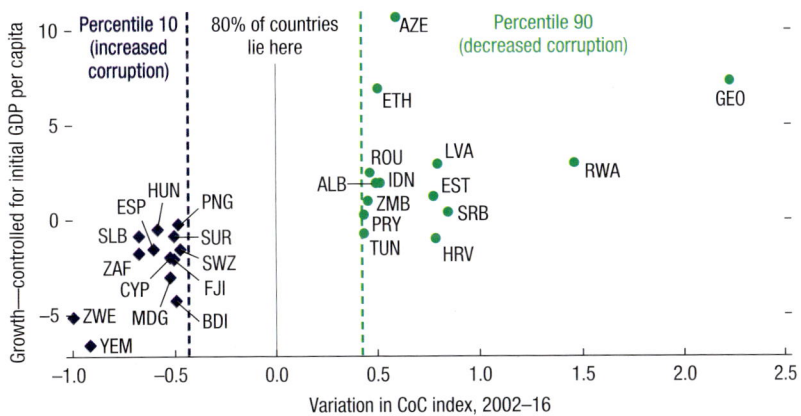

Sources: World Bank; and authors' calculations.
Note: CoC = control of corruption. Data labels in the figure use International Organization for Standardization (ISO) country codes.

---

[7]The average growth rate for countries between the dashed lines is 0.06 percent.

Figure 18.10. Economic Development and Corruption

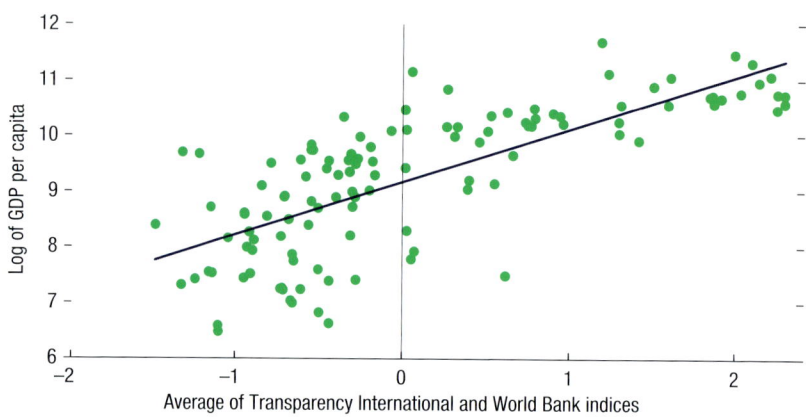

Sources: Acemoglu and others (2001); and authors' calculations.

Again, this is not a formal proof of a causal relationship, but it does get close, as large variations in corruption perceptions are likely to have been led by policy measures and institutional reforms, not "feel-good" effects owing to economic growth being better than normal.

CORRUPTION AND DEVELOPMENT

From an economic development viewpoint, focusing on income levels instead of growth rates makes more sense, for two key reasons: (1) what matters for welfare is income levels, not rates of growth; and (2) growth is a noisy variable, influenced largely by cyclical factors. Of course, if a long enough time series on growth rates is available, none of this matters, but only 20 years of data are available.

Statistical analysis using GDP per capita levels, however, presents even more problems from the point of view of endogeneity (Figure 18.10). Richer countries may have become richer because they managed to curb corruption, but the reverse is just as likely. It is easier to fight corruption if more resources are available with which to do so.[8] In sum, when it comes to development and corruption, causation runs both ways.

The endogeneity problem relating development to institutional variables has plagued the development literature, and there is no easy way out of it. Are rich countries richer because of better institutions, or are their institutions of higher quality because the countries are rich? A possible solution to this problem, which has been widely used in the past two decades, is to look for instrumental variables

---

[8]Another explanation is that "low corruption" is a normal good. Voters will demand more of a clean political environment after other basic needs are taken care of.

Figure 18.11. Control of Corruption and Colonial Origins

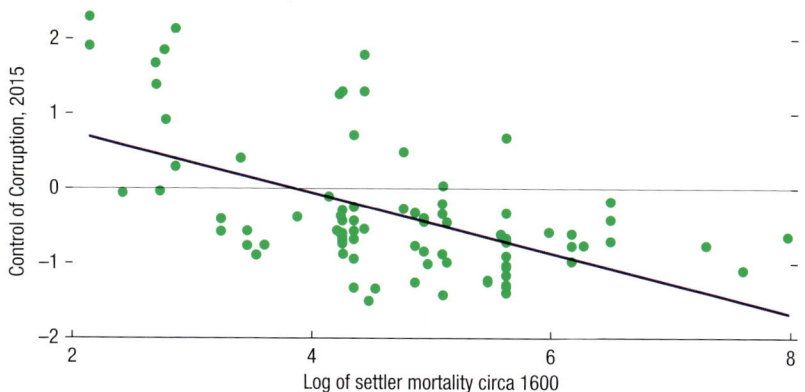

Sources: Acemoglu and others (2001); and authors' calculations.

that are able to capture exogenous variations in institutional quality. Researchers have gone back in history to identify factors that allowed the establishment of colonies by colonial powers.

The central idea behind what is commonly known as the colonial-origins literature is that 400 years ago the physical environment differed greatly across different regions of the globe, which either facilitated or impeded the establishment of European colonies and colonists. Where colonists stayed, so goes the argument, they transplanted their open-order, democratic, inclusive institutions that are conducive to growth (and fixed their human capital, too). But where the environment was too hazardous or local land characteristics favored plantations based on gang-labor technology, their choice was to implement extractive, exclusive institutions that are detrimental to long-term development.

Acemoglu, Johnson, and Robinson (2001) then use settlers' mortality rates (together with average temperature and latitude) as a proxy for the quality of institutions today (control of executive), a measure that is arguably not endogenous to current GDP levels. If the quality of initial institutions is poor, it not only has a bearing on the protection of property rights—even though the effectiveness of property rights is the measure commonly used in the empirical branch of the development literature—it also affects the degree and persistence of corrupt practices, notably because extractive institutions generate rents, leading, in turn, to a rush for rent-seeking activities by the politically connected.

Indeed, Figure 18.11 suggests a tight first-stage relationship between these two: worse initial conditions (from the colonizers' point of view) 400 years ago are associated with more corruption (lower COC indicator) in 2016.

In the same vein, the degree of a country's ethnolinguistic fragmentation, that is, a measure of how dissimilar individuals picked at random are in ethnicity, religion, and language, may also contribute to higher corruption levels if those in

Figure 18.12. Control of Corruption and Ethnolinguistic Fractionalization

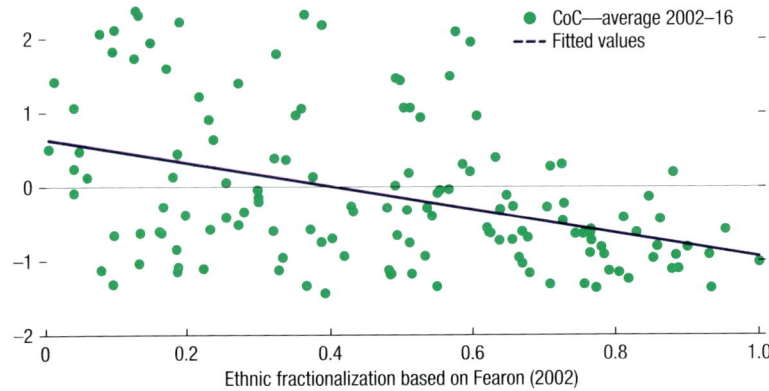

Sources: Acemoglu and others (2001); and authors' calculations.
Note: CoC = control of corruption.

power tend to favor people belonging to the same identity group (at the expense of others). If group identity matters, favoritism will be hard to extricate from public policy. Many studies point to a positive correlation between social fragmentation and corruption, a correlation that can, once again, be exploited in an instrumental variables setting (Figure 18.12).[9]

Instrumental Variables Results

This discussion uses colonial origins and ethnolinguistic fragmentation as instruments for corruption in a regression in which the explained variable is income per capita in 2016.

Arguably, this strategy goes a long way toward solving the problem of reverse causality. But does this mean these instrumental variables estimators can confidently be used to do comparative statics exercises such as "if corruption falls by P, income will eventually increase by Q"? Caution should be exercised: variables like expropriation risks, law enforcement, quality of bureaucracy, quality of regulatory framework, control of executive, corruption, and so on are all strongly correlated among themselves. Substitute "expropriation risk" for "corruption" in the regressions and little is changed.

Theoretically, these different factors are likely to affect economic development through different channels—for example, a lack of private investment, poor-quality public infrastructure, and inadequate risk taking—but it is hard to disentangle the influence of each of these institutional variables empirically. Moreover, institutional improvement usually takes place across the board: as expropriation risks

---

[9]The first empirical study investigating the corruption-growth link, Paolo Mauro's (1995) examination of corruption and growth, used fractionalization as an instrument.

Table 18.4. Income per Capita and Corruption[1]

Variables	Colonial Origins as Instrument lngdp2016	Fractionalization as Instrument lngdp2016
Average CoC 2000–16	0.563**	0.953**
	(0.280)	(0.433)
Years of Schooling	0.219***	0.129
	(0.0765)	(0.101)
Constant	7.524***	8.189***
	(0.629)	(0.835)
Observations	53	121
R^2	0.788	0.655

Sources: World Bank; and authors' calculations.

Note: CoC = control of corruption; lngdp = GDP in logarithms. Standard errors are in parentheses.

[1]There are more data on fractionalization than on settler mortality, which explains the difference in sample sizes.

***$p < 0.01$; **$p < 0.05$; *$p < 0.1$.

fall, so does corruption (and other similar variables move in tandem). In sum, identification remains a problem even after taking care of reverse causality.

Notwithstanding these limitations, the analysis suggests that an increase of, say, 0.5 point in Transparency International's CPI (which would be uncommonly large) would translate into a GDP gain of about 0.30 to 0.45 log point, meaning a country with income per capita of US$15,000 would eventually reach a new steady-state income of about US$20,000. This is a large effect—perhaps too large.

As noted, because of the identification problem, many institutional variables would produce similar results if substituted for "corruption" in the empirical analysis. One way to address the problem is to use two institutional variables instead of just one—a horserace of sorts—and ask whether corruption still has an impact on the level of GDP after controlling for, say, "property rights."

To run a meaningful instrumental variables estimation with two endogenous regressors, two separate sets of instruments are needed, one for each explanatory variable. The institutional variable added to this specification is a "rule of law" index compiled by the *International Country Risk Guide* and widely adopted in the development literature. The instrumental variable for "rule of law" is the log of settler mortality circa 1650; for corruption, the political science literature is followed, and the degree of ethnolinguistic fragmentation in society is used in the two-stage least squares regression.

Table 18.5 presents the results. As shown, even after controlling for rule of law, corruption is still statistically significant at the 5 percent level.

Because these indices enter the regression normalized, the reported coefficients are comparable. Judging by the size of the point estimates, rule of law appears to have a larger impact on the level of GDP than does corruption per se, at least for this relatively small group of countries. Importantly, though, corruption still has a quantitatively relevant impact on development. Now, the same hypothetical country with income per capita of US$15,000 would witness an increase in income all the way up to US$17,000 after the same (one standard deviation) 0.5 point improvement in CoC.

Table 18.5. Horserace Model–Corruption versus Rule of Law

	Two-Stage Least Squares
Variables	lngdp2016
Z_World Bank CoC Index	0.210**
	(0.102)
Z_ICRG Rule of Law Index	0.681***
	(0.0892)
Constant	8.942***
	(0.104)
Observations	56
R^2	0.552

Sources: World Bank; and authors' calculations.
Note: CoC = control of corruption; ICRG = *International Country Risk Guide*;
lngdp = GDP in logarithms. Robust standard errors are in parentheses.
***$p < 0.01$; **$p < 0.05$; *$p < 0.1$.

CONCLUSIONS

In terms of perceptions of corruption, countries in Latin America compare unfavorably with both advanced economies and, to a smaller extent, their emerging market peers in the rest of the world. Brazil, in particular, fares worse than expected given its level of development.

Corruption clearly has an adverse bearing on both growth and development, with the transmission channels likely to vary according to individual country circumstances, but caution should be exercised in using the regression estimates calibrated in this chapter.

Fighting corruption is thus not only a moral obligation but also an important component of economic development and progress. But fighting corruption is easier said than done, because dispersed benefits of a corruption-free environment and concentrated costs vitiate against collective action to fight corruption, and entrenched interests have all the incentives to maintain and promote corrupt practices and to defeat initiatives aimed at ending their rent-seeking activities.

In this context, some would argue that the process of extricating corruption is costly, pointing to the case of Brazil, which has witnessed a deep recession of historic proportions. Two arguments counter this narrative. First, the recent Brazilian recession can largely be explained by the pursuit of inappropriate macroeconomic and structural policies and weak external demand, and it should not be attributed to policy paralysis associated with the corruption investigations. Second, even if the short-term costs are real, they must be pitched against the long-term benefits, economic and otherwise, of a less corrupt society.

With regard to fighting corruption, experience suggests cosmetic measures or scattered efforts will not suffice. To uproot corruption, an institutional "big push" is needed, one that revamps the de facto law enforcement capabilities, under strong political leadership and with the support of society, including free and active media. Small pushes tend to generate waves of optimism that sooner or later fade away. Based on earlier country experiences, key elements of such a multifaceted strategy should include measures to raise transparency and accountability, strengthen public procurement and investment processes, streamline rules and regulations to reduce rent seeking, and upgrade legal frameworks.

REFERENCES

Acemoglu, Daron, Simon Johnson, and James A. Robinson. 2001. "The Colonial Origins of Comparative Development." *American Economic Review* 91 (5): 1369–401.

Fearon, James, and David Laitin. 2003. "Ethnicity, Insurgency, and Civil War." *American Political Science Review* 97 (1): 75–90.

Mauro, Paolo. 1995. "Corruption and Growth." *The Quarterly Journal of Economics* 110 (3): 681–712.

Olson, Mancur. 1971. *The Logic of Collective Action: Public Goods and the Theory of Group*s. Cambridge, MA: Harvard University Press.

CHAPTER 19

Legal Issues in Fighting Money Laundering and Related Corruption

RICHARD BERKHOUT

Much has been achieved in the 20 years since Brazil first joined international efforts against money laundering, terrorism financing, and corruption; some of the current successes against money laundering and corruption are the result of legal progress made several years ago. Yet challenges remain, and further progress is critical. This chapter examines Brazil's progress against money laundering and related corruption, discusses the main risks and mitigation measures, and presents recommendations for further improvement.

BRAZIL'S INSTITUTIONAL FRAMEWORK AGAINST MONEY LAUNDERING AND CORRUPTION

Money laundering and corruption are two distinct types of crime. Corruption is an act of abuse of trust by persons with authority, often for personal gain, and can take different forms (for example, bribery and embezzlement). Money laundering is a process by which the illicit source of assets obtained or generated by criminal activity is concealed to obscure the link between the funds and the original criminal activity. The proceeds of crime include those derived from corruption and bribery, but also from other types of crime (for example, organized crime, human and drug trafficking, environmental crimes, tax crimes).[1] These proceeds-generating offenses are also referred to as *predicate offenses.*

The relative importance of each of the predicate offenses depends on a given country's context and differs from country to country. As is the case for other countries in Latin America, and as discussed further below, for Brazil corruption and bribery are an important risk for money laundering, on a par with tax, drugs, and organized crime. However, anti–money laundering and anti-corruption tools can reinforce each other[2] and increase the effectiveness of both systems. The Brazilian authorities recognized this symbiosis at an early stage of the

---

[1]FATF (2012–17).

[2]The FATF has provided guidance on the effective use of anti–money laundering tools to fight corruption; see FATF (2012) and FATF (2013).

development of the Brazilian anti–money laundering system. Notably, the Brazilian authorities exploited the synergies between anti–money laundering and anti-corruption before the international community started to discuss links and synergies between the two.[3]

Domestic Framework

The Estratégia Nacional de Combate à Corrupção e à Lavagem de Dinheiro (ENCCLA, National Strategy to Combat Corruption and Money Laundering) is a domestic network that coordinates anti-corruption and anti–money laundering measures. Created in 2003, it currently connects 95 administrative, judicial, and legislative entities from federal, state, and municipal levels. Within ENCCLA, action items are agreed on annually, and published on ENCCLA's website. Progress is made through peer pressure: each action item is publicly assigned to a working group that is tasked to follow up on the item and to report back to ENCCLA on progress. ENCCLA's secretariat is hosted by the Ministry of Justice.[4] Over the past years, the ENCCLA framework has supported advancement in several areas, as is set out further below.[5]

The main anti–money laundering body in Brazil is the Conselho de Controle de Atividades Financeiras (COAF, the Financial Activities Control Center). COAF, Brazil's financial intelligence unit, receives and analyzes suspicious activity reports and disseminates the results of its analysis to law enforcement for use in investigations and prosecutions. Established in 1998, COAF is an administrative operationally independent unit within the Ministry of Finance. Banks and other entities submit suspicious transaction reports (as required by law) to COAF, and these submissions can be used as supporting evidence in existing investigations or trigger additional money laundering, corruption, or similar investigations. Other important competent authorities with anti–money laundering responsibilities are the Central Bank of Brazil (Banco Central do Brasil), other financial supervisors, law enforcement bodies, and the prosecution.[6]

---

[3]The FATF's first attempt to cover such links was under the South African FATF presidency. One of FATF President Kader Asmal's priorities for his presidency was to further explore the links between money laundering and corruption, in joint partnership with the Asia Pacific Group for Money Laundering (APG). This initiative, although supported by the membership of the FATF and the APG, gained little traction over the longer term. It took until 2011, under the Mexican FATF presidency of Luis Urrutia Corral, for the FATF to successfully explore the synergies between the two crimes, starting with a series of annual expert meetings and the adoption of relevant guidance (FATF 2006, 2012).

[4]See also the public website of ENCCLA at http://enccla.camara.leg.br.

[5]For more information on the history and achievements of the ENCCLA, see LaForge (2017).

[6]The following is the list of entities relevant for Brazil's anti–money laundering and anti-corruption regime, as represented in the COAF Council: Agência Brasileira de Inteligência (ABIN); Banco Central do Brasil (BCB); Comissão de Valores Mobiliários (CVM); Ministério da Transparência e Controladoria-Geral da União (CGU); Departamento de Polícia Federal (DPF); Ministério da Justiça (MJ), Procuradoria-Geral da Fazenda Nacional (PGFN); Secretaria da Receita Federal do Brasil (RFB); Superintendência de Seguros Privados (SUSEP); and

International Cooperation and Treaty Obligations

The global fight against money laundering and corruption started in the early 1990s. Brazil joined these international efforts in the early 2000s, about the same time as other Latin American countries did. Brazil became a member of the Financial Action Task Force (FATF)[7] in 2000[8] and was one of the founding members of the FATF-style regional body for Latin America, the Grupo de Acción Financiera de Latinoamérica (GAFILAT).[9] COAF had already become a member of the Egmont Group of Financial Intelligence Units in 1999.[10] Brazil was assessed twice against the international standards, first in 2003[11] (by the FATF) and again in 2010[12] (jointly by the FATF and GAFILAT). These reports analyze Brazil's money laundering and corruption risks, describe mitigation measures, and contain ratings and recommendations.

Brazil also joined international treaty efforts against money laundering and corruption, ratifying the 1988 Vienna Convention,[13] the 2000 OECD Bribery Convention,[14] the 2000 Palermo Convention,[15] the 2001 New York Terrorist Financing Convention,[16] and the 2003 Merida Anti-Corruption Convention.[17]

International legal norms, standards, and peer pressure have proved to be instrumental for the development of Brazil's anti–money laundering and anti-corruption system. Throughout the years, some of ENCCLA's action items mirrored recommended actions identified by FATF/GAFILAT (such as in relation to amending the anti–money laundering law in 2004) or directly refer to international obligations (for example, ratification of the 2005 Merida

---

Ministério da Fazenda (MF). The following entities attend the COAF meeting without voting rights: Advocacia-Geral da União (AGU); Conselho Federal de Corretores de Imóveis (COFECI); Conselho Federal de Contabilidade (CFC); Secretaria de Assuntos Econômicos (SEAE); Conselho Federal de Economia (COFECON); and the Departamento de Registro Empresarial e Integração (DREI) (http://fazenda.gov.br/orgaos/coaf, May 2018).

[7]The Financial Action Task Force (FATF), http://www.fatf-gafi.org, is the international standard setter for anti–money laundering and combating the financing of terrorism and proliferation. The FATF was established in 1989, by the Group of Seven economies (Canada, France, Germany, Italy, Japan, United Kingdom, United States).

[8]See http://www.fatf-gafi.org/countries/#Brazil.

[9]See https://www.gafilat.org/index.php/es/gafilat/quienes-somos/organismo-internacional.

[10]The Egmont Group is the international body for FIUs. See https://egmontgroup.org/en/content/brazil-council-financial-activities-control.

[11]Although the FATF at that time did not publish copies of assessment reports, the executive summary of the 2003 FATF Assessment is available as a report on the observance of standards and codes (ROSC) by the IMF (IMF 2005).

[12]FATF (2010).

[13]UN (1988).

[14]OECD (2017).

[15]UN (2000).

[16]UN (2001).

[17]UNODC (2003).

Convention). In addition, some of ENCCLA's more recent action items directly relate to preparing for the next FATF/GAFILAT assessment, such as undertaking a self-assessment against the FATF recommendations and drafting proposals to comply with revised international standards.

The IMF has also supported Brazil's efforts, notably by providing policy advice on anti–money laundering and anti-corruption efforts in Financial System Stability Assessments (2012[18]) and the IMF's surveillance framework (for example, in Article IV staff reports for 2014, 2016, and 2017[19]) when money laundering and corruption issues have been considered macrocritical for Brazil.

International peer pressure is not always sufficient to address all relevant issues. For example, with regard to terrorism financing, Brazil's shortcomings—first identified in the early 2000s—related to the need to implement targeted financial sanction requirements. Such requirements, mandated by the United Nations Security Council Resolutions,[20] have yet to be addressed despite increasing pressure via five[21] FATF public statements.[22]

MONEY LAUNDERING AND CORRUPTION RISKS AND MITIGATION MEASURES

Risks

As indicated, corruption is one of the main risks for money laundering in Brazil, as it is for the region. The 2010 FATF/GAFILAT assessment of Brazil's compliance with anti–money laundering standards further elaborated this risk. Its opening chapter contains information on money laundering and corruption risks, and it explains that the main sources of illicit proceeds in Brazil are corruption, embezzlement, and state capture (aided by impunity); financial crimes (including fraud and capital flight); drugs and weapons trafficking; organized crime; smuggling of illicit and counterfeit goods; and tax crimes. The report also finds that the banking sector (including private banking and money exchanges) is the financial sector facing the highest money laundering risks and points to the perception

---

[18]See IMF (2012).

[19]See IMF (2018).

[20]United Nations Security Council Resolutions 1267 (1999) and 1373 (2001), and relevant successor resolutions, as identified by the FATF in its current Recommendation 6.

[21]See statements on Brazil since February 2016 at http://www.fatf-gafi.org/countries/#Brazil.

[22]The FATF's follow-up policy requires countries to address shortcomings identified in reports. If they do not, the FATF has in place gradual steps to pressure countries to address their deficiencies. The use of these steps depends on the nature of the shortcoming (the FATF differentiates between regular, key, and core requirements) and the length of time since an assessment. The steps the FATF can take are a letter, a high-level visit, a public warning, suspension of membership, and termination of membership. See the procedures for assessments (FATF 2018).

that border regions and the informal economy are at a higher risk for money laundering than the formal economy.[23]

Even though the FATF/GAFILAT assessment is several years old, it remains in line with more recent sources of information, suggesting that Brazil's risk profile has not changed fundamentally. For example, the 2018 US State Department *Annual Narcotics Control Strategy Report* on money laundering[24] is consistent with the FATF's findings on Brazil. In addition, the report mentions the use of banks, shell companies, tax havens, and bulk cash smuggling as vulnerable sectors or methods for money laundering.

The next FATF/GAFILAT assessment is scheduled to be undertaken in 2020–22. At that time, Brazil will be expected to have performed a national risk assessment, showing that it understands its main money laundering risks and related predicate risks, including corruption, and to have taken relevant mitigating measures. The resulting report will have extensive coverage of risks (more so than previous assessment reports), and the main ratings will assess the effectiveness of the system.[25]

Mitigating Measures

Brazil has taken mitigating measures to address money laundering and corruption risks. These measures conform to international standards and have been adapted to Brazil's specific needs. As international standards against money laundering changed over the years,[26] so did the Brazilian anti–money laundering system.

Two different types of mitigating efforts are worth highlighting. The first concerns legal and other measures that Brazil took to increase the effectiveness of its anti–money laundering and anti-corruption system. As set out comprehensively by LaForge (2017) after 2005 authorities took measures to (1) improve domestic coordination (including by setting up ENCCLA) and reinforce existing bodies that have a role in anti–money laundering and anti-corruption (such as the CGU, the Federal Comptroller General); (2) launch the CGU's transparency portal,[27] which provides access to government data, with the aim of reducing corruption by increasing transparency; and (3) introduce data-sharing frameworks (such as those for sharing bank account data with law enforcement).

Other measures included setting up specialized financial crimes courts, which subsequently required dedicated prosecution and law enforcement bodies, and

---

[23]FATF (2010), Chapters 1.1 and 1.2.

[24]US Department of State (2018).

[25]Effectiveness/outcomes is defined by the FATF as an assessment of output against risks. See FATF (2013–2018).

[26]The FATF first issued its 40 recommendations against money laundering in 1990. In 2001, the FATF added the Eight Special Recommendations against terrorism financing, and in 2003, the FATF revised the 1990 FATF 40 recommendations against money laundering. In 2012, the FATF merged and revised the money laundering and terrorism financing requirements and issued the consolidated 2012 FATF 40 recommendations (the most current standard).

[27]See http://www.portaltransparencia.gov.br.

making improvements to asset declarations. However, the main achievements addressed amendments to the legislative framework. For example, the 1998 anti–money laundering law was amended to include, among other things, foreign bribery as a predicate offense. ENCCLA participants also drafted a bill on criminal organizations and a bill on plea bargains. Enacted between 2011 and 2014, these and other legislative proposals proved pivotal to increasing the effectiveness of the anti–money laundering and anti-corruption system.

The second type of mitigation measure concerns the increased effectiveness of law enforcement and prosecutorial measures. Based on the legal changes that had been introduced, some law enforcement and judicial authorities have been able to investigate, prosecute, and obtain convictions for money laundering, corruption, and other predicate crimes at increasingly effective levels.

For example, as of May 14, 2018, in the Lava Jato case under the jurisdiction of the state of Paraná alone, judicial authorities had instigated 1,765 court proceedings, issued 240 arrest warrants, and charged 309 defendants in 74 separate prosecutions with money laundering, corruption, and forms of organized crime.[28] Although this investigation got a lot of public attention, other corruption cases have also been pursued. These include separate Lava Jato investigations in other states (such as Rio de Janeiro and São Paulo) and at the federal level. There are also Lava Jato spin-offs (such as investigations involving Odebrecht and JBS) and numerous stand-alone corruption investigations, such as *Greenfield* (involving pension funds), *Panatenaico* (inflation of public work bids), *Zelotes* (tax appeals board investigation), and *Câmbio, desliga* (money laundering).

Brazil's investigation efforts attract much international attention; however, it should be noted that the level of corruption in Brazil may be comparable to that of other countries in Latin America. As a comparison of recent FATF and GAFILAT detailed assessment reports shows,[29] corruption is considered to be one of the main proceeds-generating offenses for money laundering across the region (that is, corruption as a predicate offense for money laundering). Within the region, corruption cases have spilled across borders, with many lawsuits involving senior politicians and businesspeople (as in the Odebrecht case[30]). This suggests that the relatively high number of money laundering and related corruption investigations and prosecutions in Brazil may be an indication of competence, independence, and impartiality of the authorities in addressing corruption, and not necessarily an indicator that corruption is more widespread in Brazil than

---

[28]The judicial authorities in the State of Paraná regularly publish updated Lava Jato numbers. See http://www.mpf.mp.br/para-o-cidadao/caso-lava-jato/atuacao-na-1a-instancia/parana/resultado.

[29]See the FATF's public website for an up-to-date list of assessment reports, with direct links to the reports of countries in Latin America (and other regions), as undertaken by the FATF and the GAFILAT. The analysis focused on the information presented in Chapter 1 of these reports. See http://www.fatf-gafi.org/countries.

[30]See IMF (2017), Box 1.

elsewhere in the region. When the FATF and the GAFILAT assess the Brazilian anti–money laundering system in 2020–22, the fact that the authorities have generated these cases will likely be considered a strength of the Brazilian anti–money laundering system.

RECOMMENDATIONS FOR FUTURE IMPROVEMENTS

Changing societal norms that enable money laundering and corruption will require continuing and intensifying the current efforts. Lava Jato alone will not have a lasting positive impact on Brazil's corruption risks unless the fight against corruption is broadened. This expansion will include taking measures to increase prevention of money laundering and corruption and to boost the effectiveness of the anti–money laundering and anti-corruption system. The current anti–money laundering and anti-corruption framework is a good starting point for authorities.

Improvements are possible in several areas, in line with international standards. Measures that authorities could consider include the following:

The completion of a national risk assessment for AML/CFT should be the authorities' main priority. This international requirement has been in place since 2012 and Brazil should complete it expeditiously. Undertaking a national risk assessment takes a considerable amount of time but is critical to any government's ability to understand and present its money laundering and related corruption risks in a comprehensive manner (to domestic policymakers and to external assessors) and to take the appropriate risk-mitigation measures. This process is a useful tool for any country; however, understanding risks and risk mitigation will also be the main focus of the 2020–22 FATF/GAFILAT assessment, which makes the completion of the national risk assessment all the more critical.

Increasing the effectiveness of the criminal justice system is another priority. Recent supreme court jurisprudence that limits the number of appeals available to convicted persons and limits the use of privileged forums for criminal trials for certain groups is positive and will help ensure that those who are found guilty of money laundering and corruption are punished. This should have a preventive effect, and authorities could consider codifying the jurisprudence. Other possible measures are pending as action items in ENCCLA or are in Congress; they include limiting the statute of limitations, increasing the efficiency of the court system to speed up cases, criminalizing illicit enrichment to facilitate the confiscation of ill-acquired assets, and improving the confiscation system itself.

Boosting the effectiveness of the criminal justice system should continue to be supported by strong and independent law enforcement and judicial authorities who can investigate and prosecute corruption cases at all levels of society.

To ensure that money launderers and those who engage in corruption cannot hide their ill-gotten gains, all relevant authorities and private sector bodies must have access to information that identifies the owner or controller of a company. Authorities have already taken some important steps requiring tax authorities and financial institutions to collect beneficial ownership information. Authorities should ensure that this information is shared with all relevant entities, and consideration could be given to having a public register of such beneficial ownership information.

Finally, in addition to further risk-mitigation measures that will be prompted by the national risk assessment, authorities should continue to increase the data that are available on the CGU's transparency portal and enhance the sophistication of the risk-based supervision of the financial sector, specifically for anti–money laundering.

CONCLUSIONS

For effective law enforcement, investigation, and prosecution of money laundering and related corruption, Brazil is setting a high bar for the region. However, repression alone will not be sufficient, and preventive measures will need to be taken to decrease money laundering and corruption risks over the long term.

REFERENCES

Financial Action Task Force (FATF). 2006. *FATF Annual Report 2005–2006.* Paris.

———. 2010. "Mutual Evaluation Report: Federative Republic of Brazil." Paris.

———. 2012. "Corruption A Reference Guide and Information Note on the Use of the FATF Recommendations to Support the Fight against Corruption." Paris.

———. 2012–17. International Standards on Combating Money Laundering and the Financing of Terrorism and Proliferation, Glossary, "Designated Categories of Offences." Paris.

———. 2013. "The Use of the FATF Recommendations to Combat Corruption," Best Practices Paper. Paris.

———. 2013–18. "Methodology for Assessing Compliance with the FATF Recommendations and the Effectiveness of AML/CFT Systems." Updated February 2018. Paris.

———. 2018. "Procedures for the FATF Fourth Round of AML/CFT Mutual Evaluations." Paris.

LaForge, Gordon. 2017. "The Sum of Its Parts: Coordinating Brazil's Fight against Corruption 2003–2016." Innovations for Successful Societies, Princeton University, Princeton, NJ.

International Monetary Fund (IMF). 2005. "Brazil: Report on the Observance of Standards and Codes—FATF Recommendations for Anti-Money Laundering and Combating the Financing of Terrorism." IMF Country Report 05/207. Washington, DC.

———. 2012. "Brazil: Financial System Stability Assessment." IMF Country Report 12/206. Washington, DC.

———. 2017. Brazil: 2017 Article IV Consultation—Press Release, Staff Report, and Statement by the Executive Director for Brazil, Washington, DC.

———. 2018. Brazil: 2018 Article IV Consultation—Press Release, Staff Report, and Statement by the Executive Director for Brazil, Washington, DC.

Organisation for Economic Co-operation and Development (OECD). 2017. OECD Convention on Combating Bribery of Foreign Public Officials in International Business Transactions, Ratification Status as of May 2017. Paris.

United Nations (UN). 1988. United Nations Convention against Illicit Traffic in Narcotic Drugs and Psychotropic Substances. Vienna.

———. 2000. United Nations Convention against Transnational Organized Crime. New York.

———. 2001. International Convention for the Suppression of the Financing of Terrorism. New York.

United Nations Office on Drugs and Crime (UNODC). 2003. United Nations Convention against Corruption, Signature and Ratification Status. New York.

US Department of State. 2018. *International Narcotics Control Strategy Report*, vol. 2, on Money Laundering and Financial Crimes, Brazil. Washington, DC, 65–67.

CHAPTER 20

Lava Jato, Mani Pulite, and the Role of Institutions

Maria Cristina Pinotti

If the highest rate of return in an economy is to piracy, we can expect that the organizations will invest in skills and knowledge that will make them better pirates. Similarly, if there are high returns to productive activities, we will expect organizations to devote resources to investing in skill and knowledge that will increase productivity.

Douglass North, 2005

INTRODUCTION

Both economic development and corruption are linked to the quality of institutions: poor countries often live with high rates of corruption, and developed economies tend to see lower rates. Both sustainable growth and reduction of corruption depend on strengthening a country's institutions, which must be designed to ensure the common good. Corruption corrodes the pillars of democracy, undermines the principle that all people are equal before the law, and distorts electoral outcomes through bribes and kickbacks. It affects the functioning of market economies by reducing efficiency and productivity—mainly through adverse selection and misallocation of resources. The objective of this chapter is to analyze the phenomenon of corruption through a multidisciplinary approach. It looks at two of the world's largest anticorruption operations—Mani Pulite ("Clean Hands") in Italy, and Lava Jato ("Car Wash") in Brazil—and at the outcome of empirical research linking economic performance and corruption, in the hope of producing lessons for the future.

The chapter first discusses the roles of formal and informal institutions in creating incentives that determine the degree of development and of corruption. It then presents a case study on Italy, considering available hypotheses for why it has been in a state of economic stagnation since the mid-1990s. To these hypotheses is added the proposition that the political system's reaction to investigations during operation Mani Pulite—weakening laws that could identify and punish

The author thanks Affonso Pastore, Flora Pinotti Sano, and Marcelo Gazzano for their invaluable comments.

crimes of corruption, along with a major media blitz against the judiciary—wore down the country's institutions, thus partly explaining its economic stagnation and the persistence of high levels of corruption. The chapter then analyzes Lava Jato, whose success is clearly no guarantee of a permanent reduction of corruption, which will only be achieved through the correction of institutional weaknesses laid bare over the years since the operation was launched, as discussed in the conclusion.

THE ROLE OF INSTITUTIONS

Advanced economies tend to present lower levels of corruption; corruption is higher in poorer countries, as corruption indicators reveal.[1] Much effort has gone into quantifying the costs of corruption, correlating it with per capita income or other appraisals of growth. Insurmountable problems involving causality and absent variables have held back progress in this exercise, but the work has made strides toward identifying major economic costs (see Pinotti 2017). In addition to misdirecting the macroeconomy, corruption provokes misallocation of resources, such as the building of "cathedrals in the desert"—overpriced and oversized projects—and the adverse selection of production factors, all of which add up to suboptimal operation of economies and lower productivity. Some promising recent research is attempting to quantify, at the firm level, the microeconomic impacts of corruption, as discussed in this chapter for the Italian case.

In another direction, studies by North (1990) and Acemoglu (2009) open the way for exploring the hypothesis that the quality of institutions is the common factor between economic development and corruption. Behind both poverty and widespread corruption, but also behind low rates of corruption, we find the quality of institutions. "Institutions are the rules of the game in a society" (North 1990, 3). To simplify, formal horizontal institutions, grounded in appropriate laws and courts, are important facilitators of contracts between savers and investors, as are vertical institutions based on the guarantee of property rights. These vertical institutions, in addition to the traditional interpretation of guaranteeing property rights over goods and inventions, must limit the right of governments, politicians, and privileged groups to expropriate the property rights of much of the population. If corruption is present, those institutions are not guided by public values but by personal enrichment that benefits corrupt groups, while poorly designed institutions lead economies to stagnation. It is important, and revealing, to ask who writes the rules, for whom, and with what purpose in mind. Formal institutions, moreover, are held up by cultural pillars; that is, informal institutions are made up of beliefs, expectations, and standards of behavior.

---

[1] According to Transparency International's Corruption Perceptions Index for 180 countries, in 2017 the five least corrupt countries were New Zealand, Denmark, Finland, Norway, and Switzerland, while the five most corrupt were Somalia, South Sudan, Syria, Afghanistan, and Yemen. Brazil slipped down that year, from the 79th to the 96th position. Italy ranked 54th. See Transparency International (2017).

Impunity undermines the belief that laws are applicable to everyone and reduces the importance of constitutional and legal provisions, for example.

Formal and informal institutions interact in a complex fashion, shaping the structure of incentives that guide individuals' behavior. As Rose-Ackerman and Palikfa (2016) recall, the detective Serpico, back in 1971, lamented that "10 percent of the cops in New York City are absolutely corrupt, 10 percent are absolutely honest, and the other 80 percent—they wish they were honest." Other authors refer to that 80 percent—an imprecise number to designate the majority—as opportunists or pragmatists, or even "more corruptible than corrupt," depending on outside pressure. The gains to be expected from joining or not joining an act of corruption depend on the number of individuals who practice that act, revealing the "contingent behavior" of those who act in accordance with their expectation of what the majority will do: if everyone is taking bribes, why shouldn't I? We can thus have a "good equilibrium" that keeps countries' corruption levels down because of rules and social sanctions, or a "bad equilibrium" in which countries' institutions foster impunity for crimes of corruption or even punish those who dare to denounce them (Fisman and Golden 2017). History is rife with examples of how hard it is to break out of the inertia of a bad equilibrium, as in the cases of Brazil and Italy.

THE CASE OF ITALY

Italy has suffered the worst economic performance and the highest rates of corruption of any developed economy. Evidence suggests that the strong reaction by the political system to the Mani Pulite investigations may have contributed to this situation.

The Puzzle of Economic Stagnation

Since the 1990s, Italy's economic growth rates have lagged behind those of other developed economies. Despite the benefits from adopting the euro (lower interest rates, lower sovereign risk, and less uncertainty for economic policymaking), economic growth, which had been strong and above average for Europe from the 1950s to the 1980s, took a turn for the worse (Pellegrino and Zingales 2017).

In the third quarter of 2017, Italy's GDP was still 5.9 percent below its previous peak, just before the global economic crisis in the first quarter of 2008. During the same period, the euro area grew 4.9 percent, France 6.5 percent, and Germany 10.9 percent (Figure 20.1).

The drop in productivity—in particular, low labor productivity[2]—was responsible for Italy's poor economic performance. From 2000 to 2010, investment rates

---

[2]Pellegrino and Zingales (2017) and Bugamelli and others (2018). "Labor productivity, defined as real GDP per hours worked, increased only 3.5 percent, while the TFP [total factor productivity] declined 7.5 percent since Italy adopted the Euro in 1999" (Giordano and others 2015, 4).

Figure 20.1. GDP in Italy, the Euro Area, and Selected Countries
(Index, 2005 = 100)

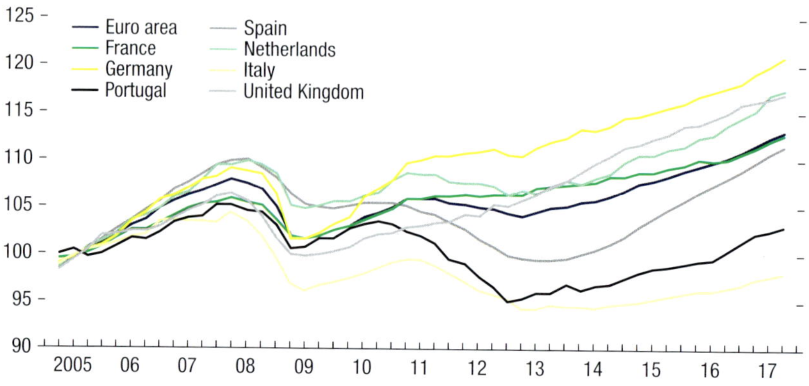

Source: Eurostat.

varied between 20 percent and 22 percent of GDP, while public investment was higher than in Germany, France, and the United Kingdom.[3] Italy stopped growing in 1995, and its total factor productivity (TFP) started to fall behind that of other developed economies in 2000, accumulating a 6 percent decline by 2016, compared with growth rates in France, Germany, and the United States of 5.1 percent, 11.3 percent, and 14.2 percent, respectively[4] (Figure 20.2). There were no wars, plagues, or climate shocks during that period that might explain such abnormal performance. Nor can it be attributed to any scarcity of physical capital, considering the high rates of investment, or some scarcity or low quality of labor (Gros 2011). What could explain this anomaly?

Pellegrino and Zingales (2017) discuss some of the explanations frequently given for that performance. The impact of China's entry into the World Trade Organization may have affected Italy more than other countries in the euro area, reducing both the market shares and productivity of Italian companies. Yet looking at the decade from 1996 to 2006, no evidence indicates that sectors most exposed to Chinese imports lagged in TFP growth rates. Pellegrino and Zingales

---

[3]Silvio Berlusconi's ambitious investment program launched in 2000 included many oversized projects, such as high-speed train expansion that required three times more passengers to be profitable and built at three times the price of those in Spain and France. Mario Draghi, while still in the Finance Ministry, asserted that while Italy's public spending was higher than that of France, Germany, and the United Kingdom over the past three decades, the absence of any cost-benefit assessment did not ensure that the projects would meet the country's needs. Flaws in the selection of projects and of their contractors heightened the risk of corruption and collusion, leading to frequent and inefficient contract renegotiations—so much so that from 1990 to 2009 only 2 percent of all public-private partnerships signed in Europe took place in Italy. See Pinotti (2017).

[4]For a detailed breakdown of real GDP growth in Italy, France, Germany, and Spain, see Bugamelli and others (2018, Table 1, 80).

Figure 20.2. Total Factor Productivity: Italy, Germany, France, and United States
Index (1998 = 100)

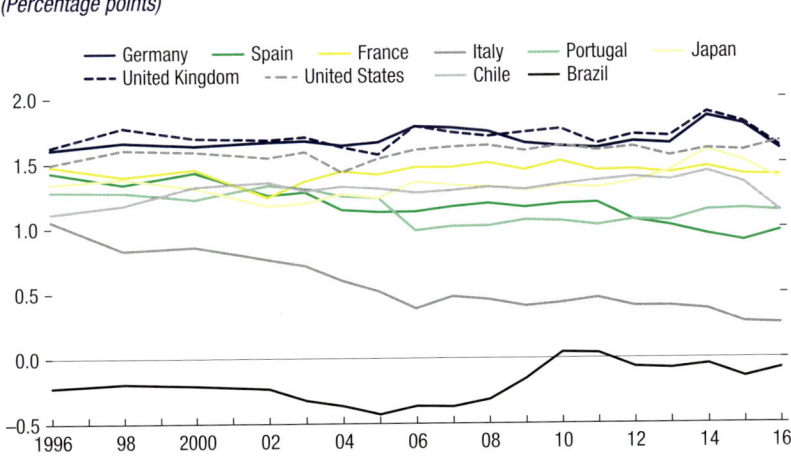

Source: Organisation for Economic Co-operation and Development.

(2017) also refute the hypothesis that Italy's historically rigid labor market may have been responsible for declining productivity, as there is no evidence of labor immobility.

From another angle, Gros (2011) finds a worsening of Italy's governance indicators as calculated by the World Bank in its Worldwide Governance Indicators since 1999–2000. The Worldwide Governance Indicators covering the rule of law (Figure 20.3), governmental efficacy, and control of corruption show an ongoing and notable decline since 1996.

Figure 20.3. Rule of Law: Selected Countries
(Percentage points)

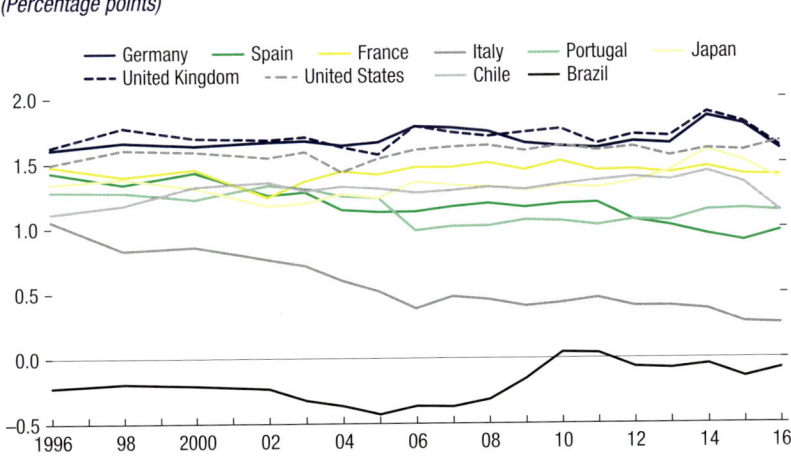

Source: World Bank.

The empirical analysis by Pellegrino and Zingales (2017) is informative. They examine the revolution brought about by information and communication technologies (ICTs) in the mid-1990s and cite several studies that show that the impact on productivity of ICT investments complements meritocratic managerial practices. The authors also observe that most Italian companies select, promote, and reward people based on loyalty rather than on merit, and find evidence that TFP in more ICT-intensive sectors grew faster in countries where companies adopted merit-based managerial methods, as measured in a survey by the World Economic Forum. Pellegrino and Zingales (2017) further develop their analysis with data collected in a firm-level survey[5] on the use of incentives and the selection of managers to measure meritocratic administration, company by company, in seven countries. They find that TFP grows faster in more meritocratic firms in sectors that are more dependent on ICT.

Why does Italy lag in adopting meritocratic managerial practices? The explanation is that in Italy more than in other countries, nonmeritocratic managerial practices—that is, those based on loyalty—confer more benefits for companies. The greatest advantage is that companies can operate in environments in which law enforcement is either inefficient or nonexistent. Among developed economies, Italy stands out both for the inefficiency of its legal system and for the widespread practices of tax evasion and kickbacks. The ICT revolution thus caught Italy with the wrong managerial system, and the country was unable to benefit from these innovative technologies. The absence of meritocracy, according to Pellegrino and Zingales (2017), explains 61 percent to 83 percent of Italy's productivity gap and leads the authors to conclude that family ties and favoritism are the ultimate causes of the "Italian disease."

Another source of inefficiency is the extent of political connections in companies. Data from 1980 through 2014 (Akcigit, Baslandze, and Lotti 2017) show that companies with political connections employ 32 percent of the country's labor force. Political connections are part of the landscape for 44 percent of firms with more than 100 employees. These companies employ more people and survive longer in the market, but their labor is less productive, they innovate less, and their performance is below average, with lower growth rates and productivity. Firms in more-regulated sectors as well as larger companies tend to have more political connections.

From 1985 to 2014, Akcigit, Baslandze, and Lotti (2017) identified a reasonable degree of stability in the percentage of companies with political connections. In the early 1990s, when Mani Pulite began, the rate declined sharply—with some 9,000 companies losing their political connections—but it soon returned to its previous level. Of greater interest is that for companies connected to higher-echelon politicians (mayors, provincial presidents, and so on), the decline in the early 1990s was followed by a strong (some 50 percent) and permanent surge in their connections. In the authors' words: "We interpret this picture as a

---

[5]Bruegel-Unicredit EFIGE firm-level data set.

smoking gun for a regime shift from a more 'under the table' relationship between firms and politicians involving corruption and bribes, towards a more formal 'moonlighting' relationship." This is important evidence of the intensification of corrupt practices after Mani Pulite.

Firms' productivity is also negatively affected by the inefficiency of the public sector, as Giordano and others (2015) show in a study based on productivity data from approximately 450,000 Italian companies. They find that "Well-functioning education or childcare and a fast and efficient judicial system are likely, for different and obvious reasons, to have a positive impact on firm productivity." They conclude that "if public sector efficiency rose to the frontier in all provinces, firm productivity, measured as output per euro spent on salaries, could increase by up to 22 percent in the sectors that depend the most on the public sector, while gross value added per employee costs could rise from 2 to 10 percent" (Giordano and others 2015).

The results of this research underscore the major negative impacts of a precarious institutional environment—and of the subsequent presence of multiple forms of corruption—on firms' productivity. What does the efficiency of a court system mean in such an environment?

THE ROLE OF EFFICIENCY IN COURT SYSTEMS

The efficiency of the judiciary is fundamental to ensuring the sustained development of countries, as Rose-Akerman and Palifka (2016) have shown. Esposito, Lanau, and Pompe (2014) state that "A well-functioning, independent, and efficient justice system is one where decisions are taken within a reasonable time, are predictable and effectively enforced, and where individual rights, including property rights, are properly protected." In addition, "Judicial independence implies that . . . judges do not have to fear negative consequences as a result of their decisions [and that they] can expect their decisions to be implemented regardless of whether they are in the (short-term) interest of other government branches" (Voigt, Gutmann, and Feld 2015).

Rose-Ackerman and Palikfa (2016) report that judicial independence and competence are positively correlated with higher levels of economic growth, lower levels of corruption, greater protection of human rights, and higher levels of political and economic freedom. An independent judiciary helps limit the siphoning off of public funds into private pockets: in a sample of 144 countries, the authors find a correlation of 0.83 between these two variables.

Low efficiency in a judicial system affects economic growth in several ways. It reduces incentives for research and technological innovation, makes the business environment less attractive for both domestic and foreign investment, limits the development of the credit market by increasing its cost, undermines stable and predictable labor relations, promotes informality and tax evasion, and is unable to inhibit high levels of corruption and organized crime.

The great majority of available indicators place Italy's judiciary among the least efficient, compared with its peers. The degree of independence of Italian courts and judges is the lowest among Europe's developed economies:[6] 57 percent of the general public (and 63 percent of businesspeople) consider it "very bad" and "bad," compared with France (37 percent and 31 percent), Germany (16 percent and 20 percent), and, finally, Denmark with the best score on this account, where only 7 percent of the public and 6 percent of businesspeople consider their courts' and judges' degree of independence to be bad or very bad. Among the reasons for such a lack of independence, 29 percent of the Italian general public (and 40 percent of businesspeople) believe that "the status and position of judges do not sufficiently guarantee their independence"; 38 percent (50 percent) blame "interference or pressure from economic or other specific interests"; and 40 percent (48 percent) blame "interference or pressure from government and politicians." The average time it took to resolve civil and commercial litigation cases in lower courts in 2015 was 527 days in Italy, compared with 346 in France and 190 in Germany.[7]

MANI PULITE AND POLITICIANS' REACTION TO ITS IMPACT

Italian institutions—and the judiciary in particular—suffered a strong blow from the political class's reaction to the Mani Pulite investigation, which began in February 1992 in Milan.[8] A sting operation based on a denunciation by the owner of a small cleaning company hired through a public tender led to the arrest of Mario Chiesa, the president of a public retirement center, who had taken a cash bribe.[9] Shortly after his arrest, the defendant agreed to a plea bargain in court and testified that he had received bribes from several other businesses, setting off a chain reaction that uncovered a widespread, long-standing system of corruption involving businesspeople, politicians, public officials, and members of the police and the judiciary. Tenders for public works were tailored for companies that bribed public officials and politicians to whom they were connected. Stable cartels had operated for decades, choosing who would win each bidding process and

---

[6]Eurobarometer data in the *2017 EU Justice Scoreboard*—Quantitative Data (EC 2017).

[7]According to the *2017 EU Justice Scoreboard*—Quantitative Data, based on CEPEJ data (EC 2017).

[8]The operation was also known as Tangentopoli, or Bribesville. This was neither the first nor the last major corruption investigation in Italy. Before it came the Ambrosiano Bank, the P2 Masonic Lodge, IMI, IN, Carceri D'Oro, and others; after Mani Pulite came the cases involving Parmalat, expo Milano 2016, and more. There is a correlation between the outbreak of corruption cases and periods of recession in Italy, whereby the reduction of public investment may increase the propensity to denounce and break up cartels and agreements (Davigo and Mannozzi 2007).

[9]Chiesa, president of the Pio Albergo Trivulzio and a candidate for mayor of Milan, received approximately 3,500 euros. For details of the operation, see Colombo (2015), Davigo and Mannozzi (2007), and Barbacetto, Gomez, and Travaglio (2012).

how the proceeds of overpriced tenders would be paid and distributed. In addition to enriching government officials personally, the bribes funded the careers and campaigns of most politicians from practically all political parties.

At first, Bettino Craxi,[10] president of the Council of Ministers at the time, commented that the arrest of Chiesa was insignificant, since he was only a "lone swindler" who had besmirched the image of a clean party. Soon afterward,[11] in the wake of an avalanche of indictments, Craxi himself denounced in Parliament a system of illicit political payments involving nearly all politicians and parties. No one in the chamber dared to contradict him, thus highlighting the amazement of everyone about the gravity and scope of the facts coming out every day. Very soon, 4,200 people had been incriminated, including four former presidents of the Council of Ministers, 12 ministers, and 130 deputies and senators (Davigo and Mannozzi 2007). By the 1994 elections, five parties had disappeared, including the Christian Democrats, who had dominated politics since the postwar period.

At that point, the political system mounted its reaction against the investigations, with the political debut of Silvio Berlusconi, a successful building contractor, closely tied to Craxi. Berlusconi also controlled a media empire, with national TV networks, newspapers, and a soccer team. Regarding the accusations of corruption investigated by Mani Pulite, he told historian and journalist Indro Montanelli in 1993, "I am obliged to go into politics. Otherwise they'll arrest me, and I'll be broke." He ran for Parliament and won in 1994, becoming prime minister with the new party Forza Italia, whose slogan was "Away with old politics. We want different, new, clean politics!" He headed a strong media attack against members of the operation, which had to face a true "sea of mud," fed by a war of fake dossiers and accusations that the judges' real objective was to eliminate all politicians. The population, alarmed by the extent of the accusations, after suffering decades of terrorist attacks and contaminated by a centuries-old omertà (code of silence) culture spread by the Mafia, began to abandon its nearly unanimous initial support for the investigations. The Italian press, beholden to economic groups and government advertising, was used to proliferating fantasized conspiracies.

Meanwhile, another lethal attack was launched not only against Mani Pulite but against Italy's very future, with a series of new laws, many of them unconstitutional and soon to be repealed, but which demonstrated that the political class and the government would do anything to put an end to the operation. Several crimes of corruption were legalized, and sentences were reduced for those that remained on the books, tying the judiciary's hands regarding punishing these kinds of crimes.

---

[10]On December 15, 1992, the first *avviso di garanzia* was issued against Craxi. On May 12, 1994, his passport was taken, but he had already fled to Hammamet, Tunisia, where he lived until his death on January 19, 2000.

[11]During a session of the Chamber of Deputies, in April 1993.

The first blow came in mid-1994 with the Biondi Decree, also known as *salva ladri* (thief saver). It simply struck provisional arrests[12] from the books for most crimes against the public administration, including corruption and extortion, as well as crimes against the financial system. The overwhelming reaction by judges and the population kept the decree from being upheld by Parliament, and it expired. Even so, it caused permanent damage, since many defendants arrested during the Milan operation were released, and the number of accomplices willing to collaborate with the courts declined.[13]

Other important legislative changes included[14] annulment of evidence obtained through letters rogatory, throwing out some of the evidence of white-collar crimes committed abroad; changes in the use of testimony taken during preliminary investigations, which also annuls evidence collected previously; and redefinition of the crime of abuse of functions, drastically reducing its punishment. One of the most significant changes for the fight against corruption and for the quality of the business environment was the depenalization of accounting fraud. In addition to creating uncertainties regarding the authenticity of corporate balance sheets, it is through unrecorded payments that major corruption cases are generally identified. The issuance of counterfeit invoices, through which most off-the-books accounting is done in Italy, was punishable by six months to five years of confinement. In 2000, penalties for those crimes were reduced to six months confinement, but only when the value of the invoice is greater than a certain limit on revenues declared by the firm. Even more devastating was the 50 percent reduction in the statute of limitations, benefiting many defendants with the extinction of their crimes.

With a demoralized judiciary, after a relentless campaign of defamation, and new laws to ensure impunity from crimes of corruption,[15] Italy's recent lackluster performance is not at all surprising. It combines the worst ranking in corruption perceptions and in the quality of other governance indicators with the lowest economic growth of any of its peers.

---

[12]The criticism of the abuse of provisional arrests was refuted by Colombo (2015) with an estimate that during the investigations in Milan, the average number of such arrests was 8,000, while during the first three years of Mani Pulite there were fewer than 1,000. Provisional arrests are important for investigations into crimes of corruption, since the participants could eliminate evidence of their crimes, hide funds obtained improperly in the country or abroad, agree on plausible alibis with accomplices, and so on.

[13]Secrecy is crucial for the success of crimes of corruption, and the absence of material evidence is very common, since clues are carefully eliminated by the authors of corruption. That is why collaboration with the court, induced by lesser penalties, is so important to finding accomplices. With greater chances for impunity, criminals cease their collaboration with the court, to the detriment of important means for investigation.

[14]Part of the following analysis on changes in penal legislation is from Davigo (2018).

[15]The number of crimes of corruption reported in Italy's judicial statistics today is lower than the rate observed in Finland, one of the world's least corrupt countries. This reveals a huge gap between the number of crimes committed and the number that actually are recorded.

BRAZIL AND THE LAVA JATO OPERATION

Two decades later, could Brazil follow in Italy's footsteps? With the arrest in March 2014 of a money changer (*doleiro*) known in Curitiba for several past crimes, members of the police, federal prosecutors, and federal judge Sergio Moro could not imagine the scale of what they would uncover in the years to come, through what came to be known as Operation Lava Jato ("Car Wash").[16] An SUV delivered as a "gift" to a former supply director at Petrobras led to the disclosure of a gigantic corruption and money-laundering scheme involving Petrobras and its main suppliers and contractors, as well as several political parties loyal to the government. Investigations revealed that the scheme went beyond Petrobras to various government agencies, amounting to a serious situation of systemic corruption.[17] As Emilio Odebrecht testified at a plea-bargain hearing in December 2016, "everything that is happening became institutionalized. It was business as usual. And with all these political parties, were they fighting over public offices? No. . . . The parties brought in their leaders to raise funds for the parties and for politicians. It's been this way for 30 years."[18]

At Petrobras, overbilled construction work contracted out to and done by some of the country's biggest civil engineering companies, organized in a cartel that lasted many years. Operated by *doleiros,* the bribes found their way into the overseas bank accounts of Petrobras directors and to the parties responsible for naming the corporation's upper echelon, to be used in election campaigns and for other purposes. Public information shows that the main parties benefiting from this scheme set up inside the company were the Partido dos Trabalhadores (PT, Workers Party), Partido do Movimernto Democrático Brasileiro (PMDB, Brazilian Democratic Movement Party), and Partido Progressista (PP, Progressive Party).[19]

Participants include members of the highest ranks of the country's political and business elite, several of them now—or recently—in prison. Former President Lula da Silva was sentenced to 12 years in prison by an appeals court and is awaiting the outcome of six other criminal cases now being heard in federal trial

---

[16]See Netto (2016), Dallagnol (2017), and the website of the Federal Prosecutor's Office/MPF (www.mpf.mp.br/) for details on this operation.

[17]Crimes of corruption were uncovered in Eletronucloear, Caixa Econômica Federal, pension funds of state-owned corporations, and others. Politicians and government officials were involved in the sale of laws or decisions by the Fiscal Appeals Administrative Board to benefit businesspeople. Several other Lava Jato–related operations are still underway throughout the country. In Rio de Janeiro, former governors are in prison and a dramatic panorama of systemic corruption and administrative dereliction has been unveiled, as the state government is near bankruptcy and currently is under intervention by the army to ensure public safety.

[18]See *Valor Econômico*, EU&Fim de Semana, May 12, 2017.

[19]The system of corruption has spread throughout the continent and beyond. Projects in a dozen countries in Latin America and Africa took loans from the Brazilian Development Bank for Brazilian contractors, generating bribes for illegal enrichment and campaign funding in Brazil and other countries.

courts.[20] Four former Petrobras directors have received prison sentences, two of them after making plea-bargain agreements. Dozens of executives in the builders' cartel were found guilty of paying kickbacks. In its 2015 annual report, Petrobras recognized it had lost 6 billion reais (about US$1.8 billion) to corruption, and in 2018 it signed a US$3 billion settlement with shareholders in the United States. Three of Brazil's largest building companies—Camargo Correa, Andrade Gutierrez, and Odebrecht—signed leniency agreements with federal prosecutors, committing themselves to abandon illicit practices and return billions of reais to the public treasury. The most outstanding single episode of generalized corruption combined with managerial irresponsibility was the construction of the Abreu e Lima refinery. With an initial budget of US$2.4 billion, its price finally hit US$18.5 billion in 2015.

With the high level of corruption in Brazil, identified by any of the ratings used internationally, it is no surprise to see the country shaken by scandals from time to time, like "Collorgate" in 1992, which led to the impeachment of President Fernando Collor; the "budget midgets" in 1992; the SUDAM case in 2001; Operation Anaconda in 2003; Operation Sanguessuga in 2006; and the Mensalão in 2005 (see Power and Taylor 2011).

What makes Lava Jato different from the previous cases? Lava Jato has been successful for several reasons. Luck put the case in the hands of Judge Moro, who has had a solid career in court as well as expertise in money-laundering crimes. Conversant with the Mani Pulite case, he was one of the first to publish an article on it in Brazil, in 2004 (see Moro 2004). Its coming in the wake of the Mensalão[21] trial was an important advantage (Moro 2018). Despite the slow pace of that trial,[22] it was the first time the Supreme Court had tried and imprisoned icons of the PT (the Workers' Party) and some government officials for crimes of corruption, criminal conspiracy, and other charges. A 2016 Supreme Court decision allowing defendants to begin serving prison sentences after their conviction was upheld on a first appeal that helped suspects recognize that they could no longer count on endless appeals to stay out of prison, thus encouraging the plea-bargaining option to reduce their impending penalties. Growing international opposition to crimes of corruption and money laundering—in battles against financial schemes

---

[20]Records at the Federal Prosecutor's Office, as of February 9, 2018, contain 1,765 procedures initiated since the onset of Operation Lava Jato, 881 search and seizure warrants issued, 101 precautionary arrest warrants and 111 temporary arrest warrants issued, 340 requests filed for international cooperation, 163 plea-bargaining agreements signed with physical persons, and more. See Ministerio Publico Federal (2018).

[21]In 2005, a member of the Chamber of Deputies, Roberto Jefferson, denounced a scheme that had made monthly bribe payments since 2002 to congressional supporters of the government in exchange for supporting President Lula, then in his first term. Since most of them had a right to be tried in a special forum, the federal prosecutor filed charges in the Supreme Federal Court in 2006, and in November 2007 the Supreme Court opened formal criminal proceedings, in Penal Suit 470. Five years later, of the 40 original defendants, 37 were tried and 24 were found guilty.

[22]The slow pace of procedures at the Supreme Court is due to the excessive number of suits brought—more than 100,000 in 2017. See Falcão and others (2017).

for terrorism, drug trafficking, and corruption—facilitated Brazil's collaboration with countries where the proceeds of corrupt acts had been deposited. Modern ICT has also been used well in the operation, including the rapid publication of testimony and denunciations and live broadcasts of trials.[23] Access to information, along with a free, high-quality press in Brazil, ensured strong public support for the operation, with noisy street and online demonstrations every time Lava Jato appeared to be threatened.

By confronting gigantic, deep-rooted interest groups, Lava Jato became a symbol of the fight against corruption, but it also gave rise to a horde of stakeholders interested in its ruin. Several bills in Congress tried to reduce the independence of judges, to legalize off-the-books campaign donations, to grant amnesty to politicians on the take, and so on. There is an ongoing (2018) attempt to overturn a Supreme Court ruling on the enforcement of a prison sentence after a defendant is convicted by the first appeals court, particularly with regard to the prosecution of former President Lula. Time will tell if Brazil will turn this sad page in its history or fall back under the yoke of powerful interest groups to the detriment of the majority of the population.

As it nears its conclusion and having dealt with the subject matter for which it was created, Lava Jato can be deemed to have been a successful operation, but it is still incomplete—only because of the naturally slow pace of Supreme Court deliberations on accusations against politicians who enjoy special forum privileges.[24] Even so, one cannot expect Lava Jato to put an end to corruption in the country. The skill of the prosecution and the rapid punishment meted out for crimes of corruption, which Lava Jato pioneered, represented necessary, albeit insufficient, steps toward reducing corruption once and for all in Brazil. To reduce corruption meaningfully, it will be crucial to ensure the population's ongoing engagement in the fight against corruption, breaking with old cultural habits, and the emergence of political leaders who embrace the anticorruption agenda. Here, as in other countries where the political system has a vested interest in keeping itself corrupt, the overriding challenge is to change the country's laws to make the judiciary and the fight against corruption more efficient, even when doing so goes against the interests of many of those who write the laws. The sad fate in Congress of the bill known as "Ten Measures against Corruption,"[25] drafted by public prosecutors and filed as a popular petition with more than 2 million signatures in 2016, is one example of how invested players still rule Brazilian politics.

---

[23]An example is the photograph released by the federal police of boxes with 51 million reais in cash (US$16 million at today's exchange rate) that were found in the apartment of President Michel Temer's former chief of staff, Geddel Vieira Lima.

[24]More than 50,000 people hold "special forum" privileges in Brazil. The Supreme Court tries the president, the vice president, federal ministers, senators, and federal deputies (members of the lower house). Governors and mayors are tried by the Superior Court of Justice and by regional federal courts, respectively. Judges, appeals judges, state assembly members, and state secretaries are judged directly by second- or third-level appeals courts.

[25]See Dallagnol (2017) and www.dezmedidas.mpf.mp.br.

CONCLUSIONS

Ever since the work of Gary Becker (1968), corruption has been known to be a rational crime, from beginning to end. Targets are chosen rationally, as are the means for obtaining an advantage, and, at the end, steps are taken to hide the proceeds, possibly via sophisticated techniques to launder and hide the money in tax havens. Penalties for corruption must therefore not be viewed as a judge's personal vendetta but simply as a good way to provide corrective incentives that raise the cost of corrupt practices. We presume, therefore, that the laws will be suitable and their legal enforcement effective.

People still complain, in Italy, that "the judges wiped out the political parties" and that this opened the way for Berlusconi. This chapter shows that, from the inception of Mani Pulite, judges simply enforced the law, but when they caught politicians, the laws were changed. What remains is a hostile setting for the fight against corruption that has degraded the notions of justice and of economic efficiency. In Brazil, judges are also enforcing the laws, and—so far—Italy's example has been significant enough that threats to rework institutions have been avoided.

In addition to allowing Lava Jato to run its course, Brazil needs profound reforms that will make political parties work more transparently, shielded from corruption. The special forum must be reduced to put an end to impunity and to the adverse selection of politicians. The possibility of imprisonment to enforce convictions following the first appeal must be preserved to make justice more effective. The public sector, including regulatory agencies, must become more efficient by establishing clearer rules for the contracting of public officials, reducing political sway over nominations.

The Brazilian case is made more dramatic by high rates of inequality in the distribution of income and wealth, which provides fertile ground for populist, nondemocratic government proposals. The country is emerging from one of its worst recessions, caused by irresponsible macro- and microeconomic policies adopted by populist governments with the purpose of sharing favors with friends and encouraging families to consume through indebtedness, so individuals could keep their hold on power while generously distributing bribes and kickbacks to fuel their own parties and a continent-wide project of political power. The public debt soared from 50 percent to more than 75 percent from 2014 to 2018 and will continue to grow unless profound, and unpopular, reforms are adopted.

REFERENCES

Acemoglu, D. 2009. *Introduction to Modern Economic Growth.* Princeton and Oxford: Princeton University Press.

Akcigit, U., S. Baslandze, and F. Lotti. 2017. "Connecting to Power: Political Connections, Innovation, and Firm Dynamics." Bank of Italy. Rome.

Barbacetto, G., P. Gomez, and M. Travaglio. 2012. *Mani Pulite: The True Story 20 Years Later.* Milan: Chiare Lettere.

Becker, G. 1968. "Crime and Punishment: An Economic Approach." *Journal of Political Economy* 76: 169–217.

Bugamelli, M., and others. 2018. "Productivity Growth in Italy: A Tale of a Slow-Motion Change." Occasional Paper No. 422, Bank of Italy, Rome.

Colombo, G. 2015. *Letter to a Son on Mani Pulite*. Milan: Garzanti

Dallagnol, Deltan. 2017. *The Fight against Corruption—The Lava Jato and the Future of a Country Marked by Corruption*. Rio de Janeiro: Editora Primeira Pessoa.

Davigo, P. 2017. *Il Sistema Della Corruzione*. Rome: Editori Laterza.

———. 2018. "Some Notes on Corruption in Italy." unpublished.

Davigo, P., and G. Mannozzi. 2007. *Corruption in Italy: Social Perception and Criminal Control*. Rome: Editori Laterza.

Esposito, G., S. Lanau, and S. Pompe. 2014. "Judicial System Reform in Italy—A Key to Growth." IMF Working Paper WP/14/32, International Monetary Fund, Washington, DC.

European Commission (EC). 2017. *2017 EU Justice Scoreboard*. Quantitative Data. Brussels.

Falcão and others. 2017. *V Supreme Report on Numbers—The Privileged and Supreme Forum*. Rio de Janeiro: FGV Direito Rio.

Fisman, R., and M. Golden. 2017. *Corruption—What Everyone Needs to Know*. New York: Oxford University Press.

Giordano, R., S. Lanau, P. Tommasino, and P. Topalova. 2015. "Does Public Sector Inefficiency Constrain Firm Productivity? Evidence from Italian Provinces." IMF Working Paper 15/168, International Monetary Fund, Washington, DC.

Gros, D. 2011. "What Is Holding Italy Back?" CEPS Commentary, Center for European Policy Studies Commentary, Brussels.

Klitgaard, R. 2017. "On Culture and Corruption." BSG Working Paper Series, Blavatnik School of Government, University of Oxford, Oxford.

Ministerio Publico Federal. 2018. "The Lava Jet in Numbers in Paraná." Teresina, Brazil.

Moro, S. F. 2004. "Operation Considerations Mani Pulite." Revista CEJ 8(26): 56–62.

———. 2018. "Preventing Systemic Corruption in Brazil." Unpublished.

Netto, V. 2016. *Judge Sergio Moro and the Backstage of the Operation that Rocked Brazil*. Rio de Janeiro: Editora Primeira Pessoa.

North, D. 1990. *Institutions, Institutional Change and Economic Performance*. Cambridge: Cambridge University Press.

———. 2005. *Understanding the Process of Economic Change*. Princeton, NJ: Princeton University Press.

Pellegrino, B., and L. Zingales. 2017. "Diagnosing the Italian Disease." NBER Working Paper 23964, National Bureau of Economic Research, Cambridge, MA.

Pinotti, M. C. 2017. "Economic Effects of Corruption." In *Infrastructure—Efficiency and Ethics*, edited by Affonso Pastore, Elsevier Editora Ltda.

Power, T., and M. Taylor, eds. 2011. *Corruption and Democracy in Brazil—The Struggle for Accountability*. Notre Dame, IN: University of Notre Dame Press.

Rose-Ackerman, S., and B. Palikfa. 2016. *Corruption and Government—Causes, Consequences and Reform*. New York: Cambridge University Press.

Rossi, S. 2017. "Finance and Development." Speech by the Director General of the Bank of Italy and President of IVASS, Rome, October 4.

Transparency International. 2017. *Corruption Perceptions Index 2017*. Berlin.

Voigt, S., J. Gutmann, and L. Feld. 2015. "Economic Growth and Judicial Independence, a Dozen Years On: Cross-Country Evidence Using an Updated Set of Indicators." *European Journal of Political Economy* 38(C): 197–211.

CHAPTER 21

Lessons from Italy's Anti-Corruption Efforts

ALESSANDRO MERLI

Since it began in 2014, the vast anticorruption investigation underway in Brazil, Operation Lava Jato, or "Car Wash," and related inquiries have been compared with the Italian inquiry called Mani Pulite, or "Clean Hands," of the 1990s. One of the main prosecutors in the Brazilian investigation, Sergio Moro, started studying the Italian case as far back as the early 2000s (Moro 2004). Both investigations showed that the extent of corruption in the respective countries reached the highest levels of the political and business establishments.

It is useful for Brazil to examine the Italian case of Clean Hands and analyze its results and aftermath, which the first part of this chapter summarizes. On the political front, Mani Pulite decapitated two of the ruling parties of that time, the Christian Democrats and the Socialists, and created a power vacuum, which was filled mainly by a newcomer to politics: the television and real estate tycoon Silvio Berlusconi. As Berlusconi himself became embroiled in several corruption cases, open conflict between the political system and the judiciary began. This situation was partly responsible for a backlash against the investigating magistrates and the adoption of several laws that blunted their powers. On the economic side, although Mani Pulite initially led to a reduction in corruption cases and in the costs of public projects—which had been inflated by kickbacks—many high-profile cases that have emerged over the past few years show that corruption remains widespread in Italy.

The second part of the chapter reviews some of the measures that were taken to counter corruption, starting in 2012 and especially during Matteo Renzi's government in 2014–16. It also offers some lessons for Brazil, including the need for the actions of the magistrates to have the support of public opinion beyond the initial phase of the inquiry and the need for at least part of the political class to take the necessary legislative steps to achieve long-term results against corruption, intervening on its prevention as well as its repression.

The author thanks Edmund Amann, Juliano Basile, Carlos A. Primo Braga, Lorenzo Forni, and Erik Jones for their helpful suggestions and comments.

CORRUPTION IN ITALY AND THE MANI PULITE INVESTIGATION

Corruption, according to a definition accepted by both the IMF and the World Bank, is "abuse of public office for private gain" (IMF 2018). The United Nations Convention against Corruption, ratified by 183 countries, identifies a core set of corrupt acts (UNODC 2003).

Italy has long been considered one of the most corrupt advanced economies and certainly has a long history of scandals. At the beginning of the 20th century, the economist Vilfredo Pareto (1916) observed, "In Italy we can note that all the newly acquired wealth has its roots in public bids, railway constructions, state-funded companies, and custom protection. . . . As a result, this order appears to experienced politicians as a lottery, which grants prizes, some large and some smaller ones." According to criminologist Letizia Paoli (2002), however, until the late 1960s, corruption was by and large confined to the country's ruling elite. From then on, "it became a common and socially accepted behavior, spread across all social strata and involving an even larger number of low- and middle-level politicians and bureaucrats."

The complexity of legal and bureaucratic rules and the inefficiency of the bureaucracy, together with insufficient social capital, are often cited as factors that contribute to the spread of corruption. They are compounded by the pervasive presence of organized crime, especially in Italy's southern region.

It is, in fact, impossible to examine the problems created by corruption for Italy's economy and society without considering other factors that interact with it. It is no coincidence that in his book on "the seven deadly sins of the Italian economy," the former director of the fiscal department of the IMF, Carlo Cottarelli (2018), puts corruption at number two; however, no fewer than four of the other capital sins are quite closely linked to it: tax evasion, the excess of bureaucracy, the slowness of justice, and the North/South gap. Some indirect evidence comes from the World Bank's *Doing Business* report (2017).

In introducing the IMF's stepped-up engagement on corruption, its managing director, Christine Lagarde (2018), noted a need for a broader focus. The work on corruption undertaken at the IMF "will be embedded in [its] general work that promotes good governance in key areas such as public financial management, financial sector oversight, and anti-money laundering. . . . Governance weaknesses are harmful in their own right, but they also open the door to widespread corruption. To be truly effective, anticorruption strategies must go beyond merely throwing people in jail. They require broader regulatory and institutional reforms." Italy is one of the countries—together with the other Group of Seven (G7) members, Austria, and the Czech Republic—that have agreed to submit their legal and institutional frameworks to the IMF for an assessment with regard to corrupt practices by private actors on the payment of bribes and the laundering of dirty money.

The judges on the Mani Pulite (also known as Tangentopoli, or Bribesville) inquiry advanced many explanations as to why, at the beginning of the 1990s, the system was ripe for attack. The main one is that the system had become increasingly costly, which, together with the difficulties in the economy, made it uneconomical.

Because of its very (illegal) nature, corruption is inherently difficult to measure. Vannucci (2009) tries to quantify it using official statistics on the number of cases and persons indicted, which peaked in the mid-1990s, and the number of convictions, which peaked a few years later. In the first years after the 1992 start of Mani Pulite, six former prime ministers, more than 500 members of Parliament, and several thousand public officials, together with the heads of some of the most prominent companies in Italy, were under investigation. Another indicator of the scale of corruption in Italy is the cost of public works as it compares with that of other countries. But the image of Italy as a country more corrupt than most is based not as much on hard data as on several indices of perceptions of corruption. The most frequently quoted is Transparency International's Corruption Perceptions Index, which in 2017 ranked Italy 54th, with a score of 50 out of 100—a distinct improvement over 2012, when the latest wave of anti-corruption efforts started and Italy was in 79th place (with a score of 42 out of 100), but still behind most other European Union countries. Brazil, by way of comparison, is 96th, with a score of 37 out of 100 (Transparency International 2018a). Other measures, such as the World Bank's Control of Corruption rating in its World Development Indicators and the Eurobarometer surveys, paint a similar picture.

Perception matters: It influences confidence and investment decisions, in addition to more generally affecting the behavior of economic agents, including their willingness to trust the judiciary and pay taxes (Cardoso 2006).

The Italian anti-corruption authority, Autorità Nazionale Anticorruzione (ANAC), is now trying to develop a new set of corruption risk indicators. These indicators are differentiated by territory, sector, and level of government and initially applied to the areas of waste management, education, social services, and procurement. The objective is to identify anomalies in public contracts that may raise red flags for the anticorruption authorities (ANAC 2017, 55–66).

Studies accompanying the IMF's most recent framework (2018) on governance and anti-corruption show that there is a negative correlation between corruption and long-term per capita income, investment, and tax revenues and a positive correlation with higher inequality. Calculations for Italy made by the economist Luca Paolazzi for Confindustria, the employers' federation, indicate that, were Italy to reduce corruption (as measured by the World Bank's Control of Corruption rating) to Spain's level, economic growth would be 0.6 percent higher. If it managed to lower it to France's level, per capita income in 2014 would have been 5,000 euros higher (Paolazzi 2014).

More generally, Lagarde observes that "sliding down from the 50th to 25th percentile in an index of corruption or governance is associated with a fall in the annual rate of growth of GDP per capita by half a percentage point or more, and a decline in the investment-to-GDP ratio by 1.5 to 2 percentage points. [The IMF's] results show that corruption and poor governance are associated with higher inequality and lower inclusive growth."

Because of the inherent difficulty in measuring bribery, it is unclear whether corruption in Italy has increased or decreased since Mani Pulite. On the economic front, the strongest effect, at least in the short term, was the steep drop in the cost of public projects. Construction costs for the Milan underground went from 300–350 billion lire (L) per kilometer in 1991 to L97 billion per kilometer in 1995. Total costs for the Milan cross-rail dropped from L1,994 billion to L1,452 billion. The budget for the extension of Malpensa Airport was L4,200 billion, while the actual cost was eventually L1,990 billion (Vannucci 2012).

A misleading value about the cost of corruption for the Italian economy that pops up from various sources sets the figure at 60 billion euros a year, equivalent to 3.5 percent of GDP. The origin of this figure is uncertain, but it does not seem to be grounded in reality.[1] Arguably, Mani Pulite's biggest impact was on the political system. The investigation decapitated the two political parties that had been the mainstays of government coalitions for most of the post–World War II era, the Christian Democrats and the Socialists, as well as some smaller political parties; the inquiries ended up overwhelming them and condemning them to extinction. Some analysts attribute the start of Mani Pulite to the fact that, after the fall of the Berlin Wall, the Christian Democrats were no longer seen as a bulwark against communism and therefore an indispensable ally with the United States. The demise of the two parties left a huge vacuum at the center of the political spectrum. This vacuum was filled by Berlusconi, who was able to portray himself as the expression of a new way of doing politics; he also exploited his history as a successful businessman, his superior marketing skills, and the support of his extensive media ownership. His arrival on the scene, where he would stay for the next 20 years, is the first element that invites a comparison with Brazil's current situation: the collapse of the political party structure (already much more amorphous in Brazil than in the Italy of the early 1990s) can open the way for politicians with a populist bent—in the case of Berlusconi, with a formidable media machine.

As Berlusconi himself became a target of several judicial investigations, including the corruption of judges, he initiated a powerful pushback against the magistrates, who had enjoyed a considerable degree of public support in the first phase of Mani Pulite. He not only used the means at his disposal on the media front, subjecting the judiciary to a relentless attack, but also mobilized his majority in Parliament to approve legislation that would severely restrict the magistrates' actions. The most important measure was undoubtedly the law that imposed a stricter statute of limitations. The impossibility of concluding the majority of the trials within the new deadlines was one of the factors in the public's loss of trust in the magistrates' actions. The fact that several of these magistrates entered politics themselves (an aspect that is already present in Brazil as well) helped give credence to the image of a politicized judiciary. Antonio Di Pietro, the most

---

[1] Cottarelli (2018) makes a brave and amusing, albeit largely unsuccessful, attempt at finding out where it came from; the question is not at all irrelevant, since the figure is constantly quoted by official sources.

famous face of the investigating "pool" of Mani Pulite in Milan, for instance, founded his own party (Italia dei Valori) and was twice minister in center-left governments, riding the popularity of the inquiry and fading with it from the political scene. Many others were elected to Parliament.

The inquiries were unable to sustain original levels of public support. According to Paoli (2002), "ordinary Italians were never forced to ask uncomfortable questions about their own behavior, i.e. the extent to which the culture of Tangentopoli was in fact their own." The historian Paul Ginsborg maintains that "Tangentopoli remained very much a spectator sport, far removed from the realities of everyday life."[2]

Almost 20 years after Mani Pulite, the emergence of new scandals, sometimes involving the same people,[3] has shown that something has changed (the financing of politics had, if anything, become even more opaque, going not directly to the parties but through foundations and associations with few, if any, obligations of transparency), but much has remained the same. Some new large-scale investigations (for instance, on the construction of the MOSE tidal barriers in Venice, the Expo in Milan, and the Mafia Capitale inquiry in Rome) show that corruption was alive and well and the political system was still vulnerable to it.

These were followed by a renewed legislative attack on corruption, this time trying to achieve a better balance between repression and prevention, starting with the Severino Law in 2012. The Renzi government then intensified efforts in 2014–16. The prevention role of the anti-corruption authority ANAC was strengthened, and the appointment of respected anti-Mafia magistrate Raffaele Cantone as its head gave impulse to its efforts, also in the public arena. However, Cantone himself lamented the budget constraints imposed on ANAC, which, he claimed, risked endangering the exercise of its growing functions. ANAC has penetrating powers of intervention, especially on public procurement, one of the areas most infested with corruption, where more transparency was introduced.

In 2015 the statute of limitations was reformed to provide more time for trials to be completed, partly removing one of the elements that had contributed to the eventual failure of several strands of the Mani Pulite inquiry. However, the calculation formula for the limitations was left unchanged, which, according to some critics, may reduce the effectiveness of the law. The crime of false accounting, which often reveals other illicit activities, including corruption, and had been abolished under Berlusconi, was reintroduced. Penalties were made harsher for both the perpetrators and the beneficiaries of corruption.[4] Conversely, some measures were introduced, such as an increase of the ceiling on the amount of cash payments, that may facilitate the payment of bribes.

---

[2]Ginsborg, cit. in Paoli (2002), 179.

[3]Polo and Vannucci (2014). The title of their article, à la Tomasi di Lampedusa, is "I gattopardi delle mazzette," or "The Leopards of the Bribes."

[4]Vannucci (2016).

It is probably too early to tell if these efforts will bear fruit and if full implementation will follow the adoption of European-standard rules. Much remains to be done, moreover, to tackle one of the underlying causes of corruption by simplifying rules and red tape (Berselli 2008; Cottarelli 2018, 63).

LESSONS FOR BRAZIL

To what extent participation in international efforts will be of help to both Italy and Brazil also remains to be seen. Since the Brisbane Summit of 2014, the Group of 20 (G20), to which both countries belong, has promoted biennial anti-corruption action plans. Italy was also at the forefront of similar efforts during its presidency of the G7 in 2017. The G20 has adopted, for instance, high-level principles on beneficial ownership—often a gray area that favors corruption. Italy has a "very strong framework" in this field, according to a Transparency International report (2018b), and Brazil a "strong framework," after substantial improvement in the past two years. However, "membership of the G20," observes the Transparency International report (2018b), "is not in and of itself a major driver for change."

The Organisation for Economic Co-operation and Development (OECD) in its most recent survey of Brazil devoted a number of recommendations to the area of anti-corruption policies.[5] Some of the issues that came to the surface after Lava Jato are indeed similar to what emerged in Italy after Mani Pulite. The OECD indicators on several points go in the same direction as the actions taken in Italy in the 1990s, especially over the past few years. "Corrupt practices and kickbacks such as those revealed in recent years," says the OECD country survey, "waste public resources and exacerbate income inequalities by allowing relatively prosperous public officials and businessmen to divert taxpayer resources."

The OECD points out that "evidence has mostly surfaced in the context of public procurement, including by state-owned companies, credit subsidies, or tax benefits to specific companies and sectors. Infrastructure concessions are also vulnerable to collusion among bidders and corruption, as estimates suggest that corporate campaign donations by companies have significantly increased the probability of being awarded public contracts.

Regulating the financing of political parties and campaigns, which Brazil is currently discussing, is crucial to prevent powerful special interests from capturing the policy process, which makes growth less inclusive and decreases trust in government." The latest issue is still unresolved in Italy as well: despite a 1993 referendum to abolish public financing of political parties and several interventions by successive governments (the latest in 2014), the discipline is unclear and leaves room for abuse.

---

[5]OECD (2018, 42–43). Brazil, although not a member country, is a "key partner" of the OECD and cooperates closely with the Paris-based organization on several issues.

The OECD praises recent progress in exposing and prosecuting corruption charges and the strength of Brazil's judiciary; however, it notes that although the country already has a transparency law and progress has been made at the federal level, enforcement is "uneven" in states and municipalities. Essential information about procurement contracts whose disclosure is mandated by law is often not provided, and institutions charged with combating corruption have sometimes failed to collaborate, despite a national anti-corruption and anti–money laundering strategy.

The chasm between laws and regulations and their enforcement resembles what is observed in Italy in some areas.

The issues for which the OECD recommendations to Brazil mirror what was undertaken in Italy are in particular the assessment of public procurement laws to limit complexity and exemptions; the strengthening of the rules concerning conflicts of interest, incompatibilities, and impartiality; the use of centralized purchasing bodies with systematic training of procurement officials to design tenders and detect collusive practices; and new whistle-blowing procedures.

The Italian model following Mani Pulite and the results of Italy's subsequent anti-corruption efforts do not necessarily lead to optimism in Brazil about the outcome of Lava Jato. According to World Bank Executive Director Otaviano Canuto (2017), in Brazil "there is potential for change in at least three economic dimensions. First, the cost effectiveness of public spending can improve substantially. . . . Second, the investigation is likely to lead to extensive changes in those sectors of the economy where there is significant interaction with the public sector. . . . Third, there will be an improvement in the perception of Brazil's rule of law, a boon for attracting foreign investors." The Italian experience is positive on the first point, only partially successful on the second, and does not seem to be borne out by the evidence on the third. Concerns about corrupt practices remain at the top of the list of reasons given by foreign investors for not investing in Italy (Paolazzi 2014).

The main lesson from Italy, however, is probably on the issue of the interaction between the investigations and politics. The more judges are, or appear to be, politicized (which unfortunately seems increasingly to be a feature in Brazil), the harder the clash with the political system, endangering some of the results of the inquiries and creating a backlash. The question of what happens in national politics after traditional parties become involved in investigations and ample room is left for populist figures is not for the magistrates to answer, but it is one to keep in mind on the basis of the Italian experience. For Brazil this interaction may be complicated, as compared with the Italian case of the 1990s, by a very different political structure in which only three truly national parties (all involved in the Lava Jato investigations) exist and politicians owe their allegiance as much, if not more, to their state of origin as to party affiliation. A "political solution" to the judicial investigations may therefore be even more difficult than in Italy.

A final, very important, element is the balance between prevention and repression of corruption. Although prevention takes much longer to produce an impact, it is an indispensable complement to the repression, as concluded by

Italy's Raffaele Cantone (Cantone and Caringella 2017). Even in Italy, not everyone agrees. One of the members of the Mani Pulite investigative "pool" in Milan, Piercamillo Davigo, thinks not enough is done on the repression front (Davigo 2017). Sergio Moro, the judge on the front line of Lava Jato, has reached the same conclusion as Cantone: "We shouldn't be under the illusion that the problem of corruption can be solved merely by the criminal-justice system. It just treats its most evident symptoms" (Moro, as quoted in Magalhaes and Pearson 2017). It is at least an encouraging sign that, having devoted the better part of the past two decades to studying the Italian lesson, he has taken on board one of its main messages.

REFERENCES

Autorità Nazionale Anticorruzione—National Anti-Corruption Authority (ANAC). 2017. *Relazione annuale 2016*. Rome.

Berselli, Edmondo. 2008. "Moral Question: The Inverted Scenario." *La Repubblica*. December 8.

Cantone, Raffaele, and Francesco Caringella. 2017. *La corruzione spuzza*. Milan: Mondadori.

Canuto, Otaviano. 2017. "Dissolving Corruption in Brazil." *OMFIF Bulletin*, Official Monetary and Financial Institutions Forum. London.

Cardoso, Eliana. 2006. *Fábulas Econômicas*. São Paulo: Prentice Hall.

Cottarelli, Carlo. 2018. *I sette peccati capitali dell'economia italiana*. Milan: Feltrinelli.

Davigo, Piercamillo. 2017. *Il sistema della corruzione*. Bari: Laterza.

Ginsborg, Paul. 2001. *Italy and Its Discontents*. London: Penguin.

International Monetary Fund (IMF). 2018. "Review of the 1997 Guidance Note on Governance—A Proposed Framework for Enhanced Fund Engagement." Washington, DC.

Lagarde, Christine. 2018. "Shining a Bright Light into the Dark Corners of Weak Governance and Corruption." *IMFBlog*, April 22.

Magalhaes, Luciana, and Samantha Pearson. 2017. "Judge Warns on Brazil Graft." *Wall Street Journal*, October 18.

Moro, Sergio Fernando. 2004. "Considerações sobre a Operação Mani Pulite." *Legal Journal of the Center for Judicial Studies* (R. CEJ) 26 (July/September): 56–62.

Organisation for Economic Co-operation and Development (OECD). 2018. *Brazil*. Paris: OECD Economic Surveys.

Paolazzi, Luca. 2014. "La corruzione zavorra per lo sviluppo." Slide Presentation, Confindustria, Rome, December 17.

Paoli, Letizia, 2002. "Crime, Italian Style." *Daedalus* 130(3): 157–85.

Pareto, Vilfredo. 1916. *Trattato di sociologia generale*. Florence: Giunti-Barbera.

Polo, Michele, and Alberto Vannucci. 2014. I gattopardi delle mazzette. *lavoce.info*, May 20.

Transparency International. 2018a. *Corruption Perception Index 2017*. Berlin.

———. 2018b. *G-20 Leaders or Laggards?* Berlin.

UN Office of Drugs and Crime (UNODC). 2003. United Nations Convention against Corruption. United Nations, New York.

Vannucci, Alberto. 2009. "The Controversial Legacy of 'Mani Pulite': A Critical Analysis of Italian Corruption and Anti-Corruption Policies." *Bulletin of Italian Politics* 1(2): 233–64.

———. 2012. *Atlante della corruzione*. Turin: Edizioni Gruppo Abele.

———. 2016. "Tempi più duri per corrotti e corruttori?" *lavoce.info*, March 4.

World Bank. 2017. *Doing Business 2018*. Washington, DC.

Author Biographies

Fernando Coppe Alcaraz is the undersecretary for regional integration and foreign trade at Brazil's Ministry of Finance, a position that deals with all major issues in Brazil's international trade and investment policies. As a government official, he has more than 16 years of experience in positions of increasing responsibility in the areas of international trade and international economics. He holds a BA in business administration from the University of São Paulo, in Brazil, and an MA in international law and economics from the World Trade Institute of the University of Bern, in Switzerland.

Ravi Balakrishnan is the IMF mission chief for Peru and heads the regional group on inequality and poverty in the IMF's Western Hemisphere Department. Previously, he helped manage the US team and was mission chief for Bolivia. He was also the IMF's resident representative in Singapore during 2010–13, with regional responsibilities, and has worked on the *World Economic Outlook*. His research interests and publications cover labor dynamics, inequality, inflation dynamics, exchange rate dynamics, and capital flows. He holds a BA from the University of Cambridge and a PhD in economics from the London School of Economics.

Richard Berkhout is a senior counsel in the IMF Legal Department, where he focuses on anti–money laundering and combating the financing of terrorism (AML/CFT) and anti-corruption. He is involved in surveillance, assessments, policy issues, research, and capacity development. Previously he was a senior policy analyst at the Financial Action Task Force (FATF) Secretariat, where he was responsible for the FATF's mutual evaluation program and led assessments of Australia, Oman, Saudi Arabia, and Singapore and the follow-up program with Brazil. Before that he worked at the Dutch Ministry of Finance as a senior policy advisor for AML/CFT. He holds a master's degree in law and political science from the University of Leiden in the Netherlands.

Nina Biljanovska is an economist in the IMF's Western Hemisphere Department, currently covering Brazil and Ecuador. Previously, she worked in the IMF's Institute for Capacity Development. Her research focuses mainly on policy design, uncertainty, and behavioral finance and has been published in academic journals and IMF publications. She holds a PhD in economics from Goethe University Frankfurt.

Fabian Bornhorst was the IMF's resident representative in Brazil during 2014–18. Prior to that he was an economist in the IMF's European and Fiscal Affairs Department. Before joining the IMF, he was an Overseas Development Institute fellow in Namibia. His research focuses on fiscal policy and the impact of public and private indebtedness on growth. He holds an MSc in economics from University College London and the Free University of Berlin and earned his PhD in economics from the European University Institute in Florence.

Steen Byskov is a senior financial economist in the World Bank's Finance Competitiveness and Innovation Global Practice and is currently in the Latin America and Caribbean group. He works on topics related to financial stability and financial development. He has led or participated in the joint World Bank–IMF Financial Sector Assessment Program in Barbados, Guyana, Romania, Suriname, Turkey, and Uruguay. He has also led several World Bank lending operations to develop business financing and mortgage lending and has worked in the East Asia and Pacific and the Europe and Central Asia regions. Previously he was at the IMF. He has a master's degree in economics from the University of Copenhagen and an MBA from the University of Maryland.

Yan Carrière-Swallow is an economist in the Western Hemisphere Department of the IMF, where he covers Argentina. His analysis of fiscal and monetary policies in Latin America and the Caribbean has appeared regularly in the IMF's *Regional Economic Outlook*. Prior to joining the IMF in 2012, he was an advisor at the Central Bank of Chile in Santiago. His research focuses on international macroeconomics and policies in emerging markets.

Alfredo Cuevas is an assistant director in the IMF's European Department and is the mission chief for Portugal. Previously he led the Brazil mission team in the Western Hemisphere Department (2014–17) and headed the Regional Studies Division in the IMF's African Department (2012–14), where he coordinated the production of the IMF's *Regional Economic Outlook for Sub-Saharan Africa*. He has also served as the IMF senior resident representative in South Africa and as mission chief for several countries covered by the African Department. He spent several years in the IMF's Fiscal Affairs Department, where he led technical assistance missions on social security reform and other public finance topics to several Latin American countries. He was also a senior economist in the Research Department of the Mexican Central Bank and taught public finance at El Colegio de Mexico. He has a BA in public administration from El Colegio de Mexico and an MA in public affairs and a PhD in economics from Princeton University.

Isabela Ferreira Duarte is an advisor to the secretary at Brazil's Ministry of Finance Secretariat for Productivity and Competition Advocacy and an economics PhD candidate at the Pontifical Catholic University of Rio de Janeiro (PUC-Rio). Her research is focused primarily on the use of economic models and quantitative tools to evaluate and design public policy. She has conducted research in the areas of development, education, and credit markets. Her current research studies the impact of a major student loan program in Brazil on tuition, enrollment, occupational choice, and achievement. She holds a BA in economics from the University of Brasília and an MA in economics from PUC-Rio.

Mark Dutz is lead economist in the World Bank's Macroeconomics, Trade and Investment Global Practice. He is responsible for productivity growth and its interaction with poverty reduction and shared prosperity. He has worked in all World Bank geographic regions, as its enterprise policy anchor, and in the Office of the Chief Economist. His other experience includes as senior consultant with Compass Lexecon Inc.; senior advisor to the State Minister of Economic Affairs and Treasury, Turkey; principal economist in the Office of the Chief Economist, European Bank for Reconstruction and Development; and consultant to the Organisation for Economic Co-operation and Development, World Trade Organization, World Intellectual Property Organization, and Canada's Networks of Centers of Excellence. He has taught at Princeton University and holds an MA in public affairs from Princeton's Woodrow Wilson School and a PhD in economics from Princeton University.

Marcello Estevão is secretary for international affairs at Brazil's Ministry of Finance and is responsible for the country's international economic agenda. He is also G20 finance deputy, chairman of the board of directors of the New Development Bank (Shanghai), and a member of the governing board of FUNCEF (one of Brazil's largest pension funds). He has a PhD in economics from the Massachusetts Institute of Technology and has worked as a policymaker, manager, and researcher; with many academic and policy publications; and at the IMF, the Federal Reserve Board, and Tudor Investment Corporation, Greenwich, Connecticut.

Nayara Freire is a public accounts analyst at the Federation of Industries of the state of Rio de Janeiro (FIRJAN). Her projects in subnational governments include a new measure of deficit, transparency, and compliance. In past years, she worked on several studies about Rio de Janeiro, fiscal crises in Brazil's states, and a rating system for Brazil's municipalities: the FIRJAN Index of Fiscal Management. She has a BA in economics from the Federal Rural University of Rio de Janeiro and is currently pursuing a master's degree in public policy regulation and evaluation at the Getúlio Vargas Foundation.

Carlos Góes is senior economic advisor at the Executive Office of the President of Brazil and chief research officer of Instituto Mercado Popular, a São Paulo–based think tank. He previously worked as an economic analyst at the IMF and at US think tanks. His academic research has been featured in *The Wall Street Journal, The Financial Times, El País,* and *Le Monde*. He holds an MA in international economics from the Johns Hopkins University and is pursuing a PhD in economics at the University of California, San Diego.

Carlos Eduardo Gonçalves is an economist in the Western Hemisphere Department of the IMF. He previously held a position in the IMF's Research Department. Prior to joining the IMF, he was a full professor of economics at the University of São Paulo in Brazil. He has a PhD in economics from the University of São Paulo and has published in leading academic journals, such as the *Journal of International Economics, Journal of Development Economics,* and *Journal of Money, Credit and Banking*. He has also published many books in Portuguese aimed at teaching economics to the general public.

Izabela Karpowicz is a senior economist in the European Department of the IMF and desk economist for Austria. Since she joined the IMF in 2004, she has held positions in several departments, working as an economist on low income as well as systemic factors in emerging market economies across various regions. Her interests and research fall under a broad area of fiscal topics, including pensions, the government's wage bill, public-private partnerships, and intergovernmental relations. She has also conducted research on income inequality and financial inclusion in Latin America. Before joining the IMF she was a World Bank consultant. She is a graduate in economics from Bocconi University in Milan and holds an MS in economics from Central European University in Budapest. She is also a graduate in macroeconomic policy research of the Kiel Institute for World Economics Program.

Eduardo Leoni is division chief of productive infrastructures at the Executive Office of the President of Brazil. He has been an analyst at IBGE, the Brazilian national statistics agency, since 2010. He previously worked as a statistical consultant at Harvard University and Columbia University and in the private sector in Brazil and the United States. He holds a BA and an MA from the University of Brasília and an MPhil from Columbia University.

Paulo de Carvalho Lins is a former associate researcher at the Brazilian Institute of Economics at the Getúlio Vargas Foundation, where he worked on issues related to productivity and infrastructure in Brazil. He has a BA in economics from the Federal University of Minas Gerais and an MSc in economics from the University of São Paulo. He is an economics PhD student at the University of Rochester, and his research focus is on macroeconomics in general, especially monetary and fiscal policies and their interaction.

Vivian Malta is an economist in the Strategy, Policy, and Review Department of the IMF, where she has been working on analytical projects that tackle both macroeconomic issues (income) and gender inequality. Prior to joining the IMF, she worked in the Macroeconomics and Fiscal Management Department at the World Bank's office in Brazil as part of a large public expenditure review project. She has years of experience as a macroeconomist in the financial sector in Brazil. She holds a BA in industrial engineering from the Pontifical Catholic University of Rio de Janeiro and a PhD in economics from Escola Brasileira de Economia e Finanças, where she studied monetary and international economics.

Troy Matheson is a senior economist in the Western Hemisphere Department of the IMF, where his recent research has focused on Brazil and Canada. He previously worked in the IMF Research Department. Prior to joining the IMF, he was an advisor in the Modelling Division at the Reserve Bank of New Zealand. He holds a postgraduate degree in economics from the University of Canterbury, New Zealand. He has published papers in international journals in the fields of macroeconomic modeling, monetary policy, time series modeling, and forecasting.

Paulo Medas is a deputy division chief in the IMF Fiscal Affairs Department. He has led technical assistance missions to several countries on fiscal issues, including developing robust fiscal frameworks. He was the IMF's resident representative in Brazil during 2008–11 and worked with several emerging market and advanced economies. His recent areas of research include fiscal crises, governance and corruption, fiscal management in resource-rich countries, and fiscal risks.

Guilherme Mercês is chief economist at the Federation of Industries of the state of Rio de Janeiro. He is a former budget consultant for the local parliament and professor of macroeconomics at the State University of Rio de Janeiro. With a focus on macroeconomics and public finances, he has had several studies and analyses published in specialized journals and in Brazil's mainstream media. During the past 10 years, he has led studies on debt sustainability and state fiscal crises in Brazil and developed a rating for all Brazilian municipalities. He has an MA in economics from the State University of Rio de Janeiro and executive background in strategy from the INSEAD business school, in scenario planning from Oxford University, and in public management from Columbia University.

Alessandro Merli is associate fellow of the Johns Hopkins University School of Advanced International Studies, Europe. He was previously Frankfurt correspondent and European Central Bank watcher at *Il Sole 24 Ore,* the Italian financial newspaper, where he also was London correspondent, financial editor, and columnist and is still a contributor. He has taught at the universities of Modena and Parma and the Bologna Business School. He is a graduate in Law of the Università di Modena and earned an MA in economics at the University of Illinois. He was a visiting scholar at the Massachusetts Institute of Technology.

Alexandre Messa is senior economic advisor at the Brazil Trade Board and an economist at the Institute for Applied Economic Research. He specializes in microfounded general equilibrium models for policy analysis, international trade, corporate finance, and contract theory. He holds an MA in business economics from the Getúlio Vargas Foundation and a PhD in economics from the University of São Paulo.

Luís Gustavo Montes is technical advisor at the Executive Office of the President of Brazil and a foreign trade analyst at the Ministry of Industry, Foreign Trade and Services. Previously he was coordinator of labor market policies for Pronatec-MDIC, a program designed to match reskilling efforts with regional labor demand. He also previously worked at the Superior Court of Justice and the Ministry of Health. He holds a BA in international relations from the University of Brasilia and an MBA in trade remedies from IBMEC, a university in Brazil that specializes in teaching and research in Latin American business and economics in Latin America.

Carlos Mulas-Granados is a senior economist in the IMF European Department. Since joining the IMF in 2012, he has led research for flagship publications such as the *European Regional Economic Outlook*, *Fiscal Monitor,* and *World Economic Outlook* and has worked on country-specific fiscal issues in Brazil, Costa Rica, Croatia, Portugal, and Senegal and the euro area. He is also a tenured professor of applied economics at Complutense University of Madrid (on leave) and has served as a deputy director of the Spanish prime minister's economic office. He has authored or coedited four books and has published articles in areas including political economy, fiscal adjustment, debt reduction, public investment, research and development, and inequality. He holds an MA in international affairs (international political economy concentration) from Columbia University, a PhD in economics from Cambridge University, and a European doctorate in economics from Complutense University of Madrid.

Armando Castelar Pinheiro is coordinator of applied economics research at the Brazilian Institute of Economics at the Getúlio Vargas Foundation and professor of economics at the Federal University of Rio de Janeiro. Previously he worked at Gávea Investimentos, the Institute of Applied Economic Research, and the National Development Bank. He earned a BA in electronic engineering from the Instituto Tecnológico de Aeronáutica, MAs in statistics from the Instituto de Matematica Pura e Aplicada and business administration from the COPPEAD Graduate School of Business, and a PhD in economics from the University of California, Berkeley. He is a member of the Economic and Social Development Council and pens monthly columns for the *Valor Econômico* and *Correio Braziliense* newspapers.

Roberto Perrelli is a senior economist in the IMF's Strategy, Policy, and Review Department. He has served on the teams for Brazil, Greece, Ireland, Malta, South Africa, Venezuela, and the Eastern Caribbean Currency Union. He has worked on a broad range of policy and country issues, including early warning systems of balance of payments crises, financial programs, and debt restructuring. Before joining the IMF, he taught econometrics at the University of Illinois, Urbana-Champaign, where he obtained his MSc in statistics and PhD in economics. Early in his career, he worked on banking issues at Price Waterhouse in Brazil. His research interests include monetary policy, international trade and finance, and econometrics. He has published in top academic journals.

João Manoel Pinho de Mello is currently on leave from his position as professor of economics at Insper. His research interests cover several areas of applied economics. After receiving his PhD in economics from Stanford University in 2005, he joined the faculty of the Economics Department at the Pontifical Catholic University of Rio de Janeiro, where he was an assistant (2005–10) and an associate (2011–13) professor. He was a founder and cohead of the America Latina Crime and Policy Network, a network of researchers sponsored by the Latin American and Caribbean Economic Association. During the 2016–17 academic year, he was a visiting professor at Harvard University, a fellow at the Center of International Development, and the Lemann Scholar at the David Rockefeller Center for Latin America Studies. In 2017, he was appointed deputy minister of finance of Brazil responsible for microeconomic reforms. He currently heads the recently established Secretariat for the Promotion of Productivity and Competition Advocacy and is a researcher for the Brazilian National Counsel of Scientific and Technological Development. In addition to academic activities, he has worked extensively with the private sector as a consultant, economic analyst, and expert witness in numerous litigation, arbitration, and antitrust cases.

Maria Cristina Rondelli Pinotti has been a partner with the macroeconomic consulting firm A.C. Pastore & Associados for the past 25 years, working on topics relevant to analysis of the Brazilian economy, such as growth, fiscal and monetary policy, exchange rate policy, and international economics. Previously she was an economist at Unibanco and DIVESP and with MB Associados. She coauthored Affonso Pastore's 2014 book *Inflações e Crises: o Papel da Moeda*. Her latest research includes theory and empirical evidence of the economics of corruption, in particular in Brazil (Lava Jato) and Italy (Mani Pulite). She authored a chapter in the 2017 book *Infraestrutura: Eficiencia e Ética*, coedited by the Brazilian think tank Centro de Debates de Políticas Públicas, where she is a member of the advisory board. She has an undergraduate degree in public administration and a graduate degree in economics.

Carlos Pio is undersecretary for strategic planning at the Executive Office of the President of Brazil. He specializes in the political economy of trade, particularly in the Brazilian trade liberalization process of the early 1990s, and has taught international political economy at the University of Brasília for the past 20 years. He was visiting professor at the University of California, Berkeley; the University of Oxford; and the Australian National University. He holds a PhD in political science from the Rio de Janeiro Research Institute.

Shaun Roache is an economist at the Singapore government–owned investment firm Temasek. Before joining Temasek, he worked at the IMF covering Brazil, China, and other major emerging market economies. He has a PhD in economics from Birkbeck College, University of London.

Damiano Sandri is a senior economist working on the Brazil desk in the Western Hemisphere Department of the IMF. He is also associate editor of the IMF *Economic Review*. Prior to joining the Brazil team, he worked for several years in the IMF Research Department, focusing on macro-financial issues. He holds a PhD in economics from the Johns Hopkins University, and his research has been featured in top academic journals and IMF publications.

Mauricio Soto is a senior economist at the IMF. He has collaborated with the authorities of more than 20 countries in analyzing fiscal issues over the past decade. Prior to joining the IMF, he worked as a researcher on retirement issues, first at the Center for Retirement Research at Boston College and most recently at the Urban Institute. He has authored and coauthored several papers on pensions and social insurance. His peer-reviewed research has been published in the *Journal of Accounting Research, Labour, Journal of Pension Economics and Finance, Ageing International,* and *Journal of Financial Planning.*

Antonio Spilimbergo received his undergraduate diploma in economics from Università Bocconi and his PhD in economics from the Massachusetts Institute of Technology. Since 1997, he has worked at the IMF, where he is currently assistant director in the Western Hemisphere Department. He has been mission chief for Brazil, Italy, Russia, Slovenia, and Turkey. He is a research fellow of the Center for Economic Policy Research, William Davidson Institute, and CreAm. His areas of interest are international trade, development, labor economics, political economy, and macroeconomics. His papers have been published in leading academic journals, including the *American Economic Review*, Review of Economic Studies, Review of Economics and Statistics, *American Economic Journal: Macroeconomics*, and *Journal of International Economics*. He coedited the book *Getting Back on Track: Growth, Employment, and Rebalancing in Europe.*

Krishna Srinivasan is currently a deputy director in the Western Hemisphere Department of the IMF, which he joined in 1994. In this capacity, he oversees the institution's work on several countries in Latin America and the Caribbean, the department's research activities, and its flagship product, the *Regional Economic Outlook for Latin America and the Caribbean*. Most recently, he coedited a book titled *Unleashing Growth and Strengthening Resilience in the Caribbean*. He was previously in the European Department, serving as the IMF's mission chief for the United Kingdom and Israel, and before that in the Research Department, where he led the IMF's work on the G20 and was the lead editor of the IMF book *Global Rebalancing: A Roadmap for Economic Recovery*. He received his MA from the Delhi School of Economics, India, and his PhD in international finance from Indiana University and has published several papers both at the IMF and in leading academic journals.

Marina Mendes Tavares is an economist at the IMF and leader of the UK Department for International Development working group on the interconnections between macroeconomic policy and income inequality. This group developed the Macroeconomic and Distributional Analysis Model, which has been used extensively at the IMF to operationalize inequality in surveillance and program countries. She has a BA in economics from the Pontifical Catholic University of Rio de Janeiro, an MA in mathematical economics from the Instituto de Matematica Pura e Aplicada, and a PhD in economics from the University of Minnesota. Prior to joining the IMF, she worked for two years as an assistant professor at the Instituto Tecnológico Autónomo de Mexico.

Frederik Toscani is an economist in the IMF Western Hemisphere Department. He previously worked in the Fiscal Affairs Department. His research has focused mainly on issues in public economics, political economy, and economic growth. He holds a BSc in economics from the London School of Economics and an MPhil and PhD in economics from the University of Cambridge.

Mauricio Vargas is an economist in the IMF Western Hemisphere Department currently working on countries in the Caribbean I Division. Previously he worked in the Research Department for four years, contributing to the external sector report and external balance assessment. Prior to joining the IMF, he worked at various public and private institutions in Bolivia and Chile. His research focuses on topics related to international economics, informality, and poverty and inequality. He holds an MSc and a PhD in economics from the Universidad de Chile.

Alejandro Werner assumed his current position as director of the IMF Western Hemisphere Department in 2013. A Mexican citizen, he has had distinguished careers in the public and private sectors as well as in academia. He was Mexican undersecretary of finance and public credit (2006–10) and head of corporate and investment banking at BBVA Bancomer (2011–12). Previously, he was director of economic studies at the Bank of Mexico and professor at the Instituto Tecnológico Autónomo de México, Instituto de Empresa, and Yale University. He has published widely. He was named Young Global Leader by the World Economic Forum in 2007 and received his PhD from the Massachusetts Institute of Technology in 1994.

Juan Yépez is an economist in the Regional Studies Division of the IMF's Western Hemisphere Department. Previously, he worked in the World Economic Studies Division of the Research Department. He holds a PhD in international economics from the University of Notre Dame. His research interests include financial markets, monetary policy, and international macroeconomics and finance.

Index